SERIAL KILLER INVESTIGATIONS

SERIAL KILLER INVESTIGATIONS

THE STORY OF FORENSICS AND PROFILING THROUGH THE HUNT FOR THE WORLD'S WORST MURDERERS

COLIN WILSON

HYLAS PUBLISHING

Hylas Publishing®
129 Main Street, Ste. C
Irvington, NY 10533
www.hylaspublishing.com

Publisher: Sean Moore
Publishing Director: Karen Prince
Art Director: Gus Yoo
Designer: Erika Lubowicki
Senior Editor: Lisa Purcell
Junior Editors: Michael Smith, Kristin Maffei
Proofreader: Suzanne Lander

ISBN: 0-681-63116-3

Library of Congress Cataloging-in-Publication Data

Wilson, Colin, 1931–
Serial killer investigations : the story of forensics and profiling through the hunt for the world's worst murderers / by Colin Wilson. — 1st American ed. p. cm.
Includes bibliographical references and index.
ISBN-13: 978-1-59258-274-7 (alk. paper)
1. Serial murder investigation—Psychological aspects. 2. Forensic psychology. 3. Criminal behavior, Prediction of. 4. Serial murderers—Psychology. I. Title.
HV8079.H6W55 2006
364.152'30922—dc22
2006024685

Printed and bound in Canada
Distributed in the United States by Publishers Group West
Distributed in Canada by Publishers Group Canada
First American Edition published in 2006
2 4 6 8 10 9 7 5 3 1

To Robert K. Ressler

A Plague of Murder

In 1977, FBI Special Agent Robert Ressler first used the term "serial killer" after a visit to Bramshill Police Academy, near London, where someone referred to a "serial burglar." The inspired coinage was soon in general use to describe killers such as necrophile Ed Kemper (10 victims), schizophrenic Herb Mullin (14), and homosexual mass murderers Dean Corll (27) and John Wayne Gacy (32). Then in 1980, in Colombia, Pedro Lopez, the "Monster of the Andes," confessed to murdering 310 prepubescent girls; three years later, a derelict named Henry Lee Lucas claimed to have killed 350 victims. Clearly, these sprees were on a scale beyond anything known in the history of crime—even the French "Bluebeard," Gilles de Rais, executed in 1440, was believed to have killed no more than 50 children. In more recent years, the American "Pee Wee" Gaskins killed an estimated 110, "Red Ripper" Andrei Chikatilo 56, his fellow Russian Anatoly Onoprienko 52, and the British doctor Harold Shipman between 215 and 260. There was an obvious need for Ressler's new term to describe this horrific phenomenon.

Understanding it is rather more difficult. But I can claim at least one qualification. In the late 1950s, I had decided it was about time someone compiled an encyclopedia covering all the most notorious murder cases. The subject of crime had always interested me, and I was engaged in writing my first novel, *Ritual in the Dark,* about a mass murderer based on Jack the Ripper. I had collected a considerable library of secondhand books on true crime with titles like *Scales of Justice* or *Murderers Sane and Mad.* But if I wanted to look up a specific fact about a murderer, such as the date he was hanged, I had to recollect which volume in my crime library contained a chapter about him. I decided to remedy this deficiency by writing an alphabetical encyclopedia of murder, which was published in 1961. Since then many writers have followed suit with encyclopedias of female killers, sex killers, serial killers, even one devoted entirely to Jack the Ripper.

It was while compiling the *Encyclopedia of Murder* that I first noticed a variety of murder that I was unable to fit into the old classifications: apparently "motiveless" murders. In 1952, for example, a nineteen-year-old clerk named Herbert Mills sat next to a forty-eight-year-old housewife in a Nottingham cinema and decided that she would make a suitable victim for an attempt at the "perfect murder"; he met her by arrangement the next day, took her for a walk, and strangled her under a tree. It was only because he felt the compulsion to boast about his "perfect" crime that he was caught and hanged.

In July 1958, Norman Foose stopped his jeep in the town of Cuba, New Mexico, raised his hunting rifle, and shot dead two Mexican children; pursued and arrested, he said he was trying to do something about the population explosion.

In February 1959, a pretty blonde named Penny Bjorkland accepted a lift from a married man in California and, without provocation, killed him with a dozen shots. After her arrest she explained that she wanted to see if she could kill "and not worry about it afterwards." Psychiatrists found her sane.

In April 1959, a man named Norman Smith took a pistol and shot a woman (who was watching television) through an open window. He did not

BLIND-MAN'S BUFF.
(As played by the Police.)
"TURN ROUND THREE TIMES, AND CATCH WHOM YOU MAY!"

An 1888 Punch *cartoon satirizes the police's inability to find the Whitechapel murderer. The nineteenth century saw the advent of the "sex crime."*

know Hazel Woodard; the impulse had simply come over him as he watched a TV show called *The Sniper.*

The *Encyclopedia of Murder* appeared in 1961, with a section on "motiveless murder"; by 1970 it was clear that this was, in fact, a steadily developing trend. In many cases, oddly enough, it seemed to be linked to a slightly higher-than-average IQ in the murderers. Herbert Mills wrote poetry and read some of it above the body of his victim. The "Moors Murderer" Ian Brady justified himself by quoting de Sade, and in a later correspondence with him I had ample opportunity to observe that he was highly intelligent. Melvin Rees, a mild, quiet-spoken jazz pianist, committed a series of sex murders, including the slaying of an entire family, and told a friend: "You can't say it's wrong to kill—only individual standards make it right or wrong." Charles Manson evolved an elaborate racist ideology to justify the crimes of his "Family." San Francisco's "Zodiac" killer wrote his letters in cipher and signed them with signs of the zodiac. John Frazier, a dropout who slaughtered the family of an eye surgeon, Victor Ohta, left a letter signed with suits from the tarot pack. In November 1966, Robert Smith, an eighteen-year-old student, walked into a beauty parlor in Mesa, Arizona, ordered five women and two children to lie on the floor, and then shot them all in the back of the head. Smith was in no way a "problem youngster"; his relations with his parents were good and he was described as an excellent student. He told the police: "I wanted to get known, to get myself a name."

But certain basic facts seem fairly clear. One of the prime motivations of the serial killer is resentment—not just directed at society, but at life itself. Ian Brady shook his fist at the sky after killing one of his child victims and shouted, "Take that, you bastard." The multiple killer and rapist Gerald Gallego told a prison psychiatrist: "All I want is to kill God." The 1930s killer Carl Panzram explained that he was trying to make society "pay" for the miseries and indignities he had suffered at its hands.

Studying the history of murder, I was struck by an interesting insight: that its nature changes from century to century. In the eighteenth century, most crime had a material motive and was connected with robbery. In the second part of the nineteenth century a new category of crime began to emerge: "sex crime." In 1867, a clerk named Frederick Baker killed an eight-year-old girl, Fanny Adams, and hacked her to pieces. He pleaded his innocence, but his diary gave him away: "Killed a young girl today. It was fine and hot." Yet the notion of murder committed solely for sex was so strange that when the unknown killer dubbed "Jack the Ripper" began killing prostitutes in London in 1888, contemporaries did not recognize the murders as sex crimes; there was a widely held theory that the Ripper was a religious crank who wanted to clean up the licentious streets of London.

And in the 1950s another new category of crime emerged: the "self-esteem murder." Herbert Mills wanted to feel he was more than an ordinary bank clerk: that he was a man who had committed the perfect murder. Robert Smith killed because he "wanted to become known."

A major factor in such crimes is the desire to feel potent—not just sexually but also psychologically. FBI agent Roy Hazelwood remarked that a "sex crime isn't about sex, it's about power." He described a habitual rapist who would stalk his victims for days or weeks before making his way into her bedroom. He would then stand by her bed and count to ten in increments of a half. When Hazelwood asked why, he explained: "Rape is the least enjoyable part of the entire crime." "In that case," said Hazelwood, "why didn't you turn around and leave?" "Pardon the pun, but after all I'd gone through to get there, it would have been a crime not to have raped her." In other words, the real pleasure lay in the long chase and the effort it involved.

But there is still another factor that is perhaps more important than either of these: violence seems to be oddly addictive. Serial killers tend to get "hooked" on it as they might get hooked on crack cocaine. On October 16, 1977, Los Angeles pimps Angelo Buono and Kenneth Bianchi picked up Yolanda Washington, a prostitute, with the intention of killing her. Their motive was revenge on the madam for whom she worked, against whom they had a grudge. Before strangling her they decided that they might as well rape her. But the violence of the act proved addictive; Washington's became the first of a dozen murders that earned them the label "the Hillside Stranglers."

Donald "Pee Wee" Gaskins was a serial burglar who had spent years in prison for two attacks on women, and who decided that in future, he would kill any woman he raped to make sure that she could never testify against him. But the first time he killed a hitchhiker who rejected his advances he found the pleasure of the act so overwhelming that it was the first of dozens of sex murders.

When Ted Bundy first decided to commit rape, he waited for a woman who was approaching along the street, with a length of two-by-four in his hand. But she stopped before she reached him and went into a house. He was so horrified at the compulsion that had gripped him, he swore that this would be the last time. But Bundy was a Peeping Tom; the obsession was stronger than he was. He later broke into a student's bedroom after watching her undress, knocked her unconscious with a piece torn from the bed frame, and then sexually assaulted her with it. From then on, he would confess later, he was periodically taken over by a violent alter ego he called the "hunchback," under whose control he committed some forty murders.

The "Gainesville Ripper," Danny Rolling, was another Peeping Tom who broke into a house and committed his first rape after he was served with divorce papers. After the attack, he was tormented by remorse, and the next day went back to the house with the intention of begging his victim's forgiveness. When two powerfully built men came out of her front door he changed his mind and hurried away. But the next time he was in a state of rage and resentment after being dismissed from his job, he broke into the house of a young woman he had been spying on as she undressed, murdered two of her male relatives, and then raped and murdered her. Rolling also became convinced that he was possessed, not by some sinister alter ego, but by a demonic entity that ordered him to kill. In a letter to me, he claimed not only that this demon had helped him to kill and rape, but had also attacked him in his prison cell and sat on his chest.

Nietzsche once said that happiness is the sense that obstacles are being overcome and that power is increasing. This seems to be the basic element that serial killers share with most human beings. Conversely, it is the absence of this sense of power that characterizes the sort of person who becomes a serial killer. British homosexual murderer Dennis Nilsen, who strangled and dismembered a dozen victims in north London, told the crime writer Brian Masters that the character of Hannibal Lecter in *Silence of the Lambs* was an absurdity because he represented a fantasy of potency; he himself, said Nilsen, had never felt potent in his life.

This, then, enables us to understand one of the basic motives behind serial murder, and to see what Roy Hazelwood meant when he said, "sex crime isn't about sex, it's about power."

The thought is frightening because it is difficult to see an end to it. If crime has changed so much in a few decades, what will it be like in a century or in two centuries? This is the kind of reflection provoked by any volume on crime written more than a hundred years ago. There is a vast Victorian compilation called *Chronicles of Crime, or The New Newgate Calendar,* by Camden Pelham, published in 1886 and covering the period from the beginning of the century. Of its five hundred or so cases (mostly murder, but with an admixture of forgery, burglary, piracy, and treason), only seven are rapes. Four of the seven rapists were executed, one imprisoned, and two transported to Australia. Obviously, the Victorians took rape very seriously indeed. What would they have thought of the rape statistics in any modern city? They would have felt that our society has turned into a kind of Sodom and Gomorrah, and foretold its imminent extinction by an outraged deity. As to serial murder, the thought would have struck them as too frightening to believe—just as even a fairly hardened crime writer such as myself prefers not to dwell on some of the cruelties inflicted by serial killers.

"SEX CRIME ISN'T ABOUT SEX, IT'S ABOUT POWER."

Even so, I would argue that the situation is not quite as bad as it looks. As baffling and complex as serial murder first appears, it has many features that are easy to recognize and classify. And problems that can be classified and understood can also be solved. That is fortunate for the police who hunt the perpetrators, for most cases of serial murder would otherwise be virtually unsolvable, since there is no obvious link between killer and victim—the killer might be any one among millions.

These classifiable features have led to the development of the science of psychological profiling, which can often provide that first vital lead. The core of this book is the story of psychological profiling, and of the United States' Federal Bureau of Investigation's BSU, the Behavioral Science Unit, at Quantico, Virginia.

1

The Science of Profiling

1 The Science of Profiling

In 2002, the U.S. Crime Index showed that a violent crime occurred every twenty-two seconds, an aggravated assault every thirty-five seconds, a rape every five minutes, and a murder every thirty-five minutes. At least the murder rate showed a slight improvement from 1988 when a murder occurred every twenty-eight minutes.

These hair-raising statistics produce an unsettling sense that violence is spinning out of control. But although it is true that the U.S. murder rate has trebled in the post–World War II period, the mid-1990s saw it peak at around 23,000 a year, and it has been falling steadily to a thirty-five-year low.

There are several reasons for this steady decline. One is undoubtedly the zero tolerance policies introduced by Bill Clinton, which drastically reduced the number of gang-related murders. Another was the implementation of practical, commonsense anticrime measures—for example, in 1992 close to forty taxi drivers were murdered in New York. When bulletproof partitions and digital surveillance cameras were introduced inside the vehicles, these murders ceased.

But a major reason for the declining crime rate has certainly been the increased efficiency of crime-detection techniques. The most important of these was undoubtedly genetic, or DNA, fingerprinting, discovered by British scientist Alec Jeffreys in 1986. Genetic fingerprinting was perhaps the most important innovation in crime detection since digital fingerprinting in the 1880s, yet it took more than a decade before it could be implemented efficiently. A major problem was the speed at which such tests could be carried out; eventually it was increased from weeks to hours. Another major problem occurred if there was not enough DNA material for testing, or if it was old or degraded. But the discovery of methods of extracting usable DNA from old samples, and then multiplying the quantity by the method known as STR, or short tandem repeats, streamlined the process and dramatically increased the solution rate for sex crimes. It also led to a review of thousands of unsolved, or "cold cases," from earlier years.

But where catching serial killers is concerned, the most important advance is undoubtedly "criminal profiling." For all practical purposes, this began in 1950 with the series of explosions in New York City attributed to the "Mad Bomber."

On April 24, 1950, an explosion wrecked a phone booth outside the New York Public Library on Fifth Avenue. During the next sixteen years, the bomber planted twenty-eight more explosive devices in sites around the city that included Grand Central Station, Radio City Music Hall, the Capitol Theater, Rockefeller Center, the Port Authority bus terminal, and the Consolidated Edison plant on Nineteenth Street. By chance, no one was seriously hurt in any of these incidents. Then, on December 2, 1956, a bomb exploded in the Brooklyn Paramount Movie Theater, injuring seven people, one seriously.

In reality, the first Mad Bomber crime had not occurred in 1950, but instead nearly ten years earlier, on November 16, 1940, when a homemade metal pipe bomb had failed to explode on a windowsill in the Consolidated Edison plant on West Sixty-fourth Street. A note wrapped around it said: "CON EDISON CROOKS—THIS IS FOR YOU." Three months later, a second pipe bomb was found a few blocks away. When the war broke out, the Bomber wrote a letter to Manhattan police headquarters pledging to cease his attacks for the duration. It was after the Brooklyn bomb that the editor of a New York newspaper, the *Journal American,* decided to publish an open letter to the bomber. Appearing the day after Christmas 1956, it begged him to give himself up, offering to allow editorial space for a full airing of his grievances. Two days later, a bomb was found in the Paramount Theater, in an opening slashed in a seat; a police bomb squad deactivated it. Like the others, it was a homemade device consisting of a length of piping with nuts at both ends. But on that same Friday afternoon, the *Journal American* received a reply to its letter:

> *I read your paper of December 26—placing myself in custody would be stupid—do not insult my*

intelligence—bring the Con Edison to justice—start working on Lehmann—Poletti—Andrews . . .

It was signed "F.P."

The men named were the former governor of New York State, a former lieutenant governor, and a former industrial commissioner. The bomber went on to promise a "truce" until mid-January, and to list fourteen bombs he had planted in 1956, many of which had not so far been discovered. The police later found eight pipe bombs: five were dummies, but three were still live and unexploded—the crude chemical detonating mechanism had failed to work.

Police Commissioner Stephen P. Kennedy asked the newspaper not to print the letter, in case it caused public panic; instead, the editor inserted an advertisement in the personals column:

We received your letter. We appreciate truce. What were you deprived of? We want to hear your views and help you. We will keep our word. Contact us the same way as previously.

But other newspapers spotted the item, and the secret was out. The *Journal American* decided to print most of the bomber's letter, together with yet another appeal. The result was another letter from the bomber, promising a truce until March 1, and offering an important piece of information:

I was injured on a job at Consolidated Edison Plant—as a result I am adjudged totally and permanently disabled. I did not receive any aid of any kind from company—that I did not pay for myself—while fighting for my life—section 28 came up.

Section 28 of the New York State Compensation Law limits the start of any legal action to two years after an injury. The letter-writer went on to accuse Con Edison of blocking all of his attempts to gain compensation, and to criticize Lehmann, Poletti, and Andrews for ignoring his letters. Like the previous letter, this was signed "F.P."

Here, then, were clues that could lead to the bomber's identity. Yet, Con Edison is a giant energy company, supplying New York City with its electric, gas, and steam, and has numerous power plants. If the bomber had been injured before 1940—the date of the first bomb—the chances were high that his records had long ago been destroyed or lost. The same problem applied to Lehmann, Poletti, and Andrews; they probably received a hundred letters a day during their terms of office, and most of them would have ended up in the wastepaper basket. No politician files all of his crank letters.

The police decided on a curious expedient—to consult a psychiatrist for his opinion on the bomber. This was the decision of Inspector Howard F. Finney of the crime laboratory. The man he chose was Dr. James A. Brussel, who had been working

WHERE CATCHING SERIAL KILLERS IS CONCERNED, THE MOST IMPORTANT ADVANCE IS UNDOUBTEDLY "CRIMINAL PROFILING."

for many years with the criminally insane. Finney handed Brussel the file on the bomber, together with the letters. Brussel studied the letters, and his first conclusion was that the bomber was an immigrant; the letters contained no Americanisms. Further, stilted Victorian phrases such as "they will pay for their dastardly deeds" suggested a member of the older generation. The bomber, said Brussel, was obviously a paranoiac, a man far gone in persecution mania, one who has allowed himself to become locked into an inner world of hostility and resentment; everyone is plotting against him and he trusts no one. But because he is so close to the verge of insanity, he is careful, meticulous, highly controlled—the bomber's block-capital letters were beautifully neat. Brussel's experience of paranoia suggested that it most often develops in the mid-thirties. Since the first bomb was planted in 1940, this suggested that the bomber must now be in his mid-fifties.

Brussel was a Freudian—as were most psychiatrists of that period—and he observed that the only letters that stood out from the others were the *Ws*, formed from two rounded *Us*, which resembled breasts. From this Brussel deduced that the bomber was still a man with strong sex drives, and that he had probably had trouble with his mother. He also noted that the cinema bombs had been planted inside W-shaped slashes, and that these again had some sexual connotation. Brussel's final picture of the bomber was of a man in his fifties, Slavic in origin, neat and precise in his habits, and who lived in some better part of New York with an elderly mother or female relative. He was—or had been—a good Catholic. He was of strong build. And finally, he was the type who wore double-breasted suits.

Some of these deductions were arrived at by study of the letters—the meticulousness, obsessive self-control—and others by a process of elimination: the bomber was not American, but the phrasing was not German, Italian, or Spanish, so the likeliest alternative was a Slav. The majority of Slavs are Catholic, and the letters sometimes revealed a religious obsession . . .

Meanwhile, the *Journal American* had printed a third appeal, this one promising that if the bomber gave further details of his grievances, the newspaper would do its best to reopen his case. This brought a typewritten reply that contained the requested details:

> *I was injured on September 5, 1931. There were over twelve thousand danger signs in the plant, yet not even First Aid was available or rendered to me. I had to lay on cold concrete . . . Mr. Reda and Mr. Hooper wrote telling me that the $180 I got in sick benefits (that I was paying for) was ample for my illness.*

Again, the signature was "F.P."

Now that investigators had a date, Con Edison clerical employees were put to work searching the corporation's voluminous personnel files. There was still no guarantee that a file dating back to 1931 would exist, but a worker named Alice Kelly eventually located it. The file concerned George Metesky, born in 1904, who had been working as a generator wiper in 1931 at the Hell Gate power station of the United Electric & Power Company, later absorbed by Con Edison. On September 5, 1931, Metesky had been caught in a boiler blowback and inhaled poisonous gases. These caused hemorrhages, which most likely brought on his subsequent pneumonia and tuberculosis—although there was no definitive proof. His doctors sent him to Arizona to recuperate, but he'd been forced to return to Waterbury, Connecticut—where he lived—because of lack of funds. He had received only $180 in sick benefits, and the file contained letters from the men called Reda and Hooper that he had mentioned.

The police lost no time in getting to Waterbury, taking with them a search warrant. The man who opened the door of the ramshackle four-story house in an industrial area wore gold-framed glasses, and peered mildly at the policemen from a round, gentle face. He identified himself as George Metesky, and allowed the officers to come in. He lived in the fourteen-room house with two elderly half-sisters, May and Anna Milausky, daughters of his mother's previous marriage. On that matter, Brussel's "guess" had been remarkably accurate.

A search of the house revealed nothing, but in the garage police found a workshop with a lathe, and a length of the same kind of pipe used to construct the bombs. Rechecking the house, they found in a bedroom a typewriter that would later be identified through forensic examination as the one used to write the letters. An hour later, at the police station, Metesky confessed that he was, indeed, the Mad Bomber, and that the initials "F.P." stood for "fair play." A photograph of him taken immediately after his arrest showed that, as Brussel had predicted, he wore a double-breasted suit.

Psychiatrists at Bellevue Hospital found Metesky to be insane and therefore incapable of standing trial; he was committed to Matteawan State Hospital for the Criminally Insane in Beacon, New York, where he spent the remainder of his life.

The next major investigation involving "psychological profiling" was rather less successful, and brought a certain amount of discredit to the new science.

Between June 1962 and January 1964, thirteen women were strangled and raped in the Boston area; the press referred to the unknown assailant of eleven of them as the "Boston Strangler." But on January 4, 1964, the killings suddenly stopped. The Strangler's last presumed victim was nineteen-year-old Mary Sullivan; he bit her all over her body, masturbated on her face, and left her with a broom handle rammed inside her vagina.

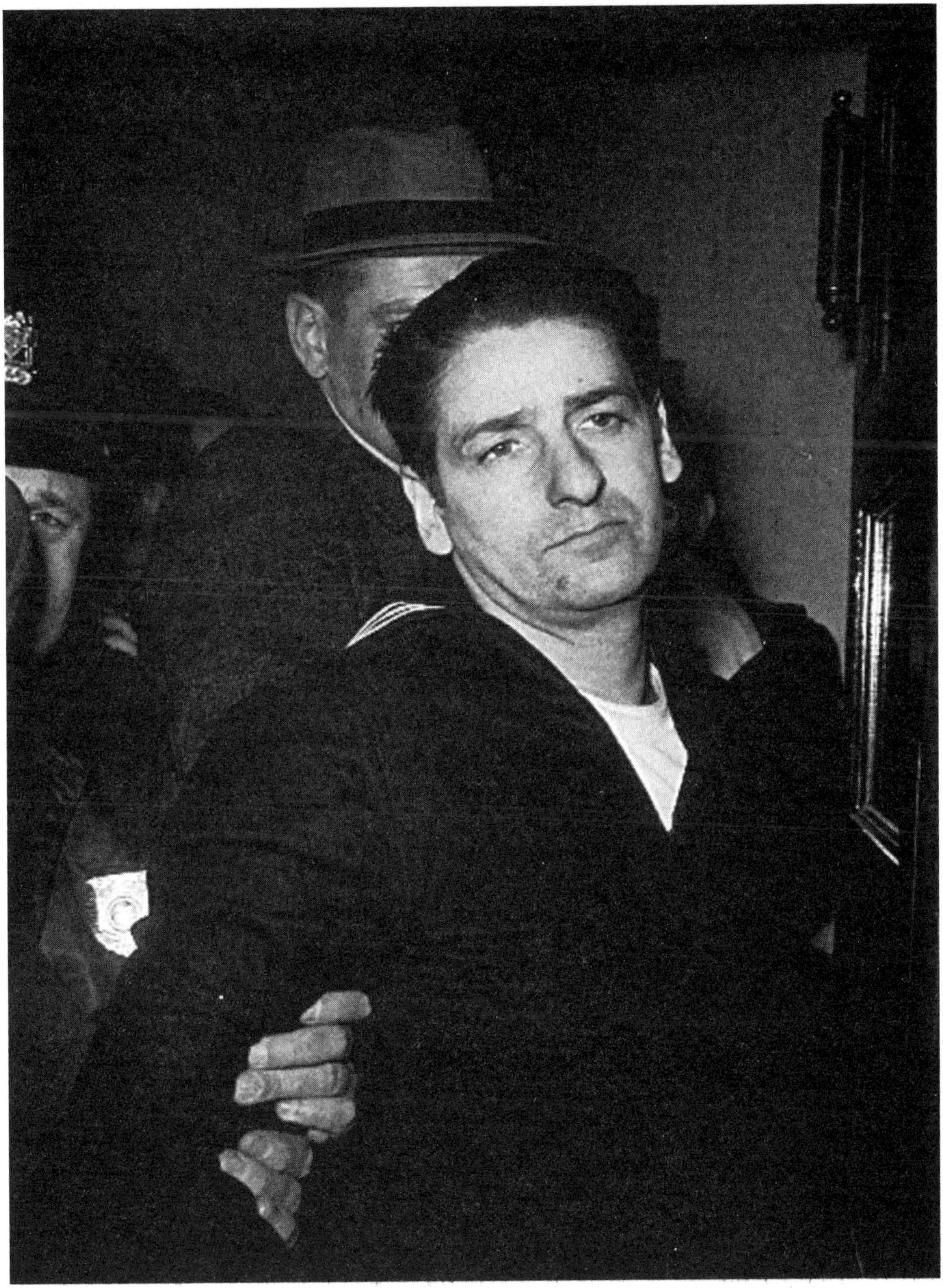

Self-confessed "Boston Strangler," Albert DeSalvo, minutes after his capture on February 25, 1967. Described as "charming" by many people who met him, DeSalvo may be the only serial killer who killed his way to some kind of "maturity." (Associated Press)

A rash of rapes continued in the Boston area, but this rapist seemed to be a polite and gentle sort of person; he always apologized before he left, and if the woman seemed too distressed, even omitted the rape. The descriptions of this "gentle rapist," known as the "Green Man" because he wore green pants, reminded the police of an offender who had been jailed for two years in 1960. He had been dubbed the "Measuring Man" because he talked his way into apartments by posing as an executive from a modeling agency, and persuaded young women to allow him to take their measurements. Occasionally he ventured a few indecent caresses. A few of the women allowed him to make love to them as a bribe—although the promised modeling jobs, of course, never materialized.

The Measuring Man was arrested, and proved to be a husky young ex-soldier named Albert DeSalvo; he was sentenced for "lewd and lascivious behavior," as well as for attempted breaking and entry.

DeSalvo was identified by the Green Man's rape victims after his arrest in November 1964, and in February 1965 was sent to the Bridgewater State Hospital for observation; there he was diagnosed schizophrenic and deemed incompetent to stand trial. Soon after his permanent committal to Bridgewater, he confessed to fellow inmate George Nassar that he was the Boston Strangler. Nassar informed his lawyer, who happened to be the controversial F. Lee Bailey, well-known for his involvement in the Sam Sheppard murder case. In taped interviews with Bailey, DeSalvo confessed in detail to the thirteen Boston murders. The police were at first inclined to be skeptical, but soon became convinced by DeSalvo's detailed knowledge of the crimes. As a result, DeSalvo was sentenced to life imprisonment; he had served only six years when he was found stabbed to death in his cell by a fellow prisoner who was never identified.

In January 1964, while the Boston Strangler was still at large, the assistant attorney general of Massachusetts, John S. Bottomly, decided to set up a committee of psychiatrists to attempt to establish some kind of "psychological profile" of the killer. One of the psychiatrists who served on that committee was Dr. James A. Brussel, the man who had been so successful in describing the Mad Bomber. When he attended his first meeting, Brussel discovered that there was a sharp division of opinion within the committee. One group believed that there were two stranglers, one of whom killed older women, and the other young ones. The opposing group thought that there was only one Boston Strangler. (To this day, the controversy continues over the irrefutable identity of the culprit, or culprits.)

It was at his second meeting of the committee—in April 1965—that Brussel was hit by a sudden hunch as he listened to a psychiatrist pointing out that in some cases, semen was found in the vagina, while in others it was found on the breasts, thighs, or even on the carpet. When it was his turn to speak, Brussel outlined the theory that had suddenly come to him "in a flash."

"I think we're dealing with one man. The apparent differences in MO, I believe, result from changes that have been going on in this man. Over the two-year period during which he has been committing these murders, he had gone through a series of upheavals . . ." The first four victims, said Brussel, were women between the ages of fifty-five and seventy-five, and there was no seminal fluid found at the scenes.

BRUSSEL OUTLINED THE THEORY THAT HAD SUDDENLY COME TO HIM "IN A FLASH."

The women had been manipulated in other ways—"a type of sexual molestation that might be expected of a small boy, not a man. . . . A boy gets over his sexual obsession with his mother, and transfers his interest to girls of his own age. The Strangler . . . achieved this transfer—achieved emotional puberty—in a matter of months." Now he wanted to achieve orgasm inside younger women. And with the final victim, Mary Sullivan, the semen was in her mouth and over her breasts. The Strangler was making a gesture of triumph and of defiance: "I throw my sex in your face."

This man, said Brussel, was a physically powerful individual, probably in his late twenties or early thirties, the age at which the paranoid reaction reaches its peak. He hazarded a guess that the Strangler's nationality was Italian or Spanish, since garroting is a method used by bandits in both countries. Brussel's final "guesses" were startlingly to the point. He believed that the Strangler had stopped killing because he had worked it out of his system. He had, in effect, grown up. And he would finally be caught because he would be unable to resist talking about his crimes and his newfound maturity.

The rest of the committee was polite but skeptical. But one year later, Brussel was vindicated when DeSalvo began admitting to his cellmate George Nassar that he was the Boston Strangler.

In 1966, Brussel traveled to Boston to interview DeSalvo. He had been half expecting a misshapen monster, and was surprised to be greeted by a good-looking, polite young man with a magnificent head of dark hair. (Brussel had even foretold that the Strangler would have well-tended hair, since he was obsessed by the impression he made on women.) Brussel found him charming, and soon realized how DeSalvo had talked his way into so many apartments: he seemed a thoroughly nice young man.

What then had turned him into a murderer? As usual, it proved to be the family background. DeSalvo's father was the worst kind of brute. He beat his wife and children mercilessly—on one occasion he broke his wife's fingers one by one. He beat one son with a hose so badly—for knocking over a box of fruit—that the boy was not allowed on the beach all summer because he was covered in black-and-yellow bruises. He often brought a prostitute home and had sex with her in front of the children. His mother was also less than satisfactory. Indifferent and self-preoccupied, she had no time for the children. As a child Albert had been a "loner," his only real friend a dog that lived in a junkyard. He developed sadistic compulsions at an early age. He and a playmate called Billy used to place a dog and a cat in two compartments of an orange crate and starve them for days, and then pull out the partition, and watch as the cat scratched out the dog's eyes. But, like so many psychopaths he could display considerable charm and make himself liked.

The real key to DeSalvo was sex. And in that sense he is typical of a majority of serial killers. From an early age he was insatiable, "walking around with a rail on most of the time, ready to take on any broad or fag come along, or to watch some broad and masturbate . . . thinking about sex a lot, more than anything, and needing it so much all the time. If only somebody could've seen it then and told me it was not normal, even sick . . ." DeSalvo is here exaggerating; a large proportion of healthy young males go around in much the same state. And DeSalvo's environment offered a great deal of sexual stimuli. He participated in sex games with his brothers and sisters when he was five or six years old. At the age of eight he performed oral sex on a girl at school, and was soon persuading girls to do the same for him. Combined with the lack of moral restraint that resulted from his family background, his tremendous sex urge soon led him to rape—his own estimation was that he had raped or assaulted almost two thousand women. During the course of the Green Man attacks, he raped four women in a single day, and even then tried to pick up a fifth.

This was something that Brussel had failed to recognize. The Strangler had not been "searching for his potency," as Brussel speculated; he had always been potent. During his teens, a neighbor had asked him if it was true that he had a permanent erection, and when he modestly admitted it, invited him into her apartment. "She went down on her knees and blowed me and I come almost right off and she said: 'Oh, now you went and come and what am I going to have to get screwed with?' and I said: 'Don't worry, I'll have a hard-on again in a few minutes.'" When he left her, she was exhausted, but he was still unsatisfied. It was *not* potency DeSalvo was searching for, but emotional stability.

Yet Brussel was undoubtedly correct about the main motivation: that DeSalvo's murders were part of an attempt to grow up. The murders of older women were acts of revenge against the mother who had rejected him; but the murder of a young black woman named Sophie Clark signaled a change. When he knocked on her door DeSalvo had no idea that she would be so young—he was looking for elderly or middle-aged women, like his mother. Clark's white dress and black stockings excited him. He talked his way into her apartment by claiming to be a workman sent to carry out repairs—the method he invariably used—then, when she turned her back, hooked his arm round her neck and squeezed until she was unconscious. After that he raped her and then strangled her. The experience taught him that he preferred girls to older women, and caused the change in his method. Hence the change in the type of victim he selected that so misled the profiling team that they assumed there were two stranglers.

Brussel was also correct about the reason DeSalvo stopped killing. The last victim, Mary Sullivan, tried to reason with him, to talk him out of raping her. Her words struck home. "I recall thinking at the time, yes, she is right, I don't need to do these things any more now." And as he tied her up he realized, "I would never be able to do it again." It was his last murder, and he returned to rape, the only known serial killer to have murdered his way to some kind of maturity.

2

Fighting Monsters

Fighting Monsters

By the mid-1970s, it was obvious to some of America's leading analysts that the police were losing the battle against the rising murder rate. In 1960 it had been around 9,000 a year; by 1975 it was 20,500. Twenty years earlier, virtually all murders had been solved, but by the time the figure had risen to 20,000 a year, a quarter of the cases were remaining unsolved. And the rate was still climbing.

This was one of the chief concerns felt by the training staff at the FBI Academy at Quantico, Virginia. The new facility had been opened in 1972 on a marine base in the midst of 385 acres of woodland, and it was seen as the successor of the old National Police Academy in Washington, D.C. This had been the base of J. Edgar Hoover, whom many regarded as a dead hand on the FBI, and it may or may not have been coincidence that 1972 was also the year of his death.

And at least one of the instructors, ex–Los Angeles cop Howard Teten, brought some new ideas to the problem of crime solving. He and James Brussel had spent a great deal of time discussing the new technique of criminal profiling, and Teten thought that this might prove a technique worthy of development. As instructors in Applied Criminology, he and his colleague Patrick J. Mullany were trying to teach a thousand recruits a year to think themselves inside the mind of the criminal. The Mad Bomber case and the Boston Strangler murders seemed to prove that a competent policeman should be able to form a picture of a criminal from a thorough examination of the facts at the crime scene.

In the 1950s, another Los Angeles detective, Pierce Brooks, had been struck by a closely related idea. Three women had vanished in the L.A. area. The first, a pretty model named Judith Ann Dull, had agreed to be photographed on July 30, 1957, by a jug-eared man who called himself Johnny Glenn. He told her he was a magazine photographer. She left her apartment with him and vanished; her remains were found five months later in the desert 130 miles away.

On March 8 of the following year, Shirley Ann Bridgeford, a twenty-four-year-old divorcée, accepted a blind date with a man who called himself George Williams; he had obtained her phone number by enrolling in a lonely hearts club. He drove off with her into the desert, and she also vanished. Sergeant David Ostroff, who had investigated the disappearance of Judy Dull, noted that the man who arrived to take Shirley square dancing was scruffy and jug-eared, and concluded that he and Johnny Glenn were probably the same person.

Three months later, another model disappeared from her flat; she was Ruth Rita Mercado, a striptease dancer who also posed nude. No one saw the man who abducted her, but her profession made it likely that she was another victim of Johnny Glenn.

The case was handed to Pierce Brooks, a former naval officer and blimp pilot. It seemed a good bet to Brooks that the same offender was responsible for other crimes in the surrounding counties, and so he began his own search through local newspaper files. He felt frustrated because it seemed so likely that the same criminal was responsible for the murders, and a computer file of similar crimes would have been a far more efficient method of finding out. But although computers existed in those days, they were far too bulky and far too expensive for the LAPD.

In fact, Johnny Glenn was caught only by chance. Two patrolmen near the small town of Tustin spotted a couple struggling in the glare of their cruiser's headlights. As they approached, the woman broke free from the man and pointed a gun at him. She lowered it at one of the patrolmen's order, and explained that the gun belonged to the man, who had tried to rape her. The man made no attempt to deny the accusation, and he was taken into custody. The woman, Lorraine Vigil, was a model who had agreed to go on a magazine assignment with the man, who said his name was Frank Johnson, because a friend who had originally agreed to take the job had pulled out and offered it to her. Instead of driving to his studio, as he had promised, he drove north, stopped on a quiet and dark road, where he pointed the gun at her and told her that he was going to tie her up. She made a grab for the gun, which went off, and forced open the door. As they struggled in the dark, she succeeded in snatching the gun, mere seconds before the patrolmen arrived.

At the Santa Ana police station the man gave his name as Harvey Murray Glatman, thirty, a TV repairman. He did not deny the attempt at assault, but claimed it was a sudden impulse.

When Pierce Brooks received a bulletin about the arrest, he noted that Glatman lived close to Ruth Mercado. The house proved to be a shabby building on South Norton Avenue, and police who searched it found the walls covered with nude pinups, in which some of the women were bound and gagged. There were also a number of lengths of rope—it seemed Glatman took an interest in bondage. Brooks realized that he had his man.

Glatman agreed to take a lie detector test, and when Ruth Mercado's name was mentioned, the stylus gave a nervous leap. A few minutes later, Glatman was confessing to murdering her.

He described how he had obtained Mercado's number from one of the numerous Los Angeles modeling agencies that booked girls who were willing to pose clothed, semi-clad, or in the nude (agencies freely gave out their client's contact information in those days). Introducing himself as Frank Johnson, he spoke to the twenty-four-year-old stripper. When he called on her on July 22, 1958, some instinct made her plead illness. The following evening, however, he showed up at her apartment with his automatic pistol, and took her to her bedroom. There he tied her up and raped her. Then, telling her they were going for a picnic, he marched her down to his car. He drove her out to the desert, and spent a day taking photographs of her—bound and gagged—and raping her. In between rapes he released her and allowed her to eat. Then he told her that he would take her home. On the way, he stopped the car for "one more shot," tied her up once more, and strangled her with a rope.

He then went on to describe the murder of Judy Dull. Calling on a model who had recently arrived from Florida, he had looked at her portfolio—but he was fascinated by a photograph he saw on the wall of nineteen-year-old Judy. She was married, with a fourteen-month-old daughter, but separated from her journalist husband. Glatman obtained her telephone number, and the following day he called her and asked her to pose for photographs later that afternoon. Dull was initially reluctant until he explained that they would have to shoot at her apartment, since his own was being used. Posing in her own home seemed safe enough, but when Glatman arrived there, he told her that he had managed to borrow a studio from a friend. It was, in fact, his own apartment.

Once there, he ordered her to take off her dress and put on a skirt and sweater. He then explained that he had to tie her hands behind her—he was taking a photograph for the cover of a "true detective" magazine. Dubious but compliant, she allowed him to tie her hands behind her, bind her knees together, and place a gag in her mouth. He snapped several photographs, then unbuttoned her sweater, pulled down her bra, and removed her skirt. After that he shot more photographs. Finally, when she was clad only in panties, he laid her on the floor and started to fondle her. She struggled and protested through the gag. Glatman became impotent if a woman showed signs of having a mind of her own—total passivity was required for his fantasy. He threatened her with a gun until she promised not to resist, and then raped her twice. After that, both sat naked on the sofa and watched television. Judy promised that if he would let her go she would never tell anyone what had happened. Glatman pretended to agree—he wanted her cooperation. He assured her that he would drive her out to a lonely place and release her, and then he would leave town. Then he drove into the desert near Phoenix, Colorado, and strangled her, after first taking more photographs. He buried her in a shallow grave.

Glatman then confessed to the murder of twenty-four-year-old divorcée Shirley Ann Bridgeford, a mother of two children, whom he contacted through the Patty Sullivan Lonely Hearts Club; he registered as George Williams, a plumber by profession. He made a date with Shirley Ann over the telephone to go square dancing on March 8, 1958, but when he picked her up at her mother's home in Sun Valley, he told her he would rather take her for a drive in the moonlight. After stopping for dinner he continued his drive until they were nearly a hundred miles south of Los Angeles before pulling the car over. He tried to fondle her; when she protested he produced a gun and ordered her into the back seat; there he raped her. Then, in the Anza Borrego desert, he tied her up, snapped his lurid photographs, and strangled her with a rope. He kept her red panties as a keepsake.

At the end of his two-hour confession, he led the detectives to the bones of Shirley Ann and Ruth.

Confessed murderer Harvey Glatman, at right, stands over bones, in San Diego, California, October 31, 1958, which he told officers were those of Shirley Ann Bridgeford. Bridgeford was one of three women he was charged with strangling. Often assuming the persona of Johnny Glenn, magazine photographer, Glatman was a fantasist whose crimes were the outcome of sexual frustration. (Associated Press)

In court in San Diego in November 1958, G
pleaded guilty to all three murders, rejecting his l
advice to plead guilty but insane on the grounds that he would rather die than spend the rest of his life behind bars. Superior Court Judge John A. Hewicker duly obliged, and on September 18, 1959, Glatman was put to death in the gas chamber at San Quentin. Pierce Brooks attended his execution.

Psychologically speaking, Harvey Glatman was the archetypal serial killer, a fantasist whose crimes were the outcome of sexual frustration. Scrawny and unattractive, he felt from the beginning that he would never be able to possess the kind of woman he dreamed about unless he took her by force.

Born in Denver, Colorado, in 1928, he was a mama's boy who did not get on with other children. Girls at school found the scrawny boy with the sticking-out ears unappealing; he therefore made his bid for attention by snatching their purses, running away, and then flinging them back at them. His mother is quoted as saying: "It was just his approach."

When he was twelve he discovered the pleasures of masochism, learning that tightening a noose around his throat induced sexual satisfaction. His mother, noticing the marks around his neck, took him to see the family doctor, who reassured her that the boy would outgrow the behavior. But by the age of seventeen his sexual frustrations had still found no other outlet, so he tried force, pointing a toy gun at a teenaged girl and ordering her to undress. She screamed and he fled, only to be picked up by the police. He broke his bail, and absconded to New York, where he satisfied his aggressive urges against woman by robbing them at gunpoint; he became known as the "Phantom Bandit." He was caught and sentenced to five years in Sing Sing Correctional Facility, and was released in 1951. He then returned to Colorado, where he became a television repairman, and in 1957 moved to Los Angeles, where his mother set him up in the TV repair business. And he soon took on the identity of Johnny Glenn, magazine photographer, and on August 1, 1957, called at the flat of Judy Dull.

Pierce Brooks never forgot the effort it had cost him to check whether there had been any similar abductions in the Los Angeles area, and he now began to try to convince his superiors of the importance of logging crimes, solved and unsolved, on a computer system where similarities could be observed. In due course, he became chief of homicide detectives in Los Angeles, then went on to become chief of police in Springfield and Eugene, Oregon, and in Lakewood, Colorado. His dream of computerizing crime reports eventually became the system known as VICAP, the Violent Criminal Apprehension Program. And the newly formed FBI Academy at Quantico looked like the ideal place to set it up. There Howard Teten and Patrick J. Mullany were teaching the concept of psychological profiling of criminals to their students.

> ALTHOUGH HE WAS NOT BROUGHT TO TRIAL—DAVID MEIRHOFER HANGED HIMSELF IN HIS CELL—HE BECAME THE FIRST SERIAL KILLER TO BE CAUGHT WITH THE AID OF THE FBI'S NEW INVESTIGATIVE TECHNIQUE.

In June 1973 came their first opportunity to put it into practice when seven-year-old Susan Jaeger from Farmington, Michigan, was abducted from a Rocky Mountains campsite in Montana. Sometime in the early hours an intruder slit open her tent with his knife and overpowered her before she could alert her parents, William and Marietta Jaeger, who slept close by. Once the alarm was raised, an intensive search failed to reveal any trace of the missing child, or any clue to the identity of her abductor. When the FBI was later called in, the case was referred to Quantico through Agent Pete Dunbar, then stationed in Bozeman, Montana.

Combining their own investigative experience with the police report, photographic evidence, and Dunbar's local knowledge, Teten, Mullany, and a recently arrived instructor named Robert K. Ressler, employed the new crime analysis to try to track down the child's abductor. They concluded that he was a homicidal Peeping Tom who lived in the vicinity of the camp—this was a remote area—and spotted the Jaegers during the course of a periodical summer's night snoop around the campsite. Statistics pointed to a young, male, white offender (sex killers are almost invariably young men: white because Susan Jaeger was white, and such offenses are usually intraracial).

The absence of any clues to his identity, the fact that he carried a knife with him to and from the campsite, and made off with his victim without any alarm being raised indicated an organized violent criminal. Sexually motivated murder frequently occurs at an early age, yet this was not the handiwork of some frenzied teenager. This bore the stamp of an older person, perhaps in his twenties. Statistical probability made him a loner, of average or possibly above average-intelligence.

Gradually the three instructors fitted together each piece of the behavioral jigsaw puzzle. The length of time the girl had been missing without word—and no sign of a ransom demand—persuaded them that Susan Jaeger had been murdered. They thought it likely that her abductor was that comparatively rare type of sex killer who mutilates his victims after death—sometimes to remove body parts as "souvenirs."

Early on in the investigation an informant contacted Agent Dunbar with the name of a possible suspect—David Meirhofer, a local twenty-three-year-old single man who had served in Vietnam. By chance, Dunbar knew Meirhofer, who to him seemed quiet and intelligent. More important, there was no known evidence to connect him with the abduction.

In January 1974, the charred body of an eighteen-year-old girl was found in nearby woodland. She had rejected Meirhofer's advances and avoided his company; otherwise he had no known connection with the crime. Yet, inevitably he again became a suspect, and even volunteered for both a lie detector test and interrogation under the "truth serum" sodium pentothal. He passed both tests so convincingly that Dunbar concluded that he must be innocent.

The Quantico profilers felt differently. They had noted that psychopaths can have dual personalities, Dr. Jekyll and Mr. Hydes so to speak, so that as Jekyll takes the test, he genuinely feels innocent. Experience had also taught the profilers that many sex killers deliberately seek ways of inserting themselves into an investigation, partly to find out how much the authorities know, but also out of a desire to play some active part in the drama. This is why they advised Susan Jaeger's parents to keep a tape recorder by their telephone. It was switched on on the first anniversary of their daughter's disappearance, when an anonymous male caller rang their home in Farmington and boasted to Marietta Jaeger that he was keeping Susan alive, and that she was in Europe. Instead of upbraiding him, Marietta responded gently, and by turning the other cheek reduced her anonymous caller to tears.

Analysis of the tape identified the voice as Meirhofer's. But that was not enough evidence under Montana law to obtain a warrant to search his apartment. Mullany reasoned, however, that if Marietta Jaeger could reduce David Meirhofer to tears by telephone, a face-to-face meeting might prove even more rewarding. Marietta had the courage to agree, and her husband escorted her to Montana where she met Meirhofer in his lawyer's office. He appeared in complete control, and said nothing to incriminate himself. The Jaegers returned home, thinking the plan had failed; but they were wrong. Shortly afterwards they received another phone call—this time from Salt Lake City, Utah, some four hundred miles south of Bozeman—from a man calling himself "Mr. Travis." He told Marietta that he was the man who abducted her daughter—but she recognized the voice, and called his bluff. "Well, hello, David," she said.

Backed now by Marietta Jaeger's sworn affidavit, Agent Dunbar in Bozeman obtained his search warrant. As the Quantico profilers had predicted, he unearthed various "souvenirs"—body parts, taken from both victims—that proved Meirhofer's guilt. At that, the man who had passed both "truth tests" so convincingly also confessed to two more unsolved murders (of local boys). Although he was not brought to trial—David Meirhofer hanged himself in his cell—he became the first serial killer to be caught with the aid of the FBI's new investigative technique.

It was a breakthrough that, within a decade, was to lead directly to the accurate, systematic profiling technique known as the "Criminal Investigative Analysis Program," or CIAP.

Both the Glatman and Meirhofer cases offered the psychological profilers some important clues to certain types of sex criminal. In childhood they are loners who feel alienated from their peer group. Robert Ressler writes in *Whoever Fights Monsters*: "As the psychologically damaged boys get closer to adolescence, they find that they are unable to develop the social skills that are precursors to sexual skills and that are the coin of positive emotional relationships. . . . By the time a normal youngster is dancing, going to parties, participating in kissing games, the loner is turning in on himself and developing fantasies that are deviant. The fantasies are substitutes for more positive human encounters, and as the adolescent becomes more dependent on them, he loses touch with acceptable social values." And he adds: "Most were incapable of holding jobs or living up to their intellectual potential."

The psychologist Abraham Maslow coined the phrase "deprivation needs" to refer to the basic needs that must be fulfilled before someone can reach his or her normal potential. A child who has been half-starved will lack certain vitamins that are essential to growth. And a child who is emotionally starved is likely to lack certain psychological vitamins, which may form an obstacle to satisfactory relationships. Ressler comments that although the result may not be murder or rape, "it will be some other sort of demonstration of dysfunction." In such people, the Dr. Jekyll aspect, shocked by what Mr. Hyde is doing, may become suicidal—hence Glatman's plea to be executed and Meirhofer's self-destruction.

Observations such as these would become the basis of Ressler's insight into the minds of serial killers.

A CHILD WHO IS EMOTIONALLY STARVED IS LIKELY TO LACK CERTAIN PSYCHOLOGICAL VITAMINS, WHICH MAY FORM AN OBSTACLE TO SATISFACTORY RELATIONSHIPS.

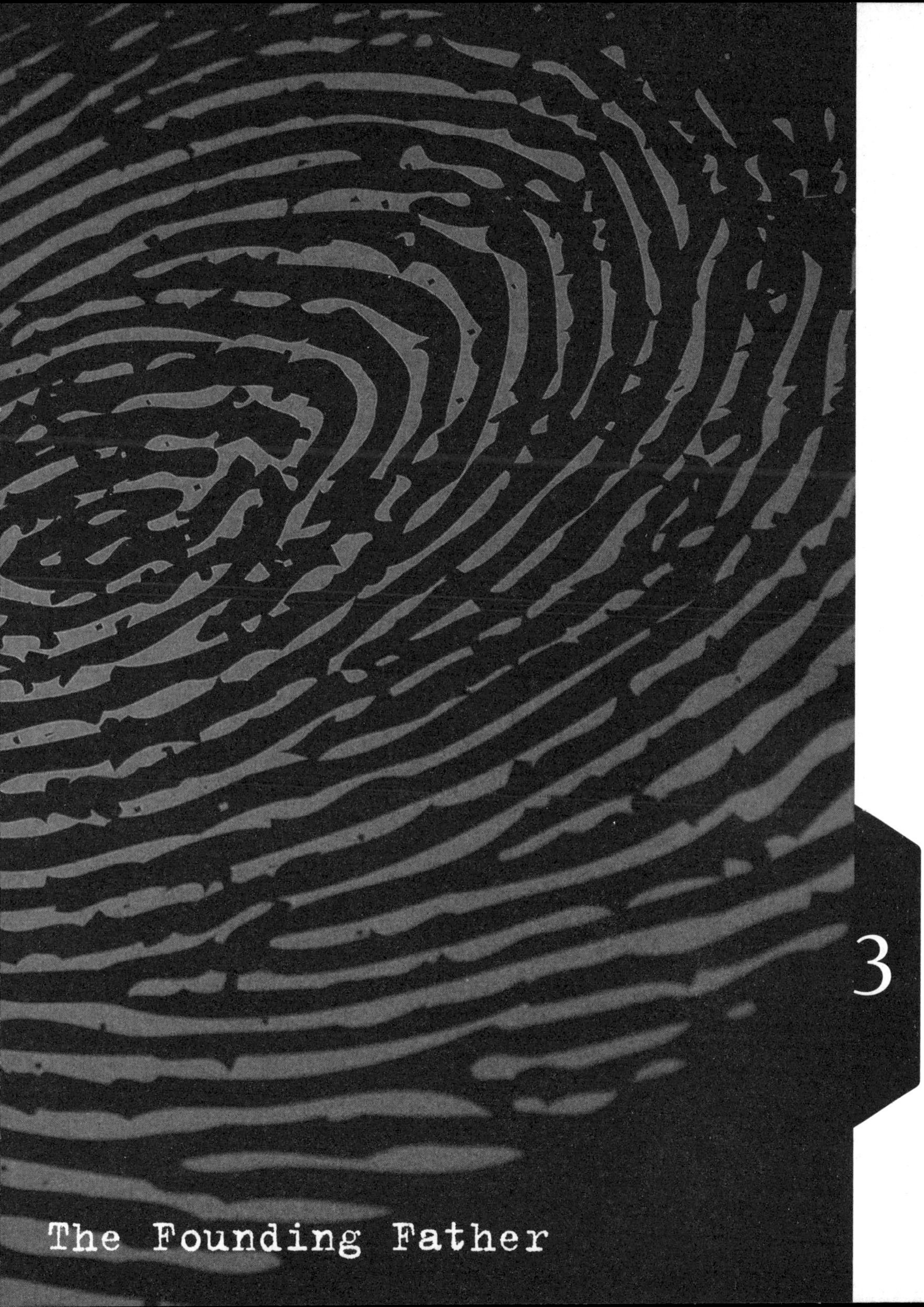

3

The Founding Father

3

The Founding Father

By the time he was a nine-year-old boy, Robert K. Ressler knew that monsters were not confined to fairy stories; there was a real one roaming the streets of his hometown, Chicago, Illinois.

On June 5, 1945, forty-three-year-old widow Josephine Ross had been stabbed to death when she had awakened to find a burglar in her apartment. Six months later, on December 10, 1945, a thirty-year-old ex-Wave named Frances Brown was discovered kneeling unclothed by the side of her bath, a knife driven through her throat with such force that it had come out the other side. On the wall above her bed someone had written in lipstick: "For heavens sake catch me before I kill more—I cannot help myself." There was no sign of rape.

Four weeks later, on the morning of January 7, 1946, James E. Degnan went into the bedroom of his seven-year-old daughter, Suzanne, and saw that she was not in her bed and that the window was wide open. He called the police, and it was a policeman who found the note on the child's chair; it said she had been kidnapped and demanded $20,000 for her return. Later that afternoon, Suzanne's head was discovered beneath a nearby manhole cover. In another sewer, police found the child's left leg. The right leg was found in another sewer, and the torso in a fourth. The arms were discovered—also in a sewer—some weeks later. The horrifically brutal case shocked the nation, but the police seemed unable to develop any definite leads.

Six months later, on June 26, 1946, a young man walked into an apartment building in Chicago, and entered the apartment of Mr. and Mrs. Pera through the open door. Mrs. Pera was in the kitchen preparing dinner. A neighbor who had seen the young man enter called to Mrs. Pera to ask if she knew a man had walked into her apartment. The young man immediately left, but the neighbor called out for him to stop. Instead, he dashed down the stairs, pointing a gun at the neighbor before running out of the building. Minutes later, he knocked on the door of a nearby apartment and asked the woman who answered for a glass of water, explaining that he felt ill. She sensed something wrong and rang the police. In fact, an off-duty cop had already seen the fleeing youth and ran after him. When cornered, the young man fired three shots at the cop; all missed. As the on-duty police answered the call, the burglar and the cop grappled on the floor. Then one of the other policemen hit the burglar on the head—three times—with a flowerpot, and knocked him unconscious.

Their prisoner turned out to be seventeen-year-old William George Heirens, who had spent some time in a correctional institution for burglary. When his fingerprints were taken, they were found to match one found on the Degnan ransom note, and another found in the apartment of Frances Brown. In the prison hospital, Heirens was given the "truth drug" sodium pentothal, and asked: "Did you kill Suzanne Degnan?" Heirens answered: "George cut her up." At first he insisted that George was a real person, a youth five years his senior whom he met at school. Later, he claimed that George was his own invisible alter ego. "He was just a realization of mine, but he seemed real to me." Heirens also admitted to a third murder, that of Josephine Ross. In addition to this, he had attacked a woman named Evelyn Peterson with an iron bar when she started to wake up during a burglary, and then tied her up with lamp cord; he had also fired shots through windows at two women who had been sitting in their rooms with the curtains undrawn.

The story of William Heirens, as it emerged in his confessions, and in interviews with his parents, was almost predictably typical of a serial sex killer. Born on November 15, 1928, he had been a forceps delivery. An underweight baby, he had cried and vomited a great deal. At the age of seven months he fell down twelve cement steps into the basement and landed on his head; after that he had nightmares about falling. He was three years old when a brother was born, and he was sent away to the home of his grandmother. He was frequently ill as a child, and broke his arm at the age of nine. The family background was far from happy; his mother had two nervous breakdowns accompanied by paralysis, and his father's business failed several times.

Heirens matured sexually very early—he had his first emission at the age of nine. Soon after this, he began stealing women's panties from clotheslines and

William Heirens stands in his cell on September 5, 1946, in the Cook County Jail in Chicago, after he was sentenced to serve three consecutive life terms for the murder of a little girl and two women. Heirens, although he claims to have been railroaded by the police, has been behind bars more than fifty years in the sensational Chicago murder case in which "Catch me before I kill more" was left scrawled in lipstick on a bathroom mirror. (Associated Press)

basement washrooms, and putting them on. (After his arrest, police found forty pairs of pink and blue rayon panties in a box in his grandmother's attic.)

He came to think of sex as something "dirty" and forbidden. This was confirmed when, at the age of thirteen, he walked into the school washroom and found two boys playing sexually with a mentally retarded boy; he refused to join in. Being a good-looking boy, he was attractive to girls; on eight occasions he attempted some form of sex play, touching their breasts or pressing their legs, but this had the effect of upsetting him so much that he cried. There was a deep conflict between his sexual obsession and his rigid Roman Catholic upbringing. He found normal sexual stimulation repellent.

From the age of thirteen he had been burgling apartments, entering through the window, and experiencing sexual excitement—to the point of emission—as he did so. After this, he lost interest in underwear, and began to experience his sexual fulfillment by entering strange apartments through the window. He often urinated or defecated on the floor. He also began lighting small fires.

He was arrested for the first time at the age of fourteen, charged with eleven burglaries and suspected of fifty; in many of them he had stolen guns and women's dresses. He was sentenced to probation and sent to a semicorrectional Catholic institution. After a year there he transferred to a Catholic academy, where he proved to be a brilliant student—so much so that he was allowed to skip the freshman year at the University of Chicago.

Back in Chicago, the sexual obsession remained as powerful as ever, and led to more burglaries. If he resisted the urge to burgle for long, he began to experience violent headaches. On one occasion, he put his clothes in the washroom and threw the key inside in order to make it impossible to go out; halfway through the night, the craving became too strong, and he crawled along the house gutter to retrieve his clothes.

Once inside an apartment, he reached such a state of intense excitement that any interruption would provoke an explosion of violence. This is why he knocked Evelyn Peterson unconscious with an iron bar when she stirred in her sleep. On another occasion he was preparing to enter what he thought was an empty apartment when a woman moved inside; he immediately fired his gun at her, but missed.

He raped none of the victims—the thought of actual sexual intercourse still scared him. Sexual fulfillment came from the "forbiddenness," the excitement of knowing he was committing a crime. After the ejaculation, he felt miserable; he believed that he was a kind of Jekyll and Hyde. He even invented a name for his Mr. Hyde—"George." Although he later admitted that the invention of an alter ego was partly an attempt to fool the psychiatrists, there can be no doubt that he felt that he was periodically "possessed" by a monster. This is why he scrawled the message in lipstick on the wall after killing Frances Brown. It may also explain why he eventually courted arrest by wandering into a crowded apartment building in the late afternoon and entering a flat in which a married woman was cooking dinner as she waited for her husband to return from work. Mr. Hyde was turning into Dr. Jekyll.

In July 1946, Heirens was sentenced to three terms of life imprisonment in Joliet Penitentiary.

Ressler states that as a nine-year-old boy he used to fantasize about catching Suzanne Degnan's killer—although he admits that the fantasy was a way of coping with his fear. But the detective fantasies lasted all that year of Heirens's arrest.

After a stint in the army, Ressler took a course in criminology and police administration at Michigan State University. But when he applied for a job with the Chicago police force, he was passed over; they were not interested in recruits with too much schooling because they "might make trouble."

He reenlisted into the army, and was posted to Germany, where he was named provost marshal of a platoon of MPs in the small town of Asschaffenburg, and, in effect, became its chief of police. Back in the United States, four years later, he opted to remain a soldier when offered a job as CID commander of a plainclothes investigation unit at Fort Sheridan, near Chicago. He was in charge of a complex operation to penetrate a narcotics ring, when a number of his undercover agents came close to being exposed and murdered. (They were posing as troublemakers awaiting dishonorable discharge.) Finally, in exchange for signing on for two more years, the army paid for him to complete his master's degree in police administration, and he applied to join the FBI. It was 1970, he was thirty-two, and his real career was about to commence.

An irritating but oddly significant incident almost prevented this from happening. Told to report to a certain classroom by 8 a.m. on a February day in 1970, he arrived in plenty of time only to find a notice saying the class had been shifted to another room several blocks away. On arriving there, he was bawled out by the instructor for being late. He replied that he had been ten minutes early at the other classroom. Irritated, the instructor sent him to see a high official, Joe Caspar, deputy assistant of the Training Division, known as the "Ghost" after the cartoon character Casper the Friendly Ghost. Caspar informed him that everyone had been sent a letter about the change of venue. Ressler replied that he hadn't received it. He added that he had been in the army for several years and knew all about orders, both giving and receiving them. "I thought steam was going to come out of the Ghost's ears as he threatened me with being kicked out of the FBI at that very minute." Ressler said maybe that would be best for everyone, if the FBI didn't know how to treat new agents. Caspar gave way and told him to hold up his right hand to be sworn in, adding sourly: "We'll be watching you."

This was typical of Hoover's old FBI, with its "do it by the book" ethos, and this would not be the last time Ressler encountered it. But it was doubly significant in that Caspar's downright refusal to admit that he was in the wrong is also typical of the behavioral pattern of a certain type of criminal to which the majority of serial killers belong. This behavioral pattern, which will recur many times in the course of this book, may well be worth further discussion here.

In the early 1960s, the Los Angeles science-fiction writer A. E. Van Vogt had a brilliant psychological insight that has considerable application to criminology: a concept that he called the "Right Man," or the "Violent Man." The Right Man is one who belongs to what zoologists call the "dominant 5 percent," for 5 percent of all animals are more dominant than their fellows. This dominance is inborn. But if a person is too young to be aware of his dominance, or if circumstances have never allowed the expression of that dominance, he will feel oddly frustrated and resentful, without understanding why. Such people have "a chip on their shoulder," and are inclined to be aggressive and self-assertive. His self-esteem depends upon feeling himself to be always in the right: he cannot bear to be thought in the wrong, and will go to any length to deny that he can ever make a mistake. Van Vogt also called him the Violent Man, because if you can prove that he is in the wrong, he would rather hit you in the face than acknowledge it.

Such a person's work colleagues may not notice his dominance, for if he wants to be liked, it is important to appear easygoing and nonaggressive. But for his wife and family he can be intolerable, for the Right Man's determination to be absolute master in his own home may be enforced by bullying.

Men like this, says Van Vogt, are at their worst in their intimate relations with women, since their sensitive egos make them wildly unreasonable if any disagreement arises. In one case he cites, the husband had divorced his wife and set her up in a suburban home, on condition that she remained unmarried and devoted herself to the welfare of their son. The husband was promiscuous—and always had been—but because his wife had confessed that she had not been a virgin when she met him, he treated her as a whore who had to be reformed at all costs. During their marriage he was violently jealous and often knocked her down. It was obviously essential to his self-esteem to feel himself her lord and master.

But perhaps the most curious thing about the violent male, Van Vogt observed, is that he is so basically dependent on the woman that if she leaves him, he experiences a total collapse of self-esteem that sometimes ends in suicide. For she is the foundation stone of a tower of fantasy. His self-esteem is built upon this notion of himself as a sultan brandishing a whip, with a submissive and adoring girl at his feet. If she leaves him, the whole fantasy world collapses, and he is faced with the prospect of an unlivable life. Van Vogt suggests that many dictators were Right Men—Hitler, Stalin, Mao—and that their urge to dominate was based upon this need to make the world conform to their fantasy of infallibility. Since submissive and adoring girls are hard to find, particularly for men like Glatman and Meirhofer, the serial killer is choosing this extreme method to ensure that the woman conforms to his fantasy.

A dominant person is, by definition, a person with a craving to be a "somebody." And if lack of talent or social skills frustrates this urge, the result is anger, self-assertiveness, and mild paranoia. This may happen very early in the career of the Right Man, and become so much a character trait that subsequent success makes no difference—it has come too late as far as he is concerned. This is why a Hitler, a Stalin, a Saddam, remains a Right Man all his life.

Freud once said that a child would destroy the world if it had the power—which explains why Right Man criminals are so dangerous. They regard society itself as the enemy that is frustrating them, with the result that they commit their crimes entirely without conscience, with a grim feeling of justification. Society is "getting what it deserves" for treating them so badly. The American mass murderer Carl Panzram, executed in 1930, declared: "If I couldn't injure those who had injured me, then I would injure someone else." Panzram committed twenty pointless murders, engaged in a weird and totally illogical principle of "reciprocity."

So it may be regarded as significant that Ressler's career as an FBI agent was nearly aborted because of an encounter with a Right Man.

Following his FBI training, Ressler spent the early 1970s doing fieldwork in Chicago, New Orleans, and Cleveland, before being transferred to Quantico in 1974, in time to participate in the profiling and capture of David Meirhofer. And here Ressler was able to observe an element that is typical of a certain kind of killer: telephoning the kidnapped child's parents on the anniversary of her disappearance. The serial killer wishes to see himself as a "mover," one who can change events. There is a need for dramatization that leads him to scan newspapers for every item referring to his crime, and to revisit the crime scene. The German sadistic mass murderer of the 1920s, Peter Kürten (on whom Fritz Lang based his film *M*) regularly returned to the crime scene after the victim had been found, enjoying the horror of the spectators and often achieving a sexual climax. If investigators had known this at the time, he might well have been caught sooner.

"IF I COULDN'T INJURE THOSE WHO HAD INJURED ME, THEN I WOULD INJURE SOMEONE ELSE."

Ressler soon observed this central role played by fantasy in the life of the serial killer (although in fact, it would be another decade before he coined the term). He would comment later: "They are obsessed with a fantasy, and they have what we must call nonfulfilled experiences that become part of the fantasy and push them on towards the next killing."

A major step in the development of his new techniques was his involvement in teaching hostage negotiation. A large number of FBI recruits came out of the military after the end of the Vietnam War; many of them were trained crack marksmen and became involved in SWAT teams (Special Weapons and Tactics). SWAT snipers were used to kill criminals, and heavy weapons often used in attempts to free hostages—which led to a great deal of needless slaughter. Rather than sending in SWAT teams, however, the New York City Police Department pioneered the use of bargaining by trained negotiators. This demanded an understanding of criminal psychology of the kind that obsessed Ressler. The new approach was slow to replace the old one, partly because many old-school cops disliked what they saw as compromise with criminal scum (an attitude that made the *Dirty Harry* movies of Clint Eastwood so popular). But this attitude had its practical disadvantages, not least of which were expensive lawsuits against the police for excessive use of force.

Ressler took note of the new approach and melded it into the idea that was taking shape in his mind, and that would become his own brand of criminal profiling.

What fascinated him was the psychology of the criminal. What drove Charles Manson, Sirhan Sirhan, "Son of Sam" David Berkowitz, and the Texas Tower Sniper, Charles Whitman (who had killed sixteen people from the University of Texas Tower)? But the books about these killers contained insufficient information for a full assessment of their motives. As to his colleagues at the FBI, he comments wryly on the "Bureau's belief that if there was something worth knowing about criminals, the Bureau already knew it."

By the late 1960s and mid-1970s, however, a whole series of bizarre mass murders made it clear that there was a great deal to be learned. The five killings at the house of film star Sharon Tate on August 9, 1969, followed by the slaying of supermarket owner Leno LaBianca and his wife, Rosemary, the next day, traumatized the American public. When it emerged that December that an ex-convict named Charles Manson had ordered his drug-dependent "Family" to commit the murders, there was universal bafflement about his motive, which the subsequent trial failed to disperse.

Between December 1968 and October 1969, five apparently "motiveless" murders were committed in the San Francisco area by a killer who called himself "Zodiac," and who signed letters to newspapers with a cross over a circle, the astrological sign of the zodiac. The killings and the letters ceased abruptly, although whether this was because of the death of the killer, or some other reason, is still unknown.

On Halloween 1970, eye surgeon Victor Ohta and his family and secretary were murdered near Santa Cruz, California, by a dropout named John Linley Frazier, who left a note saying that World War III had just begun and would not cease until "misusers of the environment" had all met the same fate; the killer proved to be a local hippie on a bad mescaline trip.

In October 1972, another dropout, Herb Mullin, committed the first of fourteen murders in the Santa Cruz area, ordered by "voices in his head."

In May 1972, Ed Kemper, a six-foot nine-inch ex–mental patient, began a series of sex murders of coeds, also in the Santa Cruz area, decapitating and mutilating six of them. He concluded his spree in April 1973 by killing and beheading his mother and her best friend. He had earlier spent five years in an institution after murdering his grandparents.

In January 1974, failed law student Ted Bundy committed in Seattle the first of a long series of sex murders that continued until his final arrest in Florida in April 1978, and probably exceeded forty victims. He seemed such a good-looking, intelligent, charming person that many people felt there must be some mistake and the wrong man had been arrested.

If New Yorkers felt like congratulating themselves that the craziest killers seemed to originate on the West Coast, they were forced to think again when a series of apparently motiveless shootings commenced in July 1976, and continued until the arrest of David Berkowitz, known as "the Son of Sam," a year later.

Clearly, something strange was happening; murder had ceased to be as straightforward as in the days of Harvey Glatman, or even the Boston Strangler. Ever since the first police forces had been created in the nineteenth century, crime detection had taken its starting point from the concept of motive; killers like Zodiac, Frazier, Kemper, and Berkowitz seemed to defy the normal classification. Which is why, it seemed to Ressler, it would be sensible to talk to some of these killers and find out what had driven them to murder.

One of the earliest successes of "criminal profiling" involved the murder of a schoolgirl. On September 2, 1977, fourteen-year-old Julie Wittmeyer disappeared on the way home from school in Platte City, Kansas. Her clothing—minus her panties—was found in a field a few days later, and her naked and mutilated body the next day. The local police turned to the FBI's new Behavioral Science Unit at Quantico. After studying the evidence, BSU sent back a "profile" of the offender: he knew the victim, he was a sexually frustrated "loner," probably of below-average intelligence and of more than average physical development, and his contemporaries probably regarded him as "strange." Police Chief Marion Beeler exclaimed: "Sure as shootin', that's him"—for the description fitted a youth named Mark Sager. In fact, Sager was found guilty of the crime and sentenced to ten years.

While the Criminal Research Project was still waiting for approval, Ressler decided to talk to a killer who was largely responsible for his interest in murder, William Heirens, who was now in the Vienna Correctional Center in Southern Illinois. At the time Ressler went to see him, he had been a model prisoner for more than thirty years. What Ressler knew about him was that he had become a panty fetishist in adolescence, and began burgling apartments to obtain them. What Ressler wanted to know was about the development of Heirens's sexual urges.

He was to be disappointed. Ever since his 1946 conviction, Heirens had been pleading his innocence. Why then had he confessed to three murders? Because, he explained, the cops had decided that he was guilty, and had told him that unless he confessed, he would be sentenced to death on the evidence they had. Naturally, he decided to confess.

What about the burglaries and the stealing of panties? Ressler writes: "Heirens did acknowledge having had some sexual problems and having committed the break-ins that he now deprecated as adolescent pranks . . ." But Heirens insisted that he was innocent of all the other crimes. Understandably, Ressler did not believe him. Here was a man who admitted burglary and "sexual problems," and who had been arrested during the course of a break-in and tried to shoot the policeman who arrested him. If he was just an ordinary burglar, why risk becoming a cop-killer? Ressler left the prison feeling slightly disgruntled.

I had written about Heirens in the *Encyclopedia of Murder*. To me, his confession sounded authentic enough, since I had personal acquaintance with fetishism. Even as a child of preschool age, I had been fascinated by my mother's knickers, and put them on when she was out of the house. With the awakening of adolescent sexual urges, I found myself continually glancing furtively at knickers in shop windows or on clotheslines. I never actually stole any, but when the opportunity presented itself, used them for autoerotic purposes. Unlike Heirens, however, I never suffered agonies of guilt about my fetish, and when the opportunity of trying the real thing with girlfriends came along, found that my appreciation of how they looked in their underwear enhanced the pleasure. When I eventually came across biologist Rupert Sheldrake's theory of "morphic resonance"—the notion that forms of learned behavior can be socially transmitted by a kind of telepathy (see the epilogue)—it seemed to me a way to explain how a three-year-old child had wanted to pull on his mother's knickers.

In August 1991, I saw an advertisement in an American bookseller's catalogue for a new book, *William Heirens: His Day in Court* by Dolores Kennedy, published by Bonus Books of Chicago, and sent off for it. To my astonishment, the author argued that Heirens was innocent. Kennedy had been legal secretary to the lawyer who represented the Degnan family, who, oddly enough, believed that Heirens should be released. In 1983, a federal magistrate did order the release of Heirens—after thirty-seven years in jail—because the parole board had failed to comply with his parole requirements. There was immediate uproar, and the attorney general declared: "I am going to make sure that kill-crazed animal stays where he is." The magistrate's decision was reversed.

Dolores Kennedy's father began to work for Heirens's release, and when he died, she went to see Heirens in the Vienna Correctional Center in Illinois to discuss what further could be done. She found Heirens likable—as do most people who meet him—and helped form a committee for his release. But Heirens himself presented a curious obstacle. He argued that he did not want to be released on parole—or at least, that he was not willing to pacify the parole board by taking what they regarded as the essential first step in considering him for parole: admission of guilt. He declared: "In 1946 I had to plead guilty to live. I was seventeen years old and I wanted to live, and sometimes I wanted to die. I am sixty years old now and I will never admit to murders I did not commit." In other words, he had been forced to plead guilty only because the alternative to this "plea bargain" was the electric chair. As Kennedy looked into the case, she began to "uncover the magnitude of the misrepresentations connected with his conviction," and decided to write a book about it.

My immediate reaction to her book was skepticism. At least 50 percent of criminals claim that they have been "framed." Where Heirens was concerned, the case against him seemed to hang together so well that I found it virtually impossible to believe in his innocence. And as I read the book, it seemed to me that Dolores Kennedy deliberately underplayed the most powerful evidence—the box of panties found in the house of Heirens's grandmother. I wrote to her to tell her so. She replied politely, declaring that Heirens had concocted the fetishism story because he hoped to be found insane. She said that Heirens himself would write and confirm this.

In March 1992, I received a letter from Heirens in which he did exactly that. He pointed out that although he had twice been arrested for burglary in his early teens, there had been no suggestion of stealing panties. "None of these examinations remotely indicated fetishism." He also pointed out that, at his arrest, it was the police who fired the three shots, not he. He went on to explain how, when he was nine, he had found a trunk of old clothes on a garbage dump near his grandmother's home, and had taken from it various items, which included women's underwear—bloomers and slips—as well as some men's swimming trunks. He put these in a cardboard box and hid them behind the chimney in his grandmother's house. "None of the underwear was of the frilly sort common with panty fetishism." In fact it was made of cotton and was of the prewar variety. There were no semen stains, as there would have been if it had been used in masturbation. And, according to Heirens, it was only after he had agreed to the plea bargaining, which included the fetishism story, that he told the police of the whereabouts of the box, which had been there for almost ten years.

On the whole, I was not convinced. Yet I had to admit that his refusal of parole unless he was given the opportunity to establish his innocence was a persuasive argument in his favor. My wife suggested that perhaps he didn't really want to be released. After all, a man in his sixties is likely to find the modern world a bewildering place after forty or so years in jail. He replied to this comment by pointing out that his prison "is not as comfortable as you seem to believe . . . it is still a prison where you are told what to do and when . . ." I asked him if there was any documentary evidence indicating that the box found in his grandmother's attic contained a mixture of male and female clothing; he replied that, as far as he knew, no inventory had been made.

When in 1993 a publisher asked me to compile an anthology of murders of the 1940s, it was obvious to me that Heirens had to be included, and that I had to make some mention of Dolores Kennedy's belief that he was innocent. That is why I decided to write to Heirens and ask him to write me a simple and brief account of his own side of the story, which I would print alongside my own account of the case. It began:

> *My name is William Heirens. I have been imprisoned in Illinois for forty-seven years for murders I did not commit. Many of you over the age of fifty will remember the murder and dismemberment of six-year-old Suzanne Degnan in January of 1946. If you are younger, you may have read about it in crime anthologies or studied the case in classes. And, based on your reading, you may*

have been satisfied that the person responsible is paying for the crime.

I did not murder Suzanne Degnan. I did not murder Frances Brown and Josephine Ross—two women whose unsolved murders I was also forced to take the blame for to save my life.

Over the years many writers have canvassed my case in crime anthologies. Almost without exception they have been carelessly written with no regard for the facts.

The account was impressive, and there was no point where I could fault it or point to distortions of fact. So I concluded my piece on Heirens by saying that, while I was not convinced of his innocence, I was now rather less certain of his guilt.

And so matters rested over the next few years. But in 2000, I was involved in editing a crime part-work called *Murder in Mind,* and one of the issues I had to read and check was on the Heirens case. It was many years since I had looked at the case, and I had forgotten many of the details. And at that point I came across something that suddenly left me in no doubt that Heirens was guilty.

On October 5, 1945, a retired army nurse, Lieutenant Evelyn Peterson, was in bed sleeping late in her flat not far from the University of Chicago when someone struck her on the head with a metal bar. When she woke up she found that she was tied hand and foot with electrical cord. She worked her way free, and noticed that $150 was missing from her purse.

As she was about to call the police there was a knock on her door. She opened it to find a dark-haired young man. He seemed greatly concerned about the blood on her face, and said he would notify the apartment manager that she needed help. Then he left. When the police arrived, they discovered that the apartment had been wiped clean of fingerprints. The dark-haired young man—Heirens—was nowhere to be seen.

So what was Heirens doing knocking on a stranger's door at nine in the morning?

Heirens's story, as told in Dolores Kennedy's book, is that, arriving early for classes, he had decided to commit a quick burglary in the apartment block where Evelyn Peterson lived. He saw a woman banging on Peterson's door and asked if he could help. The woman, Peterson's sister, Margaret, said she couldn't get in and her key would not turn in the lock. Assuming that her sister must be deeply asleep, she went off to get some breakfast. Heirens left with her, but as soon as she was out of sight, went back up to the apartment with the intention of breaking in. As a precaution, he knocked on the door. And it was opened by a woman with blood on her face.

This is Heirens's story, and in my view it is preposterous. He is asking us to believe that, by pure chance, he decided to try to break into an apartment where, by some extraordinary coincidence, another burglar had already knocked Evelyn Peterson unconscious—a million-to-one likelihood, like lightning striking the same place twice.

I wrote to Dolores Kennedy and told her that, with the greatest regret, I could no longer entertain the slightest doubt of Heirens's guilt. Being a nice lady, she replied patiently that while she could see my point, she still believed his story, a million-to-one likelihood or not.

What must have happened strikes me as fairly obvious. Heirens had broken in, knocked the sleeping woman unconscious, and rifled her purse. He then cleaned off any fingerprints he might have left and departed. Then, in the manner of a guilty person wondering if there is some trace of his presence that he had overlooked, he decided to go back to check. He returned, but found her sister trying to get in. Clearly, Peterson was still unconscious. So he left the building with Margaret, and then slipped back, only to find that Peterson was by then fully conscious. It must have been an embarrassing moment when she opened the door. How could he explain why he was knocking on her door? He made his excuse about summoning help and left—for good this time.

If it was Heirens who knocked Peterson unconscious—and who else could it have been?—then he was not the fairly harmless teenager he wanted Dolores Kennedy to believe. He could have cracked her skull or caused brain damage. And as soon as we have this image of Heirens striking a sleeping woman with an iron bar—if he was so harmless, why not just take her purse and vanish?—we also glimpse the person who beat and stabbed Frances Brown, killed and dismembered Suzanne Degnan, and stabbed Josephine Ross through the throat.

Why did he not, in order to obtain parole, simply tell the truth? Because, I suspect, his shame about the sexual aspect of the murders made him incapable of admitting that his victims had seen him masturbating at the side of their beds, and driven him to kill to expunge the humiliation.

Ressler goes on to say that, although the interview with William Heirens was a disappointment, even the failure left him doubly certain that this direct contact with criminals could bring new insights.

4

Fantasy Finds a Victim

4

Fantasy Finds a Victim

In early 1978, Ressler, due to travel to northern California on a teaching assignment, decided that this would be a good time to make a start with his project of interviewing killers. In theory, he should have obtained permission from his superiors. But he had been present at lecture by a naval computer expert who had described her own scheme for cutting through bureaucratic red tape. It was better, said Grace Hopper, to ask forgiveness than to ask permission, because permission might be refused, whereas one could always apologize later for transgressions. Ressler took her point, and contacted a friend in California who was the liaison officer for the prison system, and asked him the whereabouts of the murderers he wanted to interview: these included Charles Manson, Edmund Kemper, Herbert Mullin, John Linley Frazier, Juan Corona (a killer of migrant workers), and Sirhan Sirhan (the assassin of Robert F. Kennedy). Because FBI agents could enter any prison in the country by showing their badges, and did not have to give a reason for wanting to talk to inmates, all of this presented no problems.

Sirhan happened to be the first interviewee on the list. He had shot Robert Kennedy ten years earlier, on June 5, 1968, as Kennedy was on his way to a press conference at the Ambassador Hotel in Los Angeles, after winning the California presidential primary. Kennedy was making his way through the food service area when Sirhan began shooting with a .22 revolver. Convicted of first-degree murder, Sirhan, a Palestinian, was sentenced to death, but a decision of the U.S. Supreme Court brought an end to the death penalty in 1971, before he could be executed.

Sirhan had been diagnosed a paranoid schizophrenic, and his demeanor bore this out. Ressler says: "He entered the room with his eyes wild, frightened and apprehensive. He stood against the wall, his fists clenched, and refused to shake hands." Sirhan seemed to believe that Ressler had some connection with the Secret Service, and declined to be tape-recorded. But when Ressler asked his view of the prison system, he became more forthcoming, and talked angrily about a cellmate who had betrayed him by giving an interview to *Playboy*. But finally he relaxed and sat down at the table.

He told Resssler that he had been instructed to assassinate Kennedy by voices in his head, and that when he had been looking in a mirror, he had seen his face cracking and falling in pieces. Ressler noted that he referred to himself in the third person—Sirhan did this and Sirhan did that—and believed that he was in protective custody because the authorities were treating him with more respect than common criminals (whereas the truth was that other prisoners might attack him).

He shot Kennedy, he explained, because Kennedy had once supported the selling of jet fighters to Israel, and if he became president, he might be pro-Israeli and anti-Arab. He believed that in killing Kennedy he had changed the course of world history, and that when he returned to Jordan he would be carried shoulder high as a hero. The parole board was afraid to release him, he said, because they feared his personal magnetism.

Ressler describes how, at the end of the interview, Sirhan stood by the door, pulling in his stomach and flexing his muscles, which he had kept in trim with weight lifting, and as he left asked: "Well, Mr. Resssler, what do you think of Sirhan now?" It was clear that he believed he had made a strong impression. "Obviously," said Ressler, "he felt that to know Sirhan was to love him."

The next three interviews—with Juan Corona, Herb Mullin, and John Linley Frazier—were unrewarding, offering no real insights. Corona, a Mexican labor contractor who had killed and then buried twenty-five tramps and migrant workers in 1971, was originally believed to have killed them to avoid paying their wages. But the fact that many of the men—mostly alcoholics—had their trousers around their ankles suggested a sexual motive. Corona, argued his defense, was a "hopeless heterosexual" who was married with children, and was therefore unlikely to be guilty. But he had formerly been diagnosed as schizophrenic, and the violence of some of the murders certainly hinted at a disturbed personality. Unfortunately, since Corona was "entirely uncommunicative," Ressler was unable to form any assessment.

The Frazier case had caused some panic at the time, since the Manson murders were fresh in everyone's minds. After shooting Victor Ohta, his wife and two children, and his secretary, Frazier had dumped them in the swimming pool, and then set the house on fire. Under the windshield wiper of Ohta's Rolls Royce was a grandiloquent note signed with the four suits of the tarot pack, suggesting some kind of occult group, or perhaps another Zodiac. The doctor's station wagon had been left in a railway tunnel in the obvious hope of causing a serious accident, but the goods train that struck it was traveling so slowly that it only pushed it out of the tunnel.

RESSLER ALSO FOUND THIS INTERVIEW DISAPPOINTING, COMMENTING ONLY THAT FRAZIER WAS "THE PRISONER OF HIS DELUSIONS."

Questioning a group of hippies in the nearby woods pointed the investigation in the direction of a twenty-four-year-old car mechanic who had left his wife to live with hippies, and fingerprints on the door of the Rolls Royce confirmed this. John Linley Frazier had been studying the tarot and books on ecology, and concluded that American society lacked spirituality. He had burgled the Ohtas' expensive home before the crime, and subsequently told someone that the Ohta family was too materialistic and should be killed. (In fact, Dr. Ohta had founded a hospital in Santa Cruz to which he gave financial support, and gave free treatment to patients who could not afford his fees.) After his arrest, Frazier had remained silent throughout his trial but had nonetheless been sentenced to death because his guilt was established beyond reasonable doubt. Like Sirhan, he had been saved by the abolition of the death penalty in 1971.

Ressler also found this interview disappointing, commenting only that John Linley Frazier was "the prisoner of his delusions."

Herb Mullin had first shown symptoms of schizophrenia after the death of his closest friend in a car accident, and by the time he was twenty-one (in 1969) was hearing voices that told him to shave his head and burn his penis with a lighted cigarette. In 1972, driving along a highway in the mountains he saw an old tramp; he asked him to take a look at his engine, and then, as the man leaned over the car, killed him with a baseball bat. Ten days later, as he was giving a lift to a college student, he stabbed her in the heart, and then disemboweled her. A month later he killed a friend and his wife, and then a woman and her sleeping children. In a Santa Cruz state park he shot to death four teenagers who were camping, and finally, at random, an old man in his front garden. A neighbor who witnessed the shooting called the police and Mullins was arrested.

These murders, he explained at his trial, had saved thousands of lives by averting natural disasters such as earthquakes. Oddly enough, he was deemed to be sane and sentenced to life. One psychiatrist blamed his murder spree on Governor Ronald Reagan's closing of mental hospitals in California to save money.

Ressler found Mullin docile and polite, but with nothing to say.

Ressler's conclusions about his interviewees so far was that, apart from Sirhan they belonged to a category his fellow profiler Roy Hazelwood called "disorganized" killers; these are fundamentally weak personalities whose crimes tend to be spontaneous and are poorly and inadequately planned. He writes: "The disorganized offender's actions are usually devoid of normal logic; until he is caught and tells us his version of the crimes, chances are that no one can follow the twisted reasoning he uses to pick his victims."

Organized killers such as Ed Kemper and Charles Manson proved to be a more complex proposition.

"I'm sorry to sound so cold about this," Kemper explained to Ressler, "but what I needed to have was a particular experience with a person, and to possess them in the way I wanted to, I had to evict them from their human bodies."

Edmund Emil Kemper III, born on December 18, 1948, had started to show signs of severe psychological disturbance as a child. His mother and father separated when he was seven; he was one of those children who badly needed a man to admire and imitate, and became an ardent fan of John Wayne. He had been a boy scout and was taught to shoot and handle a knife at summer camp. He claimed that his mother, Clarnell, ridiculed him, and he grew up with a highly ambivalent attitude towards her. As a child, he played games with his sister in which she led him to die in the gas chamber, and he once cut the hands and feet off her doll.

At thirteen he cut the family cat into pieces. He had sadistic fantasies which included killing his mother, and often went into her bedroom at night with a gun, toying with the idea. He grew up to be six feet nine inches tall and weighing 280 pounds. He also had fantasies of sexual relation with corpses. In spite of his powerful sexual interest in women from an early age, he was pathologically shy; when his sister once joked with him about wanting to kiss his teacher he replied, "If I kissed her I'd have to kill her first." Which is precisely what he did to his victims in manhood. Like English sex murderer John Christie, he seems to have killed women because he would have been impotent with a living woman.

THE IMPORTANCE OF THE ROLE OF FANTASY IN THE EARLY LIVES OF SERIAL KILLERS COULD HARDLY BE EXAGGERATED.

At thirteen Ed ran away to his father. But his sullen demeanor and his sheer size made his stepmother nervous, and she prevailed on her husband to return him to his mother. He was then sent to live with his father's parents on a ranch in California. His mother rang her ex-husband to warn him that he was taking a risk in sending Ed to live with them; she said, "You might wake up one day and find they've been killed." Which is exactly what happened. When he lost his temper with his domineering grandmother one day in August 1963, he pointed a rifle at the back of her head and shot her. He then stabbed her repeatedly. When his grandfather came home, he shot him before he could enter the house. He then telephoned his mother and waited for the police to arrive. Donald Lunde, a psychiatrist who examined him later, remarked: "In his way, he had avenged the rejection of both his mother and father."

After five years in mental hospitals, he was sent back to his mother. She moved to Santa Cruz, where she became an administrative assistant in a college of the University of California. She and Ed had violent, screaming quarrels, usually about trivial subjects. Kemper loathed her. He bought a motorcycle and wrecked it, suing the motorist involved, and then did the same with a second motorcycle. Using the insurance money he bought himself a car, and began driving around, picking up hitchhikers, preferably female. And on May 7, 1972, he committed his first sex murder, picking up Anita Luchessa and Mary Anne Pesce, both students at Fresno State College, in Berkeley. He produced his gun, drove to a quiet spot, and made Anita climb into the trunk while he handcuffed Mary Ann and put a plastic bag over her head. She seemed unafraid of him, and tried to talk to him reasonably. He stabbed her several times in the back, then in the abdomen; finally he cut her throat. After this he went to the trunk, and stabbed the other young woman repeatedly. He then drove home—his mother was out—carried the bodies up to his apartment, and decapitated and dissected them. Later, he buried the pieces in the mountains.

On September 14, 1972, he picked up fifteen-year-old Aiko Koo hitchhiking to a dance class in San Francisco. He produced his gun, drove her to the mountains, and then taped her mouth. He suffocated her by placing his fingers up her nostrils; she fought fiercely but vainly. When she was dead, he laid her on the ground and raped her, achieving orgasm within seconds. He took her body back to his apartment, cut off the head, becoming sexually excited as he did so, then her hands, and dissected the body. He took the remains out to the mountains above Boulder Creek and buried them. By then, newspapers were reporting that the "Chopper" or the "Coed Butcher" was preying on young women.

On January 8, 1973, he picked up Cynthia Schall, who usually hitched a lift to Cabrillo College. He produced the gun, drove her to the little town of Freedom, and stopped on a quiet road. For a while he played a game of cat and mouse with her, assuring her that he had no intention of harming her, enjoying the sensation of power. Then he shot her, dumped the body in the trunk, and drove home. She was a heavy girl, and he staggered with her into his bedroom and stuffed her into his closet. His mother came home, and Kemper talked to her and behaved normally.

As soon as she was gone the next morning, he took out the body and engaged in various sex acts. He then dissected it with an axe in the shower, and drove out to Carmel, with the pieces in plastic sacks, and threw them off cliffs. This time, parts of the body were discovered only a day later, and identified as Cynthia Schall.

After another violent quarrel with his mother on February 5, 1973, he drove to the local campus, and picked up Rosalind Thorpe, who was just coming out of a lecture. Shortly after, he picked up twenty-one-year-old Alice Liu. As they drove along in the dark, he shot Rosalind in the head. Alice covered her face with her hands, and he shot her several times in the head.

He then put both bodies in the trunk, and drove home. His mother was at home, so he couldn't carry them in. Unable to wait, he took his big hunting knife (which he called "the General") and hacked off their heads in the trunk. The next morning, after his mother left for work, he carried Alice into the bathroom, cleaned off the blood, and had sexual intercourse with the headless corpse. He also cleaned up Rosalind, although it is not clear whether he again performed necrophiliac sex. He placed both bodies back in the trunk, cut off Alice's hands, then drove to the coast highway south of Pacifica and disposed of the heads; the bodies were dumped in Eden Canyon, Alameda. They were found nine days later.

Meanwhile, media coverage in the Santa Cruz area heightened the atmosphere of terror. Shortly after the discovery of Rosalind Thorpe and Alice Liu, a policeman checking through gun licenses realized that Ed Kemper had a criminal record, and had not declared this. He drove to Kemper's house, and found him in his car with a young blonde woman. Kemper handed over the gun, and the policeman drove off. The visit probably saved the life of the blonde hitchhiker.

Kemper felt that he was going to "blow up" soon, commit a crime so obvious that he was going to be caught. He decided to kill his mother first. On the morning of Easter Sunday 1973 Kemper walked into Clarnell's bedroom and hit her on the head with a hammer. He then cut off her head with the General, "humiliated" her body in some unspecified way, and then dumped it in a closet wrapped in a blanket.

He felt sick and went out for a drive. On the way he saw an acquaintance who owed him $10 and they went for a drive in his friend's car: his friend offered him the $10, which, said Kemper later, "saved his life." But he felt the craving to kill again, so he rang a friend of his mother's, Sara Hallett, and invited her to dinner with him and his mother. When she arrived, she was breathless, and said, "Let's sit down. I'm dead." Kemper took this as a cue, hit her, and then strangled her, crooking his arm round her neck from behind and squeezing as he raised her from the floor. Later, in removing her head, he discovered that he had broken her neck.

That night he slept in his mother's bed. The next day he drove west in Mrs. Hallett's car. Then, using money he had taken from the dead woman, he rented a Hertz car. At one point he was stopped by a policeman for speeding, and fined $25 on the spot. The policeman did not notice the gun on the back seat.

Kemper had been expecting a manhunt, but when, after three days, there was still no news on the radio of the discovery of the bodies, he stopped in Pueblo, Colorado, and telephoned the Santa Cruz police to confess to being the "co-ed killer." They asked him to call back later. He did, several times, before he finally convinced them that he was serious. They sent a local policeman to arrest him. In custody in Pueblo, he showed himself eager to talk loquaciously about the killings, describing them all in detail—even how he had buried the head of one victim in the garden, facing towards the house, so that he could imagine her looking at him, and how he had cut out his mother's larynx and dropped it in the trashcan "because it seemed appropriate after she had bitched me so much." He explained that he had driven to Pueblo before turning himself in because he was afraid that if he went straight to the local police they might shoot first and ask questions later, and he was "terrified of violence."

Kemper was adjudged legally sane, and sentenced to life imprisonment.

Ressler obviously felt that Kemper, unlike Frazier, Mullin, and Corona, was well worth the trip to Vacaville Prison—in fact, he visited there three times. Kemper told him how, at the age of ten, he had returned home one day to find that all his belongings had been moved to the windowless basement, his mother explaining that his size made his sisters feel uncomfortable (they were in their teens). She also spent much of her time belittling him—another unpleasant characteristic of many parents of serial killers. So Kemper was virtually condemned to fantasy.

The importance of the role of fantasy in the early lives of serial killers could hardly be exaggerated. Kemper admitted that he had killed thousands of women in fantasy before he did it in reality. In his classic *Sex Perversions and Sex Crimes* (1957), James Melvin Reinhardt, professor of criminology at the University of Nebraska, starts by underlining the central role played by fantasy in sexual aberration, and adds: "These tend to generate their own psychic energies"—that is to say, the fantasy takes over. The result, says Reinhardt, "is that they can bring about a "deterioration that leads to criminality, alcoholism and other modes of escape."

One of the oddest of the cases in which fantasy played a central part concerns the shooting of Eddie Waitkus, first baseman of the Philadelphia Phillies baseball team, by an admiring fan. On June 15, 1949, nineteen-year-old Ruth Anne Steinhagen, an attractive six-foot brunette, left a note for Waitkus in the Edgewater Hotel in Chicago saying that she had to see him urgently. When he came to her room, she let him in, and then shot him with a rifle she had bought in a pawnshop. It collapsed his right lung, but struck no vital organs.

She explained in a letter to her court-appointed psychiatrist: "As time went on I just became nuttier and nuttier about the guy. I knew I would never get to know him in a normal way, so I kept thinking I will never get him, and if I can't have him nobody else can. Then I decided I would kill him."

With other fans she would wait for hours outside the baseball park to see him leave. Yet when he finally emerged, she always hid. Her fantasy had built up so much psychic energy that it was unable to endure the least contact with reality.

What strikes us odd is that her adoration was transformed—not into hatred, but into a kind of sadism. The thought of killing her hero convulsed some strange sexual nerve. We can see the parallel with Harvey Glatman, snatching girl's purses in the playground and then flinging them back at them. It is as if both he and she are saying: "If you won't take an interest in me, then you'll pay for it." And in Glatman's case, women did literally pay for it with their lives.

Here we are coming close to the basic motivation of the serial killer, and how desire can be transformed into violence.

Another case cited by Reinhardt involved a huge white-haired rapist named Carl J. Folk, a carnival owner who had been released from a mental hospital after tying a girl to a tree and raping and beating her.

In December 1953, Folk engaged in conversation at a gas station a young couple, Raymond and Betty Allen, who were towing a trailer en route to their new home in California. Folk followed them all day, and that night entered their trailer, knocked Allen unconscious, and then spent the night raping and torturing his wife, while Allen, tied hand and foot, was forced to listen to her screams. Finally Allen succeeded in freeing his legs and escaping from the trailer; a passing motorist untied his hands, and Allen went and got his revolver from his car. As Folk poured gasoline over Betty and her baby, with the intention of burning the trailer, Allen shot him in the stomach, disabling but not killing him. His wife proved to be dead—Folk had strangled her after burning her with matches and cigarettes and biting her all over.

Folk was executed in the gas chamber in March 1955. In view of the fact that he was middle-aged, it seems likely that Betty Allen was not his first murder victim. Folk had obviously spent a lifetime engaged in sadistic fantasies. What seems surprising about Kemper is that he had reached the same stage by the age of twenty-three.

That Ressler was aware of Kemper's continued potential for violence is illustrated by an amusing story he tells of their third interview. On this occasion he had been alone with Kemper, and at the end of a four-hour session that included detailed discussion of appalling depravities, Ressler pushed the buzzer to summon the guard to come and let him out. When no one came, he simply carried on the conversation. But there was not much more to say. Ressler buzzed again. Then again.

He says: "A look of apprehension must have come over my face, despite my attempts to keep calm and cool, and Kemper, keenly sensitive to other people's psyches (as most killers are) picked up on this." He told Ressler to relax; the guards were serving meals and might take twenty minutes. He stood up, emphasizing his huge bulk. Then, sensing Ressler's rising tension, he said: "If I went apeshit in here, you'd be in a lot of trouble, wouldn't you? I could screw your head off and place it on the table to greet the guard."

It was obviously a possibility, and although Ressler did his best to appear calm, his pulse began to race. He tried bluffing, saying he was armed; Kemper was clearly unconvinced. Ressler was deeply relieved when the guard finally showed up.

It is a curious story, because the reader has come to feel that, no matter how much of a threat he might be to women, Kemper would certainly not represent a danger to a federal agent who had been interviewing him. The anecdote suddenly makes us aware that this is not correct; locked in with this massive psychopath, Ressler could easily have found himself in trouble. From then on, he made sure he had a partner during the interviews.

We also note that Kemper talked about screwing off Ressler's head. He clearly had a fetish about heads, which meant he experienced sexual excitement at the thought of removing them. When he arrived home with the bodies of Rosalind Thorpe and Alice Liu in the trunk, and found his mother already home, he went and severed the heads in the car because he could not wait. But how does one develop sexual excitement at the thought of beheading somebody? A psychiatrist consulted before his trial suggested that he associated it with symbolic removal of his penis (which was undersized), but that sounds far-fetched. Another psychiatrist suggested at Kemper's trial that he might not be a sociopath but a classic sadist, and that must surely be closer to the truth. Certain types of sadism may be inborn, possibly some kind of undesirable genetic inheritance—that is, an inherent tendency to associate cruelty with sex. And he seems to have been only about four when he cut off the heads of his sister Allyn's dolls. The reason may have been the noisy quarrels between his father and mother, both over six feet tall, both with loud voices. He also fantasized about killing his other sister, Susan, six years his senior, and his mother.

Ressler uncovered another interesting clue to the behavior of serial killers. Kemper admitted that his first murder—otherwise unrecorded—occurred after a quarrel with his mother, in the spring of 1972, when he left the house in a fury and swore he would kill the first attractive young woman he saw. It was a case of rage and frustration overcoming normal inhibitions, (since Kemper was basically a mild person), like an angry person driving too fast.

In an interview in Margaret Cheney's book on Kemper, *The Co-ed Killer*, Kemper explains: "It's kind of hard to go around killing somebody just for the hell of it. It's not a kicks thing, or I would have ceased doing it a long time ago. It was an urge, I wouldn't say it was on the full moon or anything, but I noticed that no matter how horrendous the crime had been or how vicious the treatment of the bodies after death, still at that point in my crimes the urge to do it again coming as often as a week or two weeks afterwards—a strong urge, and the longer I let it go the stronger it got, to where I was taking risks to go out and kill people—risks that normally, according to my little rules of operation, I wouldn't take because they could lead to arrest."

As with so many serial killers, it became an addiction, a strange compulsion, not unlike demonic possession.

Ressler's interviews with Ed Kemper occurred in 1978. During the same period, Ressler went to interview Charles Manson.

Manson had always maintained that he was not guilty of any crimes. He had not been present at any of the murders, and he had not ordered his followers to commit them. Strictly speaking, this was true—although Manson had tied up the LaBiancas before he sent Tex Watson, Leslie Van Houten, and Patricia Krenwinkel in to kill them.

Manson was a little man who looked harmless. But the staring, hypnotic eyes betrayed a man of high dominance. When he arrived in San Francisco in 1967, he was thirty-two years old, and had spent most of his adolescent and adult life in reform school or prison. His mother, Kathleen Maddox, was fifteen when she became pregnant with him; a few years later she was in jail for armed robbery. Manson was placed in a children's home when he was twelve and began his career of burglary soon after. By the time he emerged from a ten-year jail sentence in 1967—for car theft, check fraud, and pimping—he had been institutionalized for more than half of his life and would have preferred to stay in prison.

HOW DID THIS MILD, INOFFENSIVE, GUITAR-PLAYING HIPPIE TURN INTO THE MANIAC WHO MADE HIS FOLLOWERS BELIEVE THAT HE WANTED THEM TO KILL HALF A DOZEN PEOPLE HE HAD NEVER MET?

Yet, San Francisco in the age of the flower children proved to be a revelation to him. Suddenly he was no longer an ex-jailbird but a member of the "counterculture." He was well qualified, having learned to play the guitar from Alvin "Creepy" Karpis, a former Public Enemy Number One and last surviving member of the infamous Ma Barker gang. Busking outside the university in Berkeley, he met a librarian named Mary

Brunner and soon moved in with her. He acquired a second girl—Lynette "Squeaky" Fromme—when he found her crying on the pavement after a quarrel with her family. Manson told her, "I am the god of fuck." After years in prison he was as sexually active as a rabbit.

He attracted young women because he had a striking personality, yet seemed unthreatening—almost a father figure to them. He once told a friend: "I'm a very positive force . . . I collect negatives." A prison report on him had stated: "Charles Manson has a tremendous drive to call attention to himself." But now he no longer had to call attention to himself; teenaged girls stuck to him as if they were fragments of colored paper and he possessed some kind of static electricity.

Another young woman he picked up was nineteen-year-old Susan Atkins, who had left home at sixteen and served some time for associating with criminals. She invited him back to her apartment, and as they lay naked, he told her to imagine that it was her father who was making love to her. She claimed that it was the greatest orgasm of her life. Later she was to say of him: "He is the king and I am his queen. And the queen does what the king says."

The drugs undoubtedly helped. Manson and his "Family" never used heroin; they preferred pot and psychedelics. It was on an LSD trip that Manson saw himself as Christ, and went through the experience of being crucified. It made a deep impression. His followers later said that he had "Christlike vibes." He liked to point out that his surname meant "Son of Man."

He somehow acquired a battered Volkswagen bus, and with his "Family" of young women, now grown to half a dozen or so, he shuttled around between California, Oregon, and Washington, gradually acquiring more followers. They exchanged the Volkswagen for a yellow school bus and removed most of the seats from it so that they could sleep in it.

How did this mild, inoffensive, guitar-playing hippie turn into the maniac who made his followers believe that he wanted them to kill half a dozen people he had never met? When he arrived in San Francisco, he saw himself as a gentle pacifist, trying to spread the gospel of love and understanding. Within six months he had a group of followers over whom he exercised almost absolute control. He found the role of leader hard work; at one point he even announced the dissolution of the group and sent most of them away. But they soon drifted back, and he realized that, whether he liked it or not, he had to play the role of patriarch and guru.

The gruesome Tate and LaBianca slayings of 1969 shocked the American public. Here, the accused Charles Manson walks into the courtroom in Santa Monica, California, on October 13, 1970. When his name was called to enter his plea, Manson stood, folded his arms, and turned his back on the judge. Susan Atkins, seated, a fanatic member of his family of followers, did the same. (Associated Press)

But what is a patriarch and guru supposed to do? He has to demonstrate his power. Unlike many "messiah" figures, Manson never claimed to be God, or even Moses—although his sermons on modern corruption could also last for hours. He merely claimed to be a good musician—as good as the Beatles—but no one in the music business seemed to agree with him. Little by little, he became accustomed to exercising power. When he and disciple Paul "Tex" Watson came upon a rattlesnake, Manson ordered Watson to sit in front of it. Watson did ("I must have been crazy, but that's the kind of effect he had on me"), and the snake rattled and slid away. Watson was convinced Manson had some strange power over animals. When Charles Melton, whom Family member Linda Kasabian had robbed of $5,000, went after them in search of his money, Manson handed him a knife and said he was welcome to kill him if he had any quarrel. Melton said he hadn't, but he wanted his money. Manson said that in that case, he had better kill Melton, to prove that death did not exist. Melton decided to leave without the money.

When a drug dealer named Crowe went in search of $2,400 worth of marijuana he had paid for, Manson pointed a revolver at him and pulled the trigger. Nothing happened, and he fired again; this time Crowe collapsed with a bullet in his torso. Manson left, convinced that he had killed Crowe; in fact, Crowe survived, but did not report the shooting. Again, Manson had proved his ability to protect "his own."

When another follower, Bobby Beausoleil, was ordered to persuade a musician named Gary Hinman to give the Family $20,000, Hinman refused, and Beausoleil rang Manson. Manson arrived with a sword, with which he slashed Hinman's face, half severing his ear. After this, Manson left, leaving Beausoleil to try to beat Hinman into divulging the whereabouts of his money. When this failed, Beausoleil rang Manson again and asked what he should do, and Manson ordered him to kill Hinman. Beausoleil did not hesitate. He stabbed him twice in the chest, and Hinman died from loss of blood.

Two weeks after Hinman's death, on August 8, 1969, four of Manson's followers—Tex Watson, Susan Atkins, Patricia "Katie" Krenwinkel, and Linda Kasabian—set out to commit murder at a house in Cielo Drive, where an acquaintance in the music business lived. They encountered a friend of the houseboy, Steven Earle Parent, about to leave the drive, and Watson shot him in the head. After this, they went into the house and held up its inhabitants at gunpoint—film star Sharon Tate (who was eight months pregnant) and three friends, coffee heiress Abigail Folger, Polish writer Voytek Frykowski, and hair stylist Jay Sebring, who were there for dinner. When the Manson clan left, all four were dead—brutally stabbed or shot.

The following night, Manson walked into the house of supermarket owner Leno LaBianca, held up LaBianca and his wife, Rosemary, at gunpoint, and tied them up. After that, he left, and Watson, Krenwinkel, and Van Houten stabbed the LaBiancas to death.

Two months later, Susan Atkins was in custody, being questioned about the Gary Hinman murder, and confided to a fellow prisoner her part in the Tate killings. The prisoner told someone else, who told the authorities. In December 1969, Manson, Watson, Atkins, Krenwinkel, Kasabian, and Van Houten were charged with the murders. In March the following year, Manson, Atkins, Krenwinkel, and Van Houten were sentenced to death (Linda Kasabian turned state's evidence). This was reduced to life imprisonment when the death penalty was abolished in California in 1972. Watson, because of legal complications, did not stand trial with the rest of the Family, but was instead found guilty of murder in a separate trial several months later.

BUT WHAT IS A PATRIARCH AND GURU SUPPOSED TO DO?

After encountering the mild—if alarmingly huge—Kemper, Ressler could hardly have encountered anyone less similar. Manson was completely nonthreatening, but highly—almost maniacally—articulate.

Ressler made a point of studying the lives of his interviewees before he confronted them, and in the case of Manson, this quickly established a rapport. Manson explained to him how he became a kind of guru to the hippies of Haight-Ashbury. He was, as Ressler noted, physically unprepossessing, at five foot six inches and 130 pounds, and more than a decade older than most of the kids he encountered—a father with unkempt hair, dressed in tattered jeans, and carrying a guitar. He told Ressler: "I became a negative, a reflection of these kids." What he meant, he explained, was that he thought they used him as a kind of mirror in which they saw their own faces. And that, he implied, was why he should be regarded as innocent.

At one point in the interview, Manson jumped up on the table to demonstrate the way the guards controlled prisoners. Ressler would have been willing to let it pass, but his fellow interviewer John Conway said sternly "Charlie, get off the table, sit down and behave," and Manson did as he was told, and tried to make up by talking about his techniques of mind control. Then he asked for a souvenir, and attempted to take Ressler's FBI badge. Ressler compromised by giving him a pair of sunglasses.

What was happening, fairly clearly, was that Manson was deliberately behaving like a naughty schoolboy, as if to demonstrate his harmlessness. He was obviously delighted when, on his way back to his cell, the guard found the sunglasses, assumed he had stolen them, and marched him back to Ressler—who then confirmed that he had given them to him. Manson was demonstrating to the guard that he had a powerful authority figure on his side.

Manson's plea of innocence becomes absurd when we recollect how he had slashed off half of Gary Hinman's ear and then told Beausoleil to kill him. Ressler obviously realized this, since he speaks of Manson "with the sunglasses incongruously perched on his face—hiding these fearsome eyes." He recognized that Manson was a king rat merely pretending to be a playful mouse.

This is undoubtedly the real key to Manson—high dominance. And to fully understand him it is also necessary to know something about the psychology of "rogue messiahs." People such as Manson, who discover that they can exert their charisma on a group of followers, quickly become intoxicated with a sense of power. The Reverend Jim Jones, who committed suicide with a thousand followers in Guyana in 1978, and cult leader David Koresh, who died in the FBI siege at Waco in 1993, demonstrate the same mechanisms at work. Dominating their followers, and being allowed to take their sexual pick of the females, is obviously as addictive as sex murder is to the serial killer, but has the additionally strange characteristic of developing into paranoia that quickly turns murderous. It was Manson's ability to control his followers, and the heady delight of exercising dominance, that led to the Tate and LaBianca murders.

Ressler went on to interview Tex Watson, who had killed Sharon Tate and the LaBiancas. As he expected, Watson was not a dominant male, although he had led the girls who helped him in the killings. Manson had permitted this, presumably as a kind of reward to his lieutenant, but had told Ressler that letting "that SOB Watson have too much power in the Family" was the dumbest thing he had ever done. Ressler noted that "the rivalry between Manson and Watson, which I learned about from both men, was a definite factor in the dynamics of the murders."

Watson had made his own kind of peace with society by his conversion to born-again Christianity; he had become a renowned preacher and, Ressler noted, "walked around as if he owned the place." So, in a paradoxical sense, Watson had achieved his aim of becoming the dominant male, even though he had paid for it with his freedom. Watson had written a book placing all the blame on Manson, claiming that Manson had ordered them to kill. Manson had not turned him into a homosexual, as he had done with others, said Watson, but he had wrapped him around his finger, like an old convict with a new one. The psychedelic drugs, he said, were used by Manson to bring people under his control. Every night after dinner, when everybody was high, Manson climbed up on a mound at the back of the ranch and preached for hours.

All this, says Ressler, gave him the insight he wanted. Manson was not a homicidal maniac, but a cunning manipulator. And when Ressler got back to Quantico, he verified this by interviewing two of the Manson girls, Squeaky Fromme and Sandra Good, who were in a nearby prison. The two wore matching hooded outfits, and approached him like nuns, walking in unison. Manson had obviously done a brilliant job of brainwashing them; they said they were "sisters in the church of Charles Manson, and that they had kept the faith." The faith, apparently, was that our egos prevent us from seeing the truth. We must let go of the ego, "cease to exist," as Manson sang in one of his songs. Once you cease to exist, you become totally free.

Ressler comments that they were simply inadequate personalities who had submitted their destinies to a male whom they adored. One day, they believed, Charlie would come out of jail, and they would be waiting, ready to start where they had left off. They had both proved their fidelity: Good by writing letters to directors of large corporations threatening them that unless they stopped polluting the earth, Manson disciples would kill them; Fromme by pointing a revolver at President Gerald Ford and pulling the trigger. (Fortunately a Secret Service agent had aborted the assassination attempt by interposing his hand between the hammer and the firing pin.)

In fact, when Sandra Good was released in 1991, she moved to a town close to Manson's prison in California.

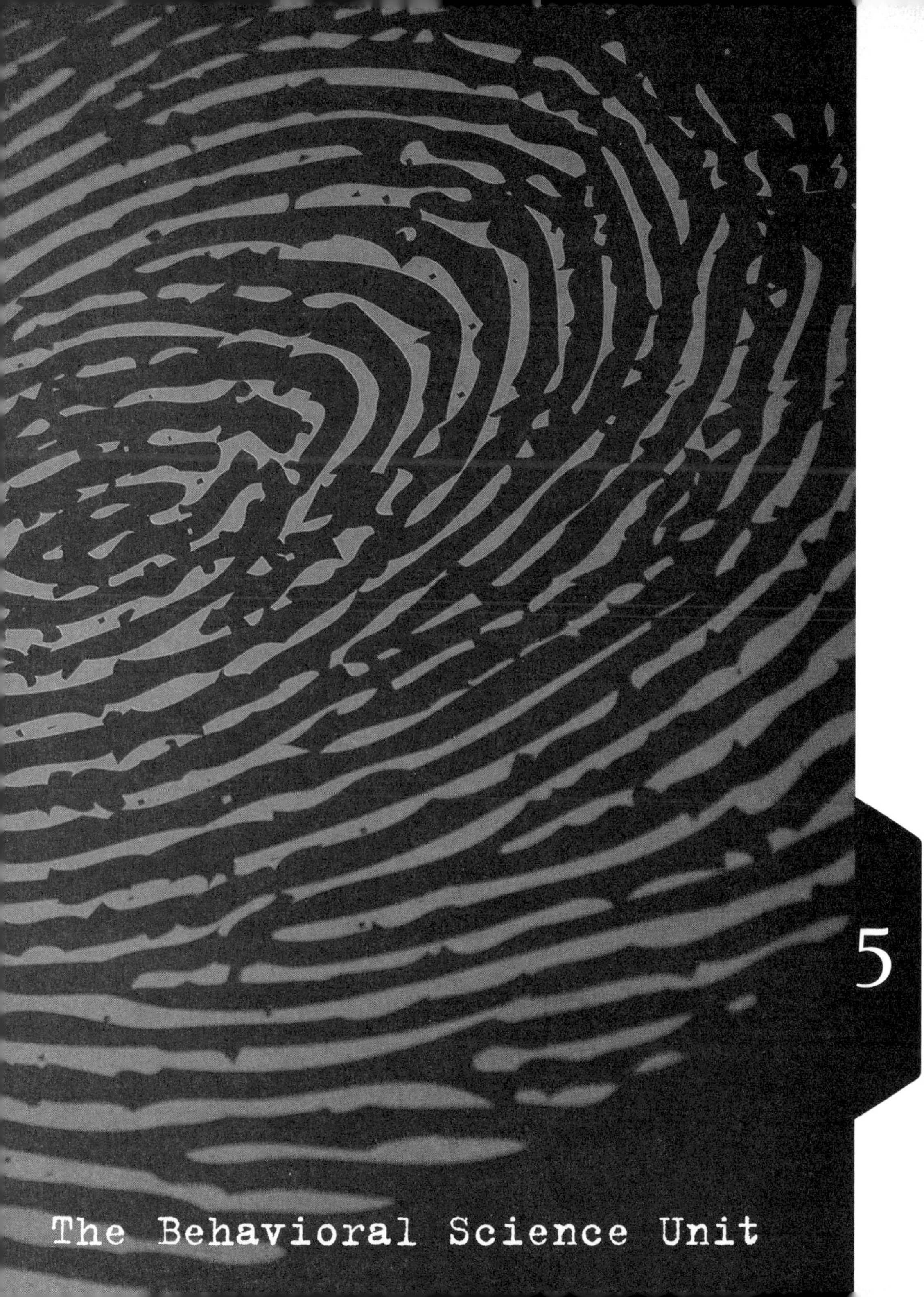

5

The Behavioral Science Unit

5

The Behavioral Science Unit

When he returned to Quantico from California, Ressler told his immediate superior, Larry Monroe, what he had been doing. Monroe was aghast. "You saw who?" But he allowed Ressler to visit Squeaky Fromme and Sandra Good on condition that he did not officially know about it, and that Ressler would later make it official by putting something on paper when he got back.

But their scheme was revealed prematurely. A colleague to whom Ressler had spoken about his interviews talked to someone about them in the lunchroom, within earshot of the FBI Academy chief, Ken Joseph, a member of the Hoover old guard. Monroe and Ressler were ordered to present themselves in Joseph's office.

Asked why he had not been told about the initiative, Ressler was able to point out that Joseph has issued a memo a few months ago encouraging instructors to do research. That, Ressler said, is what he was planning.

Joseph pointed out that interviewing people like Sirhan and Manson could cause problems for the Bureau. Ressler replied that he had put his intentions in a memo before he left for California, and Joseph said he hadn't seen it (which was inevitable, since no memo had been written). Ressler was told to go and dig out the memo. He did this promptly, by writing one up, backdating it, and crumpling and Xeroxing it to make it look bedraggled. It said that he planned to interview some serial killers to see if they would be willing to participate in the research. He called it the Criminal Personality Research Project.

Ressler was told to expand it and explain its long-term objectives. He did this, adding that he would not need to spend money on the project, since it could be done in the course of his road schools.

The memo was then sent out to John McDermott, the Bureau's second-in-command in Washington. McDermott lost no time in turning it down flat. The Bureau's job, he said, was to catch criminals, not to behave like social workers.

There was nothing for it but to forget the idea until McDermott retired. Fortunately, that was later the same year. The forward-looking William Webster replaced him. Ken Joseph also retired, and his replacement, James McKenzie, was enthusiastic about the idea. At a working lunch presided over by Webster, Ressler presented his idea, adding that the previous director had turned it down. Whether or not this influenced Webster, the project was approved. As a result, the Behavioral Science Unit (BSU) was set up with a grant of $128,000 from the National Institute of Justice, with Howard Teten as an adviser.

The Behavioral Science Unit provides a preliminary idea of the sort of person the police should be looking for. It was obviously of central importance that this idea should be accurate, otherwise it would send the police looking in the wrong direction. Interviewing murderers gives the profilers the necessary background to begin to formulate a picture of the man they are looking for. The wider the range of their knowledge of such criminals, the more profilers can trust intuition.

Sometimes the details of a case seem to offer no possible clue to the culprit. At the time Ressler was brooding on the idea of psychological profiling, there occurred in Yorkshire, England, a series of violent attacks on women that recalled the Jack the Ripper murders that took place in London's East End in 1888. The Yorkshire murders, mostly of prostitutes, began in the summer of 1985, when the man who became known as the Yorkshire Ripper attacked two women with a hammer, and then slashed them with a knife. Both victims recovered. The third victim, Wilma McCann, was knocked unconscious with a hammer, dragged into a sports field, and had injuries inflicted on her stomach, chest, and genital area with a knife. The fourth victim was battered beyond recognition with a hammer, and then stabbed fifty times in the chest. Two more prostitute murders followed, but the eighth victim, sixteen-year-old Jayne MacDonald, was a pretty schoolgirl, made it look as if the notion that the killer was driven by a hatred of prostitutes was inaccurate after all.

When Robert Ressler came to England in 1978, he was accompanied by a young and flamboyant agent named John Douglas, who had come to Quantico as a visiting counselor and then joined the Behavioral

Science Unit on Ressler's recommendation. Douglas would accompany Ressler during his second interview with Ed Kemper.

Ressler and Douglas were at the Bramshill Police Academy, where Ressler had coined the phrase "serial killer," and they were drinking at a nearby bar when one of the leading investigators in the three-year-old Ripper case, John Domaille, walked over to speak to them, with several other detectives. They sketched out for the benefit of the FBI agents the background of the case, and the scenes of the crimes. The man in charge of the case, Chief Inspector George Oldfield, had received a cassette containing a message that purported to be from the killer. Ressler and Douglas had heard the tape in the United States, and Douglas now commented: "Based on the crime scenes you've described and the audiotape, that's not the Ripper. You're wasting your time with that."

Douglas then sketched out his own notion of the killer. He would be an almost invisible loner in his late twenties or early thirties, with a pathological hatred of women, a school dropout, and possibly a truck driver, since he seemed to get around quite a bit. The murders were his attempt to punish prostitutes in general.

In fact, the Ripper was caught by accident in January 1981, after thirteen murders and four serious attacks. Two policemen doing a routine check on a parked Rover interrupted prostitute Olivia Reivers, and her client, who gave his name as Peter Williams. Recognizing Reivers as a convicted prostitute with a suspended sentence, the policemen checked the number plate of the car and found it to be false—in fact it came from a scrapyard for used cars. When they ordered Reivers into their car, the man asked if he might relieve himself, and went behind an oil storage tank before being taken to the police station. There he gave his correct name, Peter Sutcliffe, aged thirty-five, but continued to insist that he had done nothing wrong. But when one of the policemen, acting on a sudden hunch, returned to the storage tank, he found a hammer and a knife that Sutcliffe had dropped among the leaves. After forty-eight hours in custody, Sutcliffe confessed to being the Ripper. The massive hunt for him had taken six years.

Psychologically speaking, Peter Sutcliffe proved to be as strange and complex as Ed Kemper. This working-class young man was the last person in the world anyone would have expected to become the sadistic disemboweler of women. As a child he had been so gentle and timid that he seemed destined for a life of self-effacement. His father, who was mad about cricket and football and was regarded as something of a ladies' man, treated him with a kind of irritable contempt, which reflected his feeling that his eldest son would always remain a sissy.

John Sutcliffe's large family was terrified of him. He was the kind of man who would walk into the room when everyone was watching television, and change the channel on to a sports program. Then he would sit in front of it, so close that no one could see past him. One of his daughters admitted that she daydreamed of murdering him.

Peter, born in June 1946, was undersized and shy, a scrawny, miserable little boy who spent hours staring blankly into space. He learned to walk quite literally by clinging to his mother's skirts. And he continued to cling to them for years after.

At school he was so withdrawn and passive that after his arrest, most of his teachers could not even recall his face. His headmaster remembered him because Peter had once played truant for two weeks because he was being bullied. When his father found out, he made such a scene at the school that from then on, the headmaster took great care that Peter would never be bullied again.

The Sutcliffe home in Bingley, Yorkshire, was no background for an introspective child. With a dominant, self-assertive tyrant for a father, Peter inevitably took his mother's side. But his younger brothers were more like their father. One of them once floored the local boxing champion by punching him in the testicles. The house was always jammed with people, and John Sutcliffe enjoyed "feeling up" any girl who strayed too close. The atmosphere was heavy with sex, and even Peter's mother, a quiet doormat of a woman, had an affair with a local police sergeant. When her husband found out, he retaliated by moving in with a deaf woman who lived a few doors down the street.

Peter was twenty-three when the unthinkable happened, and he discovered that his mother, the woman he regarded as his ideal, his vision of what a woman ought to be, loving, hard-working, self-sacrificing, always warm and sympathetic, had been having an extramarital affair. His father later confessed to a female reporter that he thought this had "turned Peter's mind."

John Sutcliffe had learned about the affair when his wife mistook his voice on the phone for that of her lover. (They had never before spoken on the phone, and he was not wearing his teeth.) He arranged to meet her in a hotel room, arrived three hours early, and persuaded a member of staff to let him into the room. He had taken his children with him to witness her shame.

"I REMEMBER PETER WERE JUST STANDING THERE—HE WERE SHOOK RIGID. HE HAD A LOOK ON HIS FACE LIKE AN ANIMAL, IT WERE. I THINK IT MAY HAVE TURNED HIS MIND."

When Kathleen Sutcliffe came into the room, carrying a bag with her nightclothes, she was confronted by her family, including Peter and his fiancée, Sonia. Her husband began to shout at her, calling her a prostitute. He then made her open her night bag, take out the expensive negligee she had packed for her tryst, and hold it up. John later told the reporter: "I remember Peter were just standing there—he were shook rigid. He had a look on his face like an animal, it were. I think it may have turned his mind."

There was another factor: Kathleen's lover was a policeman. This made it even worse. Coppers were not held in high esteem in their house. John had been arrested for breaking and entering. The second brother was always in and out of jail, and some of Peter's best mates were burglars. The infidelity of Peter's mother with one of the "enemy" must have convinced him that even the nicest women were whores at heart.

By this time, Peter himself was no longer the pathologically shy boy. Ashamed of being so weak, he had flung himself into bodybuilding until by his late teens he had the physique of a wrestler. As soon as he could afford it, he had bought his first car, and used to drive at eighty miles an hour through the narrow Bingley streets. For as much as he disliked his father, he also admired him, and wanted to be more like him.

Where women were concerned he could never match his father or his brothers. He liked to drive around the red-light district of Bradford and stare at the women, but he never dared to accost one, even though he boasted to his mates about his nonexistent sexual experience. With his obsessive, semi-incestuous feelings about his mother, Peter Sutcliffe was undoubtedly a psychological mess.

Then he finally found himself a girlfriend. She was a Czech émigrée named Sonia Szurma, who was even shyer than he was, and so plain that even his father did not try to put his hand up her skirt.

And it was the timid Sonia, oddly enough, who started the train of events that turned him into a killer. For when she began having an affair with an Italian who owned a sports car, Sutcliffe was thrown into a frenzy of jealousy. It was like his mother all over again; this young woman who seemed so shy and withdrawn was just like the rest of them. Peter finally took the plunge and went to a prostitute. But even this turned out to be a fiasco. He was unable to raise an erection, and the girl swindled him out of five pounds. Worse still, when he saw her later in a pub, and asked for his change, she jeered at him and told the whole story at the top of her voice, so he became a laughingstock. For the introspective boy who had been fighting all his life to feel like a man, the humiliation bit deep, and turned poisonous.

One day, eating fish and chips in a friend's minivan, he thought he saw the prostitute, and followed her. He was carrying in his pocket a brick inside a sock that was precisely for this kind of opportunity. He hit her on the back of the head and then ran back to the van. But she succeeded in taking its number, and police questioned him. He managed to convince them that it had been an ordinary quarrel, and they let him go.

But that act of hitting a prostitute had taken possession of his imagination. He realized that it had given gave him some deep and strange satisfaction that was intensely sexual. He became a kind of dual personality. While the Peter known to his friends and Sonia remained genial and courteous, another Peter enjoyed stopping his car by prostitutes and asking what they charged. When they told him, he would shout, "Is that all you're worth?" and drive off.

In 1975, a prostitute turned him down and released once more the wellspring of rage; he followed her and hit her with a hammer, then raised her clothes and took out a knife. Someone called out, and he ran away. But the feverish excitement that swept through him again made him realize that what he really wanted was to assert his masculinity by killing a prostitute. A month later he again crept up behind a woman and hit her with a hammer; again he was disturbed and was forced to flee. But now it was only a matter of time before he committed murder.

It happened two months later, when he picked up a drunken hooker who was thumbing a lift. He took her to a playing field, where he once again proved to be impotent. He then made up for it by hitting her with a hammer and stabbing her repeatedly in the breasts and stomach.

What he had failed to realize, as he daydreamed of revenge on "whores," is that he was handing himself over to a demon who would give him no peace. He would have to carry on murdering and disemboweling woman after woman, even when he knew perfectly well that they were not prostitutes, because only this could make him feel fully alive. Roy Hazelwood was right: "Sex crime isn't about sex, it's about power." A murderer such as Sutcliffe is the living illustration of what he meant.

The hunt for the Yorkshire Ripper was the biggest police operation ever mounted in the United Kingdom. It cost $10 million, and involved 200,000 interviews—including four with Sutcliffe—and 30,000 searches of homes. But it taught the British police the same lesson that the FBI had learned through Manson, Kemper, and the rest: there had to be some more logical way of trapping serial killers. The Yorkshire police reached the conclusion Pierce Brooks had reached in 1948: the answer lay in computerisation. In the United Kingdom, this happened in the early 1980s, and would later help to trap serial killers such as Duffy and Mulcahy, the "Railway Rapists."

In the United States, it also began to happen in the early 1980s, when Pierce Brooks persuaded the Department of Justice to host a conference at Sam Houston State University, and the Violent Criminal Apprehension Program was approved. It was decided to run it from Quantico, and in May 1985 Brooks was appointed its first director, and joined the team there.

By that time, Ressler had already inaugurated a new project that he called the National Center for the Analysis of Violent Crime (NCAVC), which sprang from that plan to interview killers—Ressler's original "Criminal Personality Research Project" of 1978. The idea, as Ressler put it, was to "bring together the fragmented efforts from around the country so they could be consolidated into one national resource center available to the entire law enforcement community."

But at the time Ressler and Douglas were advising the British police about the Yorkshire Ripper, all this lay some years in the future. And on the other side of the Atlantic, in New York, another series of random and apparently motiveless killings was underlining the need for some method of psychological profiling.

It had started in the stiflingly hot early hours of July 29, 1976, as two young women sat talking in the front seats of an Oldsmobile on Buhre Avenue in the Bronx; they were eighteen-year-old Donna Lauria, a medical technician, and nineteen-year-old Jody Valenti, a student nurse. Donna's parents, on their way back from a night out, passed them at about 1 a.m., and said good night. A few moments after they reached their apartment, they heard the sound of shots and screams. A man had walked up to the car, pulled a gun out of a brown paper bag, and fired five shots. Donna was killed immediately; Jody was wounded in the thigh.

Total lack of motive for the shooting convinced police that they were dealing with a man who killed for pleasure, without knowing his victims.

On October 23, 1976, three months after the Bronx murder, twenty-year-old Carl Denaro shared a few beers with friends at a Queens bar. At 2:30 a.m., he left with Rosemary Keenan and parked his car near her house. Suddenly a man appeared and fired five shots into the car; one of them struck Carl in the head. Rosemary raced the car back to the bar and his friends, who rushed him to the hospital. Surgeons replaced a part of his skull with a metal plate.

Just a month later, on November 26, two young women were talking on the stoop in front of a house in the Floral Park section of Queens; it was half an hour past midnight when a man walked toward them, started to ask if they could direct him, then, before he finished the sentence, pulled out a gun and began shooting. Donna DeMasi, sixteen, and Joanne Lomino, eighteen, were both wounded. A bullet lodged in Joanne's spine, paralyzing her.

On January 30, 1977, a young couple were kissing goodnight in a car in the Ridgewood section of Queens; there was a deafening explosion, the windscreen shattered, and Christine Freund, twenty-six, slumped into the arms of her boyfriend, John Diel. She died a few hours later in hospital.

On March 8, 1977, Virginia Voskerichian, an Armenian student, was on her way home, and only a few hundred yards from her mother's house in Forest Hills, Queens, when a gunman walked up to her, and shot her in the face at a few yards' range; the bullet went into her mouth, shattering her front teeth. She died immediately. Christine Freund had been shot only three hundred yards away.

By now police recognized that the bullets that had killed three and wounded four had all come from the same gun, an uncommon .44 Charter Arms Bulldog revolver. And this indicated a homicidal psychopath who would probably go on until he was caught. The problem was that the police had no clues to his identity, no idea of where to begin searching. Unless he was caught during an attempted murder, the chances of arresting him seemed minimal. New York City mayor Abraham Beame called a press conference in which he announced: "We have a savage killer on the loose." He was able to say that the man was white, about five feet ten inches tall, well groomed, with hair combed straight back." The press dubbed the unknown shooter "the .44-Caliber Killer."

Despite the media frenzy and the intensive police manhunt, on the morning of April 17, 1977, there were two more deaths. Alexander Esau and Valentina Suriani were sitting in a parked car in the Bronx when the killer shot both of them. Valentina died instantly; Esau died later in the hospital, three bullets in his head. Only a few blocks away was the spot where Donna Lauria and Jody Valenti had been shot.

In the street near the victims, a policeman found an envelope. It contained a letter addressed to Captain Joseph Borrelli, and it was from the killer. The handwritten missive was littered with misspellings: "I am deeply hurt by your calling me a weman-hater. I am not. But I am a monster. I am the Son of Sam. I am a little brat . . ." It claimed that his father, Sam, was a brute who beat his family when he got drunk, and who ordered him to go out and kill. "I love to hunt. Prowling the streets looking for fair game—tasty meat. The wemen of Queens are prettyist of all . . ." It was reminiscent of the letters that Jack the Ripper and so many other "thrill killers" have written to the police, revealing an urge to "be somebody," to make an impact on society. A further rambling, incoherent note, signed "Son of Sam," was sent to New York *Daily News* columnist Jimmy Breslin.

The next attack, on June 26, 1977, was like so many of the others: a young couple sitting in their car in the early hours of Sunday morning, saying good night after a date. They were Salvatore Lupo and Judy Placido, and the car was in front of a house on 211th Street, Bayside, Queens. Four shots shattered the windshield. The assailant ran away. Fortunately, his aim had been bad; both these victims were only wounded, and recovered.

It was now a year since the Son of Sam had killed Donna Lauria; on the anniversary of her death, Queens and the Bronx were swarming with police. But the Son of Sam had decided that these areas were dangerous, and that his next shootings would be as far away as possible. On July 31, Robert Violante and Stacy Moskowitz were sitting in a parking lot close to the Brooklyn shore; it was 1:30 a.m. on Sunday morning. The windshield exploded as four shots were fired. Both were hit in the head. Stacy Moskowitz died hours later in hospital; Robert Violante recovered, but was blinded.

But this shooting brought the break in the case. A woman out walking her dog had noticed two policemen putting a ticket on a car parked near a fire hydrant on Bay Seventeenth Street, a block from the crime scene. Minutes later, a man ran up to the car, leapt in, and drove off. Only four parking tickets had been issued in the Coney Island area that Sunday morning, and only one of those was for parking near a hydrant. The carbon copy of the ticket contained the car's registration number. And the Division of Motor Vehicles was able to identify its owner as David Berkowitz, aged twenty-four, of Pine Street, Yonkers.

On the Wednesday after the last killing, detectives found the Ford Galaxie parked in front of an apartment building on Pine Street. They peered in through its window, and saw the butt of a gun, and a note written in the same block capitals as the other Son of Sam letters. A police team staked out the car. When David Berkowitz approached it at 10:15 that evening, Deputy Inspector Tim Dowd, who had led the hunt, said, "Hello, David." Berkowitz looked at him in surprise, and then said, "Inspector Dowd! You finally got me!"

After the terror he had aroused, the Son of Sam was something of an anticlimax, a pudgy little man with a beaming smile, and a tendency to look like a slightly moronic child who has been caught stealing sweets.

He proved to be a paranoid schizophrenic who lived alone in a room lit by a naked light bulb, sleeping on a bare mattress. The floor was covered with empty milk cartons and bottles. On the walls he had scrawled messages such as "In this hole lives the wicked king." "Kill for my Master." "I turn children into killers."

His father, who had run a hardware store in the Bronx, had retired to Florida after being robbed. Nat Berkowitz was not the Son of Sam's real father. David Berkowitz, born June 1, 1953, was illegitimate, and his mother had offered him up for adoption. He had felt rejected from the beginning, and longed to find his biological mother.

He reacted to his poor self-image by boasting and lying—particularly about his sexual prowess. In

David Berkowitz, aka the "Son of Sam," during an interview at Attica prison in New York in 1979. Berkowitz killed six people and wounded seven others in New York City in 1976 and 1977. He claimed to have been driven by an "unknown urge to kill." (Associated Press)

reality, he was afraid of women. He told the police that demons began telling him to kill in 1974. Living alone in apartments that he allowed to degenerate into pigsties, kept awake at night by the sound of trucks or barking dogs, he slipped into paranoia, telling his father in a letter that people hated him and spat at him as he walked down the street. "The girls call me ugly, and they bother me the most." On Christmas Eve 1975, he began his attempt at revenge on women by taking a knife and attacking two of them. The first one screamed and he ran away. The second, a fifteen-year-old schoolgirl, was badly cut and had one lung punctured, but recovered. The blood disturbed him, which is why he traveled to Texas to buy a gun. Seven months later, he used it in his first murder.

The name Sam seems to have been taken from a neighbor called Sam Carr, whose black Labrador sometimes kept Berkowitz awake. He wrote Carr anonymous letters, and on April 27, 1977, shot the dog—which recovered. He also wrote anonymous letters to people he believed to be persecuting him. He had been reported to the police on a number of occasions as a "nut," but no one suspected that he might be the Son of Sam.

Berkowitz was judged legally sane, and was arraigned on August 23, 1977. He pleaded guilty, saving New York the cost of a trial. He was sentenced to 365 years in prison.

The aftermath is worth describing. His Yonkers apartment building became a place of pilgrimage for sensation-seekers. They stole door-knobs, cut out pieces of carpet, even chipped pieces of paint from Berkowitz's door. In the middle of the night, people shouted, "David, come out," from the street. Berkowitz's apartment remained empty, and a quarter of the building's tenants moved out, even though the landlord changed its number from 25 to 42 Pine Street to try to mislead the souvenir hunters.

Even after Berkowitz was arrested, most Americans found the crimes incomprehensible. One psychiatrist who interviewed him was convinced that his story of "voices" was an attempt to establish a defense of insanity. On the other hand, journalist Maury Terry became convinced that Berkowitz had not acted alone, but that he was a member of a satanic cult who committed some of the murders attributed to Berkowitz, and filmed the shootings to sell as "snuff movies."

Two years after Berkowitz's arrest, Ressler and Douglas went to interview him—three times. As usual, they prepared by learning everything about Berkowitz that was on record. One important discovery was that Berkowitz was an arsonist, and that he had set at least 1,488 fires in New York, which are documented in his diary. He had also triggered hundreds of false alarms. For a long time now, arson has been recognized as basically a sex crime—many arsonists masturbate as they watch the flames. This helped confirm Ressler's suspicions that the Son of Sam shootings were sexual in origin.

Ressler found Berkowitz to be shy, reserved, polite, and low key, and that he spoke only when spoken to. When Ressler tried to touch on the possible sexual aspect of the murders, Berkowitz flatly denied that they had any, claiming that he had had a normal sex life, with girlfriends, and that the murders were just shootings. This, Ressler discovered, was an attempt to mislead. Berkowitz had never had girlfriends, and this was the root of his trouble. In that respect he resembled Harvey Glatman, feeling that he lacked the physical attractiveness to appeal to women.

Where Glatman attempted to satisfy his desires through kidnapping and rape, Berkowitz was far too shy and withdrawn to attempt anything so ambitious. He lacked the aggression to be a true predator. So every evening he went out with a .44, looking for lone women or girls, or couples necking in cars. As he stalked them and then shot them, he admitted, he became sexually excited, and would masturbate afterwards. The men were shot simply because they happened to with the young women, the true targets.

On the nights when he couldn't find a victim, he told them, he would drive to the scenes of earlier murders and replay them in his imagination. If there were still bloodstains visible on the pavement, he would sit in his car and masturbate.

Ressler was pleased that he had made another discovery: that it was true that murderers returned to the scene of their crimes, so offering the manhunters a chance to catch them.

It gave support to another of Ressler's theories: that aberrant behavior is an extension of normal behavior. Teenaged boys ride their bicycles past the homes of teenaged girls, or hang around them and "engage in impetuous spontaneous behavior." Mark Twain had observed the same thing in the scene where Tom Sawyer sets out to attract the attention of Becky Thatcher in the school playground—and we have already noted that Harvey Glatman did the same thing at school, and how the playful snatching of purses developed into armed robbery and then rape.

Berkowitz would have liked to attend the funerals of his victims, but was afraid of being spotted. But he stayed away from work on the day of the funeral, and hung around diners near police stations hoping to hear cops discussing his crimes. (He never succeeded.)

In all, it seems clear that Berkowitz belonged to a class of killers who are basically "wannabes." While most people attempt to achieve a sense of value or worth by doing something that their fellows regard as admirable or useful, people whose self-esteem is irretrievably low daydream of shocking or outraging them, so that they can at least regard themselves as mavericks or rebel outsiders. Berkowitz told Ressler how, as a teenager, he wanted to get to Vietnam, daydreaming of receiving medals and "being recognized as an important individual, and thereby fashioning an identity for himself." It was not to be. His army career—in Korea—was undistinguished and a visit to a prostitute resulted in syphilis.

Back in New York, he began trying to trace his natural mother, Betty Falco, and finally succeeded through an old telephone directory. There was an emotional reunion at her home in Coney Island in May 1975. He also met his half-sister, Roslyn, thirty-seven, who welcomed him to her home. But although he was glad to have found his family, it was too late. He was too frustrated and unfulfilled to find satisfaction in his new role as a son and brother. He began suffering from frequent headaches. And on Christmas Eve 1975, he took a hickory-handled hunting knife and went out in search of a woman to stab. On Co-Op City Boulevard he double-parked and followed a woman who came out of a supermarket. She was wearing a long, heavy coat, and he raised the knife and brought it down on her back. The knife failed to penetrate the thick material, but the woman turned, saw a man with his arm raised to strike again, and screamed. Berkowitz turned and ran away.

He wandered around until he saw another female approaching; this was a fifteen-year-old schoolgirl named Michelle Forman. He followed her across a pedestrian bridge, and stabbed her in the head, and then the upper body. As she turned he saw she was pretty; she lashed out at him, and then fell down. When she tried to grab his leg, he ran off.

As he began to describe the attacks and murders, Berkowitz started to repeat the story he had told to psychiatrists: that he killed because Sam Carr's dog, possessed by a three-thousand-year-old demon, had barked orders at him. Douglas called his bluff. "Hey David, knock off the bullshit. The dog has nothing to do with it." When Berkowitz persisted, they told him the interview was over. "We want the factual basis for these crimes." As they started to leave, Berkowitz laughed and admitted that the demon dog story was false, designed to back his defense of insanity.

The real motive, it seemed, was the desire to become known, to become notorious. There was a sense of potency in holding a whole city to ransom, in seeing the crowds who bought the newspapers that described the latest shooting. That is why he began communicating with the police and with journalist Jimmy Breslin. Ressler has some harsh words to say about the journalists who kept feeding the media frenzy, even when there were no new developments to write about. They, he believed, simply encouraged Berkowitz to continue, like a child who enjoys attention.

Yet what emerged from these interviews is that Berkowitz was not simply a nonentity looking for action to give him a sense of identity. There had been a touch of sadism in his makeup since childhood, when he had poured ammonia into his adoptive mother's fish tank to kill the fish, and killed her pet bird with rat poison, getting pleasure from watching it die slowly. He enjoyed torturing mice and moths. In adolescence, his masturbation fantasies were mixed with violence. And when he graduated to arson, he enjoyed watching bodies being carried out of burning buildings.

As to the stories about the evil spirits in his head that told him to kill, these were, he admitted, an invention. His insistence that he had been enslaved by demonic voices—which would become the basis of the standard book on the case, *Son of Sam* by Lawrence D. Klausner (1981)—were designed to achieve the effect they did, in fact, achieve, to allow him to plead guilty to second-degree murder, with the eventual possibility of parole.

At the end of the interview, Berkowitz told them that if he had been able to settle into a relationship with a good woman who would fulfill his fantasies, he would not have committed the killings. Ressler comments that he does not believe it for a moment. Berkowitz's problem was that he felt inadequate and compensated with violent fantasies, which made him incapable of the give and take of a relationship. Ressler concludes: "Like so many of the criminals I interviewed, he had grown up to murder."

The psychologist Dorothy Otnow Lewis had once made the controversial remark that she felt some criminals were just "born bad." Ressler seemed to be saying the same thing in a different way.

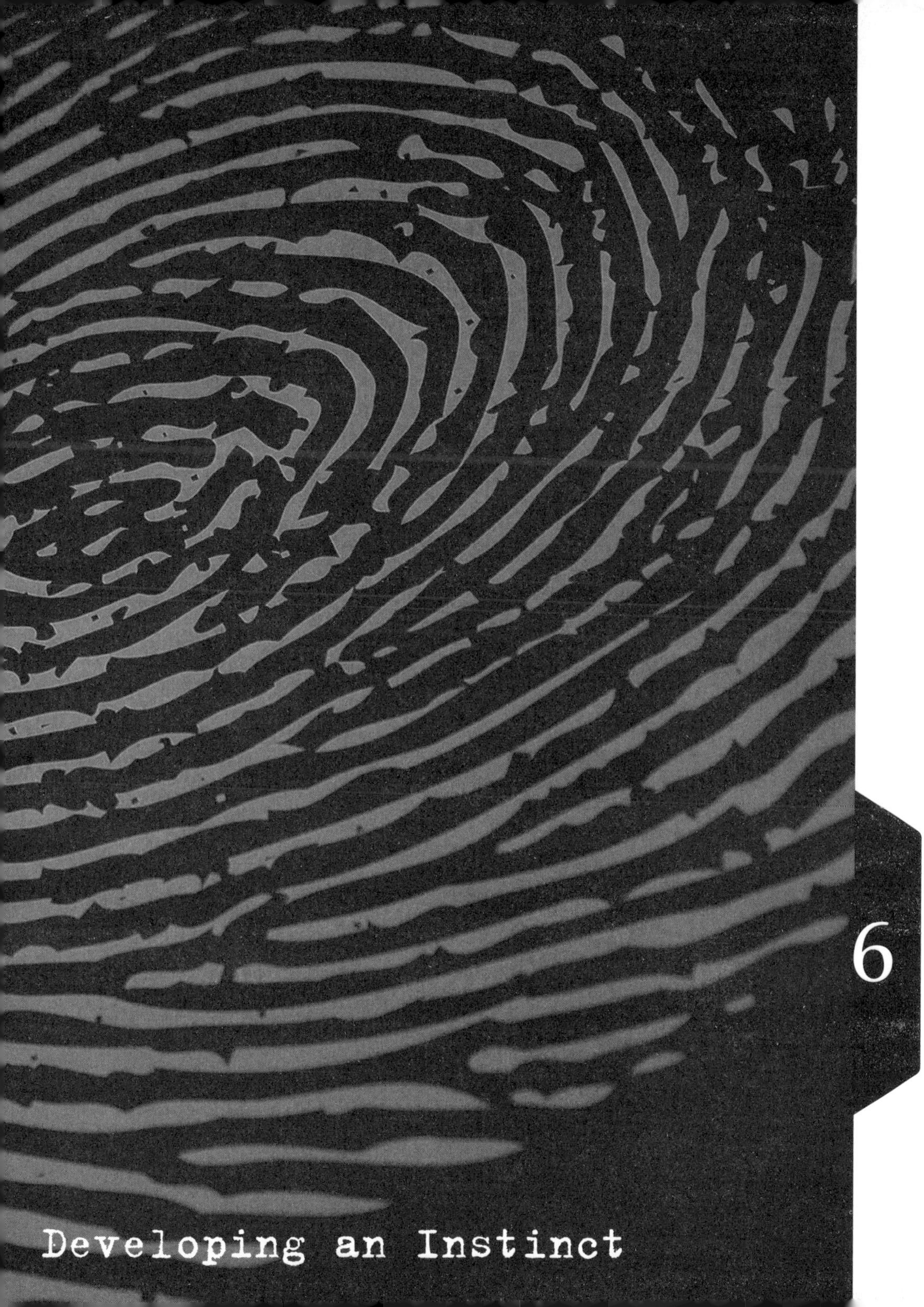

6

Developing an Instinct

6 Developing an Instinct

What Ressler was learning was that once you had talked to enough killers, you began to develop an instinct about what kind of person would commit a particular crime.

In early 1978 he used it to help a colleague, homicide detective Russ Vorpagel, in Sacramento, California.

On January 23, an intruder walked into the house of newly married Teresa Wallin, twenty-two, in the Watt Avenue area of Sacramento, shot her three times, and then mutilated the body with a knife. There was no sign of rape, but there was evidence that the killer had drained some of her blood into a yoghurt cup and drank it.

In his profile of the killer, Ressler said:

White male, aged 25–27 years; thin, undernourished appearance. Residence will be extremely slovenly and unkempt and evidence of the crime will be found at the residence. History of mental illness, and will have been involved in use of drugs. Will be a loner who does not associate with either males or females, and will probably spend a great deal of time in his own home, where he lives alone. Unemployed. Possibly receives some form of disability money. If residing with anyone, it would be with his parents; however, this is unlikely. No prior military record; high school or college dropout. Probably suffering from one or more forms of paranoid psychosis.

Ressler explains:

I had plenty of reasons for making such a precise description of the probable offender. Though profiling was still in its infancy, we had reviewed enough cases of murder to know that sexual homicide—for that's the category into which this crime fit, even if there was no evidence of a sex act committed at the scene—is usually perpetrated by males, and is usually an intraracial crime, white against white, or black against black. The greatest number of sexual killers are white males in their twenties and thirties; this simple fact allows us to eliminate whole segments of the population when first trying to determine what sort of person has perpetrated one of these heinous crimes. Since this was a white residential area, I felt even more certain that the slayer was a white male.

Now I made a guess along a great division line that we in the Behavioral Sciences Unit were beginning to formulate, the distinction between killers who displayed a certain logic in what they had done and those whose mental processes were, by ordinary standards, not apparently logical—"organized" versus "disorganized" criminals. Looking at the crime-scene photographs and the police reports, it was apparent to me that this was not a crime committed by an "organized" killer who stalked his victims, was methodical in how he went about his crimes, and took care to avoid leaving clues to his own identity. No, from the appearance of the crime scene, it was obvious to me that we were dealing with a "disorganized" killer, a person who had a full-blown and serious mental illness. To become as crazy as the man who ripped up the body of Terry Wallin is not something that happens overnight. It takes eight to ten years to develop the depth of psychosis that would surface in this apparently senseless killing. Paranoid schizophrenia is usually first manifested in the teenage years. Adding ten years to an inception-of-illness age of about fifteen would put the slayer in the mid-twenties age group. I felt that he wouldn't be much older, for two reasons. First, most sexual killers are under the age of thirty-five. Second, if he was older than late twenties, the illness would have been so overwhelming that it would already have resulted in a string of bizarre and unsolved homicides. Nothing as wild as this had been reported anywhere nearby, and the absence of other notable homicides was a clue that this was the first killing for this man, that the killer had probably never taken a human life before. The other details of the probable killer's appearance followed logically from my guess that he was a paranoid schizophrenic, and from my study of psychology.

For instance, I thought this person would be thin. I made this guess because I knew of the studies of Dr. Ernest Kretchmer of Germany and Dr. William Sheldon of Columbia University, both dealing with body types. Both men believed there was a high degree of correlation between body type and mental temperament. Kretchmer found that men with slight body builds (asthenics) tended toward introverted forms of schizophrenia; Sheldon's categories were similar, and I thought that on his terms, the killer would be an ectomorph [i.e thin, intellectual type]. These body-type theories are out of favor with today's psychologists—they're fifty years old and more—but I find, more often than not, that they prove to be correct, at least in terms of being helpful in suggesting the probable body type of a psychopathic serial killer.

So that's why I thought this was bound to be a thin and scrawny guy. It was all logical. Introverted schizophrenics don't eat well, don't think in terms of nourishment, and skip meals. They similarly disregard their appearance, not caring at all about cleanliness or neatness. No one would want to live with such a person, so the killer would have to be single. This line of reasoning also allowed me to postulate that his domicile would be a mess, and also to guess that he would not have been in the military, because he would have been too disordered for the military to have accepted him as a recruit in the first place. Similarly, he would not have been able to stay in college, though he might well have completed high school before he disintegrated. This was an introverted individual with problems dating back to his pubescent years. If he had a job at all, it would be a menial one, a janitor perhaps, or someone who picked up papers in a park; he'd be too introverted even to handle the tasks of a deliveryman. Most likely he'd be a recluse living on a disability check.

I didn't include some other opinions in the profile, but I did believe that if this slayer had a car, it, too, would be a wreck, with fast-food wrappers in the back, rust throughout, and an appearance similar to what I expected to be found in the home. I also thought it likely that the slayer lived in the area near the victim, because he would probably be too disordered to drive somewhere, commit such a stunning crime, and get himself back home. More likely, he had walked to and from the crime scene. My guess was that he had been let out of a psychiatric-care facility in the recent past, not much more than a year earlier, and had been building up to this level of violent behavior.

Sherlock Holmes could not have explained his methods better. Using this profile, cops on the beat began questioning people in the area. Around that time, many of them had reported seeing a dirty, disheveled man in an orange jacket, who sometimes knocked on doors and made incomprehensible demands.

Four days later, thirty-eight-year-old Evelyn Miroth, the mother of three sons, was found shot and mutilated on her bed, and a boyfriend, Danny Meredith, was found shot dead in the next room. One of her sons, six-year-old Jason, had also been shot. A twenty-two-month-old baby, David Ferreira, whom the victim had been babysitting, was missing. Evelyn Miroth's other two sons were away from home at the time. The postmortem showed that Evelyn had been sodomized.

Again, there was evidence that the killer had drunk some of his victim's blood.

Finally, Ressler's profile paid off. A woman named Nancy Holden thought she recognized it, and told the police about an encounter she had had with a man named Richard Chase on the day of the Wallin murder. Chase, who had been at school with her, had accosted her in a store and tried to persuade her to give him a lift. Worried by his wild appearance, she had made some excuse.

The police checked on Chase and discovered that he had a record of mental illness. When they called at his apartment to interview him, Chase tried to run away; he was finally handcuffed before he could draw a gun.

The body of David Ferreira was found—decapitated—in a box near a church.

On January 2,1979, Richard Chase was tried on six counts of murder. It became clear from the evidence that one of his peculiarities was to dabble his fingers in the intestines of his victims—hence the nickname the "Dracula Killer." Chase was sentenced to death, but on December 26, 1980, he committed suicide with an overdose of his antidepressants, which he had been saving up for weeks.

Ressler makes the vitally important observation that Chase's mental problems can be traced back to his mother, who was "schizophrenic, emotionally unable to concentrate on the task of socializing her son or to care for him in a loving way." And he goes on to note that no less than nineteen of his serial killers had inadequate mothers. The psychologist Abraham Maslow used the term "schizophrenogenic" about his own mother, explaining that it meant the kind of mother who made her kids crazy, and told me (when I was working on a book about him) that if it had not been for a maternal uncle who loved children, and who took care of Abe and his younger brother, he would not be sane, that his uncle "may have saved my life psychically." If a person like Maslow, brought up in a protective family background, can come close to being "psychically wrecked," it underlines how easy it is for the kind of offenders Ressler was dealing with.

Another serial killer to whom Ressler devotes several pages in *Whoever Fights Monsters* was Gerard Schaefer, perhaps one of sickest sex killers of the twentieth century. In his early lectures to police academies, Ressler would use Schaefer as a typical example of the organized serial killer. In fact, Schaefer fit the pattern so well that members of the audience often accused Ressler of taking the details of the organized serial killer directly from Schaefer.

ONCE YOU HAD TALKED TO ENOUGH KILLERS, YOU BEGAN TO DEVELOP AN INSTINCT ABOUT WHAT KIND OF PERSON WOULD COMMIT A PARTICULAR CRIME.

Ressler was not involved in catching Schaefer; he was arrested before Ressler had developed the idea of criminal profiling. But the pages about him in *Whoever Fights Monsters* show the importance Ressler attaches to the case.

In 1973, there had been so many disappearances of young women in Brevard County, Florida, that the police were in the process of putting together a task force when the man responsible fell into their hands. He was Gerard John Schaefer, a twenty-nine-year-old police officer.

On July 22, 1972, Schaefer stopped his police cruiser to confront two hitchhikers, Nancy Trotter, seventeen, and Pamela Sue Wells, eighteen, in the town of Stuart in Martin County. He issued them a warning about hitching rides, but also offered to give them a ride to the beach the next day. He drove them out to the then swampy and isolated Hutchinson Island on the pretext of showing them a Spanish fort. The young women must have felt that they could hardly be in safer hands.

Once out on the island, he suddenly started to verbally abuse them, accusing them of being runaways (which they were not). He then forced them from the car at gunpoint, and handcuffed them both. All this was plainly designed to reassure them that this was a legitimate arrest, to make them feel that this was a mistake that would soon be cleared up when they reached the police station. But when he went on to gag them with old rags from the trunk of his car, they must have realized that this was no arrest.

Schaefer then forced Pamela Sue to balance on the giant roots of a cypress tree, where he tied her. Next he made Nancy stand on the roots of another cypress, some distance away, with a noose around her neck. Trapped there, the young women were forced to listen to his taunts of selling them into white slavery. His aim was obviously to terrify them—if possible, until they lost control of their bowels, which seems to have been one of the things that sexually excited him. But then he was interrupted by a call on the police radio. He left the pair only to return to find them gone. Realizing that Pamela Sue and Nancy could identify him, he went home and rang the sheriff—his boss—and told him that he had done "something foolish." His intention, he explained, was to frighten the girls and make them realize that hitchhiking was dangerous. He described where he had left them, and in about a quarter of an hour, the sheriff found the petrified young women wandering in the woods—still handcuffed and gagged.

Schaefer was dismissed from the police force immediately, and charged with assault and imprisonment. He was released on $15,000 bail, and ordered to appear for trial in November 1972.

My own interest in Schaefer arose from the fact that he had been the first love of a friend of mine, a woman named Sandy Steward, who later became the crime writer Sondra London. After his arrest she kept in touch with him, published some of his writings under the title *Killer Fiction,* and persuaded me to write an introduction to them.

When Sondra met Gerard Schaefer in Florida at a high school dance in 1964, she was seventeen and he was eighteen—handsome, gentle, and well-mannered. Her parents liked him so much that they invited him to go with them on their vacation, and her grandmother told her she was lucky to meet such a nice boy. Sandy and Gerry decided that they were in love, walked hand in hand, and made love among the tombstones in the old graveyard. They had been together for a year when he confessed to her that he experienced terrifying sadistic urges towards women, and daydreamed of hanging them dressed only in their underwear. Sometimes he sobbed as he told her about these compulsions. He even talked to the school counselor about them, but she was unable to help him. Eventually, Sandy broke off their engagement because, she said, she had no desire to be his mother-confessor.

Schaefer also spied on a woman who sunbathed in her garden in a bikini. One night, when she came home late and slightly drunk, he broke into her house, and woke her up by pressing a knife to her throat and threatening her with instant death if she moved, and then made her lie on her face. He removed his trousers and masturbated on her, then urinated on her pillow. Before he left, he threatened to kill her if she told anyone.

The experience proved to be addictive. But it was not rape to which he became addicted, but the terror he could inspire in his victims. For this reason, Schaefer liked abducting two victims together, so one could watch as he killed the other. This is undoubtedly what he had in mind when he drove Nancy and Pamela Sue into the woods that day in 1972, a decision that cost him his job, but unfortunately not his liberty. For soon after being released on bond, he went back to killing.

On September 27, 1972, Schaefer introduced himself to Susan Place, eighteen, and her friend Georgia Jessup, seventeen. He went with them to Susan's home and told her parents that they were going to the beach to "play some guitar."

Mrs. Place thought the man—who said his name was Jerry Shepherd—looked too old for the girls (he was twenty-six). A feeling of vague unease prompted her to note down the license-plate number of his blue Datsun.

When neither girl returned home, Mrs. Place notified the police. But when they checked the license number she had noted down, it proved to belong to another make of car, whose owner was totally unlike the genial, plump-faced "Jerry Shepherd."

A month later, on October 23, 1972, two more teenaged girls vanished—this time, they were only fourteen. Elsie Farmer and Mary Briscolina had set out to hitchhike when they too disappeared. In January 1973, their skeletons were found in undergrowth near Fort Lauderdale, and identified by dental records.

Meanwhile, in November 1972, Schaefer had been sentenced to six months for the Trotter and Wells kidnapping, and while he was in jail, his luck ran out. As Susan Place's mother was driving through Martin County, she noticed that all car license plates began with "42." The license number of the blue Datsun had started with a 4, which was the number of Pinellas County, near Saint Petersburg. Had she noted down the number incorrectly? Mrs. Place decided to act on the assumption that she had, and when she found that the same number, but starting with 42, belonged to a blue Datsun, she suspected that she was at last on the right track. When further research revealed that its owner, Gerard Schaefer, was in jail for kidnapping two teenage girls, she knew she was. At the county sheriff's office, she was able to identify Schaefer as Jerry Shepherd.

A search of Schaefer's home—where he lived with his mother—revealed various items that belonged to the missing young women, and some extremely explicit pornography, written and illustrated by Schaefer himself, describing murder, rape, and acts of necrophilia.

Schaefer was indicted and sentenced to two life terms for the murders of Susan Place and Georgia Jessup. But the items found in Schaefer's room convinced the police that he had killed at least twenty women, and even two children of eight and nine. Evidence recovered later suggested that even this could be less than half the total. Sondra London was shaken when Schaefer came to trial in 1973, and as she began to realize that Schaefer had already committed murder when he was her lover, her fascination with the problem of serial killers increased.

Finally, in February 1989, Sondra addressed a letter to Schaefer in Florida State Prison. He replied effusively: "How could I not remember you, the great love of my life?" Soon he agreed to allow Sondra to work on a book about him.

As the correspondence continued, she asked him if he still wrote pornographic stories, like those the police had found in his home. By way of reply he forwarded her some of his more recent efforts.

A typical one, "Grand Theft," describes how he picks up a hooker, a "girl with an ass like jello on springs," in a burger bar. In her room she performs oral sex with "misty eyed pleasure." Then, as they are leaving the room, he slips a garrote around her throat. Schaefer describes her last moments: "With her eyes, she asked me, 'Why?' 'Because,' I hissed, as the life went out of her."

Most of the stories have the same, predictable plot: he picks up a young woman, they have sex, and he kills her sadistically, strangling, shooting, or disemboweling her. "She stared in wide-eyed fascination as the ropy coils of her own intestines slid out of her belly . . ."

Yet as she interviewed him in prison, Sondra was puzzled by the paradox of a man who was "well-spoken and pleasant, funny and smart." She adds: "In the process of studying him like some kind of caged wild animal specimen, I've come to appreciate his many fine qualities. What is scary is the idea of the hideously deformed, shadowy monster lurking behind this nice, normal guy."

Sondra decided to publish Schaefer's "killer fiction" herself. "You do not have to like something to learn from it," she pointed out. It appeared in a slim, red-paper covered book, seventy pages long, costing $18. I was offered a copy by a specialist crime bookseller in New Jersey, and recognized that this was the authentic production of a sadistic sex killer.

Soon after, I entered into correspondence with Sondra, after an introduction by British publisher Paul Woods, who published her study of men on death row, *Knockin' on Joe* (a term meaning self-injury to get out of forced labor) and in due course, wrote an introduction to a new edition of *Killer Fiction*. I have to admit that I hesitated. It was so sick that it seemed to me to be interesting solely as an insight into the mind of a sadistic killer. I described Schaefer as suffering from a kind of "halitosis of the soul." Finally, though, I overcame my squeamishness, because I agree with Sondra that it is not necessary to like something to learn from it.

I have never read the entire book and do not intend to. There is a dreary sameness about the stories, an obsession with trying to provoke nausea and disgust. "I pulled off her shoes thinking it wasn't right to cornhole a woman with her panties around her knees and a bullet in her head with her shoes on." And he describes how he dug up the body several times, in spite of decomposition, and ended by cutting off the head.

Oddly enough, Schaefer would later try to sue me because his name is mentioned in my book *The Serial Killers* (1990), maintaining that he was in prison only for the murder of two teenagers. When I sent the publisher's defense attorney some photocopied pages of Schaefer's book, in which Sondra London writes of the "serial killer who loved me," and Schaefer quotes himself as telling fellow inmate Ted Bundy: "[I reckon] twenty-eight confirmed kills in South Florida alone, plus my collection of heads," Schaefer's case against me was dismissed. I suspect that he only started it to introduce some variety into his uneventful prison life.

Schaefer was murdered in his cell on December 3, 1995, stabbed by fellow inmate Vincent Rivera. But Sondra, who attended the trial, sets it on record that she does not accept this version of his death. "His body was covered with marks of state-issued boots." She believes prison guards murdered him, and that drug-dealing lay behind it.

Since Schaefer has written hundreds of thousands of words attempting to describe his crimes and his state of mind, it ought to be possible to understand exactly why he committed them. We know that he was brought up a Roman Catholic, and that he adored his mother and hated his alcoholic father, who often beat her. Sondra once had to pull him off his father, whose head he was beating with a golf club, after he had called Schaefer's mother a whore. Plainly, Schaefer became obsessed with this idea of "whores"; he once said that there are only two types of women: whores and virgins. He obviously hated women who enjoy sex: ". . . with her left hand she tore at her panties in an effort to strip them from her own ass. Her wanton depravity was out of control. She'd become an animal in the mindless throes of sexual lust, a regular bitch in heat." This comment is a prelude (of course) to killing her.

But the story enables us to glimpse the puzzling complexity of Schaefer's psychology. He knows perfectly well that the woman in question is not a whore, just as he knew that Georgia Jessup and Susan Place and his other victims were not whores. When he broke into the bedroom of the woman who lived nearby, and set out to terrorize her, he knew she was not a whore either—she had just said good-bye to her boyfriend at the front door. But he could only achieve the maximum pitch of sexual excitement by telling himself that they *were* whores. In a sense it made no difference what they were, for they were simply tools of his masturbatory fantasy, like illustrations in some pornographic magazine. He had conditioned himself to be excited by the idea of whores, and perpetrating violence on them, just as some men need a prostitute to dress in a schoolgirl's gym slip, or a nurse's uniform.

Which leaves the interesting question: What originally caused Schaefer's obsession with "whores"? Was it, perhaps, his adoration of his mother, and his father's assertion that she was a whore? Sondra London believes that he was sexually obsessed with his mother, and that since he was allowed into the marital bed until he was sixteen, such an obsession had plenty of time to develop. We recall that the Yorkshire Ripper,

Peter Sutcliffe, was also obsessed by prostitutes; a friend describes how he would hang around brothels, fascinated by the sight of the women who went in and out. We have noted how Sutcliffe was deeply shocked when his mother, whom he adored, was caught by her husband having an affair with a policeman. Sutcliffe's mother was also bullied and humiliated by her husband, another typical Right Man. Could it be that when a child sees the mother he worships ill-treated by her husband, and accused of being a whore, the result is an emotional trauma that causes him to associate love and humiliation, purity and sadism?

There is undoubtedly another element that needs to be added to the equation: what psychologists call "hypersexuality." Most young and healthy adolescent males experience a powerful sex drive that usually results in repeated masturbation, perhaps several times a day; therefore most of them are potential rapists. Another serial killer, Danny Rolling, commented in a letter to me that the difference between the rapist and the normal male is smaller than we assume, and he refers to a study in which a hundred college men were asked if they would rape a pretty girl if they were sure they could get away with it, and all replied yes.

In some males the sex drive is so abnormally powerful that it is almost insatiable. We have seen that Albert DeSalvo, the "Boston Strangler," needed sex up to a dozen times a day, and on more than one occasion, raped two women the same day. When the sex drive is this strong, particularly in an adolescent lacking in self-confidence, the result is inevitably masturbation accompanied by fantasies. Like Heirens, Schaefer became an underwear fetishist when he was twelve; like Harvey Glatman, he also discovered the pleasures of bondage: "I would tie myself up to a tree, struggle to get free, and I'd get sexually excited and do something to hurt myself." And he began to fantasize about hurting women.

In persons with an abnormally strong sex-drive, fantasy can easily build up into what I have sometimes called "superheated sex," in an analogy with superheated steam. In Schaefer's case this led him to killing livestock, beheading them with a machete before having sex with the carcases. The desire to kill things became so strong that he even experienced the urge to shoot at cows, and thought about joining the army because he liked the idea of killing human beings. But by the time he was old enough for the draft, in 1968, he had changed his mind. He later claimed that he had obtained deferment by wearing women's underwear.

There followed unsuccessful attempts to become a priest, then a schoolteacher. He lost the latter job at Plantation High School after a few weeks because of "persistent efforts to impose his moral and political views on the students." The same thing happened when he became a student teacher at Stranahan High School, revealing the same obsessive need to exercise authority.

His first murder seems to have occurred in September 1969. The victim was Leigh Hainline Bonadies, a schoolmate of Sondra, whom Schaefer had lusted after when he was her neighbor and tennis partner. In August 1969 she married, but it was not a success, and after two weeks she walked out, leaving a note saying that she was going to Miami. According to Schaefer, she asked him for a lift to the airport, but never arrived at his house. But she vanished, and when Schaefer was arrested in 1973, some of her jewelry was found in his bedroom. He never admitted to killing her.

> WHAT IS SCARY IS THE IDEA OF THE HIDEOUSLY DEFORMED, SHADOWY MONSTER LURKING BEHIND THIS NICE, NORMAL GUY.

Two months later, on December 18, 1969, Carmen Hallock, a twenty-two-year-old cocktail waitress, told her sister-in-law that she intended to meet a schoolteacher who had offered her undercover work for the government, with "lots of money." This was the last time she was ever seen alive.

On December 29, 1970, nine-year-old Peggy Rahn and eight-year-old Wendy Stevenson vanished from Pompano Beach. A clerk identified photographs of the two girls and said he had seen them with a six-foot-tall man in his twenties who was buying them ice cream. Neither girl was ever found, and Schaefer later claimed—perhaps jokingly—that he had killed them and eaten their flesh cooked with onions and peppers, having been reading about the 1930s child killer Albert Fish, who claimed to have eaten an eight-year-old girl.

Another twenty-two-year-old cocktail waitress, Belinda Hutchens, was last seen on January 5, 1972, driving off in a blue sedan before she vanished. Her drug-addict husband later identified the car as the one belonging to Schaefer.

There is no exact record of Schaefer's murders, but when his mother's house was searched in April 1973, items found included a purse owned by Susan Place; three pieces of jewelry belonging to Leigh Bonadies; two teeth and a shamrock pin belonging to Carmen Hallock; news clippings on the Bonadies and Hallock cases; an address book belonging to Belinda Hutchens; a passport, diary, and book of poetry owned by nineteen-year-old Collette Goodenough, last seen in January 1973; the driver's license of nineteen-year-old Barbara Wilcox, who vanished with Goodenough; a piece of jewelry owned by Mary Briscolina, missing with a female friend since October 1972; an envelope addressed to "Jerry Shepherd"; eleven guns and thirteen knives; photos of unknown women and of Schaefer dressed in women's underwear; and more than a hundred pages of writings and sketches, detailing the torture and murder of "whores."

Schaefer's writings in *Killer Fiction* detail many other murders that sound oddly authentic—in that they do not seem to have been written merely to gloat—including one of a woman whose body was dumped in a water-filled quarry in an automobile.

It is apropos to Schaefer that Ressler has a passage describing the organized serial killer:

> *. . . let me point out the attributes of the organized offender that are present so far in the narrative. The abductor personalized the victims by talking with them, used his own vehicle, and conned the women into his car by means of his verbal skills. He brought his own threatening weapon to the scene and took it away with him, had a rape kit, and was plainly planning to complete sexual acts with the women prior to torture and murder. After the murder, he was going to hide and dispose of the bodies. He displayed mobility and adaptive behavior during the crime when he left the women tied up and went to pay attention to some other aspect of his life, telling them that he would return and finish them off later.*

In short, Schaefer feels utterly relaxed and at ease with his intended victims, cool and systematic. It can be seen why Ressler regarded him as the perfect example of the organized serial killer.

Perhaps the most basic characteristic of the serial killer is one that he shares with most other criminals: a tendency to an irrational self-pity that can produce an explosion of violence.

In that sense, Paul John Knowles may be regarded not merely as the archetypal serial killer but as the archetypal criminal.

Knowles, who was born in 1946, from the age of nineteen had spent an average of six months of every year in jail, mostly for car thefts and burglaries. In Florida's Raiford Penitentiary in 1972, he began to study astrology, and initiated a correspondence with a divorcée named Angela Covic, whom he had contacted through the personals ads in an astrology magazine. Angela flew down to Florida, was impressed by the gaunt good looks of the tall redheaded convict, and agreed to marry him. She hired a lawyer to work on his parole, and he was released on May 14, 1972. Knowles hastened to San Francisco to claim his bride, but by then she had second thoughts; a psychic had warned her that she was mixed up with a very dangerous man. Knowles stayed at her mother's apartment, but after four days Angela told him she had decided to return to her first husband, and gave him his airline ticket back to Florida. Knowles exploded with rage and self-pity; he later claimed that he went out on to the streets of San Francisco and killed three people. This was never verified, but it is consistent with the behavior of the disorganized serial killer.

Back in his hometown of Jacksonville, Florida, on July 26, 1974, Knowles got into a bar fight and was locked up for the night. He escaped, broke into the home of a sixty-five-year-old teacher, Alice Curtis, and stole her money and her car. But he rammed a gag too far down her throat and she suffocated. A few days later, as he parked the stolen car, he noticed two children looking at him as if they recognized him—their mother was, in fact, a friend of his family. He forced them into the car and drove away. The bodies of seven-year-old Mylette Anderson and her eleven-year-old sister, Lillian, were later found in a swamp.

What followed was a completely unmotivated murder rampage, as if Knowles had simply decided to kill as many people as he could before he was caught.

The following day, August 2, 1974, in Atlantic Beach, Florida, he broke into the home of Marjorie Howie, forty-nine, and strangled her with a stocking; he also stole her television set. A few days later he

With cigarette dangling from his mouth and his long hair disheveled, Paul John Knowles appears to be the archetypal criminal. In 1974, the Florida parolee was charged and convicted of six slayings in several states. (Associated Press)

strangled and raped a teenage runaway who hitched a lift with him. On August 23, he strangled Kathie Pierce in Musella, Georgia, while her three-year-old son looked on; Knowles left the child unharmed. On September 3, near Lima, Ohio, he had several drinks with an accounts executive named William Bates, and later strangled him, driving off in the dead man's white Chevrolet Impala. After driving to California, Seattle, and Utah (using Bates's credit cards) he forced his way into a trailer in Ely, Nevada, on September 18, 1974, and shot to death an elderly couple, Emmett and Lois Johnson. On September 21, he strangled and raped forty-two-year-old Charlynn Hicks, who had stopped to admire the view beside the road near Sequin, Texas. On September 23, in Birmingham, Alabama, he met an

PERHAPS THE MOST BASIC CHARACTERISTIC OF THE SERIAL KILLER IS ONE THAT HE SHARES WITH MOST OTHER CRIMINALS: A TENDENCY TO AN IRRATIONAL SELF-PITY THAT CAN PRODUCE AN EXPLOSION OF VIOLENCE.

attractive woman named Ann Dawson, who owned a beauty shop, and they traveled around together for the next six days, living on her money; she was murdered on September 29, 1974.

For the next sixteen days, he drove around without apparently committing any further murders; but on October 16 he rang the doorbell of a house in Marlborough, Connecticut; sixteen-year-old Dawn White, who was expecting a friend, answered it. Knowles forced her up to the bedroom and raped her; when her mother, Karen, returned home, he raped her too, and then strangled them both with silk stockings. He left with a tape recorder and Dawn's collection of rock records.

Two days later, he knocked on the door of fifty-three-year-old Doris Hovey in Woodford, Virginia, and told her he needed a gun and would not harm her; she gave him a rifle belonging to her husband, and he shot her through the head and left, leaving the rifle beside her body.

In Key West, Florida, he picked up two hitchhikers, intending to kill them, but was stopped by a policeman for pulling up on a curb; when the policeman asked to see his documents, he expected to be arrested; but the officer failed to check that Knowles was the owner of the car, and let him drive away.

On November 2, Knowles picked up two hitchhikers, Edward Milliard and Debbie Griffin; Milliard's body was later discovered in woods near Macon, Georgia; Griffin's body was never found.

On November 6, 1974, in a gay bar in Macon, he met a man named Carswell Carr and went home with him. Later that evening, Carr's fifteen-year-old daughter, Mandy, heard shouting and went downstairs, to find Knowles standing over the body of her father, who was tied up. It emerged later that Carr had died of a heart attack; Knowles had been torturing him by stabbing him all over with a pair of scissors. He then raped Mandy—or attempted it (no sperm was found in her)—and strangled her with a stocking. The bodies were found when Carr's wife, a night nurse, returned home.

The next day, in a Holiday Inn in downtown Atlanta, Knowles saw an attractive redhead in the bar—a British journalist named Sandy Fawkes; she went for a meal with him and they ended up in her bedroom. But he proved impotent, in spite of all her efforts to arouse him. He had introduced himself to her as Daryl Golden, son of a New Mexico restaurant owner, and the two of them got on well enough for her to accept his offer to drive her to Miami. On the way there, he hinted that he was on the run for some serious crime—or crimes—and told her that he had a premonition that he was going to be killed some time soon. He also told her that he had tape-recorded his confession, and left it with his lawyer, Sheldon Yavitz, in Miami. In another motel, he finally succeeded in entering her, after first practicing cunnilingus and masturbating himself into a state of excitement. But even so, he failed to achieve orgasm—she concluded that he was incapable of it.

Long before they separated—after six days together—she was anxious to get rid of him. She had sensed the underlying violence, self-pity, and lack of discipline. He pressed hard for another night together; she firmly refused, insisting that it would only make the parting sadder. He waited outside her Miami motel half the night, while she deliberately stayed away; finally, he gave up and left.

The following day, she was asked to go to the police station, and there for the first time realized what kind of a man she had been sleeping with. On the morning after their separation, "Daryl Golden" had driven to the house of some journalists to whom he had been introduced four days earlier, and offered to drive Susan Mackenzie to the hairdresser. Instead, he took the wrong turn, and told her that he wanted to have sex with her, and would not hurt her if she complied. When he stopped the car and pointed a gun at her, she succeeded in jumping out and waved frantically at a passing car. Knowles drove off. Later, alerted to the attempted rape, a squad car tried to stop Knowles, but he pointed a shotgun at the policeman and drove off.

Knowles knew that he had to get rid of the stolen car. In West Palm Beach, he forced his way into a house, and took a woman named Barbara Tucker hostage, driving off in her Volkswagen, leaving her sister (in a wheelchair) and a six-year-old child unharmed. He held Barbara Tucker captive in a motel in Fort Pierce for a night and day, and then finally left her tied up and drove off in her car.

The next day, Patrolman Charles F. Campbell flagged down the Volkswagen—now sporting altered license plates—and found himself looking down the barrel of a shotgun. He was taken captive and driven off, handcuffed, in his own patrol car. But the brakes were poor, and, using the police siren, Knowles forced another car—that of businessman John Meyer—off the road, and then drove off in Meyer's car, with Meyer and the patrolman in the back seat. In Pulaski County, Georgia, Knowles took them into a wood, handcuffed them to a tree, and shot each man in the back of the head.

Soon after killing the two men, Knowles spotted a police roadblock ahead, and drove on through it, losing control of the car and crashing into a tree. He scrambled from the wreck and ran into the woods. A vast manhunt was now launched, involving two hundred police personnel, tracker dogs, and helicopters. Knowles was in the end arrested by a courageous civilian, who saw him from a house, and he gave himself up quietly.

THE DAILY STORIES OF THE WOMEN IN HIS LIFE HAD TURNED HIM INTO A CASANOVA KILLER . . . DILLINGER AND JESSIE JAMES ROLLED INTO ONE.

The day after his appearance in court, as he was being transferred to a maximum-security prison, Knowles unpicked his handcuffs and made a grab for the sheriff's gun; FBI agent Ron Angel shot him dead. Knowles had been responsible for at least eighteen, possibly as many as twenty-four murders.

Sandy Fawkes had seen Knowles in court, and was overwhelmed by a sense of his "evil power." But she had no doubt that on that day he now had what he had always craved: he was famous at last.

And enjoying his notoriety. The newspapers were filled with pictures of his appearance at Midgeville and accounts of his behavior. The streets had been lined with people. Sightseers had hung over the sides of balconies to catch a glimpse of him, manacled and in leg irons, dressed in a brilliant orange jumpsuit. He loved it: the local coeds four-deep on the sidewalks, the courtroom packed with reporters, friends, and Mandy Carr's relatives and school chums. It was an event and he was the center of it, and he smiled at everyone. No wonder he had laughed like a hyena at his capture; he was having his hour of glory, not in the hereafter as he had predicted, but in the here and now. The daily stories of the women in his life had turned him into a Casanova killer, a folk villain, Dillinger and Jesse James rolled into one. He was already being referred to as the most heinous killer in history.

He was quoted in a local newspaper as saying that he was "the only successful member of his family." At last Knowles had achieved the aim of most serial killers: "to become known, to get myself a name."

7

The Worst Mass Murderer Yet

7

The Worst Mass Murderer Yet

Despite their local notoriety, Knowles and Schaefer remained relatively unknown to the public at large. It was the Houston killer Dean Corll who first made the American public—and then the world—aware of the rise of a new kind of mass murderer. And although the case cannot compare in psychological interest with many others in this book, it must be discussed as a kind of gruesome historical landmark. Corll was the first serial killer to create the feeling that human depravity had reached a new depth.

Shortly after 8 a.m. on August 8, 1973, the telephone operator in the Pasadena Police Department received a call from someone with a boyish voice and a broad Texas accent. "Y'all better come on here now. Ah jes' killed a man." He gave the address as 2020 Lamar Drive.

Within a minute, two squad cars were on their way. Lamar Drive was in a middle-class suburb of Pasadena—a southeastern suburb of Houston—and 2020 Lamar was a small frame bungalow with an overgrown lawn. Three teenagers were sitting on the stoop by the front door: two boys and a girl. The girl, who was small and shapely, was dressed in clothes that looked even more tattered than the usual teenage outfit. All three were red-eyed, as if they had been crying. A skinny, pimply youth with an incipient blonde moustache identified himself as the one who had made the phone call. He pointed at the front door: "He's in there."

Lying against the wall in the corridor was the naked body of a well-built man, his face caked with blood that had flowed from a bullet wound. There were more bullet holes in his back and shoulder. The bullet in the head had failed to penetrate fully, and the end was sticking out of his skull. He was very obviously dead.

The three teenagers had identified themselves as Elmer Wayne Henley, seventeen, Timothy Kerley, sixteen, and Rhonda Williams, fifteen. Henley, the youth who had made the call, also acknowledged that he had shot his friend, whose name was Dean Arnold Corll. The teenagers were driven off to the Pasadena police headquarters. Meanwhile, an ambulance was summoned to take the corpse to the morgue, and detectives began to search the house.

It was obvious that Corll had moved in recently—the place was only half furnished. The bedroom outside which the corpse was lying contained a single bed and a small table. It smelt strongly of spray paint—the type used in "paint-sniffing" (similar to glue or other solvent sniffing). The oddest thing about the room was the transparent plastic sheeting that covered the entire carpet. And lying beside the bed was an eight-foot length of plywood with handcuffs attached to two of its corners, and nylon ropes to the other two. A long hunting knife in its scabbard lay nearby. A black box proved to contain a seventeen-inch dildo and a jar of Vaseline. It did not require the powers of a Sherlock Holmes to deduce that these objects were connected with some bizarre sexual ritual in which the victims were unwilling.

The new Ford van parked in the drive produced the same impression. There were navy-blue curtains that could be drawn to seal off the whole of the rear portion, a piece of carpeting on the floor, and rings and hooks attached to the walls. There was also a considerable length of nylon rope. In a large box—covered with a piece of carpet—there were strands of human hair. Another similar box in a shed had airholes drilled in its sides.

Back at the police station, Elmer Wayne Henley, nervous and chain-smoking, was explaining how he came to shoot his friend Dean Corll.

He had met Corll, he said, when he had lived in a run-down area of Houston known as the Heights. Corll, who was sixteen years his senior, had recently moved into a house that had belonged to his father; it was in Pasadena. On the previous night, he and Timothy Kerley had gone to a glue-sniffing party at Corll's house. But in the early hours of the morning, the two boys had made some excuse to go out and collect Rhonda Williams, who had just decided to run away from home. Rhonda had been in a state of tension and misery ever since her boyfriend had vanished a year earlier.

Corll had been furious when the boys arrived back at the house with Rhonda. "You weren't supposed to bring a girl," he yelled, "You spoilt everything." But after a while he seemed to control himself and regain his good humor, and the four of them settled down to paint-sniffing in the living room. Paint was sprayed into a paper bag, which was then passed around so that they could all breathe in the fumes. Within an hour, they were all stretched out unconscious on the floor.

When Wayne Henley woke up, daylight was filtering through the drawn curtains, and Corll was snapping handcuffs on his wrists; his ankles were tied together. The other two were already handcuffed and bound.

DEAN CORLL WAS THE FIRST SERIAL KILLER TO CREATE THE FEELING THAT HUMAN DEPRAVITY HAD REACHED A NEW DEPTH.

As they all began to recover their senses and struggle against their bonds, Corll revealed that his good humor of a few hours ago had been deceptive. He was seething with resentment and fury. He waved the knife at them and told them he was going to kill them all. "But first I'm gonna have my fun." Then he dragged Henley into the kitchen and rammed a revolver in his belly.

Henley decided that his only chance of escape was to "sweet talk" Corll, persuading him that he would be willing to join in the murder of the other two. It took some time, but finally Corll calmed down and removed the handcuffs. Henley would rape Rhonda while he raped Timothy Kerley. Corll went and picked up Kerley, carrying him to the bedroom like some huge spider with its prey. Then he came back and carried off Rhonda. He turned on the portable radio to its top volume to drown out any screams or protests.

When Henley went into the bedroom, Corll was naked, and was handcuffing Kerley, who was also naked, to the plywood board. Kerley, like Rhonda, was gagged. Corll handed Henley the knife and ordered him to cut off Rhonda's clothes. Rhonda was still dazed from the paint-sniffing, and was only half-aware of what was happening. But Kerley understood and struggled violently as Corll tried to sexually assault him.

Knowing he was under observation, Henley pretended to rape Rhonda; in fact, he was incapable. But as Kerley thrashed and struggled violently, trying to throw off the heavy man, Henley shouted above the music: "Why don't you let me take her outta here? She don't want to see that." Corll just ignored him. Henley saw his chance and jumped to his feet, grabbing the .22 pistol from the night table. "Back off, Dean! Stop it!" Corll lurched to his feet. "Go on, Wayne, kill me. Why don't you?" As he lunged towards Henley, the boy fired; the bullet struck Corll in the head, and he staggered past, while Henley fired another shot into his shoulder. As Corll tumbled through the door and hit the wall of the corridor, Henley emptied the rest of the bullets into his back. Corll slumped down slowly to the floor, resting finally with his cheek and shoulder against the wall.

Henley found the handcuff key and released his friends—Rhonda was still unable to take in what had happened. But when she saw Corll lying in a pool of blood, she screamed. Henley calmed her, and the three of them dressed—Rhonda making do with her slashed clothes. What should they do next? Simply leave the corpse and go away? But it would be found sooner or later, and if neighbors had seen them entering or leaving the house, they would be in serious trouble. So Henley looked up the number of the Pasadena police department and rang them. As the tension relaxed, all three of them found that they were unable to stop sobbing.

It took Henley an hour and a half to make his statement. Meanwhile, Kerley was able to confirm the story. But Kerley also mentioned something that intrigued the detectives. "While we were waiting for the police, Wayne told me that if I wasn't his friend, he could have got fifteen hundred dollars for me."

Questioned about the plywood board and the dildo, Henley told the police that Corll liked little boys, and had been paying him to procure them for him. But why, in that case, had Henley decided to kill him? "He made one mistake," said Henley. "He told me that I wouldn't be the first one he'd killed. He said he'd already killed a lot of boys and buried them in the boat shed."

The words made the detectives glance at one another. So far, they had been assuming that this was a simple case of glue-sniffing and sexual perversion, and that Corll's threats to kill the teenagers had been intended to frighten them. Henley's words raised a far more unpleasant suspicion. For nearly three years now, boys had been disappearing from the Heights area of Houston. Some of them were assumed to be runaways, but in the case of many, the parents had ruled it out as impossible—as, for example, in the case of a nine-year-old. Now the police had learned that Corll had lived in the Heights area until he moved to Pasadena, and one of his homes had been directly opposite that of the missing nine-year-old.

WAYNE HENLEY STOOD AT THE DOOR, GAZING BLANKLY INSIDE. THEN HE WALKED BACK TOWARDS THE CARS, SAT DOWN ON THE GROUND, AND BURIED HIS HEAD BETWEEN HIS KNEES.

"Where is this boat shed?"

Henley said he wasn't sure; he had been there only once. But it was somewhere in southwest Houston. He now was able to recollect three of the names that Corll had mentioned: Marty Jones, someone called Cobble, and someone called Hilligiest. Even with all these details, none of the detectives really believed that they were dealing with serial murder. It was more likely that Henley was still under the influence of the "glue." But his story had to be checked.

Detective Sergeant Dave Mullican asked Henley: "Can you remember how to get to this boat shed?"

"I think so. It's near Hiram Clark Road."

The first stop was the Houston police headquarters. There Henley was shown pictures of two boys who had been missing since July 27, thirteen days earlier. Henley identified them as Charles Cobble, seventeen, and Marty Jones, eighteen. The teenagers had shared a room, and both had good school records. Neither had any reason to run away.

The Pasadena detectives—accompanied by two of their Houston colleagues—now headed south to Hiram Clark Road. Another group of detectives was ordered to collect spades and ropes, and to meet them there. It was already late afternoon when the two cars arrived at the rendezvous point. Henley now took over the navigating. In an area of open fields dotted with grazing cattle, they finally pulled up beside a barbed-wire fence on Silver Bell Street, and Henley pointed out the corrugated iron shed standing well back from the road.

Southwest Boat Storage was virtually a parking lot for boats, with twenty roofed "stalls." The police cars drove into the compound, and Henley directed them to stall number eleven. "That's Dean's."

The double doors were padlocked, and the owner, Mayme Meynier, who lived in a large house next to the compound, told them that she had no key: the renters provided their own padlocks. When they explained that Corll was dead, she gave them permission to break in.

There was no boat inside the shed, only a half-dismantled car, a bicycle, and a large iron drum. With the sun on the roof, the place was like an oven. There were a few cardboard boxes, water containers, and—ominously—two sacks of lime. Two long strips of old carpet covered the earthen floor. A large plastic bag proved to contain a mixed lot of male clothing, including a pair of red shoes.

Wayne Henley stood at the door, gazing blankly inside. Then he walked back towards the cars, sat down on the ground, and buried his head between his knees.

The first task was to move everything out of the shed. While this was being done, a detective noted the registration numbers on the car and the bicycle and radioed them to headquarters. The answer came back quickly: the car had been stolen from a used-car lot, and the bicycle belonged to thirteen-year-old James Dreymala, who had vanished less than a week ago.

The shed was now empty; the two strips of carpet were also rolled out. Mullican pointed to a swelling in the floor near the left wall, and told two "trusties"—convicts from the local jail who had been brought along to help—to start digging.

Even with the doors open, the heat was stifling. Both men were soon perspiring heavily. Six inches down in the sandy earth, they uncovered a white substance. "That's lime," said Mullican. "Keep digging."

Suddenly, the shed was filled with a sickening stench; the detectives held their noses. The next carefully excavated shovelful revealed a face staring sightlessly up at them. The younger trusty dropped his spade and rushed from the shed, retching. A policeman calmly took up the spade and went on clearing the earth. Minutes later, the policemen found themselves looking down at a large plastic bag that contained the body of a boy. He looked about twelve or thirteen, and was naked. When the bag had been carefully lifted from the ground, it was obvious that the body inside had been recently buried. One of the detectives again radioed headquarters, this time to send for forensic experts.

Outside, the press was arriving. One radio reporter had allowed Wayne Henley to use his car telephone to call up his mother. They heard him say: "Mama, I killed Dean." Over his own microphone the reporter heard Mrs. Henley said: "Oh Wayne, you didn't." From what followed, it was clear that Henley's mother wanted to rush out to the site; a detective shook his head.

Moments later, as Henley hung up, the body was carried out from the boat shed in its plastic sheeting. Henley was clearly shaken. "It was all my fault." "Why?" asked a detective casually. "Because I introduced him to them boys." And the teenager went on to explain that, during the past two years, he had procured many boys for Dean Corll.

By the time the radio reporter went on the air at six o'clock, a second body had just been discovered. As it began to grow dark, a fire engine with a floodlight and two air-extractors arrived. Soon after that, two more bodies were uncovered. One had been shot in the head, the other strangled with a Venetian blind cord that was still knotted tightly around the throat.

As the news of the finds was broadcast, crowds of spectators arrived to peer over the barbed-wire fence. The air extractors blasted the smell of decaying corpses at them. One reporter had already minted a striking phrase: "There are wall to wall bodies in there."

Detectives questioned Mrs. Meynier about her former tenant. She described him as "the nicest person you'd ever meet," a "gentleman" with a charming smile and dimples. He had never been behind with his $5-a-week rent. But recently, she had been baffled when he told her that he wanted to rent another stall. Why should he need more space? Surely he already had plenty.

Asked how long Corll had rented the stall, she replied: "Since 1971." The detective turned away muttering: "My God!"

Henley, meanwhile, was also telling reporters how nice Corll could be. His mother liked ol' Dean and did not object to their friendship. But as the fourth body was carried out, he became nervous; it was obvious that he was suffering from a glue-sniffing hangover. At ten o'clock he was driven back to the police station. Two hours later, the body count had risen to eight, and the diggers were exhausted. They decided to call it a day.

Back in the Heights, many families with missing teenage sons were now watching their television screens for the printed messages that gave the latest news, and trying to convince themselves that their child could not be among those in the boat shed. But for those whose children had known Dean Corll, that was a slender hope. Now the parents found themselves wondering why they had failed to suspect Corll of being a sexual pervert. He and his mother had run a candy factory in the Heights, and Corll was popular with the children because he gave them candy. He also gave them lifts in his white Dodge van.

By midnight, a planeload of reporters from other parts of the country arrived in Houston. And from all over the world, reporters were converging on the corrugated iron boat shed. Dean Corll had been dead for only sixteen hours, but his name had already reached every part of the globe. If the number of his suspected victims was confirmed—and the detectives had a list of forty-two youngsters who had vanished since 1970—he would be America's worst mass murderer to date. Even the nineteenth-century Chicago killer H. H. Holmes had confessed to only twenty-eight.

Two hours after the lights went out at Southwest Boat Storage on Silver Bell Street, a car containing five people drew up at the barbed-wire fence. They identified themselves to the police on guard as the Hilligiest family. Thirteen-year-old David Hilligiest had disappeared more than two years earlier, on May 30, 1971. He had set out for the local swimming pool early that afternoon, and failed to arrive there. On that same day, another local boy, George Malley Winkle, sixteen, had vanished. The Hilligiests had spent $1,100 on a private detective, but had failed to find the slightest trace of their son. Now, after telephoning police headquarters, they had learned that Wayne Henley had mentioned David Hilligiest as one of the buried victims. They begged the guard to allow them to go to the boat stall. The police explained sympathetically that that was impossible; the lights were out and the place was now locked up. They had better go home, get some sleep, and prepare for their ordeal of the next day.

At ten the next morning, after a visit from his mother and a light breakfast, Henley was again sitting opposite Mullican in the Pasadena interrogation room. The rings under his eyes made it obvious that he had slept badly.

"Tell me about the boys you procured."

Henley explained that he had met Corll two years earlier, and that Corll had then offered him $200 each for any boys he could "bring along." For a year he did nothing; then, when he badly needed money, decided to take up the offer. Corll had not actually paid him the full $200 for the first boy he had procured. And he had not paid subsequently.

Now Henley made his most significant admission so far: he had been present when Corll had killed some of the boys. This suddenly changed the whole situation. The police had been assuming that they were dealing with an insatiable homosexual rapist and a youth he had persuaded to help him find boys. Now it began to look as if Henley had been an active partner in the murders.

They were interrupted by the telephone. It was the Houston police headquarters. A man named Alton Brooks had turned up at the police station with his eighteen-year-old son, David, explaining that David had known Corll and wanted to talk about it. And David Brooks was now giving a statement that implicated Henley in the murders.

When Mullican hung up, he told the teenager on the other side of the desk: "That was Lieutenant Porter at Houston Homicide. He says he has a boy named David Brooks in there, and Brooks is making a statement about you and Dean Corll."

Oddly enough, Henley looked relieved.

"That's good. Now I can tell you the whole story."

Mullican's next question was: "Did you kill any of the boys yourself?"

Henley answered without hesitation: "Yes, sir."

Mullican did his best to show no emotion during the statement that followed. But it was difficult to appear impassive. Wayne Henley was describing how he had lured some of his own best friends into Corll's lair, witnessed their torture and rape, and then participated in their murders.

It seemed that David Brooks had been Corll's original accomplice, as well as his lover. He had been procuring victims for Corll long before Henley came along. In fact, Henley was intended to be just another victim when he was taken along to meet Corll in 1971. But Corll soon realized that Henley would be more useful as an accomplice. He had lot of friends, and would do anything for money. In fact, said Henley, he was pretty sure that Corll still planned to kill him sooner or later, because he had his eye on Henley's fourteen-year-old brother, Ronnie, and knew he would have to kill Wayne before he could get his hands on him.

The method of obtaining victims was usually much the same. Corll would drive around with Henley until they saw a likely victim, and Corll would offer him a lift. Since there was already a teenager in the car, the boy would suspect nothing. That was how Dean had picked up that thirteen-year-old blond kid a few days ago. Dean was parked in front of a grocery store when the kid came past on his bike. Dean called him over and told him he had found some Coke bottles in his van, and the kid could go and collect the deposit on them. The boy (it was thirteen-year-old James Dreymala) took the bottles and came back a few minutes later with the money. Then Dean remembered that he had a lot more Coke bottles back in his garage, and if the kid would like to come along, he could have them, too. So James Dreymala allowed Dean to put his bike in the back of the van, and went back to Dean's house on Lamar Street. The boy said he had to ring his father to ask if he could stay out, but the father refused. After the call, Dean "had his fun," strangled the teenager, and then drove the body out to the boat shed to join the others.

At about this time, Mullican heard the latest report from the boat shed. Four more victims had been found in the past two hours, bringing the total up to twelve. And beside one of them his genitals had been found in a plastic bag. Part of Dean's "fun" was castrating his victims.

Henley's new confession went on for two more hours. It was rambling and often incoherent, but Mullican gathered that Henley had been present at the murder of at least nine boys. He admitted shooting one of them himself. The bullet had gone up the boy's nose, and the boy had looked up and said: "Wayne, why did you shoot me?" Henley pointed the gun at his head and pulled the trigger again; this time the boy died.

Had Corll buried any bodies in other places beside the boat shed? Mullican wanted to know. Oh sure, said Henley, there were some on the shores of Lake Sam Rayburn and more of them on High Island Beach, east of Galveston.

It was now past noon, but it seemed a good idea to bring Wayne Henley and David Brooks face to face. He would then persuade Henley to show them where the bodies were buried at Lake Sam Rayburn.

When they arrived at the Houston police station, Lieutenant Breck Porter took Mullican aside. David Brooks was doing plenty of "confessing," but it was all about Wayne Henley and Dean Corll. According to Brooks, he had been merely an innocent bystander.

David Brooks proved to be a tall, round-faced, long-haired youth who wore granny glasses; apparently he had recently married. He looked startled to see Wayne Henley—no one had warned him Henley was on his way. Henley stared across at his former friend. "David, I told 'em everything. You better do the same."

Brooks looked defensive. "I don't know what you're talking about."

"Yes you do. And if you don't tell everything, I'm gonna change my confession and say you was responsible for all of it."

Brooks said he wanted to talk to his father, and was taken out of the room. Later that day, he was told he was under arrest for being implicated in the murders. He was subdued and tearful as he was led away.

Henley, on the other hand, seemed to have been infused with a new life since his confession. On the way out to Lake Sam Rayburn—120 miles away, in the Angelina National Park—he talked nonstop, and made a number of damaging admissions. "I choked one of them boys until he turned blue, but Dean still had to come and finish him off." When a deputy asked how a decent boy like him could get involved in murder, he made the odd reply: "If you had a daddy that shot at you, you might do some things too."

An hour later he was leading them into the woods on the shores of Lake Sam Rayburn. He was already implicating David Brooks, although not by name. "We picked them up and Dean raped and killed them." Asked by a reporter if there had been any torture, he replied cryptically: "It wasn't what you would really call torture." But he declined to elaborate.

Then, refusing to allow reporters and photographers to accompany them, he led the police to the sites of four more bodies. One of them had been buried underneath a board; it emerged later that when Henley and Corll had returned to bury another body, they had found a hand sticking out of the ground, so had reburied it with the board on top.

Before darkness made further digging impossible, two bodies had been unearthed. The latest news from the boat shed in south Houston was that the digging was now finished, and seventeen bodies—or parts of bodies—had been found. The ones that had not been buried in plastic bags had decayed, so that little but bones remained. The body count so far was nineteen.

The following morning, it rose to twenty-one, with the uncovering of the other two bodies at Lake Sam Rayburn. By mid-morning, the convoy of police and reporters was on its way south to High Island, where Henley insisted there were eight more bodies buried.

HENLEY WAS INTENDED TO BE JUST ANOTHER VICTIM WHEN HE WAS TAKEN ALONG TO SEE CORLL.

The search of the High Island beach turned into a circus. Three helicopters had arrived with camera crews, and the reporters almost outnumbered the crowds of morbidly fascinated spectators. Henley was in good spirits, offering to race the overweight sheriff up the beach—an offer which, in view of the ninety-degree heat, the sheriff politely declined. David Brooks, who had been brought down from Houston, was much more subdued; he sat there much of the time, his arms around his knees, refusing to speak to reporters.

Only two more bodies were found that afternoon, bringing the total up to twenty-three. Later, four more would be unearthed on the beach. The other two mentioned by Henley were never discovered. But even a total of twenty-seven made Dean Corll America's worst mass murderer.

While Wayne Henley was helping the police at Lake Sam Rayburn, David Brooks was offering the first complete picture of Corll's career of homicidal perversion in the Houston interrogation room. He still insisted that he had never taken an active part in the killings, but his questioners suspected that this was because he had sworn to his father that he was innocent of murder. Henley, who seems to have been the more truthful of the two, stated that Brooks had taken an active part in several murders. The picture that emerged left little doubt that this was true.

Meanwhile, reporters were learning all they could about the background of America's worst mass murderer. For the most part, it proved to be surprisingly innocuous.

Dean Arnold Corll was born on Christmas Day 1939, in Waynesdale, Indiana, the first child of Arnold and Mary Corll, who were in their early twenties. But the parents were temperamentally unsuited; both were strong characters, and their quarrels could be violent. Mary adored her eldest son; Arnold—a factory worker who became an electrician—was a disciplinarian who found children tiresome. When Dean was six, the couple divorced, and Arnold was drafted into the Army Air Force. Mary bought a house trailer and drove to join her ex-husband at his base in Tennessee, but the quarrels continued and they separated again. An elderly farm couple agreed to look after the boys—Dean had a younger brother, Stanley—while Mary went out to work.

NOW LIVING IN AN APARTMENT OF HIS OWN, DEAN BEGAN MAKING FRIENDS WITH THE CHILDREN OF THE NEIGHBORHOOD—NOTABLY THE BOYS—GIVING AWAY FREE CANDY.

From the beginning, Dean was an oversensitive loner. Because his feelings were hurt at a birthday party when he was six, he always refused to go to other people's houses. While Stanley played with other children, Dean stayed at home.

The Corlls made yet another reconciliation attempt after the war, and in 1950 drove the trailer to Houston. But the marriage still failed to work out, and they parted again. At this point, it was discovered that Dean had a congenital heart ailment, and he was ordered to avoid sports. In fact it was hardly necessary; he was not the sporting type. Life for Mary was hard; she worked while the boys went to one school after another. In 1953 she married Jake West, a traveling clock salesman by whom she had a daughter. The family moved to Vidor, Texas, a small town where, as one commentator put it, "the big event is for the kids to pour kerosene on the cat and set it afire." Since he spent so much time without his parents, Dean became intensely protective of his siblings—a kind of surrogate mother.

Now a teenager, Dean took up skin diving, but had to quit when he fainted one day, and the doctor diagnosed a recurrence of the heart problem. But he was allowed to continue playing the trombone in the school band. He was always quiet, always polite, and never complained or "fussed."

One day, a pecan-nut salesman observed Mary's efficiency at baking pies and asked her why she didn't take up candy making. She liked the idea, and was soon running a candy business from their garage, with Jake West as traveling salesman and Dean as the errand boy and "gofer" ("go fer this, go fer that"). He was often overworked, but remained cheerful and uncomplaining. After his graduation from high school at the age of twenty, Dean went back to Indiana to be with Jake's widowed mother, while the family returned to Houston. There the candy business continued to be underfunded. Two years later, when Dean moved back to Houston, he took a job with the Houston Lighting and Power Company, and made candy at nights. Women who worked there were awed at his industry.

In 1964, Dean Corll was drafted into the army. This seems to have been a watershed in his life, for it was the time when he first recognized that he was gay. No details are available, but it seems obvious that some homosexual affair made him realize what he had so far failed to suspect. Released from the army after eleven months—pleading that his family needed him to work in the candy business—he returned to Houston to find his mother's second marriage in the process of dissolution. Mr. and Mrs. West had become business rivals rather than partners, and when Jake threw her out of the shop one day, Mary went off and started one of her own. Dean didn't mind; he had never liked his stepfather.

Now living in an apartment of his own, Dean began making friends with the children of the neighborhood—notably the boys—giving away free candy. Yet when a boy who worked for the company made some kind of sexual advance, Dean was angry and upset, and pleased when his mother dismissed him. Nevertheless, a coworker noticed that another teenaged employee always made sure that he was never left alone with Dean.

Dean's mother remained intensely protective, treating him as if he was still a teenager himself. But he was once again seeing something of his father, for whom he had great admiration.

Meanwhile, Mary now repeated her error and married yet again—this time a merchant seaman. She found him stupid and coarse, and soon began to suspect that he was psychotic. They divorced—and then remarried. He became neurotically jealous of his wife, and they separated again. But his continual attempts to force his way into the candy factory destroyed her enthusiasm for the business. When a psychic told her to move to Dallas, she took his advice, and divorced the merchant seaman yet again. And Dean, now left alone in Houston, suddenly felt that he was free to do as he liked.

Corll's Mr. Hyde aspect had at first manifested itself simply as a powerful attraction to boys, with whom he enjoyed playing the part of an elder brother. One boy said; "He acted real nice to me. He never tried to mess with me or nothing." But the desire was there, and Mr. Hyde began to break out when he realized that some boys would permit oral sex in exchange for money. Fourteen-year-old David Brooks was one of them. In fact, he was delighted to have an "elder brother," and became completely emotionally dependent on Corll—so dependent that he made no attempt to denounce him when he learned that he was a killer.

This emotional dependence of David Brooks undoubtedly played a major part in the tragedy that followed. His love for Corll meant that he was willing to subjugate his will to Corll's. And Corll, in turn, was encouraged to give way to his Mr. Hyde personality. It was a case of *folie à deux,* or "madness for two."

Brooks was a lonely schoolboy when he met Dean Corll in the Heights in 1969. The two had something in common: their parents had broken up, and they were on their own. Corll's mother had closed the candy factory she ran with her son's help, and gone off to live in Dallas. Corll had found himself a $5-an-hour job with the Houston Lighting and Power Company, and moved his few possessions into a shed. Corll propositioned Brooks, and the teenager agreed to allow Corll to have oral sex for a payment of $5.

But their relationship was not purely commercial. Corll was able to give Brooks something he needed badly—affection. Brooks, in turn, worshipped Corll. "Dean was a real good dude," and "a brilliant and generous man," he claimed. And when he returned to Houston in 1970—escaping from his disintegrating family—Brooks began to see a great deal of Corll: during the next three years they often shared rooms for brief periods.

By that time, it seems probable that Corll had already committed his first murder. A twenty-one-year-old student from the University of Texas in Austin, Jeffrey Alan Konen, had hitchhiked to his home in Houston on September 25, 1970. He had last been seen at six o'clock in the evening, looking for another lift. It seems probable that it was Corll who picked him up, and invited him back to his apartment at 3300 Yorktown. Konen's body was one of the last of those found—on the High Island beach—and was so decomposed that it was impossible to determine cause of death. But the fact that the body had been bound hand and foot suggested that Corll had killed Jeffrey Konen in order to commit sodomy.

What made Corll's murderous mission so easy was the teenage drug culture of the Heights. In the claustrophobic, run-down environment, all the kids were bored and discontented; they felt they were stuck there for life. The mere suggestion of a party was enough to make their eyes light up. They all smoked pot—when they could afford it. They also popped pills—Seconal, Nembutal, Phenobarbital, Quaaludes, even aspirin, washed down with beer or Coca-Cola. But because it was cheap, spray paint was the easiest way of obtaining a quick "high." Although one boy collapsed and died when he tried to play football after a long paint-sniffing session, it made no difference to the others; he was merely "unlucky." Moreover, the possession of spray paint was perfectly legal; and in an environment where a teenager was likely to be searched for drugs at any hour of the day, this went a long way towards making paint-sniffing the most popular form of escape.

That most of the kids were permanently broke conferred another tremendous advantage on a predatory homosexual such as Corll. Allowing a "queer" to perform oral sex was an easy and quick way of obtaining a few dollars. There can be no doubt that many of Corll's victims had been back to his room several times before his demand for a more painful form of sex caused them to balk, and led to their deaths. The fact that there were a fairly high number of runaways from the Heights meant that occasional disappearances caused little stir.

The key to the Houston murders is Corll's craving for sexual violation. At some point, oral sex ceased to satisfy him. Brooks admitted: "He killed them because he wanted anal sex, and they didn't want to." Even Brooks himself seems to have withheld anal sex. He describes how, after he had introduced Corll to Wayne Henley, the latter knocked him unconscious as he entered Corll's apartment; Corll then tied him to the bed and sodomized him. This would obviously have been pointless if anal sex had been a normal part of their relationship. Yet in spite of the rape, Brooks continued to worship Corll, and to participate in the murders and disposal of the bodies.

It also seems clear that Corll was in love with Wayne Henley. But Henley remained independent. Far more avaricious than Brooks, he became Corll's accomplice for cash. In spite of Henley's denial, there can be no doubt that Corll paid him large sums of money as a procurer. One friend of Henley's later described how Henley had suggested that they should move to Australia together and become homesteaders—Henley declared that he would provide the $1,700 each that they would need. "Where would you get it?" asked his friend. "I already have it." Henley's later assertion that Corll never paid him is almost certainly an attempt to conceal the appalling truth: that he sold his friends to Corll for $200 each.

By the end of 1970, Corll was firmly in the grip of "Mr. Hyde." Brooks later tried to justify the murders: "Most of the boys weren't good boys. This . . . probably sounds terrible, but most of 'em wasn't no great loss. They was in trouble all the time, dope fiends and one thing or another." This is almost certainly a repetition of something Corll said to Brooks—perhaps on many occasions.

Not long after the murder of Jeffrey Konen, Brooks walked into Corll's Yorktown apartment unannounced, and found Corll naked. In another room there were two naked boys strapped to a plywood board. Corll demanded indignantly what Brooks was doing there, and ordered him to leave. Later, he told Brooks that he had killed both boys, and offered him a car as the price of his silence. In fact, he gave Brooks a new Corvette. The identity of these two victims has never been established, but they were probably among the bodies found on the High Island beach.

Having accepted the Corvette, Brooks was now an accomplice. He would go "cruising" with Corll, offering lifts to teenaged boys. One unknown youth was picked up some time in November 1970, and taken back to Corll's apartment. Corll raped and murdered the boy while Brooks looked on. No further details of this murder—or victim—are known.

Corll's appetite for murder was growing. Many of the boys he once befriended in the days of the candy factory, and who had always been welcome visitors in his room, now noticed that he was becoming bad-tempered and secretive, and they stopped calling round. Many of these boys later insisted that Corll had simply been "nice" to them, without any attempt to make sexual advances. Many others, like David Brooks, had undoubtedly accepted money for oral sex.

On December 15, 1970, Brooks persuaded two boys to come back to an apartment that Corll had rented on Columbia Street. They were fourteen-year-old James Eugene Glass, and his friend Danny Michael Yates, fifteen. Both had been to church with James Glass's father, and had agreed to meet him later. Glass had already been to Corll's apartment on a previous occasion, and had taken a great liking to Corll. This time, both boys ended on the plywood board, after which they were strangled. By this time, Corll had decided that he needed somewhere closer than High Island or Lake Sam Rayburn (where his family owned a holiday cabin), so he rented the boat shed on Silver Bell Street. The two boys were the first to be buried there.

Corll had apparently enjoyed the double murder so much that he was eager to try it again. Six weeks later, two brothers, fourteen-year-old Donald Edward Waldrop, and thirteen-year-old Jerry Lynn Waldrop, were lured to a newly rented apartment at 3200 Mangum Road. (Corll changed apartments frequently, almost certainly to prevent curious neighbors from gossiping about his activities.) The father of the Waldrop boys was a construction worker who worked next door to Corll's new apartment. The boys were also strangled and buried in the boat shed. Brooks admitted: "I believe I was present when they were buried." This was typical of his general evasiveness.

On May 29, 1971, David Hilligiest, thirteen, disappeared on his way to the local swimming pool; his friend, sixteen-year-old George Malley Winkle, also vanished that day. Malley was on probation for stealing a bicycle. That same evening, just before midnight, Mrs. Malley's telephone rang; it was her son, contacting his mother to tell her that he was in Freeport—a surfing resort sixty miles to the south—with some kids. They would be on their way home shortly.

That night, Mrs. Winkle slept badly, with a foreboding that her son was in trouble. When he failed to return, she asked young people in the neighborhood if they had seen him, and learned that he had climbed into a white van, together with David Hilligiest.

The frantic parents spent weeks following up every possible lead. They had posters printed, offering a $1,000 reward, and friendly truckers distributed them all over southern Texas. So did a lifelong friend of David Hilligiest's—Elmer Wayne Henley, another child of a broken home. He tried to comfort the Hilligiests by telling them that he was sure nothing had happened to David. A psychic who was consulted by the Hilligiests disagreed: he plunged them into despair by telling them that their son was dead.

Ruben Watson, seventeen, another child of a broken home, went off to the movies on the afternoon of August 17, 1971, with a few dollars borrowed from his grandmother; he later rang his mother at work to say he would meet her outside the theater at 7:30. He never arrived. Brooks later admitted being present when Ruben was murdered.

By this time, Wayne Henley had entered the picture. He had become friendly with David Brooks, and Brooks had introduced him to Dean Corll. Henley was intended as a victim, but Corll seems to have decided that he would be more useful as a pimp. The fact that Henley was skinny and pimply may also have played a part in Corll's decision to let him live. The Hilligiests' son Greg—aged eleven—came home one day to say that he had been playing an exciting game called poker with Wayne Henley, David Brooks, and an older friend of Henley's who made candy. Dorothy Hilligiest knew the man who made candy—in the previous year, she had gone looking for David, and found him at the candy factory with Malley, Winkle, and the round-faced man who owned the place. Mrs. Hilligiest had bought a box of candy from him before she took David away.

Another friend of Henley's was fourteen-year-old Rhonda Williams, who was as anxious to escape the Heights as most of its other teenagers. Since she had been sexually assaulted as a child, her attitude to sex was inhibited and circumspect. Like so many Heights teenagers, she was part of a one-parent family—her mother had collapsed and died of a heart attack as she was hanging out the washing. Rhonda craved affection and security, and she seemed to have found it when she met nineteen-year-old Frank Aguirre. He was slightly cross-eyed, but serious-minded, and was already saving money—from his job in a restaurant—to marry Rhonda. But on February 24, 1972, Frank Aguirre failed to return home from work, and was never seen again. He left his paycheck uncollected. Rhonda was shattered and went into nervous depression for a year; she was only just beginning to recover on that evening in August 1973 when she informed Wayne Henley that she had decided to run away from home, and Henley took her to Dean Corll's house in Pasadena to stay the night.

CORLL HAD APPARENTLY ENJOYED THE DOUBLE MURDER SO MUCH THAT HE WAS EAGER TO TRY IT AGAIN.

On May 21, 1972, sixteen-year-old Johnny Delome vanished. His body was found on High Island fourteen months later; he had been shot as well as strangled. Johnny Delome must have been the youth that Henley shot up the nose, and then in the head. He was killed at the same time as Billy Baulch, seventeen, who was also buried at High Island. Six months later, Billy's fifteen-year-old brother, Michael, would become another victim of Dean Corll. In the meantime, he had killed another two boys, Wally Jay Simoneaux, fourteen, and Richard Hembree, thirteen, on October 3, 1972. Their bodies were found together in the boat shed. Another victim of 1972 was eighteen-year-old Mark Scott, whose body was one of those that was never identified; Brooks stated that he was also one of Corll's victims.

And so the murders went on into 1973: Billy Lawrence, fifteen, on June 11; Homer Garcia, fifteen, on July 7; Charles Cobble, seventeen, on July 25, who vanished with his friend Marty Jones, eighteen, on the same day. The final victim was thirteen-year-old James

Dreymala, lured to Corll's Pasadena house to collect Coke bottles, and buried in the boat shed. There were undoubtedly other victims in 1973, possibly as many as nine. Brooks said that Corll's youngest victim was a nine-year-old boy.

On Monday, August 13, five days after the death of Dean Corll, a grand jury began to hear evidence against Henley and Brooks. The first witnesses were Rhonda Williams and Tim Kerley, the two who had almost become Corll's latest victims. It was clear that Kerley had been invited to Corll's house by Henley in order to be raped and murdered—this is what Henley meant when he told Kerley that he could have got $1,500. He was exaggerating, but was otherwise telling the truth. And when Corll had snarled, "You've spoilt everything," he meant that the arrival of Rhonda Williams now made it impossible to murder Kerley. At that moment, it seems, he thought of a solution that would enable him to "have his fun": kill all three teenagers.

Rhonda Williams, it emerged, had decided to run away with Henley, whom she now regarded as her boyfriend. In fact, Corll knew all about the arrangement and had no objection—he himself was planning to move to Colorado, where his mother was living, and to take Henley and Rhonda with him. The fact that he also planned to take an old flame of his pre-homosexual days, Betty Hawkins, as well as her two children, suggests that Corll had decided to give up killing teenagers. But Rhonda had arranged to run away on August 17, nine days later; and when she arrived at Corll's house in the early hours of August 9, he felt deprived of his night of pleasure.

After listening to the evidence of various teenage witnesses, the jury indicted Henley and Brooks on murder charges. Henley was charged with taking part in the killing of Billy Lawrence, Charles Cobble, Marty Jones, Johnny Delome, Frank Aguirre, and Homer Garcia; Brooks for his part in the murders of James Glass, Ruben Watson, Billy Lawrence, and Johnny Delome. Efforts by the lawyers to have bail set were turned down.

Houston was stunned by the events of the past week, and criticism of the police department was bitter and uninhibited. The main complaint of the parents of missing teenagers was that they had been unable to get the police to take the slightest interest; they were told that their children were runaways. Police Chief Herman Short counterattacked clumsily by publicly stating that there had been no connection between the missing teenagers—implying that there would have been little for the police to investigate. The statements of Henley and Brooks—indicating that most of the victims knew one another—flatly contradicted this assertion. Short went on to say that the murders indicated that parents should pay closer attention to the comings and goings of their teenagers, a remark that drew outraged rebuttals from parents such as Dorothy Hilligiest, whose children had simply vanished on their way to or from some normal and innocent activity. Short also expressed fury at the Soviet newspaper *Izvestia,* which had referred to the "murderous bureaucracy" of the Houston police department; he pointed out that the Soviet government had a reputation for making dissenters "disappear." All of his blustering failed to impress the public or the politicians, and Short resigned three months later, after the municipal elections.

There was also criticism of the attitude of the police towards the search for additional bodies. One of Corll's ex-employees, Ruby Jenkins, had mentioned the interesting fact that, during the last years of the candy factory's existence, Corll was often seen handling a shovel and digging holes. He dug under the floor of his private room in the factory—known jokingly as the "pouting room," because he often retired there to sulk—and then cemented over the excavation. He also dug holes near the rear wall of the factory, and on a space that later became a parking lot. He always dug by night. His explanation was that he was burying spoiled candy because it drew bees and bred weevils. No one questioned this curious explanation, or asked him what was wrong with placing the spoiled candy in a plastic bag and dropping it in the trashcan. "He had this big roll of plastic sheet, four or five foot wide, and he had sacks of cement and some other stuff back in his pouting room." Clearly, this was something that required investigating. But when the police came along to look at the spots indicated by Ruby Jenkins, they dug only halfheartedly in a few places, and soon gave up. "Lady, this is old cement. There couldn't be any bodies there."

After the finding of bodies number twenty-six and twenty-seven—on High Island beach, tied together—the search for more was dropped, even though Henley insisted that another two were buried there. Another curious feature of this final discovery was that there were two extra bones—an arm bone and a pelvis—in the grave, plainly indicating a twenty-eighth victim.

Lieutenant Porter received two calls about bodies on the same morning. A Mr. and Mrs. Abernathy had been camping on Galveston Island—about fifty miles down the coast from High Island—when they saw two men carrying a long bundle over the dunes. Another man had been camping on east Galveston beach when he saw a white car and another car parked near a hole in the beach; a long plastic bundle the size of a body lay beside the hole. There were also three men. The camper identified two from photographs as Dean Corll and Wayne Henley. The third man had long blond hair—like David Brooks. As the campers sat looking at this curious

THE PARENTS OF MISSING TEENAGERS . . . HAD BEEN UNABLE TO GET THE POLICE TO TAKE THE SLIGHTEST INTEREST; THEY WERE TOLD THAT THEIR CHILDREN WERE RUNAWAYS.

scene in their own car, Henley advanced on them with a menacing expression, and they drove off.

These two events took place in March and June 1973. In fact, the first 1973 victim identified (from the Lake Sam Rayburn burial site) was Billy Lawrence, who vanished on June 11. It seems unlikely that a man who had been killing as regularly as Corll would allow a seven-month period to elapse between victims (the last known victim of 1972 is Michael Baulch, Billy Baulch's younger brother). The unidentified victims found in the boat shed had obviously been buried much earlier, probably in 1971.

The Galveston authorities flatly declined to allow the Houston police to follow up this lead, refusing to permit digging on their beach. Meanwhile, the police switchboard in Houston continued to handle hundreds of enquiries about missing teenagers—one mother, whose son had been working with a circus, and had vanished in Houston, was certain that he was one of Corll's victims. In most of these cases, the police were forced to state that they were unable to help.

When Brooks and Henley appeared for their arraignment, there was a heavy guard of armed police—dozens of threatening phone calls had been received from all over Texas. Henley's defense lawyer, Charles Melder, indicated that his defense would be one of insanity. Brooks's attorney, Ted Musick, said that he would follow the same line. At the same time, the district attorney announced that each of the accused would be tried on one charge only: Henley for the murder of Charles Cobble, and Brooks for that of Billy Lawrence.

Since Corll was already dead, and the two accused had confessed, the trial itself was something of an anticlimax. Its venue was changed, on the insistence of the lawyers, and it opened at San Antonio, Texas, in July 1974, before Judge Preston Dial. Predictably, the jury rejected the insanity defense, and Henley was convicted on nine counts (not including the shooting of Dean Corll), drawing a total sentence of 594 years. Brooks was convicted on only one count, and received life imprisonment. Henley appealed in 1979, and was convicted for a second time.

It is easy to understand the sense of shock produced by the Corll murders, and the feeling that Corll was a sadistic monster, the kind we would expect to encounter in a horror movie. But this book must have demonstrated that nothing is ever as simple as that. Some are psychotic, such as Mullin and Frazier and Chase. Some are violently oversexed, such as the Boston Strangler. Some are inspired by hatred of woman, such as the Yorkshire Ripper and Son of Sam. Some regard themselves as social rebels, such as Manson. But some, such as Corll and Shaefer, emerge simply as spoiled brats, who felt that having their own way was a law of nature, and felt no compunction about killing for a few hours of sexual pleasure. (The Chicago builder John Wayne Gacy—see the next chapter—was another such.) Corll remained emotionally a child—this aspect of his personality is caught in a photograph that shows him holding a teddy bear.

In fact, as do so many serial killers, Corll drifted into it by slow steps—as a man becomes a drug addict or an alcoholic. He wanted young boys; he bought their sexual favors. Then he began raping and killing them. It was a gentle progression down a slope, like walking slowly into a pond.

8

The Egoists

8 The Egoists

It was when Ressler was driving to his hometown of Chicago for Christmas 1978 that he heard on the radio about the discovery of bodies in a house in Des Plaines, Illinois, a Chicago suburb, close to his childhood home. He left his family with a relative and hastened to the crime scene. There he found a crowd swarming around the house that had been occupied by a building contractor, John Wayne Gacy. Among the police at the scene was a former classmate at Quantico, who quickly brought Ressler up to date on what was happening.

It seemed that police searching for a missing fifteen-year-old youth named Robert Piest, had heard that Piest had been to Gacy's home to talk about a job, and then vanished.

On December 11, Elizabeth Piest drove to the Nisson Pharmacy in Des Plaines to pick up her fifteen-year-old son, Robert; it was her birthday and she intended to throw a party. It was nine in the evening when she arrived, and the boy asked her to wait a few minutes while he went to see a man about a summer job that would pay $5 an hour. By 9:30, Robert had still not returned. She drove home to tell her husband and at 11:30 they rang the police to report his disappearance. The police investigated at the drug store, and noticed that the inside had been renovated recently; they inquired about the contractor, and were told that his name was Gacy, and that he could have been the man who had offered Robert the job.

The police already knew about John Wayne Gacy. On March 21, a twenty-seven-year-old Chicagoan, Jeffrey Rignall, had entered into conversation with a fat man who drove a sleek Oldsmobile, and accepted an invitation to smoke a joint in the car. The man had clapped a chloroform-soaked rag over Rignall's face, driven him to a house, and there spent several hours raping him and flogging him with whips. Rignall woke up in the dawn by the lake in Lincoln Park. In the hospital, it was discovered that he was bleeding from the rectum, and that the chloroform that had been repeatedly administered had permanently damaged his liver. The police said they were unable to help, since he knew so little about his molester, so Rignall hired a car and spent days sitting near motorway entrances looking for the black Oldsmobile.

Eventually, his patience paid off; he spotted the Oldsmobile, followed it, and noted the plate number. It proved to belong to John Gacy. But in spite of issuing an arrest warrant, the police still delayed. It was mid-July before they picked him up on a misdemeanor charge, but the case dragged on; the police felt that if Rignall had been chloroformed so much of the time, he might well be mistaken about Gacy.

Yet a check of Gacy's background revealed that he had been sentenced to ten years in a "correctional institution" in Waterloo, Iowa, ten years earlier. The charges involved handcuffing an employee and trying to sodomize him, paying a youth to perform fellatio on him, and then hiring someone to beat up the same youth when he gave evidence against Gacy. At that period, Gacy had been married and managing a fried chicken business; he was apparently a highly regarded member of the community. He had been paroled after only eighteen months—described as a model prisoner—and placed on probation in Chicago. In 1971, he had been arrested for picking up a teenager and trying to force him to engage in sex. The boy failed to appear in court and the case was dismissed. Another man had accused Gacy of trying to force him to have sex at gunpoint in his house, and said that Gacy had boasted that he had already killed somebody.

The police now called at Gacy's house at 8213 West Summerdale Avenue, Des Plaines, and questioned him about Robert Piest. When inside, they raised a trapdoor leading to a crawl space under the house. There was a heavy odor of decaying flesh, and the beam of the torch picked out bodies and human bones.

At the police station, Gacy admitted that he had killed thirty-three teenagers—in the course of forcing them to have sex with him—and said that twenty-nine of these had been buried or disposed of in or around his house; the remaining four—including Robert Piest—had been disposed of in other ways; Piest had been dumped in the Des Plaines River.

Seven bodies were found in the crawl space under the house, and various parts of others. In another crawl space in another part of the house, bodies were found covered with quicklime in trenches that had been dug for them. Eight more were quickly unearthed. Gacy's house was demolished in the search for more corpses; eventually, the remains of twenty-eight were discovered—Gacy had lost count by one. When he had run out of burial space around his house, he had started dumping bodies in the river.

John Wayne Gacy was born March 17, 1942, in Chicago; his mother was Danish, his father Polish. He went to business college, became a shoe salesman, and married a coworker whose parents owned a fried chicken business in Waterloo, Iowa. He was a member of the Junior Chamber of Commerce. He was known as an affable man who badly wanted to be liked, and who tried to buy popularity with generosity. He was also known as a liar and a boaster—in short, a thoroughly unstable character. Married life came to an end with his imprisonment, and his wife divorced him. (They had a son and a daughter.) In prison, Gacy worked hard, avoided homosexuals, and obtained parole.

In 1972 he married a second time, and started in business as a contractor. But his new wife found his violent tempers a strain. His sexual performance was also inadequate. And then there was the peculiar odor that hung about the house . . .

In 1976 the couple divorced. Gacy continued indefatigably to try to rise in the world and to impress people—when he became involved with the local Democrats, he had cards printed identifying himself as a precinct captain. In 1978 he was photographed shaking hands with First Lady Rosalynn Carter.

He used the contracting business to contact young males. One of these was John Butkovich, who vanished on August 1, 1975; he may have been the first victim. He had quarreled with Gacy about pay; Gacy was notoriously cheap, and refused to pay his employees for traveling time to the jobs. It was probably the stench of Butkovich's decomposing corpse that filled the house during the last year of Gacy's second marriage.

Greg Godzik came to work for Gacy in 1976; on December 11 he disappeared. A few weeks later, on January 20, 1977, a friend of Godzik's, John Szyc, vanished; he also knew Gacy. There were many others. Billy Carrol disappeared on June 10, 1976, and in the previous month, three other boys, Randall Reffett, Samuel Stapleton, and Michael Bonnin vanished. Rick Johnston was dropped off by his mother at a rock concert on August 6, and was never seen again.

Once Gacy was separated from his second wife, there was nothing to stop him from inviting young men to his house. Some of these, such as a male prostitute named Jaimie, were handcuffed and violently sodomized, but allowed to leave—with payment. The boys who resisted were killed. A nine-year-old boy who was known as a procurer was driven off in the black Oldsmobile and never seen again. The Oldsmobile became familiar in the Newtown district of Chicago, where homosexuals could be picked up in bars or on the pavement. And the disappearances continued, until the killing of the thirty-third victim, Robert Piest, finally brought police with a search warrant to the house.

AT THE POLICE STATION, GACY ADMITTED THAT HE HAD KILLED THIRTY-THREE TEENAGERS—IN THE COURSE OF FORCING THEM TO HAVE SEX WITH HIM—AND SAID THAT TWENTY-NINE OF THESE HAD BEEN BURIED OR DISPOSED OF IN OR AROUND HIS HOUSE

Ressler watched the development of the investigation with interest. On February 6, 1980, Gacy's trial began in Chicago. His plea of not guilty by reason of insanity was rejected, and he was found guilty on March 13, and sentenced to death. Ressler then requested a meeting with him, and Gacy agreed to see him, together with some associates from the Behavioral Science Unit. He proved to be a short, pudgy man with a double chin and a moustache.

Gacy claimed to recognize him from childhood, when they had lived a few streets apart, and could not only recall delivering groceries to the Ressler home, but even some unusual flowerpots outside.

He was friendly and communicative, obviously feeling that he and Ressler were on an equal intellectual footing. He was convinced that the police, psychiatrists, and courts were fools who did not understand him. Ressler by now knew enough about interviewing serial killers to remain objective and not show any sign of disapproval.

He told Gacy he suspected that there had been far more victims than the thirty-three he was accused of killing—that since he had traveled widely in the United States, he could have "trawled the homosexual transient districts for victims anywhere." Gacy neither admitted nor denied this.

His position was a strange one. Against all logic, he insisted that he was innocent. Moreover, he indignantly denied that he was homosexual. He talked contemptuously about "worthless little queers and punks." As to why he had used boys for sex, Gacy explained that he had been a hard-working businessman who found is easier to seek out quick sex with a male—getting a woman into bed required wining and dining and "romancing" her.

HE WAS CONVINCED THAT THE POLICE, PSYCHIATRISTS, AND COURTS WERE FOOLS WHO DID NOT UNDERSTAND HIM.

Gacy's view of himself was that he was a "nice guy," helpful, decent, and heterosexual. But he was virtually a multiple personality, who had inside him another Gacy, "Bad Jack," who committed murder and left Good John to dispose of the corpses. Dr. Marvyn Ziporyn, the psychiatrist at Gacy's prison (and the author of a book on Richard Speck, *Born to Raise Hell*) read Gacy's letters to various correspondents—Gacy was an indefatigable letter-writer—and wrote an analysis in which he said that Gacy was a classic sociopath, a man whose huge ego "exists solely to satisfy his own appetite . . ." His answer to the question "What is one allowed to do?" is "Whatever one can get away with." His answer to "What is good?" was "Whatever is good for me." He was also, Ziporyn said, a classic control freak, trying to control his correspondents even from the death cell. Certainly, like Gerard Shaefer and Dean Corll, he was also totally involved in his own ego.

In 1988, Ressler conducted a conference at Quantico, an International Homicide Symposium, in which both Kemper and Gacy agreed to appear on live-circuit television from their prison cells, and be interviewed by Ressler. Kemper was as frank as always, speaking in detail about his crimes and his motivations. Gacy, on the other hand, used his ninety minutes to insist on his innocence, and to try to persuade the watching law-enforcement officials to probe further into the case and uncover evidence that would lead to his release. Some of the audience later criticized Ressler for not "pinning Gacy to the wall" and forcing him to face up to his guilt. Ressler's reply was that this would have served no real purpose, since his aim was to allow the audience to see the mind of a serial killer at work, and to see Gacy's conviction of his innocence—in flat contraction to the facts—and his skill as a manipulator, one of the more frightening skills of many serial killers.

But how do we explain Gacy's refusal to accept responsibility for the murders? Was he, as he claimed, a Jekyll and Hyde who was periodically taken over by the person he called "Bad Jack"? Ressler thinks not. In such killers, he argues, "the deadly side is always there, but the murderer is frequently successful in hiding it from the outside world."

My own conviction is that the key lies in Gacy's childhood. From a fairly early age it was clear that he had psychiatric problems, and that they linked to his father. John Stanley Gacy was a violent bully and an alcoholic. He was also a Right Man. "If my father said the sun wouldn't rise tomorrow you couldn't disagree with him. He'd argue you into the ground." His father was, it followed naturally, a violent man who beat the child regularly with a razor strop, and never lost an opportunity to tell the boy he was "dumb and stupid."

His father detested him for being sickly and weak, and not interested in "manly sports." When the child was eleven he was struck on the head with a swing, and thereafter began to suffer from blackouts. Gacy senior said he was play-acting.

Certainly the number of sex killers who have suffered head injuries is so high that it is hard to deny the probable correlation. The following lists only some of the most prominent:

The "French Ripper," Joseph Vacher, a tramp who raped and disemboweled victims of both sexes in the mid-1890s, had attempted to shoot himself through the head, permanently damaging one eye and paralyzing the right side of his face. It is not known what part of the brain he damaged, but after years in an asylum he was released and began his career of sex murder, killing eleven before he was caught and executed in 1898.

Fritz Haarmann, Hanover, Germany's "cannibal killer," suffered from a concussion after a fall from parallel bars during his army training in 1900; after a period in the hospital he was judged mentally deficient. After World War I, working as an unofficial police agent, he made a habit of picking up destitute youths at the railway station and taking them to his room. The murders were not apparently preplanned; sexual frenzy would carry him away, and Haarmann would either strangle his victims, or suffocate them by fixing his teeth in their windpipes. He cut up the bodies and sold them for meat. Haarmann was executed in 1925.

America's "Gorilla Murderer " of the 1920s, Earle Nelson, was knocked down by a streetcar when he was ten years old. The fall gashed a hole in his temple, rendering him unconscious for six days, after which he suffered from recurring pain in the head and dizziness. After several periods in an asylum he escaped and began to roam the country, committing twenty-two sex murders between February 1926 and his capture in June 1927. He was hanged in January 1928.

Child-killer Albert Fish, who was born in 1870, began to suffer from severe headaches and dizzy spells, and also developed a stutter, after a fall from a cherry tree as a child. He committed his first murder—of a homosexual—in 1910, but had been raping small boys since 1895. He mutilated and tortured to death a mentally retarded boy in 1919, and between that time and his capture in December 1934 is believed to have committed fifteen more murders of children, one of whom (Grace Budd) he cooked and ate. He himself claimed to have committed four hundred murders.

Raymond Fernandez was perfectly normal until a falling hatch knocked him unconscious when he was at sea in December 1945. At thirty-one years of age, Fernandez suddenly turned into a sex maniac, contacting lonely women through advertisements in contact magazines, and seducing them—it made no difference whether they were young or old, fat or thin, beautiful or ugly; he even seduced one seriously disabled woman. He and his mistress Martha Beck became known as the "Lonely Hearts Killers" after murdering a number of women for their money, and were executed in 1951.

THE NUMBER OF SEX KILLERS WHO HAVE SUFFERED HEAD INJURIES IS SO HIGH THAT IT IS HARD TO DENY THE PROBABLE CORRELATION.

John Reginald Christie, the British sex killer of the 1940s and early 1950s, had been knocked down by a car when he first came to London, and was unconscious for several hours.

Richard Speck, who systematically and brutally slaughtered eight student nurses from South Chicago Community Hospital on one July day in 1966, had suffered a number of head injuries as a child, but began having severe headaches and blackouts at the age of sixteen after a policeman had broken up a fight by beating him on the head several times with his club. Speck died in prison in 1991.

Gary Heidnik was tried in 1988 for keeping six women prisoner in his basement in Philadelphia and subjecting them to a four-month ordeal of rape and torture, during which he killed two of them, cooking parts of one of the corpses and feeding it to the other prisoners. Heidnik had been mentally abnormal since he fell out of a tree as a child, deforming the shape of his head so that his school-fellows called him "football head."

Randy Kraft, a computer expert of Long Beach, California, was stopped on May 14, 1983, for careless driving, and was found to have the corpse of a young man propped up beside him in the passenger seat. A search of the car and his home revealed that he was the homosexual "Freeway Killer" who had been murdering and torturing young men since 1975 and dumping their bodies on the freeways. A list found in his car indicated that he had killed sixty-seven men. As a child, Kraft had fallen down a flight of concrete steps and been unconscious for several hours. He was sentenced to death in 1989.

Henry Lee Lucas (see chapter 11) was violently beaten by his drunken mother as a child, and on one occasion was unconscious for three days after she struck him on the head with a piece of wood.

Bobby Jo Long, received a fractured skull after a motorcycle accident when in the army, and remained in a coma for weeks. After this, he reported, he began thinking about sex all the time. From having sex with his wife two or three times a week he went to two or three times a day, also masturbating in between. He began committing rapes after he left the army, telephoning women who had placed classified advertisements, and if he found them alone, raping them. Then, in 1983, he changed suddenly from a rapist who left his victims alive to a sex murderer, killing nine women in the Tampa, Florida, area. After each murder he sank into a deep sleep, and when he woke up was never certain whether he had dreamed it all—he had to go out and buy a newspaper to find out. Finally, he was touched by the story of a seventeen-year-old girl who had been abused in childhood, and although he raped her, he let her go, knowing that it would lead to his arrest.

Dr. Dorothy Otnow Lewis examined Long and found that he had had more than one head injury—one after falling off a swing, one after being knocked down by a car. A PET scan showed that he had damage to the left temporal lobe, and an abnormality of the amygdala, a part of the brain associated with violence. She was inclined to believe that this was responsible for Long's hyperactive sex drive. In spite of these discoveries, Long was sentenced to death.

The British serial killer Fred West (see chapter 16) had two serious injuries to his head, the first from a motorcycle crash that left him unconscious for a week, the second when a girl pushed him off a fire escape after he put his hand up her skirt—this time he was unconscious for two days.

At the time I write these words, Dennis Rader, the "BTK" (bind, torture, kill) killer, sought by the police formore than thirty years, has explained in an interview that he was dropped on his head as a child.

All this should make us aware that we should not dismiss the view that Gacy's accident with the swing may explain a great deal that seems baffling about his crimes. He was interviewed in prison by psychologist Dr. Helen Morrison, who appeared for the defense to support his plea of insanity, and her account of him in her book *My Life Among Serial Killers* makes it obvious that by no stretch of the imagination could Gacy be described as sane. She notes that he would contradict himself, from sentence to sentence, and that he could change from reasonable behavior to rage and violence in a moment. Although Dr. Morrison was appearing in his defense, he could swing instantly from friendliness to fury, and shout that she was dumb and stupid. Gacy was a seething cauldron of violent emotions, only held together by his overwhelmingly high opinion of himself. Her prison interviews with him reads like a conversations with someone who is firmly convinced that he is Julius Caesar and is married to the queen of Sheba. It is not surprising that, after his conviction, he suddenly started declaring that he had never killed anybody, but had been framed by the police. It is also certain that, if he had taken a lie detector test, it would have registered that he was telling the truth.

When Gacy was asked by a friend of mine, Jeffrey Smalldon, what he thought of my entry on him in *An Encyclopedia of Modern Murder,* he replied predictably: "Colin Wilson doesn't understand me."

On May 10, 1994, he was executed by lethal injection at Stateville Penitentiary near Joliet, Illinois. A crowd cheered as he was pronounced dead.

It later emerged that his execution had gone badly; the ingredients of the lethal injection had been mixed in a way that caused them to solidify, so he took a long time to die. There were even rumors that his execution had been deliberately bungled to prolong his discomfort.

The demonstrations at Gacy's execution were reminiscent of the final scenes of another notorious serial killer of the 1970s, Ted Bundy, who also happens to be another textbook case of the "high-IQ killer."

On January 31, 1974, a student at the University of Washington in Seattle, Lynda Ann Healy, vanished from her room; the bloodstained bed sheets suggested

With his good looks and easy charm, Ted Bundy, shown here in Pensacola in 1977, seemed an unlikely serial killer. Bundy was convicted of three Florida slayings, although authorities considered him a suspect in as many as thirty-six killings, mostly in the Northwest. (Associated Press)

that she had been struck violently on the head. During the following March, April, and May, three other female students vanished; in June, two more. In July, two young women vanished on the same day. It happened at a popular picnic spot, Lake Sammamish; a number of people witnessed a good-looking young man, with his arm in a sling, approach Janice Ott and ask her to help him lift a boat onto the roof of his car; she walked away with him and did not return. Later, Denise Naslund was accosted by the same young man; she also vanished. He had been heard to introduce himself as "Ted."

In October 1974, the killings shifted to Salt Lake City; three young women disappeared in one month. That November, the police had their first break in the case: Carol DaRonch was accosted in a shopping center by a young man who identified himself as a detective, and informed her that there had been an attempt to break into her car. She agreed to accompany him to headquarters to view a suspect. In the car he snapped a handcuff on her wrist and pointed a gun at her head; she fought and screamed, and managed to jump out of the car. That same evening, a female student vanished on her way to meet her brother. A handcuff key was found near the place from which she had been taken.

HE WAS POLITE, WELL SPOKEN, ARTICULATE, CHARMING, THE KIND OF MAN WHO COULD HAVE FOUND HIMSELF A GIRLFRIEND FOR EACH NIGHT OF THE WEEK. WHY SHOULD SUCH A MAN BE A SEX KILLER?

Meanwhile, the Seattle police had fixed on a young man named Ted Bundy as a main suspect. For the past six years, he had been involved in a close relationship with divorcée Meg Anders, but she had called off their engagement when she realized that he was a habitual thief. After the Lake Sammamish disappearances, she had seen a composite drawing of the wanted "Ted" in the Seattle *Times* and thought it looked like Bundy; moreover, "Ted" drove a Volkswagen like Bundy's. She had seen crutches and plaster of paris in Bundy's room, and the coincidence seemed too great; with many misgivings, she telephoned the police. They assured her that they had already checked out Bundy; but at the suggestion of the Seattle police, Carol DaRonch was shown Bundy's photograph. She tentatively identified it as resembling the man who had tried to abduct her, but was obviously far from sure. (Bundy had been sporting a beard at the time.)

In January, March, April, July, and August of 1975, more young women vanished in Colorado, and their bodies—or skeletons—found in remote spots. On August 16, 1975, Bundy was arrested for the first time. As a police car was driving along a dark street in Salt Lake City, a parked Volkswagen launched into sudden motion. Curious at its haste, the policeman followed, and it accelerated. He caught up with the car at a service station, and found inside the car a pantyhose mask, a crowbar, an ice pick, and various other tools; there was also a pair of handcuffs.

Bundy, twenty-nine, seemed an unlikely burglar. He was a graduate of the University of Washington, and was in Utah to study law; he had worked as a political campaigner and for the crime commission in Seattle. In his room there was nothing suspicious—except maps and brochures of Colorado, from which five young women had vanished that year. But strands of hair were found in the car, and they proved to be identical with those of Melissa Smith, daughter of the Midvale police chief, who had vanished the previous October.

Carol DaRonch had meanwhile identified Bundy in a police lineup as the fake policeman, and bloodstains on her clothes—where she had scratched her assailant—were of Bundy's blood type. Credit card receipts showed that Bundy had been close to various places from which young women had vanished in Colorado.

In theory, this should have been the end of the case—and if it had been, it would have been regarded as a typical triumph of scientific detection, beginning with the composite drawing and concluding with the hair and blood evidence. The evidence was, admittedly, circumstantial, but taken all together, it formed a powerful case.

The central objection to it became apparent as soon as Bundy walked into court. He looked so obviously decent and clean-cut that most people felt that there must be some mistake. He was polite, well spoken, articulate, charming, the kind of man who could have found himself a girlfriend for each night of the week. Why should such a man be a sex killer? In spite of which, the impression he made was of brilliance and plausibility rather than innocence. For example, he insisted that he had driven away from the police car because he was smoking marijuana, and that he had thrown the joint out of the window.

The case seemed to be balanced on a knife-edge—nevertheless, the judge pronounced a sentence of guilty of kidnapping. Bundy sobbed and pleaded not to be sent to prison; the judge ignored his whimpering and imposed a sentence of between one and fifteen years jail time.

The Colorado authorities now charged him with the murder of Caryn Campbell, who had been abducted from a ski resort where a witness had seen Bundy. After a morning courtroom session in Aspen, Bundy succeeded in wandering into the library during the lunch recess, and jumped out of the window. He was recaptured eight days later, tired and hungry, and driving a stolen car.

Legal arguments dragged on for another six months: What evidence was admissible and what was not? And on December 30, 1977, Bundy escaped again, using a hacksaw blade to cut through an imperfectly welded steel plate above the light fixture in his cell. He made his way to Chicago, then south to Florida; there, near the Florida State University in Tallahassee, he took a room. A few days later, a man broke into a nearby sorority house and attacked four young women with a club, knocking them unconscious; one was strangled with her pantyhose and raped; another died on her way to the hospital. One of the strangled girl's nipples had been almost bitten off, and she had a bite mark on her left buttock. An hour and a half later, a student woke up in another sorority house when she heard banging next door, and a girl whimpering. She dialed the number of the room, and as the telephone rang, someone could be heard running out. Cheryl Thomas was found lying in bed, her skull fractured but still alive.

Bundy would later confess that he had again been watching girls undress outside the sorority house when he was overwhelmed by the impulse to break in and commit rape.

Three weeks later, on February 6, 1978, Bundy—who was calling himself Chris Hagen—stole a white Dodge van and left Tallahassee; he rented a room at the Holiday Inn, using a stolen credit card. The following day, twelve-year-old Kimberly Leach walked out of her classroom in Lake City, Florida, and vanished. Bundy returned to Tallahassee to take a date out for an expensive meal—paid for with a stolen credit card—then absconded via the fire escape, owing large arrears of rent. At 4 a.m. on February 15, a police patrolman noticed an orange Volkswagen driving suspiciously slowly, and radioed for a check on its number; it proved to be stolen from Tallahassee. After a struggle and a chase, during which he tried to kill the policeman, Bundy was captured yet again. When the police learned his real name, and that he had just left a town in which five young women had been attacked, they suddenly understood the importance of their capture.

Bundy seemed glad to be in custody, and began to unburden himself. He explained that "his problem" had begun when he had seen a girl on a bicycle in Seattle, and "had to have her." He had followed her, but she escaped. "Sometimes," he admitted, "I feel like a vampire."

On April 7, a party of searchers along the Suwanee River found the body of Kimberly Leach in an abandoned hut; she had been strangled and sexually violated. Three weeks later, surrounded by hefty guards, Bundy allowed impressions of his teeth to be taken, for comparison with the marks on the buttocks of the dead student, Lisa Levy.

Bundy's lawyers persuaded him to enter into plea bargaining: in exchange for a guarantee of life imprisonment—rather than a death sentence—he would confess to the murders of Lisa Levy, Margaret Bowman, and Kimberley Leach. But Bundy changed his mind at the last moment and decided to sack his lawyers.

His trial began on June 25, 1979, and the evidence against him was damning: a witness who had seen him leaving the sorority house after the attacks; a pantyhose mask found in the room of Cheryl Thomas, which resembled the one found in Bundy's car; but above all, the fact that Bundy's teeth matched the marks on Lisa Levy's buttocks. The highly compromising taped interview with the Pensacola police was judged inadmissible in court because his lawyer had not been present.

Bundy again dismissed his defense and took it over himself; the general impression was that he was trying to be too clever. The jury took only six hours to find him guilty on all counts. Judge Ed Cowan pronounced sentence of death by electrocution, but evidently felt some sympathy for the good-looking young defendant. "It's a tragedy for this court to see such a total waste of humanity. You're a bright young man. You'd have made a good lawyer. . . . But you went the wrong way, partner. Take care of yourself . . ."

Bundy was taken to Raiford Prison in Florida, where he was placed on Death Row. On July 2, 1986, when he was due to die a few hours before serial killer Gerald Stano, both were granted a stay of execution.

But at 7 a.m. on January 4, 1989, Bundy was finally led into the execution chamber at Starke State Prison, Florida; behind Plexiglas, an invited audience of forty-eight people sat waiting. As two wardens attached his hands to the arms of the electric chair, Bundy recognized his attorney among the crowd; he smiled and nodded. Then straps were placed around his chest and over his mouth; the metal cap with electrodes was fastened on to his head with screws and his face covered with a black hood. At 7:07 a.m. the executioner threw the switch; Bundy's body went stiff and rose fractionally from the chair. One minute later, as the power was switched off, the body slammed back into the chair. A doctor felt his pulse and pronounced him dead. Outside the prison, a mob carrying "Fry Bundy!" banners cheered as the execution was announced.

The Bundy case illustrates the immense problems faced by investigators of serial murders before the Violent Criminal Apprehension Program made it all simpler by computerizing crimes and suspects. When Meg Anders telephoned the police after the double murder near Lake Sammamish, Bundy's name had already been suggested by three people. But he was only one of 3,500 suspects.

Later Bundy was added to the list of 100 "best suspects" that investigators constructed on grounds of age, occupation, and past record. Two hundred thousand items were fed into computers, including the names of 41,000 Volkswagen owners, 5,000 men with records of mental illness, every student who had taken classes with the dead girls, and all transfers from other colleges that they had attended. All this was programmed into thirty-seven categories, each using a different criterion to isolate the suspect. Asked to name anyone who came up on any three of these lists, the computer produced 16,000 names. When the number was raised to four, it was reduced to 600. Only when it was raised to 25 was it reduced to 10 suspects, with Bundy seventh on the list. The police were still investigating number six when Bundy was detained in Salt Lake City with burgling tools in his car. Only after that did Bundy become suspect number one. And by that time, he had already committed a minimum of seventeen murders.

Detective Robert Keppel, who worked on the case, is certain that Bundy would have been revealed as suspect number one even if he had not been arrested.

The Bundy case is doubly baffling because he seems to contradict the basic assertions of every major criminologist of the past century. Bundy is not an obvious born criminal, with degenerate physical characteristics, as Cesare Lombroso suggested in *Criminal Man* (1876); there is (as far as is known) no history of insanity in his family; he was not a social derelict or a failure. In her book *The Stranger Beside Me,* his friend Ann Rule describes him as "a man of unusual accomplishment." How could the subtlest "psychological profiling" target such a man as a serial killer?

The answer to the riddle emerged fairly late in the day, four years after Bundy had been sentenced to death. Before his conviction, Bundy had indicated his willingness to cooperate on a book about himself, and two journalists, Stephen G. Michaud and Hugh Aynesworth, went to interview him in prison. They discovered that Bundy had no wish to discuss guilt, except to deny it, and he actively discouraged them from investigating the case against him. He wanted them to produce a gossipy book focusing squarely on himself, like bestselling biographies of celebrities such as Frank Sinatra. Michaud and Aynesworth would have been happy to write a book demonstrating his innocence, but as they looked into the case, they found it impossible to accept this; instead, they concluded that he had killed at least twenty-one women.

When they began to probe, Bundy hedged, lied, claimed faulty memory, and resorted to endless self-justification: "Intellectually," say Michaud and Aynesworth, "Ted seemed profoundly disassociative, a compartmentalizer, and thus a superb rationalizer."

Emotionally, he struck them as a severe case of arrested development: "He might as well have been a twelve-year-old, and a precocious and bratty one at that. So extreme was his childishness that his pleas of innocence were of a character very similar to that of the little boy who'll deny wrongdoing in the face of overwhelming evidence to the contrary." This gave Michaud the ingenious idea of suggesting that Bundy should "speculate on the nature of a person capable of doing what Ted had been accused (and convicted) of doing." Bundy embraced this idea with enthusiasm, and talked for hours into a tape recorder. Soon Michaud became aware that there were, in effect, two "Teds"—the analytical human being, and an entity inside him that Michaud came to call the "hunchback," the Mr. Hyde alter ego.

After generalizing for some time about violence in modern society, the disintegration of the home, and so on, Bundy got down to specifics, and began to discuss his own development.

He had been an illegitimate child, born to a respectable young woman in Philadelphia. She moved to Seattle to escape the stigma, and married a cook in the Veterans Administration Hospital. Ted was an oversensitive and self-conscious child who had all the usual daydreams of fame and wealth. And at an early stage he became a thief and something of a habitual liar—as many imaginative children do. But he seems to have been deeply upset by the discovery of his illegitimacy.

Bundy was not, in fact, a brilliant student. Although he struck his fellow students as witty and cultivated, his grades were usually Bs. In his late teens he became heavily infatuated with a fellow student, "Stephanie Brooks," as Ann Rule calls her in *The Stranger Beside Me,* who was beautiful, sophisticated, and came from a wealthy family. She responded and the couple became engaged. To impress her he enrolled at Stanford University to study Chinese; but he felt lonely away from home, and his grades were poor. "I found myself thinking about standards of success that I just didn't seem to be living up to."

"Stephanie" wearied of his immaturity and threw him over—the severest blow so far. He became intensely moody. "Dogged by feelings of worthlessness and failure," he took a job as a busboy in a hotel dining room. And at this point began the drift that eventually turned him into a serial killer. He became friendly with a drug addict. One night, they entered a cliffside house that had been partly destroyed by a landslide, and stole whatever they could find. "It was really thrilling," he remembered.

He was soon shoplifting and stealing "for thrills," once walking openly into someone's greenhouse, taking an eight-foot tree in a pot, and putting it in his car with the top sticking out of the sunroof. He also became the official driver for Art Fletcher, a black councilman who was the Republican candidate for lieutenant governor of Washington State. He enjoyed the sense of being a "somebody" and mixing with interesting people. But Fletcher lost the election and Bundy took a job as a salesman in a department store. He met Meg Anders in a college beer joint, and they became lovers—she had a gentle, easy-going nature, which brought out Bundy's protective side. But his kleptomania shocked her.

In fact, the criminal side—the "hunchback"—was now developing fast. He acquired a taste for violent pornography—then (in the 1960s) easy to buy. And one fateful day, walking round the university district, he saw a young woman undressing in a lighted room. This was the turning point in his life. He began to devote hours to walking around, hoping to spy on more young women undressing. He was back at the

THEY DISCOVERED THAT BUNDY HAS NO WISH TO DISCUSS GUILT, EXCEPT TO DENY IT . . .

university, studying psychology, but his night prowling prevented him from making full use of his undoubted intellectual capacities. He obtained his degree in due course and tried to find a law school that would take him. He failed all the aptitude tests and was repeatedly turned down. A year later, he was finally accepted at the University of Utah College of Law—he worked for the crime commission for a month, as an assistant, and for the Office of Justice Planning. His self-confidence increased by leaps and bounds. When he flew to San Francisco to see "Stephanie," the girl who had jilted him, she was deeply impressed, and willing to rekindle their romance. He was still involved with Meg Anders, and entered on this new career as a Don Juan with his usual enthusiasm. He and "Stephanie" spent Christmas together and renewed their engagement. Then he dumped her as she had once dumped him.

By this time, he had committed his first murder. As noted, he had for years been a pornography addict and a Peeping Tom. ("He approached it almost like a project, throwing himself into it, literally, for years.")

Then the "hunchback" started to demand "more active gratification." He tried disabling women's cars, but they always had help on hand. He felt the need to indulge in this kind of behavior after drinking had reduced his inhibitions. One evening, he stalked a young woman from a bar, found a heavy piece of wood, and managed to get ahead of her and lie in wait. Before she reached his hiding place, she stopped at her front door, and went inside. But the experience, he said, was like "making a hole in a dam."

A few evenings later, as a woman was fumbling for her keys at her front door, he struck her on the head with a piece of wood. She collapsed, screaming, and he ran away. He was filled with remorse, and swore he would never do such a thing again. But six months later, he followed a woman home and peeped and masturbated as she undressed.

He began to do this repeatedly. One day, when he knew she had forgotten to lock her door, he sneaked in, entered her bedroom, and jumped on her. She screamed and he ran away. Once again, there was a period of self-disgust and revulsion.

This was in the autumn of 1973. On January 4, 1974, he found a door that admitted him to the basement room of an eighteen-year-old woman. Now, for the first time, he employed the technique he later used repeatedly, attacking her with a crowbar until she was unconscious. He then savagely rammed a bar torn from the bed inside her vagina, causing internal injuries. But he left her alive.

On the morning of February 1, 1974, he found an unlocked front door in a students' house and went in. He entered a bedroom at random; twenty-one-year-old Lynda Ann Healy was asleep in bed. He battered her unconscious, and then carried her out to his car. He drove to Taylor Mountain, twenty miles east of Seattle, removed her pajamas, and raped her. When Bundy was later "speculating" about this crime for Stephen Michaud's benefit, the interviewer asked: "Was there any conversation?" Bundy replied: "There'd be some. Since this woman in front of him represented not a person, but, again, the image of something desirable, the last thing we would expect him to want to do would be to personalize her."

He then bludgeoned Lynda to death; Bundy always insisted that he took no pleasure in violence, but that his chief desire was "possession" of another person. Now the "hunchback" was in full control, and there were five more victims over the next five months. Three of the young women were taken to the same spot on Taylor Mountain and there raped and murdered—Bundy acknowledged that his sexual gratification would sometimes take hours. The four bodies were found together in the following year.

On the day he abducted the two young women from Lake Sammamish, Bundy "speculated" that he had taken the first, Janice Ott, to a nearby house and raped her. He then returned to the lake to abduct Denise Naslund, taking her back to the same house and raping her in view of Janice. He then killed them both, drove their bodies to a remote spot four miles northeast of the park, and dumped them.

By the time he had reached this point in his "confession," Bundy had no further secrets to reveal; everything was obvious. Rape had become a compulsion that dominated his life. When he moved to Salt Lake City to enter the law school—he was a failure from the beginning as a law student—he must have known that if he began to rape and kill young women there, he would be establishing himself as suspect number one. This made no difference; he had to continue. Even the unsuccessful kidnapping of Carol DaRonch, and the knowledge that someone could now identify him, made no difference to him. He merely switched his activities to Colorado.

Following his arrest, conviction, and escape, he moved to Florida, and the compulsive attacks continued, although by now he must have known that another series of murders in a town to which he had recently moved must reduce his habitual plea of "coincidence" to an absurdity. It seems obvious that by this time he had lost the power of choice. In his last weeks of freedom, Bundy showed all the signs of weariness and self-disgust.

Time finally ran out for Bundy in January 1989. Long before this, he had recognized that his fatal mistake was to decline to enter into plea-bargaining at his trial; the result was a death sentence instead of life imprisonment. In January 1989, his final appeal was turned down and the date of execution fixed. He then made a last-minute attempt to save his life by offering to bargain murder confessions for a reprieve—against the advice of his attorney James Coleman, who warned him that this attempt to "trade over the victims' bodies" would only create hostility that would mitigate against further stays of execution. That same year, Ressler attempted to arrange an interview with Bundy for his research project—

Bundy was articulate and intelligent, and Ressler hoped to add something to what he knew about the motivation of serial killers. His plan did not work out at that time, but two years later he was surprised to receive a letter from Bundy saying that he would like to become a consultant to the BSU. This was fairly obviously a long-shot attempt to delay his execution; if he could become a valuable consultant, his chances of being executed would be correspondingly smaller.

At their meeting, Bundy stuck out his hand even before Ressler extended his (establishing himself as being in charge of the situation) and told Ressler how much he admired his writing. (Ressler had at this time only cowritten one book on sexual homicide.) Bundy said he wondered why Ressler had not come to see him earlier, and Ressler replied he had tried but been unable to because Bundy's appeals were still pending. Bundy apologized, explaining that he would very much like to talk to someone on his own level of understanding—a clear attempt at manipulation reminiscent of John Gacy.

CLEARLY, THE RIGHT MAN SYNDROME IS A FORM OF MILD INSANITY.

Bundy agreed to answer questions on a "speculative" basis—as with his earlier interviews with Michaud and Aynesworth—and described how he had abducted Caryn Campbell from a hotel at a ski resort in Colorado in January 1979. But he would not admit that he had actually done this, and "after three or four hours of this sort of dancing around the issues," said Ressler, "I realized that Bundy would never talk, that he would attempt to con people . . . until executed, and I went home."

In a final attempt to bargain for his life, Bundy finally went on to confess to eight Washington murders, and then to a dozen others. Detective Bob Keppel, who had led the investigation in Seattle, commented: "The game-playing stuff cost him his life." Instead of making a full confession, Bundy doled out information bit by bit. "The whole thing was orchestrated," said Keppel, "We were held hostage for three days." And finally, when it was clear that there was no chance of further delay, Bundy confessed to the Chi Omega Sorority killings, admitting that he had been peeping through the window at girls undressing until he was carried away by desire and entered the building.

He also mentioned pornography as being one of the factors that led him to murder. Newspaper columnists showed an inclination to doubt this, but Bundy's earlier confessions to Michaud leave no doubt that he was telling the truth.

Ann Rule's book on Bundy contains another vital clue to his motivations. She comments that Bundy became violently upset if he telephoned Meg Anders from Salt Lake City—where his legal studies were foundering—and got no reply. "Strangely, while he was being continuously unfaithful himself, he expected—demanded—that she be totally loyal to him." This, of course, is the Right Man of A. E. Van Vogt, the man who will never, under any circumstances, admit he is in the wrong, and spends his life building a sand castle of self-esteem based on illusions. Such a man is often constantly unfaithful to his wife, yet demands total fidelity from her.

Clearly, the Right Man syndrome is a form of mild insanity. Yet it is alarmingly common; most of us know a Right Man, and some have the misfortune to have a Right Man for a husband or father.

The syndrome obviously arises from the sheer competitiveness of the world we are born into. Every normal male has an urge to be a "winner," yet he finds himself surrounded by people who seem better qualified for success. One common response is boasting to those who look as if they can be taken in—particularly women. Another is what the late Stephen Potter called "one-upmanship," the attempt to make the other person feel inferior by a kind of cheating—for example, by pretending to know far more than you actually know. Another is to bully people over whom one happens to have authority. Many Right Men are so successful in all of these departments that they achieve a remarkably high level of self-esteem on remarkably slender talents. Once achieved, this self-esteem is like an addictive drug and any threat of withdrawal seems terrifying. Hence the violence with which he reacts to anything that challenges it.

It would probably be true to say that all serial killers are Right Men.

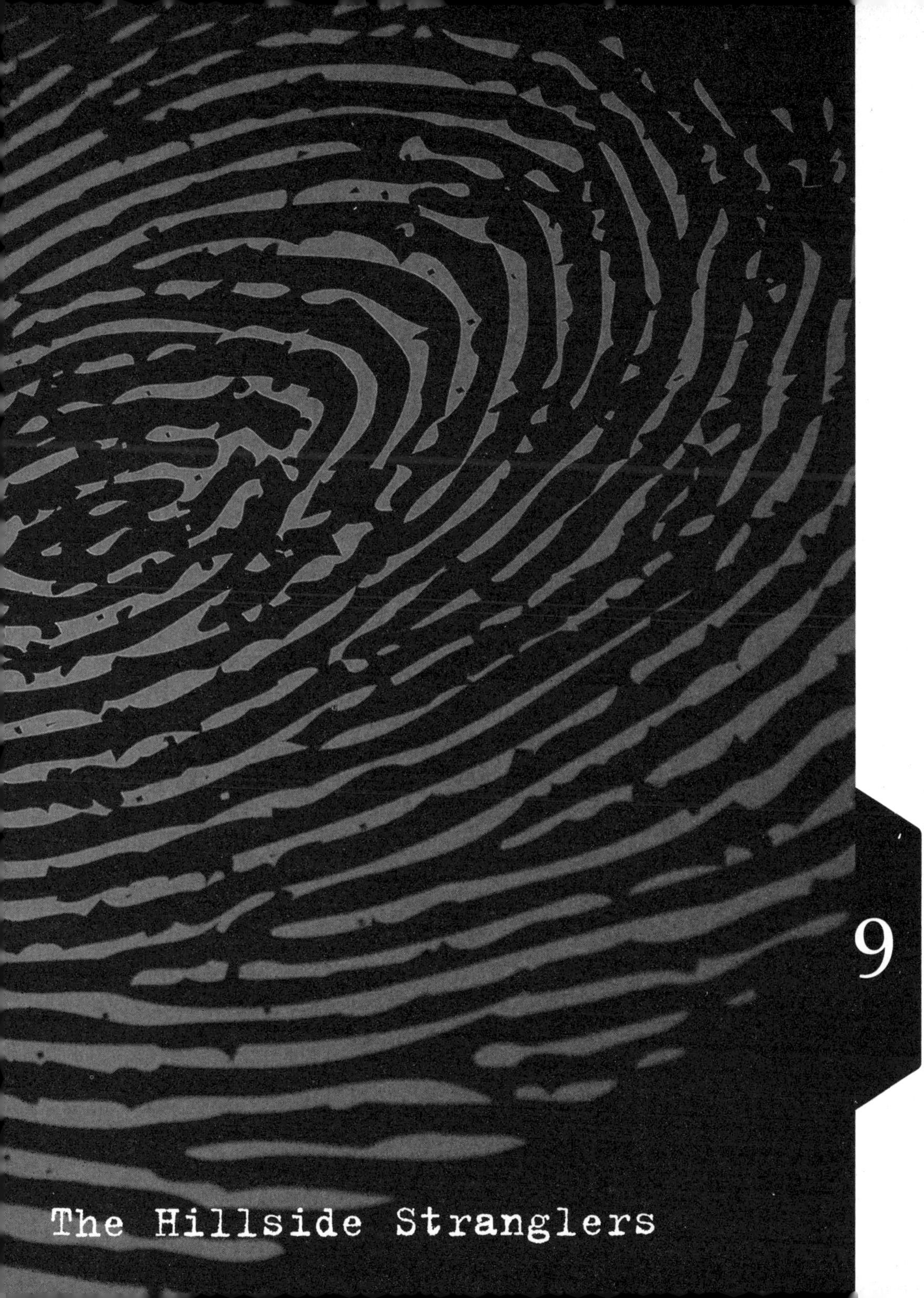

9

The Hillside Stranglers

9 The Hillside Stranglers

The most widely publicized case of the late 1980s was at the time another of those mysteries that seem to demonstrate that the police are helpless when a killer chooses to strike at random. But then, the Behavioral Science Unit was still new, and had not yet had time to find its feet.

The problem with the "Hillside Strangler"—as he was then known—was that he seemed to be a completely disorganized killer, and if luck is on their side, these are the most difficult kinds of killers to catch. Ressler explains:

> *The disorganized killer may pick up a steak knife in the victim's home, plunge it into her chest, and leave it sticking there. Such a disorganized mind does not care about fingerprints or other evidence. If police find a body rather readily, that is a clue that the crime has been done by a disorganized offender. Organized ones transport the bodies from the place that the victims were killed, and then hide the bodies, sometimes quite well. Many of Ted Bundy's victims were never found. Bob Berdella, a Kansas City, Missouri, killer who, like John Gacy, abducted, tortured, and killed young boys, cut up their bodies into small pieces and fed them to the dogs in his yard; many that were so treated could never be identified.*

Ressler then turns to the Hillside Stranglers:

> *A different dynamic seems to have been at work in the instance of the Hillside Strangler, who was later identified as two men. The victims were found, and the killers later turned out to have been quite organized offenders. Their desire seems to have been an egotistical one—to flaunt the bodies in front of the police rather than to conceal them in an effort to prevent tracing the killers through identification of the victim.*

These two killers, whose trial was one of the most costly in American legal history, differ in another significant way from killers such as Schaefer or Heirens, both of whom were tormented as they felt themselves being taken over by the urge to kill—so that so Schaefer sobbed as he told Sondra London about his compulsions, while Heirens wrote "For God's sake catch me . . ."

Kenneth Bianchi and Angelo Buono felt as little compunction as two Alsatians who team up to kill sheep. They committed rape-murder as a glutton eats: because it gave them pleasure.

The case is also of interest for another reason. The crimes of the Hillside Stranglers came about because two criminal personalities interacted, and produced an explosive combination. Psychologists sometimes refer to it as *folie à deux,* or "madness for two." When this happens, it is usually because a dominant character interacts with a weak one, and enjoys the sense of exerting power so much that he looks for ways to savor it more fully. It can be seen, for example, in the case of Leopold and Loeb, the two Chicago college students who in 1924 decided to commit a murder simply to prove to themselves that they were not like other people. Two decades later, it appears in the case of the "Lonely Hearts Killers," Raymond Fernandez and Martha Beck, who killed twenty women to gain possession of their property, and who were executed in 1951. In the 1960s, in England, the Moors Murderers, Ian Brady and Myra Hindley (see chapter 16), were a textbook case of *folie à deux*. Ten years later, came the Hillside Stranglers.

Angelo Buono and Kenneth Bianchi were cousins, Buono (born 1934) being the elder by seventeen years, and they came together when Bianchi moved to Los Angeles from Rochester, New York, in 1976. Buono had spent most of his teens in a reformatory for car theft, but nonetheless had become the successful owner of an auto body shop in Glendale, and gained a reputation as a first-class upholsterer, his clients including Frank Sinatra. Intensely macho, his infidelity and brutality had resulted in four divorces by the time he was in his late thirties.

Kenneth Bianchi, born 1951, was the son of a prostitute, and had been adopted at three months. A bright child, he had a tendency to lie compulsively. Good-looking and a plausible talker, he had no trouble finding girlfriends, but a certain weakness of character undermined his relationships. In personality type he bore many resemblances to Gerard Schaefer, including a hankering for authority that led him to try to become a policeman. When rejected, he took a job as a night security guard. But his propensity to steal led to many job changes. Eventually, with one divorce behind him, he moved to Los Angeles at the age of twenty-five.

There he was again turned down on two occasions by the LAPD, and decided instead to become a psychiatrist. He began by reading psychology textbooks, but decided to take a short cut to a career in the field: he placed a fake job advertisement in a newspaper, and then took the identity and qualifications of a graduate student who answered it.

The impact of his cousin's personality on him was profound, and his open admiration led Buono to offer him a home. There Bianchi was impressed by the ease in which his cousin bedded nubile teenagers and persuaded them to perform oral sex. Buono was brutal and coarse, but as a stud, he was awe-inspiring.

Although Buono soon tired of his fantasy-prone and weak-willed cousin and made him find a place of his own, he nevertheless suggested that they should go into the pimping business together. Bianchi quickly made a start. At a party, he met Sabra, an attractive sixteen-year-old blonde who aspired to be a model and convinced her that he could find her jobs. She moved into Buono's house, and when the jobs failed to materialize, he asked her if she had ever considered prostitution. Her first reaction was indignation, but after being stripped and beaten with a wet towel and made to perform oral sex on both men, she reluctantly submitted. They warned her that if she ever ran away, their Mafia friends would find her and kill her. On one occasion, she and Buono's teenaged girlfriend, Antoinette, served seven men at the same time, including the local police chief. Soon the cousins had a small stable of girls working for them, with all of whom Buono practiced anal intercourse. They called their agency the Foxy Ladies.

It was a slight fifteen-year-old called Becky who triggered a series of events that led to multiple murder. One evening in August 1977, Buono sent her to the Bel Air apartment of a wealthy lawyer. When he asked the sad waif how she became a prostitute, she told him the story of how two men kept her a prisoner, beat and sodomized her, and threatened her with death. He was so shocked that he put her on a plane back home to Arizona.

Enraged when he learned what had happened, Buono repeatedly telephoned him, threatening him with harm. The lawyer retaliated by calling upon the services of some biker friends, and asked Tiny, a 300-pound bouncer, to "visit" Buono's garage. Tiny took with him four equally huge companions. They walked in to find Buono working in a car, and when Tiny asked him if he was Mr. Buono, he just ignored him. Tiny then reached through the window, picked Buono up by his shirtfront, dragged him through the window, and calmly asked: "Do I have your attention, Mr. Buono?" He then ordered Buono not to bother his lawyer friend again, and left him sprawling on the garage floor.

For a Right Man such as Buono, this must have seemed the worst thing that had ever happened to him, a shattering assault on his masculinity. His reaction was murderous rage, and the determination to take it out on a woman.

Bianchi happened to be feeling the same. By this time, Sabra had also run away, and her replacement, a girl named Jennifer, had violently resisted when Bianchi tried to sodomize her. And both men were furious with a prostitute named Debbie Noble, who had swindled them by selling them a list of clients that was supposed to be of men who liked woman to come to their homes, but was in fact of men who wanted to visit a prostitute on her own premises. They both felt like murder.

On October 17, 1977, they encountered Yolanda Washington, a nineteen-year-old prostitute who happened to work with Debbie Noble. The cousins picked her up on a corner of Sunset Boulevard and Buono had sex with her in the back of the car. He then flashed her a police badge, and announced that she was under arrest. She began to scream and struggle until he handcuffed her. Then Bianchi raped her in the back seat before garroting her with a rag. Finally, the two men dumped her naked body near the entrance to Forest Lawn Cemetery, in a position where it would easily draw attention.

For Buono and Bianchi, the experience was exhilarating. Surprised at how much they enjoyed raping and killing a woman, they agreed to repeat the experience as soon as possible. They decided the time was right just two weeks later, on Halloween, but this time they wanted to do it at Buono's place. They wanted the luxury of time. They picked up Judy Ann Miller, a fifteen-year-old hooker, and in Buono's bedroom they bound and blindfolded her, and then took their turns raping her. Then they pulled a plastic bag down over her head and tied it around her neck. Bianchi sat on her legs as Buono strangled her with a cord. They dumped her body in La Crescenta, a town just north of Glendale, once again in a highly visible position.

Just a week later, the cousins were ready for more mayhem, and November 6, 1977, found them cruising for another victim. Lissa Kastin was the unfortunate target. They picked up the twenty-one-year-old waitress on her way home from her job on Hollywood Boulevard. Again they posed as policemen and instead of the station they drove her back to Buono's place. Neither of them found her sexually desirable, so they made no attempt to rape her, but instead violated her with a root beer bottle. They took nearly an hour to kill her, repeatedly tightening a cord around her neck until she was almost dead, and then releasing it. They left her naked body near the Chevy Chase Country Club in Glendale.

Three days later, on November 9, they were out "hunting" again. Bianchi spotted an attractive young woman waiting alone at a bus stop and struck up a conversation with her; she told him she was a Scientology student, and Bianchi feigned interest, asking her to tell him all about it. In the midst of the conversation, Buono drove up, pretended he hadn't seen Bianchi for months, and offered him a lift home. Jane King made the mistake of agreeing to let them drive her home, too. Back in Buono's house, they were delighted to find that her pubis was shaven. She resisted Buono's rape, and struggled so hard as Bianchi tried to penetrate her anally that they decided she needed a "lesson." She was hog-tied, and a plastic bag placed over her head while Bianchi sodomized her; by the time Bianchi climaxed she was dead. They dumped her body near an exit ramp of the Golden State Freeway. They were surprised to read later in the newspaper that Jane was twenty-eight; she looked younger.

Her shaven pubis had excited them both; it conjured images of raping a virgin. Only four days after killing Jane, they observed two schoolgirls, Dolores Cepeda, twelve, and Sonja Johnson, fourteen, boarding a bus at Eagle Rock Plaza. Now, the idea of raping two girls at once struck their fancy. They followed the bus, and when the girls disembarked near their homes, beckoned them over to the car. Bianchi identified himself as a policeman and informed them that a dangerous burglar was loose in the neighborhood. The girls were vulnerable; they had just stolen a hundred-dollars worth of costume jewelry from a department store, and were not disposed to argue with the law.

As with their other victims, there was no ride to the station, but only the drive to Buono's house. There they were both brutally violated. Sonja was murdered in the bedroom. When they came to get Dolores, the terrified girl asked: "Where's Sonja?" Buono calmly told her: "You'll be seeing her soon." The girls' corpses were dumped on a rubbish tip that Buono knew from his courting days. The police had reasoned, correctly, that whoever had dumped the bodies must have known the area intimately.

As they followed in such quick succession, the crimes began to receive extensive publicity. Because the bodies were usually dumped on slopes, the local press labeled the killer the "Hillside Strangler." Newspapers around the world soon took up the soubriquet, which had the same touch of brutality as "Jack the Ripper" or the "Boston Strangler."

The next victim was Kristina Weckler, a young woman who had spurned Bianchi's advances when they both lived in an apartment building on East Garfield Avenue in Glendale. Kristina stilled lived there and was a student at the Pasadena Art Center of Design. They knocked on her door, and Bianchi casually said, "Hi, remember me?" He told her that he was now a member of the police reserve, and that someone had crashed into Kristina's VW, parked outside the building. She went downstairs with them to check out the damage, but was instead wrestled into Buono's car and driven to his house. After raping her, they decided to try a new method of murder: injecting her with a cleaning fluid. It produced convulsions, but not death. At Buono's suggestion, they placed a bag over her head and piped coal gas into it, strangling her at the same time.

The Thanksgiving killing spree was almost over. On Monday, November 28, 1977, they saw a redheaded young woman climbing into her car, and followed it. And when Lauren Wagner pulled up in front of her parents' home, Bianchi again flashed his phony police badge and told her that she was under arrest. Even as she protested—and a dog barked loudly in a nearby house, prompting a woman to look out of the window—they bundled her into their car and drove her away. When she realized that their purpose was rape, she pretended to be cooperative, mentioning that she had spent the evening in bed with her boyfriend and was ready for more. While being raped she behaved as if she enjoyed it. Her desperate act didn't save her life; the brutal cousins strangled her anyway, after an unsuccessful attempt to electrocute her had only produced burns on her palms.

The realization that a neighbor had witnessed the abduction made them decide to use more caution. Nevertheless, three weeks later, both men were dreaming of another rape. Kimberly Martin, a call girl, was summoned to Bianchi's apartment, and taken back to Buono's house. After raping her, they agreed that she was no good in bed. Her body was dumped in a vacant lot.

SURPRISED AT HOW MUCH THEY ENJOYED RAPING AND KILLING A WOMAN, THEY AGREED TO REPEAT THE EXPERIENCE AS SOON AS POSSIBLE.

The final Hillside Strangler killing was almost an accident. On February 16, Bianchi arrived at Buono's house to find an orange Datsun parked outside. Cindy Hudspeth had called to hire Buono to make new mats for her car. The opportunity was just too good to miss. She was spread-eagled naked on the bed, her wrists and ankles tied to the posts, and then raped repeatedly for two hours. When the cousins were finally done with her, they strangled her. The Datsun was pushed off a cliff with her body in the trunk.

Bianchi had been twice questioned by the police in routine enquiries—but he was one of thousands. Buono was nonetheless becoming nervous and irritable. He was getting sick of his cousin's lack of maturity, his naïveté, and his carelessness. So when Bianchi told him that his pregnant girlfriend, Kelli Boyd, had left him and moved back to Bellingham, Washington, Buono strongly advised him to join her. At first Bianchi was unwilling—his admiration of his cousin amounted almost to worship—but as always, Buono's will prevailed.

On May 21, 1978, Bianchi drove to Bellingham and rejoined Kelli and their newborn son. He obtained a job as a security guard, and was soon promoted to supervisor. But the small town bored him. He longed to prove to his cousin that he had the makings of a master criminal. And in the first week of January 1979, his craving for rape and murder became an intolerable itch. His mind went back to Karen Mandic, an attractive twenty-two-year-old student whom he had known when he worked as a department store security guard.

On January 11, 1979, Bianchi telephoned Karen and offered her a house-sitting job in the Bayside area. He swore her to silence "for security reasons," but Karen nonetheless told her boyfriend where she was going. She also telephoned a friend who was a security guard at the university and told him about the job. Her friend was suspicious about the size of the remuneration, $100 for an evening, but he knew that the Bayside area contained many wealthy homes, full of valuables. If this was one of them, it could be worth it.

At seven o'clock that evening, Karen and her friend Diane Wilder drove to the Bayside house. Bianchi was already waiting for them in his security truck. Karen parked her car in the driveway, outside the front door, and Bianchi asked her to accompany him inside to turn on the lights, while Diane waited in the Mercury. When he reappeared a few minutes later, Diane had no suspicion that her friend was now lying dead in the basement. Like Karen, Diane walked down the stairs with Bianchi behind her, and the ligature was dropped over her head and pulled tight.

For some reason, Bianchi did not rape the girls, merely ejaculated on their underwear. He carried both bodies out to Karen's car, and lifted them into the back. He drove to a cul-de-sac, carefully wiped the car clean of fingerprints, and walked back to the Bayside house where his own truck was parked, disposing of the ligature on the way.

The Mercury was soon found, and Bianchi was interviewed by the police. He said that he had never heard of the two young women, and had certainly not offered them a house-sitting job. But a search of his home revealed all kinds of expensive items that he had stolen as a security guard.

The baffling thing about the crime was that it seemed so oddly pointless. If it was a sex crime, why were the victims not raped?

Still, the case against Bianchi looked conclusive, even though he continued to insist—with the greatest apparent sincerity—that he had no memory of the murders. His bail was posted at $150,000. And now that he was safely in jail, the police began checking on his background. Since he had been living in Glendale, north of downtown Los Angeles, an investigating detective rang the Los Angeles County Sheriff's Department to see if they knew anything about Bianchi. Detective Sergeant Frank Salerno of the Homicide Division took the call. When Salerno heard that a former Glendale resident named Kenneth Bianchi had been booked on suspicion of a double sex murder, anticipation gripped him. For the past fourteen months, Salerno had been hunting for the Hillside Strangler, whose last murder had taken place shortly before Bianchi left Los Angeles for Bellingham in the previous May.

Salerno lost no time in heading north, and within hours of arriving, he was certain that he had found at least one of the Hillside Stranglers. A large cache of jewelry had been found in Bianchi's apartment, and two items matched jewelry taken from the Hillside victims.

Bianchi, continuing to behave like an innocent man, was highly cooperative. He told the police that his only close friend in Los Angeles was his cousin, an automobile upholsterer who owned a house in Glendale. A check on

INTERVIEWED BY THE POLICE, BUONO'S ATTITUDE HAD AN UNDERTONE OF MOCKERY; HE SEEMED TO BE ENJOYING THE THOUGHT THAT THE POLICE HAD NO REAL EVIDENCE AGAINST HIM.

Buono—by an undercover agent—made it seem highly likely that he was the other Strangler. He had bushy hair, as did one of the men seen by the woman who had observed them abducting Lauren Wagner.

Interviewed by the police, Buono's attitude had an undertone of mockery; he seemed to be enjoying the thought that the police had no real evidence against him. All that, Salerno reflected with satisfaction, would change when his cousin returned to Los Angeles.

Yet, with bewildering suddenness, the whole case threatened to collapse. Kenneth Bianchi had managed to have himself declared legally insane, or, the next best thing: he was diagnosed with multiple personality disorder. In layman's parlance, MPD is a mental condition in which two or more personalities appear to inhabit one body. In Bianchi's case, he was diagnosed a Jekyll and Hyde character whose Jekyll was totally unaware of the existence of an evil alter ego.

Ever since his arrest, Bianchi had been insisting that he remembered absolutely nothing of the evening on which he killed Karen Mandic and Diane Wilder. The police, understandably, thought that was a feeble and not very inventive attempt to wriggle out of responsibility. But Bianchi's lawyer, Dean Brett, was impressed by his apparent sincerity, his protestations of horror at the thought of killing two women, and his hints that he was contemplating suicide. He called in a psychiatric social worker, John Johnston, who was equally impressed by Bianchi's charm, gentleness, and intelligence. If his protestations of amnesia were genuine, then there was only one possible conclusion: he was a victim of MPD.

Although the medical world had been debating the existence of this rare illness since the nineteenth century, the 1957 movie *The Three Faces of Eve,* based on the book by psychiatrists C. H. Thigpen and H. M. Cleckley, brought the riddle of multiple personality disorder to the general public. MPD therapists posit that the disorder is caused by severe psychological traumas in childhood, experiences so horrific (such as sexual abuse or extreme cruelty) that the personality literally blots them out and hides them away in some remote corner of the mind. In later life, a violent shock can reactivate the trauma, and the everyday self blanks out, and a new personality takes over—for hours or sometimes days or months.

Whether Bianchi knew about this rare psychological illness at this stage is a matter for debate—the police were certainly unaware that he was an avid student of psychology, who hoped one day to become a professional psychoanalyst. What is clear is that Johnston's suggestion was seized upon with enthusiasm. Equally significant for Bianchi was a showing of the made-for-television film *Sybil*—another study of multiple personality—on the prison TV. From this, he learned that "multiples" often suffer from blinding headaches and weird dreams. He also learned that psychiatrists try to gain access to the "other self" through hypnosis.

When Professor John G. Watkins, a psychologist from the University of Montana, suggested hypnosis, Bianchi professed himself eager to cooperate. And within a few minutes of being placed in a trance, he was speaking in a strange, low voice and introducing himself as someone called Steve. "Steve" came over as a highly unpleasant character with a sneering laugh. He professed to Dr. Watkins that he hated "Ken," and that he had done his best to "fix him." With a little more prompting, he went on to describe how Ken had walked in one evening when his cousin Angelo was murdering a young woman. At which point, "Steve" admitted that he had taken over Ken's personality, and made him into his cousin's willing accomplice.

Frank Salerno and his colleague Pete Finnigan were sitting quietly in a corner of the room, listening to all of this. In his notebook Salerno jotted down a single word: "Bullshit." But he knew that the investigation was in trouble. If Bianchi could convince a judge that he was a multiple personality, he would escape with a few years in a mental hospital. And since the testimony of a mental patient would be inadmissible in court, Angelo Buono would be beyond the reach of the law.

Back in Los Angeles, the investigation was looking slightly more promising. The boyfriend of Judy Miller—the second victim of the Stranglers—had identified a photograph of Angelo Buono as the "John" who had enticed Judy into his car on the evening she disappeared. And Beulah Stofer, the woman who had seen Lauren Wagner pushed into a car by two men, identified them from photographs as Buono and Bianchi. That would certainly bolster the case against Buono. But without Bianchi's testimony, it would still be weak.

The picture of Buono that had been built up through various interviews made it clear that he was brutal, violent, and dangerous. He had hated his mother, and always referred to her as "that cunt"; later in life, it became his general term for all women. From the time he left school he had been in trouble with the police, and had spent his seventeenth birthday in a reform school. His hero was Caryl Chessman, the "Red Light Bandit," who liked to hold up women at gunpoint and force them to perform oral sex. At the age of twenty, Buono had married a seventeen-year-old girl who was pregnant, but left her within weeks.

After a short jail sentence for theft, he had married again, and quickly fathered four sons. But he was always coarse and violent: one day when his wife declined to have sex, he threw her down and sodomized her in front of the children. She left him and filed for divorce. So did his third wife. The fourth one left him without bothering about divorce. After that, Angelo lived alone in his house at 703 Colorado Street, Glendale. A friend who had once shared an apartment with him described him as being obsessed by young girls. The friend had entered the room one day and found Angelo peering down at a girls' playground through a pair of binoculars and playing with himself. Angelo had boasted that he had "seduced" his fourteen-year-old stepdaughter. And one of Angelo's sons had confided that his father had raped him, too. Clearly, Angelo Buono was a man who spent his days thinking and dreaming about sex.

Back in the Whatcomb County Jail in Washington, Ken's sinister alter ego "Steve" was also telling stories of Buono's insatiable sexual appetite, and of his habit of killing girls after he had raped and sodomized them. These stories tended to contain certain anomalies—almost as if "Steve" wished to minimize his own part in the murders and throw most of the blame on Angelo—and the same applied to his later confessions to the police; but the general picture that emerged was clear enough. The first victim was the prostitute Yolanda Washington, who had been killed for revenge but raped by both men; they found the experience so satisfying that they began committing rape and murder about once every ten days.

The news that Kenneth Bianchi had accused his cousin of being his accomplice made Buono unpopular in the Glendale neighborhood, and he received several threatening letters. But it began to look increasingly likely that neither Bianchi nor Buono would ever appear in a Los Angeles courtroom. In the Whatcomb County Jail, Bianchi had not only convinced Professor Watkins that he was a multiple personality, but had also aroused equal interest and enthusiasm in another expert: Dr. Ralph B. Allison, author of a remarkable work on multiple personality, *Minds in Many Pieces*. Allison's obvious sympathy made "Steve" even more confiding, and led him to make what would later prove to be a crucial mistake. At Allison's request he revealed his last name: Walker—although at the time, this interesting and important fragment of information went unnoticed. And in the May issue of *Time* magazine,

America learned that Bianchi had been pronounced a multiple personality by two of America's most eminent psychiatrists. Ken was innocent; it was "Steve" who had killed a dozen or so young women.

At this point, the prosecution decided it was time to bring in their own expert. Dr. Martin T. Orne, of the University of Pennsylvania Hospital, who was known as an authority on hypnosis. The sessions with "Steve" had been videotaped, and Orne was given the recordings. They failed, however, to answer the question that troubled him most: Was Bianchi truly hypnotized or only pretending to be?

Dr. Orne noticed that the character of "Steve" seemed to develop during the course of the sessions. "Steve" was always coarse and foul-mouthed—his favorite term for the psychiatrists was "motherfuckers"—but he seemed to slip deeper into his role as the sessions progressed. To him, that suggested an actor rather than a true alter ego.

When the professor came to interview him, Bianchi was his usual cooperative self. Under hypnotic suggestion, he quickly slipped into a trance. Orne now decided to try a decisive experiment. Susceptible hypnotic subjects can be made to hallucinate the presence of another person; therefore, Orne told Bianchi that his defense lawyer, Dean Brett, was sitting in an empty chair. Bianchi immediately did something that Orne had never seen before in a similar situation: he leapt to his feet and shook the hand of the imaginary lawyer. At that moment, Orne was certain that Bianchi was only feigning a hypnotic state. Genuinely hypnotized subjects are content to merely talk to their hallucinations; they never try to touch them.

Dr. Orne then tried another interesting experiment. In the course of conversation, he casually dropped the information that most multiple personalities have more than one alter ego. Predictably, at the next session, Bianchi produced another "alter," a frightened child named Billy. Asked if he knew "Steve," "Billy" whispered miserably: "He's a bad egg." Now Orne knew beyond all doubt that Bianchi was faking his disorder.

But it was Frank Salerno and his partner Pete Finnigan who made the discovery that finally exploded Bianchi's claim to be a multiple personality. Listening to the Allison tape, they heard "Steve" declare that his last name was Walker. Suddenly, both men recalled that they had seen the name Steve Walker somewhere in Bianchi's papers. A careful search revealed a letter to the registrar at California State University signed "Thomas Steven Walker"—in Bianchi's handwriting—which requested a diploma without the name filled in. A little sleuthing revealed that the real Steve Walker was a graduate in psychology from California State University at Northridge, and he had answered an advertisement for a job by sending some of his academic papers. Bianchi had actually placed the advertisement, and then used Walker's name—and his papers—to obtain a phony degree in psychology.

Plainly, Bianchi was shamming and should stand trial. (Dr. Allison was later to admit that he was mistaken about Bianchi; he had meanwhile become a prison psychiatrist, and professed himself shocked to discover that criminals were habitual liars.) Dr. Martin Orne and his colleague Dr. Saul Faerstein—who had also interviewed Bianchi, at the request of the prosecution—were insistent that Bianchi was a malingerer, and it was their opinion that carried the day at the sanity hearing on October 19, 1979. At that hearing, Bianchi pleaded guilty to the two Bellingham murders and to five murders in Los Angeles, sobbing and professing deep remorse. Under Washington State law, the judge then sentenced him to life imprisonment without the formality of a trial.

But there were still five more murder charges to answer in Los Angeles. When the Los Angeles County DA's office offered Bianchi a deal—plead guilty and testify against his cousin, and he would get life with the possibility of parole—he quickly accepted. In interviews with Frank Salerno and Pete Finnigan, he described all of the murders with a precision of detail that left no doubt that it was Ken, not "Steve," who had committed them.

On October 22, 1979, Angelo Buono was finally arrested and charged with the Hillside stranglings. He was placed in the county jail, where Bianchi occupied another cell. But Bianchi was already reneging on his plea-bargaining agreement, explaining that he had made it only to save his life, and that he was genuinely innocent. The reason for his change of heart was simple. The DA's office had made the incredible decision to drop the other five Los Angeles murder charges, for which Bianchi could have been sentenced to death. He now had nothing to lose by refusing to be cooperative.

As far as Frank Salerno and Detective Bob Grogan were concerned, it did not make a great deal of difference. The jewelry found in Bianchi's house linked him to several of the victims, while a wisp of fluff on the eyelid of Judy Miller was demonstrated by forensic scientists to be identical to a foamy polyester material found in

Buono's house. Strand by strand, the case against the Hillside stranglers was becoming powerful enough to virtually ensure Buono's conviction.

For Bianchi, the case was by no means over. One of the characteristics of the psychopath is that he just never gives up. In June 1980, Bianchi glimpsed an incredible chance of proving his innocence. He received a letter signed "Veronica Lynn Compton, pen name Ver Lyn," asking for his cooperation on *The Mutilated Cutter,* a play she was writing. The plot, she explained, was about a female mass murderer who injects male semen into the vaginas of her victims, thus making the police think that the killer is a male.

Bianchi was interested. He became even more interested when Veronica Compton came to visit him, and he realized that this glamorous brunette was obsessed with him. They fantasized about how nice it would be to go on a killing spree together, and Virginia suggested that they should cut off the sex organs of the victims and keep them in embalming fluid.

Soon after that they were exchanging love letters. Finally, Bianchi confided to her his brilliant scheme for getting out of jail. All she had to do was to go to Bellingham, and transform her play into reality: strangle a woman and inject semen into her vagina through a syringe. And Bianchi would then be able to point out that the Bellingham murderer was obviously still at large, and that he must therefore be innocent. But where would she get the semen? Simple, said Bianchi, he would provide it. And he did so by masturbating into the finger of a rubber glove, which he then smuggled to her in the spine of a book.

Veronica flew to Bellingham, and registered at a motel called the Shangri-la. In a nearby bar she made the acquaintance of a young woman named Kim Breed, and had several drinks with her. When she asked Breed to drive her back to her motel, her new friend agreed. At the Shangri-la, Veronica invited her into her room for a drink. Once inside, she excused herself to go to the bathroom, armed herself with a piece of cord, then tiptoed out and sneaked up behind her unsuspecting victim, who was seated on the bed. Fortunately, Kim Breed was something of an athlete. She struggled frantically, and succeeded in throwing Veronica over her head and onto the floor. Then she fled.

When she returned to the motel with a male friend, Veronica had also fled. But the police had no difficulty in tracing her through her airline reservation. She was arrested and, in due course, the "copycat slayer," as the newspapers labeled her, was sentenced to life. As soon as he learned of her failure, Bianchi lost interest in her, thereby fueling deep resentment.

The case of Angelo Buono was due to come to court in September 1981. But pretrial hearings, before Judge Ronald M. George, began long before that. The first matter on which Judge George had to make up his mind was a motion by the defense to allow bail to the accused.

FOR BIANCHI, THE CASE WAS BY NO MEANS OVER. ONE OF THE CHARACTERISTICS OF THE PSYCHOPATH IS THAT HE JUST NEVER GIVES UP.

George turned it down. The next motion was to sever the ten murder charges from the nonmurder charges such as pimping, rape, and sodomy; this would ensure that the jury should know as little as possible about Buono's background. Because it might provide grounds for an appeal, the judge decided to grant this motion.

The next development staggered everybody, including the judge. In July, Assistant District Attorney Roger Kelly proposed that all ten murder counts against Buono should be dropped. The reason, he explained, was that Bianchi's testimony was so dubious and self-contradictory that it was virtually useless. Buono should be tried at a later date on the nonmurder charges, and meanwhile be allowed free on a $50,000 bail.

Grogan and Salerno could hardly believe their ears. It meant that even if Buono was convicted on the other charges, he would serve only about five years in jail.

The judge agreed to deliver his ruling on July 21, 1981. During the week preceding that date, morale among the police was at rock bottom; no one doubted that the judge would agree to drop the charges—after all, if the DA's office was so unsure of a conviction, they must know what they were talking about.

On the day of the ruling, Buono looked cheerful and his junior counsel, Katherine Mader, was beaming with confidence. But as the judge reviewed the evidence, it became clear that their confidence was misplaced. Whether Bianchi was reliable or not, said the judge,

BUONO, WHO HAD EXPECTED TO WALK FREE FROM THE COURTROOM, HAD TO CANCEL HIS PLANS FOR A CELEBRATORY DINNER WITH HIS LAWYERS.

the evidence of various witnesses, and the Judy Miller fiber evidence, made it clear that there was a strong case against Buono. Therefore, concluded Judge George, he was denying the district attorney's motion. And if, he added, the DA showed any lack of enthusiasm in prosecuting Buono, he would refer the case to the attorney general.

Buono, who had expected to walk free from the courtroom, had to cancel his plans for a celebratory dinner with his lawyers.

At this point the DA's office decided to withdraw from the case. Thereupon, the attorney general appointed two of his deputies, Roger Boren and Michael Nash, to prosecute Buono.

The trial, which lasted from November 1981 to November 1983, was the longest murder trial in American history. The prosecution called 251 witnesses and introduced more than a thousand exhibits. But although the transcript would eventually occupy hundreds of volumes, the trial itself held few surprises. It took until June 1982 to get to Bianchi's evidence—he was the two-hundredth witness to testify—and he at first showed himself typically vague and ambiguous. But when the judge dropped a hint that he was violating his original plea-bargaining agreement, and that he would have to serve out his time in Washington's Walla Walla—a notoriously tough jail—he became altogether less vague. Bianchi spent five months on the stand, and the results were damning to his cousin.

The defense team raised many objections, and pursued a tactic of trying to discredit witnesses and evidence. On the submission that testimony obtained under hypnosis should be inadmissible, the judge ruled that Bianchi had been faking both hypnosis and multiple personality. More serious was a motion by the defense to dismiss the whole case because one of the prosecution witnesses—Judy Miller's boyfriend—had been in a psychiatric hospital. This was also overruled: it was the defense's fault, the judge said, for failing to spot the material in the files.

Finally, the defense called Veronica Compton, the "copycat slayer," to try to prove that she and Bianchi had planned to "frame" Angelo Buono. Veronica, still seething with resentment, gave her evidence with histrionic relish. But when she admitted that she had once planned to open a mortuary so she and her lover could have sex with the corpses, it was clear that the jury found it hard to treat her as a reliable witness.

In the final submissions in October 1983, Buono's defense lawyer Gerald Chaleff argued that Bianchi had committed the murders alone, and that his cousin was an innocent man. The judge had to rebuke him for implying that the whole case against his client was a conspiracy. The jury retired on October 21, 1983, and when they had spent a week in their deliberations, the defense began to feel gloomy and the prosecution correspondingly optimistic. It emerged later that one juror, who was resentful about not being chosen as foreman, had been consistently obstructive. But finally, on Halloween, the jury announced that it had found Angelo Buono guilty of the murder of Lauren Wagner. During the following week they also found him guilty of murdering Dolores Cepeda, Sonja Johnson, Kristina Weckler, Jane King, Lissa Kastin, and Cindy Hudspeth. But—possibly influenced by the fact that Bianchi had already escaped the death penalty—they decided that Buono should not receive a death sentence. On January 4, 1984, the judge ordered that, since he had done everything in his power to sabotage the case against his cousin, Bianchi should be returned to serve his sentence in Washington. He then sentenced Buono to life imprisonment without possibility of parole, regretting that he could not sentence him to death. In his final remarks he told the defendants: "I am sure, Mr. Buono and Mr. Bianchi, that you will both probably only get your thrills reliving over and over again the torturing and murdering of your victims, being incapable, as I believe you to be, of feeling any remorse."

Asked later whether such acts as Buono and Bianchi had committed did not prove them insane, he commented: "Why should we call someone insane simply because he or she chooses not to conform to our standards of civilized behavior?"

An interesting question remains: If the Behavioral Science Unit had been called in at the time of the rampage of Hillside murders in 1977, would there have been a chance of pinpointing the killers?

The answer is probably yes. The worldwide publicity brought the LAPD a communication from a private detective in Berlin. The name of this detective has not been recorded because Detective Grogan was unable to pronounce it, and instead referred to him as "Dr. Schickelgruber." One day, he turned up, having flown to Los Angeles from Germany. He spoke no English, so a German-speaking detective was summoned. "Dr. Schickelgruber" than wrote (in German) on a blackboard:

> *Two Italians*
> *(Brothers)*
> *Aged about thirty-five.*

The doctor was politely thanked, and was driven back to the airport. No one, says Darcy O'Brien in his book *Two of a Kind,* took him seriously.

But clearly, someone should have taken him seriously and asked his reasons.

More important, if a detective from Berlin could have recognized that the Stranglers were Italian and closely related, then presumably so could the Behavioral Science Unit. And if they could have got that far, a number of simple steps could have led them to the killers.

Grogan had recognized from fairly early in the Thanksgiving killing rampage that two men were involved. He reasoned this from the fact that when Kristina Weckler's body was found on November 20, 1977, in an area between Glendale and Eagle Rock, there were no visible drag marks or disturbances in the foliage, which meant that the body must have been carried by at least two men. The same point became even clearer when the two schoolgirls were found.

On his way to Kristina Weckler's body, Grogan had already noted that the killers must be familiar with the area. The question: "Why Kristina Weckler?"—a quiet art student living alone in an apartment building—could have led to the conclusion that the killer already knew the building, and a search of former tenants would have revealed Bianchi's name. If they had been aware that their killers could be Italian, Bianchi and his cousin would have immediately become major suspects.

Unfortunately, no one thought of calling in the Behavioral Science Unit (it would have been technically possible because the two schoolgirls were kidnapped, making it a crime eligible for an FBI investigation), so these speculations must remain wishful thinking.

Angelo Buono was found dead of a heart attack in his cell at Calipatria State Prison in California on September 21, 2002; he was sixty-seven. Bianchi is serving his 118-year sentence at the Walla Walla State Penitentiary in Washington State. Bianchi had been hoping to serve his time in California, rather than in the notoriously harsh Walla Walla, but his lack of cooperation ruined his chances. Subsequently, Bianchi filed a claim against Whatcomb County seeking hundreds of thousands of dollars for lost wages and emotional distress. He argues that police and prosecutors withheld crucial evidence, leading him to his original guilty plea in 1979. Now minus his thick, curly hair, he declared in an interview in February 2004 that he was withdrawing his guilty plea and insisting on his innocence.

IF A DETECTIVE FROM BERLIN COULD HAVE RECOGNIZED THAT THE STRANGLERS WERE ITALIAN AND CLOSELY RELATED, THEN PRESUMABLY SO COULD THE BEHAVIORAL SCIENCE UNIT.

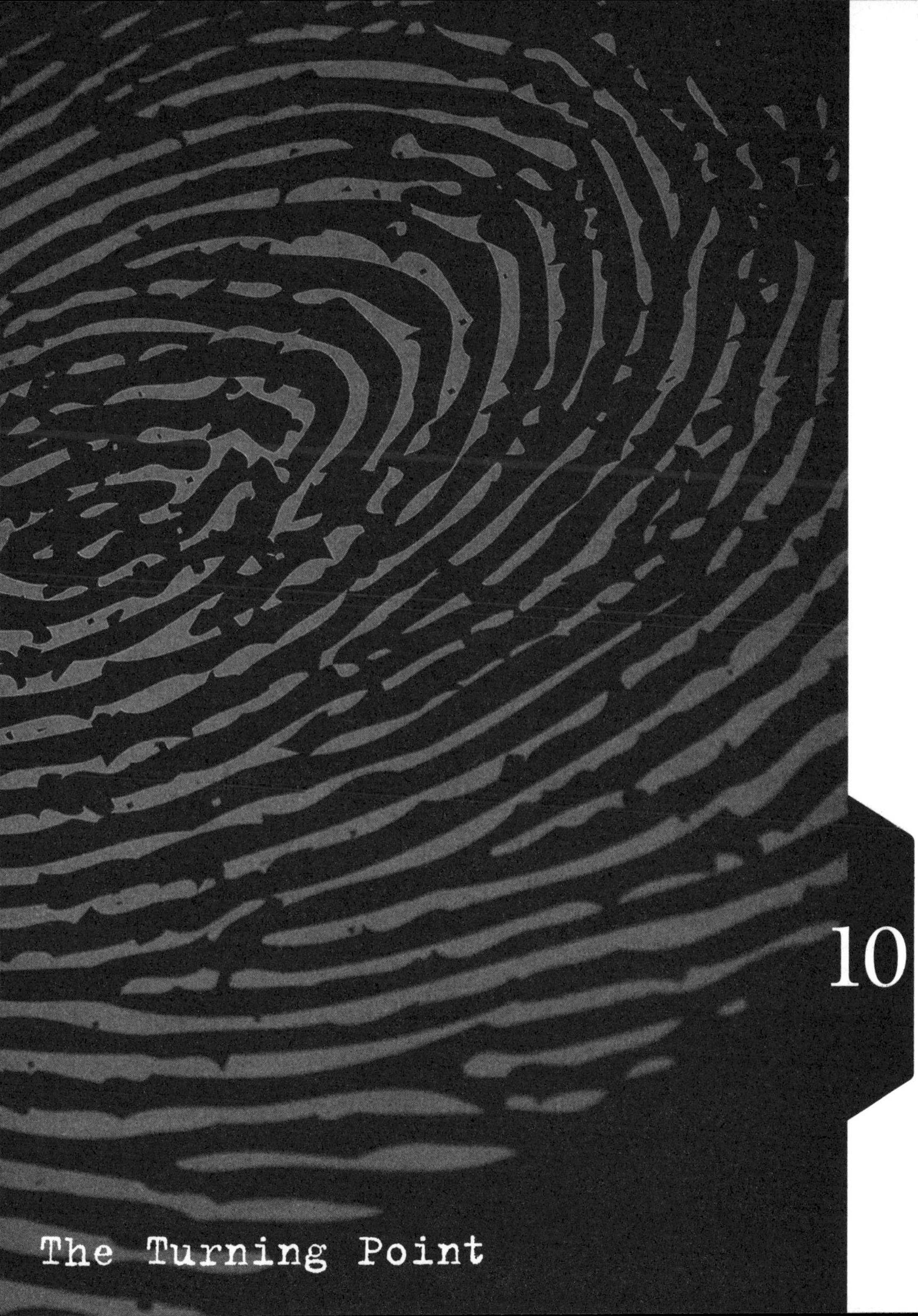

10

The Turning Point

10 The Turning Point

To law enforcement officials it must have seemed that serial murder arrived in the United States as suddenly and devastatingly as the Black Death in Europe in the fourteenth century—but was rather worse, for while the Black Death lasted for three years, from 1347 until 1350, there is still no sign of an end to this "plague of murder."

That analogy, however, makes things sound worse than they are. The Black Death wiped out one-third of the population of Europe, and continued to return down the centuries, killing millions. The "plague of murder" has caused a fractional increase in the crime rate, but already the fight against it is proving more successful than anyone could have foreseen in the mid-1970s.

For many years, not even the Behavioral Science Unit was aware of its success. In 1978, William Webster, head of the FBI, had given his official approval to allowing instructors such as Ressler and Hazelwood to offer police forces a psychological profiling service. But the FBI is a bureaucracy, and even by 1980, no one was sure if was justifying its cost. A questionnaire was sent out to all the officials and detectives who had used the service to solicit their opinion. If the answer had been negative, the BSU might have faded away. In fact, the replies demonstrated that, although many officials in the Bureau were dubious about this new departure, police themselves were full of enthusiasm. A 1981 report concluded: "The evaluation reveals that the program is actually more successful than any of us really realized. The Behavioral Science Unit is to be commended for their outstanding job."

An earlier chapter has described how in 1974, the unit was able to identify David Meirhofer as the kidnapper of Susan Jaeger, and how, when the police chief in Platte City, Kansas, telephoned the unit to describe the circumstances of the murder of Julie Wittmeyer, the profiler was able to describe the killer so accurately that the police chief cried: "Sure as shootin', it's him!"

One of Roy Hazelwood's first profiles in 1978 demonstrated the same impressive accuracy. In Saint Joseph, Missouri, a babysitter left four-year-old Eric Christgen alone in a playground while she ran to the store. When she returned, the child was missing. His sexually abused body was later found at the foot of cliffs above the river. When the local police had run out of leads, they decided to approach Quantico.

Working with crime-scene photographs and police reports, Hazelwood's own experience of criminal pedophiles led him to surmise that the killer was a white male of around fifty. This was based on witnesses to the abduction. And a middle-aged pedophile who sodomizes and strangles a child almost certainly has a police record. From the roughness of the steep hillside where the man had taken the boy, Hazelwood reasoned that the killer was powerfully built.

He judged that the man was a laborer, since he would be unlikely to have the ability or skill to hold down a more demanding job. He added that the man was a loner who had probably been drinking all day, and that this was a crime of sudden impulse.

As a final comment Hazelwood said that the criminal pedophile, like the sexual sadist, is the only sexual offender who experiences no remorse or guilt. They enjoy committing their crimes, and they fantasize about them later.

A few months after the murder, Michael Reynolds, an unemployed twenty-five-year-old cook, broke down under interrogation and confessed to killing the child. It looked as if Hazelwood had been wide of the mark. But, in 1983, a pedophile named Charles Hatcher was arrested for another crime, and confessed to the murder of Eric Christgen, and to sixteen other murders over the years. He had been fifty at the time he killed Eric. Hatcher was sentenced to life, and Reynolds was released. (False confessions, based on deep guilt feelings, are one of the problems most policemen have to contend with at some time.) Hatcher hanged himself in his cell a year later.

The prosecutor, Michael Insco, who had been in charge of the Reynolds case, later admitted to Hazelwood that he had not read the profile, since at the time the work of the Behavioral Science Unit was little known. He had come across it after Hatcher's conviction and realized that it matched on twenty-one points. If its accuracy had been recognized in 1978, Hatcher would have been prevented from killing again.

In 1979, the year Reynolds was falsely convicted, the Behavioral Science Unit had one of its most striking early successes.

Francine Elveson, twenty-six, a tiny four-foot-eleven-inches Plain Jane who suffered from a slight curvature of the spine, was found naked, badly beaten about the head and face, and with her body mutilated,

THE "PLAGUE OF MURDER" HAS CAUSED A FRACTIONAL INCREASE IN THE CRIME RATE, BUT ALREADY THE FIGHT AGAINST IT IS PROVING MORE SUCCESSFUL THAN ANYONE COULD HAVE FORESEEN IN THE MID-1970S.

spread-eagled on the roof of the Pelham Parkway Houses apartment building in the Bronx where she lived with her parents. So severe was the physical assault that her jaw and nose were both broken, and the teeth in her head pounded loose. Her nylon stockings were loosely tied round her wrists and ankles, even though no restraint had been needed: she was unconscious, or already dead, when that was done. Her underwear had been pulled over her head, hiding her battered features from view. There were tooth marks visible on her thighs and knees.

Using a pen taken from her handbag, her killer had scrawled a challenge to the police on one thigh: "You can't stop me," and on her stomach, "Fuck you." Both the pen and the dead teacher's umbrella were found thrust into her vagina, and her comb (also taken from the handbag) wedged in her pubic hair. Her pierced earrings had been removed from the lobes, and placed on either side of her head. Both breasts were mutilated, each nipple cut off and placed back on the chest.

There were no deep knife wounds: this suggested that the killer had used a small weapon—a penknife, probably—and taken it with him. A pendant that the victim habitually wore, manufactured in the shape of a Jewish good luck sign (*chai*), was missing—presumably taken by her assailant. The dead woman's limbs were positioned to simulate the shape of the pendant, as if to form a replica.

Francine Elveson was attacked within minutes of leaving her parents' apartment shortly after 6:30 a.m. on October 12, 1979. Her body was found on the roof some eight hours later, after she failed to arrive at the school for disabled children where she taught. The police report showed that the attack took place as she made her way downstairs. She was battered unconscious and carried up to the roof for the macabre ritual that followed. Medical evidence revealed that she had not been raped. The cause of death was strangulation; she had in fact been twice strangled, manually first and then with the strap of her handbag. Lack of forensic evidence—fragments of skin tissue, fibers, and the like—under her fingernails indicated that she had made no attempt to fight off her assailant. Traces of semen were found on her body, but DNA fingerprinting would not be discovered for another five years, so there were no apparent clues to the identity of her murderer.

Because of its bizarre features the Elveson case attracted a great deal of publicity, but despite an intensive police investigation that included questioning some two thousand people, and checking on known sex offenders and patients undergoing treatment in mental hospitals, the search for Francine Elveson's killer bogged down. Finally, in November 1979, local authorities called in the FBI—even though the police investigators thought it was probably a waste of time. One experienced murder squad detective was quoted as saying: "Frankly I didn't see where the FBI could tell us anything, but I figured there was no harm in trying."

Crime-scene photographs, together with the police report and autopsy findings, were duly forwarded to the Behavioral Science Unit for analysis.

Enter Special Agent John Douglas to profile the type of person responsible—from his desk at Quantico, some three hundred miles away. He knew from the police report that Francine Elveson, who was self-conscious about her size and physical deformity, had no boyfriends. That ruled out a lovers' quarrel. Moreover, it was spontaneous choice that led her to leave for work that morning via the stairs, rather than use the elevator. Those two factors meant that it was a chance encounter between victim and murderer—yet an encounter with someone who promptly spent a long time on the roof mauling his victim in broad daylight. To John Douglas that meant he was no stranger to the building; he knew its routine well enough to feel confident that he would not be disturbed during the ritual mutilation murder that ensued.

Again, the fact that he was in the building at that hour suggested someone who might live, or perhaps work there. And Elveson—this shy, almost reclusive young woman who shunned men because of her appearance—had neither screamed nor made any apparent attempt to ward off a man who suddenly lashed out as they passed on the stairs. It had to mean that either he was someone she knew, if only by sight, or who was wearing an identifiable uniform—postman, say, or janitor—whom she believed she had no reason to fear.

The offender left mixed crime scene characteristics, as many sex killers do. He used restraints (organized), yet left the body in full view (disorganized). He depersonalized his victim (disorganized), yet having mutilated her body took the knife with him (organized). On balance, however, John Douglas classified him as a "disorganized" offender, acting out a fantasy ritual that had probably been inspired earlier by a bondage article and/or sketches in some pornographic magazine. The FBI agent profiled him as white (Francine Elveson was white), male, of roughly her age (say between twenty-five and thirty-five), and of average appearance, in other words, who would not seem in any way out of character in the apartment building environment.

Statistics pointed to a school "dropout" type, possibly now unemployed. Because of the time at which it happened, the crime seemed unlikely to be either drink- or drug-related. Francine Elveson's killer was a man who found it difficult to behave naturally with women, and was almost certainly sexually inadequate. (The ritual mutilation provided the gratification he craved—a fact borne out by forensic evidence, which revealed traces of semen on the body.) He was the type of sex offender who would keep a pornography collection, while his sadistic behavior pointed to one with mental problems.

He left the body in view because he wanted it to shock and offend. That decision was part and parcel of his implied challenge to the police, inked on the victim's thigh—"You can't stop me." It was a challenge that John Douglas believed meant he was liable to kill again, should opportunity arise. His profile stressed the importance of the attacker's prior knowledge of the apartment building where the victim lived—and her apparent lack of alarm as they met on the stairs.

Once the answer to these two connected factors was found, the rest of the puzzle would slot into place.

Armed with the profile, the investigating police re-examined their list of suspects. One man in particular seemed to fit the description like a glove. His name was Carmine Calabro. He was thirty-two years old, an unmarried, out-of-work actor, and an only child with a history of mental illness. He had no girlfriends. He did not live in the apartment building where Francine was found murdered, but his father—whom he often visited—lived there and was a near neighbor of the Elvesons.

> CALABRO PROVED TO BE A HIGH-SCHOOL DROPOUT, WHO SHARED A COLLECTION OF PORNOGRAPHY—MOSTLY S&M—WITH HIS FATHER.

The problem was that it seemed impossible for Carmine Calabro to be the killer. The police had interviewed his father (as they had every other resident in the complex) before calling on the FBI for help. The father told them that his son—who lived elsewhere, and alone—was an in-patient undergoing treatment at a local psychiatric hospital, which appeared to rule him out as a possible suspect. Now enquiries were rechecked, and the police discovered that—because security was lax—patients at the hospital concerned were able to absent themselves almost at will. When they learned that Carmine Calabro was absent without permission on the evening before Francine Elveson was murdered, he was arrested—thirteen months after the body had been found.

Calabro proved to be a high-school dropout, who shared a collection of pornography—mostly S&M—with his father. He pleaded not guilty to the murder at his trial; however, the evidence given by three forensic (dental) experts—whose independent tests showed that impressions from Calabro's teeth matched the bite marks on the dead teacher's thigh—proved conclusive, and he was imprisoned for twenty-five years to life.

It had been a virtuoso performance by Special Agent John Douglas, whose startling accuracy of profiling matched that of James Brussel in the case of the Mad Bomber twenty-two years earlier. Aptly, one of the warmest tributes came from the head of the police task force assigned to the Elveson murder investigation, Lieutenant Joseph D'Amico. "They had [Carmine Calabro] so right," he said, "that I asked the FBI why they hadn't given us his phone number too."

Douglas applied the same technique to a case involving the kidnapping and murder of Betty Shade in Logan, Pennsylvania, in June 1979. Her mutilated body was found on a garbage dump, and there was evidence that she had been raped after death. The injuries to her face convinced Douglas again that the killer knew the victim well, and had killed her in a fury of resentment; but the mutilations had been performed after she had died, suggesting that the killer was too frightened to inflict them while she was alive. This indicated a young and nervous killer. Yet, Betty had been driven from her babysitting job to the dump in a car, requiring a degree of organization. The necrophilic sex also suggested a killer who was taking his time. To Douglas, all this pointed unmistakably to two killers, and again, his "profile" pointed the police in the right direction. The young woman lived with her boyfriend, and it seemed unlikely that he would rape her after death, which is why he had originally been eliminated from the inquiry. But the boyfriend had an elder brother who owned a car. Both men were eventually convicted of the murder. The younger man had killed and mutilated her; the brother had raped her dead body.

Agent Howard Teten, who taught one of the original FBI courses in applied criminology at the Academy, also seemed to have a natural talent for "profiling" random killers, which he had been applying since the early 1970s. On one occasion, a California policeman had contacted him about a case in which a frenzied killer had stabbed a young woman to death. The frenzy suggested to Teten that the murderer was an inexperienced youth, and that this was probably his first crime, committed in a violently emotional state. And, as in the later case of the Bronx schoolteacher, Teten thought the evidence pointed to someone who lived close to the scene of the crime. He advised the policeman to look for a teenager with acne, a loner who would probably be feeling tremendous guilt and would be ready to confess. If they ran across such a person, the best approach would be just to look at him and say, "You know why I'm here." In fact, the teenager who answered the door said, "You got me" even before the policeman had time to speak.

The FBI's new insight into the mind of the killer and rapist began to pay dividends almost immediately. In 1979, a woman reported being raped in an East Coast city; the police realized that the modus operandi of the rapist was identical to that of seven other cases in the past two years. They approached the FBI unit with details of all the cases. The deliberation of the rapes seemed to indicate that the attacker was not a teenager or a man in his early twenties, but a man in his late twenties or early thirties. Other details indicated that he was divorced or separated from his wife, that he was a laborer whose education had not progressed beyond high school, that he had a poor self-image, and that he was probably a Peeping Tom. In all probability, the police had probably already interviewed him, since they had been questioning men wandering the streets in the early hours of the morning. This "profile" led the police to shortlist forty suspects living in the neighborhood, and then gradually, using the profile, to narrow this list down to one. This man was arrested and found guilty of the rapes.

It soon became clear that psychological profiling could also help in the interrogation of suspects. The agency began a program of instructing local policemen in interrogation techniques. Their value was soon demonstrated in a murder case of 1980.

On February 17, the body of a woman was found in a dump area behind Daytona Beach Airport in Florida; she had been stabbed repeatedly, and the body was in an advanced state of decomposition, which indicated that she had been dead for a matter of weeks. She was fully dressed and her panties and bra were apparently undisturbed; she had been partially covered with branches and laid out neatly and ritualistically on her back, with her arms at her sides. The FBI team would immediately have said that this indicated a killer in his late twenties or early thirties.

From missing person reports, Detective Sergeant Paul Crowe identified her as Mary Carol Maher, a twenty-year-old swimming star who had vanished at the end of January, more than two weeks previously. She had been in the habit of hitching lifts.

Towards the end of March, a local prostitute complained of being attacked by a customer who had picked her up in a red car. She had been high on drugs, so could not recollect the details of what caused the disagreement. Whatever it was, the man had pulled a knife and attacked her—one cut on her thigh required twenty-seven stitches. She described her assailant as a heavily built man with glasses and a moustache, and the car as a red Gremlin with dark windows. She thought that he had been a previous customer, and that he might live in or near the Derbyshire Apartments.

Near these apartments an investigating officer found a red Gremlin with dark windows; a check with the Department of Motor Vehicles revealed that it was registered to a man named Gerald Stano. And the manager of the Derbyshire Apartments said that he used to have a tenant named Gerald Stano, who drove a red Gremlin with dark windows. A check revealed that Stano had a long record of arrests for attacking prostitutes, although no convictions; he apparently made a habit of picking up hitchhiking hookers.

A photograph of Stano was procured, and shown to the prostitute, who identified him as her attacker.

It was at this point that Detective Crowe heard about the case and reflected that Mary Carol Maher had also been in the habit of hitching lifts—she had been an athletic young woman who was usually able to take care of herself. Crowe's observations at the crime scene told him that Mary's killer had been a compulsively neat man; he was now curious to see Stano.

The suspect was located at an address in nearby Ormond Beach, and brought in to police headquarters for questioning. Crowe stood and watched as a colleague, whom he had primed with certain questions, interrogated Stano. But his first encounter with Stano answered the question about compulsive neatness; Stano looked at him and told him that his moustache needed a little trimming on the right side.

What Crowe wanted to study was Stano's body language, which was as revealing as a lie detector. And Stano was an easy subject to read. When telling the truth, he would pull his chair up to the desk or lean forward, rearranging the objects on the desktop while talking. When lying, he would push back his chair and cross his legs, placing his left ankle on his right knee.

It was not difficult to get Stano to admit to the attack on the prostitute—he knew that she could identify him. Then Crowe took over, and explained that he was interested in the disappearance of Mary Carol Maher. He showed Stano the young woman's photograph, and Stano immediately admitted to having given her a lift. "She was with another girl," he said, pushing back his chair and placing his left ankle on his right knee. After more conversation—this time about the fact that Stano was an orphan—Crowe again asked what had happened with Mary Carol Maher. Pushing his chair back and crossing his legs, Stano declared that he had driven her to a nightclub called Fannie Farkel's—Crowe knew that this was one of Mary's favorite haunts, a place frequented by the young set—but that she had not wanted to go in. Crowe knew that the truth was probably the opposite; Stano had not wanted to mix with a younger crowd (he was twenty-eight). He asked Stano if he had tried to "get inside her pants." Stano pulled the chair up to the desk and growled, "Yeah."

"But she didn't want to?"

"No!"

Crowe recalled being told by Mary's mother that her daughter had, on one occasion, "beaten the hell" out of two men who had tried to "get fresh."

"She could hit pretty hard, couldn't she?"

"You're goddam right she could," said Stano angrily.

"So you hit her?"

Stano pushed back his chair and crossed his legs. "No, I let her out. I haven't seen the bitch since."

Crowe now had the advantage. As he pressed Stano about the young woman's resistance, it visibly revived the anger he had felt at the time. And when Crowe asked: "You got pretty mad, didn't you?" Stano snorted: "You're damn right I did. I got so goddam mad I stabbed her just as hard as I could." Then he immediately pushed back his chair, crossed his legs, and withdrew his statement. But when Crowe pressed him to tell how he stabbed her, he pulled his chair forward again and described stabbing her backhanded in the chest, then, as she tried to scramble out of the door, slashing her thigh and stabbing her twice in the back—Crowe had already noted these injuries when he first examined the body. After this admission, Stano drove with Crowe to the dump behind the airport, and pointed out where he had hidden the body.

It was after Stano had signed a confession to killing Mary Carol Maher that one of Crowe's fellow detectives showed him a photograph of a missing black prostitute, Toni Van Haddocks, and asked: "See if he knows anything about her." When Crowe placed the photograph in front of Stano, Stano immediately sat back in his chair and placed his left ankle on his right knee. He denied knowing the woman. Two weeks later, on April 15, 1980, a resident of Holly Hill, near Daytona Beach, found a skull in his back garden. Local policemen discovered the scene of the murder in a nearby wooded area—bones scattered around by animals. When Crowe went to visit the scene, he immediately noted that four low branches had been torn off pine trees surrounding the clearing, and recognized Stano's method.

Back at headquarters, he again showed Stano the photograph, asking: "How often do you pick up black girls?" Stano pushed back his chair. "I hate them bastards." "But you picked her up." Stano stared at the photograph, his legs still crossed. "That's the only one I ever picked up." It was at this point that Crowe realized that he was talking to a multiple killer.

Stano persisted in denying that he had killed Toni Van Haddocks. Crowe stood up to leave the room. "I know you did because you left your signature there." Stano stared with amazement, and then called Crowe back: "Hey, wait. Did I really leave my name there?" Realizing that he had virtually admitted to killing her, he went on to confess to the crime. But these two murders, he insisted, were the only ones he had ever committed.

Crowe did not believe him. Now he knew that Stano was a ritualistic killer, and that ritualistic killers often kill many times. There had been no other recent disappearances in Daytona Beach, so Crowe studied the missing persons files and records of past murders. He found many. In January 1976, the body of Nancy Heard, a hotel maid, had been discovered in Tomoka State Park, near Ormond Beach, where Stano lived. Reports said the death scene looked "arranged." She had been last seen alive hitchhiking. Ramona Neal, an eighteen-year-old from Georgia, had been found in the same park in May 1976, her body concealed by branches. In Bradford County, a hundred miles away, an unknown young woman was found concealed by tree branches, while in Titusville, to the south, another young woman had been found under branches—a young woman who had last been seen hitchhiking on Atlantic Avenue in Daytona Beach. When Stano had moved to Florida in 1973—from New Jersey—he had lived in Stuart. A check with the Stuart police revealed that there had been several unsolved murders of young women there during the period of Stano's residence.

WHAT CROWE WANTED TO STUDY WAS STANO'S BODY LANGUAGE, WHICH WAS AS REVEALING AS A LIE DETECTOR.

Stano's adoptive parents told Crowe that they had fostered Gerald even after a New York child psychiatrist had labeled him "unadoptable." He had been taken away from his natural mother as a result of "horrible neglect." In all probability, Stano had never received even that minimum of affection in the first days of his life to form any kind of human bond. He had never shown any affection, and he had been compulsively dishonest from the beginning, stealing, cheating, and lying. He preferred associating with younger children—a sign of low self-esteem—and preferred women who were deformed or crippled—he had once impregnated a retarded young woman. He had married a compulsive overeater, but the marriage quickly broke down.

Crowe traced Stano's wife, who was living with her parents in a house of spectacular untidiness—Crowe admitted that it reminded him of the home of the TV character Archie Bunker, who spends most of his time in his undershirt. There Stano's ex-wife answered questions as she rested her huge breasts on the kitchen table. Stano's sexual demands had been normal, as was only to be expected "with his itty-bitty penis." But he had a peculiar habit of going out late at night, and returning, exhausted, in the early hours of the morning.

The lonely, frigid countryside outside Anchorage, Alaska, proved to be the perfect setting for Robert Hansen's deadly games. If a prostitute did not satisfy him, he would take her to a remote spot, release her, and then hunt her down as if she were a game animal. (Shawn Clark/Shutterstock)

What had now emerged about Stano convinced Crowe of the need for further psychological profiling, and he called in an Ormond Beach psychologist, Dr. Ann MacMillan, who had impressed police with her profile of mass killer Carl Gregory. The result of tests on Stano revealed a psychological profile almost identical with those of Charles Manson and David Berkowitz; she believed that it meant that his crimes were predictable, and that he belonged to a group that might be labeled "born killers."

Over many months, Crowe's interrogation of Stano continued. At some point, Stano realized that Crowe was reading his physical signals, and changed them. But his compulsive nature made it inevitable that he developed new ones, and Crowe soon learned to read these, too.

Eventually, Stano confessed to killing thirty-four women; then, typically, he declared that this had been a stratagem to make him appear insane. His memory of his crimes was remarkably detailed—for example, he was able to describe a prostitute whom he had picked up in Daytona Beach as wearing a brown leather jacket, brown shoes, and a shirt with an inscription: "Do it in the dirt." When he led them to the woman's skeleton—covered with branches—the police found that it was wearing precisely these clothes. With plea-bargaining, Stano finally agreed to admit to six murders. On September 2, 1981, he was sentenced to three consecutive terms of twenty-five years—seventy-five years in all—and was taken to the Florida state prison. But a later trial resulted in a death sentence.

One of the most widely publicized cases of these early years of profiling began in Anchorage, Alaska, with the disappearance of a number of "exotic" dancers. In Anchorage, the temperature is so low that it is impractical for prostitutes to walk the streets. The majority of them solve the problem by working in topless bars and making appointments with clients for after hours. Few people notice when such a girl vanishes, although bar owners were often puzzled when their dancers failed to show up to collect their pay.

When, in 1980, building workers on Eklutna Road discovered a shallow grave, which had been partly excavated by bears, containing the half-eaten body of a woman, it seemed likely that she was one of the missing women. Because the advanced state of decay made it impossible to identify the body, she became known in the records as "Eklutna Annie."

Two years later, on September 12, 1982, hunters found another shallow grave on the bank of the Knik River, not far from Anchorage; this time it was possible to identify the body in it as twenty-three-year-old Sherry Morrow, a dancer who had vanished the previous November. She had been shot three times, and shell casings near the grave indicated that the weapon had been a high-velocity hunting rifle that fires slugs—a .223 Ruger Mini-14. Here, once again, the investigation reached a dead end. It was impossible to interview every owner of such a rifle. An odd feature of the case was that the clothes found in the grave bore no bullet holes, indicating that the woman had been naked when she was killed.

A year later, on September 2, 1983, another grave was found on the bank of the Knik River; the woman in it had also been shot with a .223 Ruger Mini-14. The victim was identified as Paula Goulding, an out-of-work secretary who had found herself a job as an exotic dancer in a topless bar. She had started work on April 17, 1983, and had failed to return eight days later, leaving her paycheck uncollected. The bar owner commented that he had been reluctant to hire her because she had obviously been a "nice girl," who had only resorted to dancing because she was desperate for money. Again, there were no clues to who might have killed her.

Investigators checking the police files made a discovery that looked like a possible lead. On the previous June 13, a scared and frantic seventeen-year-old prostitute had rushed into the motel where she was staying, a handcuff dangling from her wrist, and told her pimp that a client had tried to kill her. A medical examination at police headquarters revealed that she had been tortured. She told of being picked up by a red-haired, pockmarked little man with a bad stutter, who had offered her $200 for oral sex. She had accompanied him back to his home in the well-to-do Muldoon area, and down to the basement. There he had told her to take off her clothes, then snapped a handcuff on her, and shackled her to a support pillar. The tortures that followed during the next hour or so included biting her nipples and thrusting the handle of a hammer into her vagina. Finally, he allowed her to dress. He told her that he owned a private plane, and was going to take her to a cabin in the wilderness. The young woman guessed that he intended to kill her—she knew what he looked like and where he lived. So as the car stopped beside a plane, and the man began removing things from the trunk, she made a run for it, and succeeded in flagging down a passing truck.

Her description of the "John" convinced the police that it was a respectable citizen: Robert Hansen, a married man and the owner of a flourishing bakery business, who had been in Anchorage for seventeen years. Driven out to the Muldoon district, the young woman identified the house where she had been tortured; it was Hansen's. She also identified the Piper Super Cub airplane that belonged to him. The police learned that Hansen was at present alone in the house—his family was on a trip to Europe.

When Hansen was told about the charge, he exploded indignantly. He had spent the whole evening dining with two business acquaintances, and they would verify his alibi. In fact, the two men did this. The prostitute, Hansen said, was simply trying to "shake him down." Since it was her word against that of three of Anchorage's most respectable businessmen, it looked as if the case would have to be dropped.

After the discovery of Paula Goulding's body three months later, however, the investigating team led by Sergeant Glenn Flothe decided that the case was worth pursuing. If Hansen had tortured a prostitute, then decided to take her out to the wilderness, he could well be the killer they were seeking.

The investigators contacted the Behavioral Science Unit in Quantico. What they wanted was not a profile of the killer—they already had their suspect—but to know whether Robert Hansen was a feasible suspect.

Flothe spoke to Roy Hazelwood, who told them not to tell him anything about their suspect, but to begin by giving him the details of the crimes, and the story of the prostitute who had been tortured. When they had finished, Hazelwood gave them a word picture of the kind of person they could be looking for—some local businessman who loved hunting, who was psychologically insecure, and possibly had a stutter.

The Alaska CID was impressed. Hazelwood's account was full of hits, including the stutter. And at that point they told Hazelwood about Robert Hansen—that he was a well-known big-game hunter who had achieved celebrity by bagging a Dall sheep with a crossbow in the Kuskokwim Mountains. Douglas's answer was that Hansen was indeed a feasible suspect. A big-game hunter might well decide to hunt women. And he was a trophy collector; it would be likely that he had kept items belonging to his victims. If the police could obtain a search warrant, they might well find their evidence.

What was also clear was that if Hansen knew he was a suspect, he would destroy the evidence; it was therefore necessary to work quickly and secretly. The first step was to try to break his alibi. No doubt his friends had been willing to provide a false alibi because it would cost them nothing. If they were convinced that perjury could cost them two years in prison, they might feel differently. The police approached the public prosecutor and asked him to authorize a grand jury to investigate the charges of torture against the prostitute.

HE GAVE THE WOMAN A START, AND THEN WOULD STALK HER AS IF HUNTING A GAME ANIMAL.

The businessmen were then approached, and told that they would be called to repeat their stories on oath. It worked; both men admitted that they had provided Hansen with an alibi merely to help him out of a difficult situation. They agreed to testify to that effect.

Next, the police arrested Hansen on a charge of rape and kidnapping. A search warrant authorized the police to enter his home. There they found the Ruger Mini-14 rifle, which a ballistics expert identified as the one that had fired the shells found near the graves. Under the floor in the attic the searchers found more rifles, and items of cheap jewelry and adornment, including a Timex watch. Most important of all, they found an aviation map with twenty asterisks marking various spots. Two of these marked the places where the two bodies had so far been found. Another indicated the place where the unidentified corpse of a woman had been found on the south side of the Kenai Peninsula in August 1980, a crime that had not been linked with the Anchorage killings.

The investigators discovered that her name was Joanna Messina, and that she had last been seen alive with a redheaded, pockmarked man who stuttered.

At first Hansen denied all knowledge of the killings, but faced with the evidence against him, he finally decided to confess. The twenty asterisks, he admitted, marked graves of prostitutes. But he had not killed all the women he had taken out to the wilderness. What he wanted was oral sex. If the woman satisfied him, he took her back home. If not, he pointed a gun at her, ordered her to strip naked, and then run. He gave the woman a start, and then would stalk her as if hunting a game animal. Sometimes the woman would think she had escaped, and Hansen would allow her to think so—until he once again flushed her out and made her run. Finally, when she was too exhausted to run another step, he killed her and buried the body. Killing, he said, was an anticlimax, "the excitement was in the stalking."

In court on February 28, 1984, the prosecutor told the judge (a jury was unnecessary since Hansen had pleaded guilty): "Before you sits a monster, an extreme aberration of a human being. A man who has walked among us for seventeen years, selling us doughbuts [*sic*], Danish buns, coffee, all with a pleasant smile on his face. That smile concealed crimes that would numb the mind." Judge Ralph Moody then imposed sentences totaling 461 years.

For the investigating detectives, the most interesting part of Hansen's confession was the explanation of why and how he had become a serial killer. Born in a small rural community—Pocahontas, Iowa—he had been an ugly and unpopular child. His schoolfellows found his combination of a stutter and running acne sores repellent. "Because I looked and talked like a freak, every time I looked at a girl she would turn away." He had married, but his wife had left him—he felt that it was because he was ugly. He married again, moved to Alaska, and started a successful bakery business—his father's trade. But marriage could not satisfy his raging sexual obsession, his desire to have a docile slave performing oral sex. Since Anchorage had so many topless bars and strip joints, it was a temptation to satisfy his voyeurism in them; then, sexually excited, he needed to pick up a prostitute. What he craved was fellatio, and many of them were unwilling. Hansen would drive out into the woods, and then announce what he wanted; if they refused, he produced a gun.

Because he was by nature frugal, he preferred not to pay them. In fact, it emerged in his confession that he was a lifelong thief, and that this was a result of his miserliness. "I hate to spend money . . . I damn near ejaculate in my pants if I could walk into a store and take something. . . . I stole more stuff in this damn town than Carter got little green pills." Yet his next sentence reveals that it was more than simply miserliness that made him steal. "Giving stuff away, you know, walk out in the parking lot and walk to somebody's car, and throw it in the damn car. But I was taking it . . . I was smarter than people in the damn store. It would give me—uh—the same satisfaction—I don't know if you want to call it that—but I got a lot of the same feeling as I did with a prostitute." The link between stealing and oral sex was "the forbidden." This seems to explain why many serial killers—Ted Bundy is an example—begin as habitual thieves.

The murders had started, Hansen said, with Joanna Messina, a woman he had met in the town of Seward. She was living in a tent in the woods with her dog, waiting for a job in a cannery. Hansen had struck up a conversation with her and taken her out to dinner. Afterwards, they went back to her tent, near a gravel pit, where Hansen hoped she would be prepared to let him stay the night. When they were in bed, she told him she needed money. His natural cheapness affronted, he called her a whore and shot her with a .22 pistol; he then shot her dog, destroyed the camp, and dumped her body into the gravel pit.

According to Hansen, he was violently sick after the murder. Not long afterwards, he picked up a prostitute and asked her if she would fellate him. She agreed, and they drove out along the Eklutna Road. Then, according to Hansen, she became nervous and ran away; when he gave chase, she drew a knife. He took it from her and stabbed her to death. That was how the unidentified corpse known as Eklutna Annie came to lie in a shallow grave, to be dug up by a hungry bear.

> "BECAUSE I LOOKED AND TALKED LIKE A FREAK, EVERY TIME I LOOKED AT A GIRL SHE WOULD TURN AWAY."

With this victim Hansen did not feel nauseated. In fact, he said, when he looked back on the murder, he experienced an odd pleasure. He then began to fantasize about how enjoyable it would be to hunt down a woman as if she were an animal. Like so many other serial killers, Hansen had discovered that murder is addictive.

Over the next three years he drove about sixty prostitutes out into the wilderness and demanded oral sex. If the woman complied satisfactorily, he drove her back to Anchorage. If not, he forced her to strip at gunpoint, then to flee into the woods. When the hunt was over and the woman lay dead, he buried the body, and made a mark on a map—he even tried to guide officers back to some of the murder sites, but had usually forgotten exactly where they were. Once, when they were hovering over Grouse Lake in a helicopter, he pointed down. "There's a blonde down there. And over there there's a redhead with the biggest tits you ever saw."

John Douglas, who traveled to Anchorage to help the police, makes a penetrating remark about Hansen. "[Prostitutes] were people he could regard as lower and more worthless than himself." This was Hansen's problem—a deep sense of worthlessness that could only be transformed into self-esteem by exercising his power over someone he regarded as lower than himself. And, as Douglas says, hunting a naked female through the snow would have been the "ultimate control."

This lack of self-esteem is a recurrent characteristic of serial killers, and explains cases that otherwise seem baffling. It can be seen clearly in another case that was ongoing at the time Hansen was killing: "the .22-Caliber Killer," or "Buffalo Bill"—a nickname that would be borrowed a few years later by the crime novelist Thomas Harris for the killer in his *Silence of the Lambs*.

On September 22, 1980, two black youths stopped at a supermarket in Buffalo, New York, where one of them intended to cash his paycheck. When he returned to the car, his companion, fourteen-year-old Glenn Dunn, was slumped in his seat, shot in the head. A nurse who had entered the supermarket a few minutes earlier had noticed a slim white man in a hooded sweatshirt sitting outside, as if waiting for a lift; he was carrying a brown paper bag. Glenn Dunn proved to have been killed by a .22-caliber bullet.

It was the first of four shootings that occurred over thirty-six hours. The following day, Harold Green, thirty-two, an engineer, was shot in the temple as he ate in his car outside a fast-food restaurant in nearby Cheektowaga. That night, Emmanuel Thomas, thirty, was killed in the same neighborhood as he was crossing the road with a friend. The following day the .22-Caliber Killer moved farther afield, to Niagara Falls, and shot Joseph McCoy, forty-three, in front of a church.

Because all of the victims were black, there was anger in the black community, and much criticism of the police.

Two weeks later, on October 8, the killings took an even more bizarre twist. An abandoned taxicab was found on a construction site in the Buffalo suburb of Amherst. A police patrolman found an empty wallet under the driver's seat, and the license of Parker Edwards, seventy-one. In the trunk they found Edwards, his skull smashed in. The killer had also cut out his heart.

The next day another black taxi driver, Ernest Jones, forty, was found on the bank of the Niagara River, his heart cut out of his chest. His cab, also covered in blood, was found two miles away.

The following day, October 10, a strange incident occurred in the Buffalo General Hospital. Just as visiting hours were nearly over, a white man in a baseball cap enquired for the room of Collin Cole, thirty-seven, an inmate of the local jail who was recovering from a drug overdose. A nurse on her rounds saw the visitor strangling the struggling Cole with a ligature; the attacker fled, but Cole reported that he had snarled, "I hate niggers."

The Behavioral Science Unit was consulted, and John Douglas traveled to Buffalo. His feeling was that the .22-Caliber Killer was a man who felt he had a mission to kill blacks. Douglas surmised that he was the kind of person who might join a right-wing hate group. Just possibly, such a person, with his "group" mentality, might join the military, but would probably soon be discharged because of failure to adjust. Such a person, Douglas said, was often a loner until about the age of twenty-eight, when he was likely to explode. Such men were obsessed by weapons and often had a large gun collection. Nevertheless, the crimes showed him to be rational and organized.

The heart-remover killer was disorganized and pathological, someone whose hatred had probably been building up over several years. And unless he had undergone a sudden deterioration after the shootings, he was not the same person.

For two months, there were no more killings in the Buffalo area.

On December 22, four black men and one Hispanic were stabbed in Manhattan over a thirteen-hour period by a killer who was dubbed the "Midtown Slasher." The first victim, John Adams, twenty-five, was knifed by a white assailant at 11:30 a.m.; he recovered. At 1:30 p.m., Ivan Frazier, thirty-two, was attacked by the other passenger in a subway carriage, but deflected the blow with his arm. The attacker fled. At 3:30, messenger Luis Rodriguez was attacked by a man who demanded his wallet; when he fought back, the man stabbed him twice; he later died. Around 6:50, the victim was Antoine Davis, thirty, stabbed in front of a midtown bank; he also died. So did Richard Renner, twenty, stabbed about 10:30 on Forty-ninth Street. Around midnight, the killer stabbed another subway passenger, Carl Ramsey, who succeeded in dragging himself up to street level before he died.

The .22-Caliber Killer had changed his MO. On December 29, Wendell Barnes, twenty-six, was stabbed in Rochester, and died; the next day in Buffalo, Albert Menefee recovered from the knife wound that nicked his heart. On January 1, there were two separate attacks, but both victims, Larry Little and Calvin Crippen, survived.

The case went cold again for several months, until the Buffalo police received a call from the army's Criminal Investigative Division in Fort Benning, Georgia. A twenty-five-year-old army private, Joseph Christopher, whose home was in Buffalo, was in the hospital under guard. On January 13, he had tried to slash a black GI, and been placed under restraint. He had then attempted to castrate himself. And he had told the medical officer attending him, Captain Dorothy Anderson, that he had killed black men in Buffalo and New York.

Police went to his mother's home, and in his bedroom found the sawed-off rifle used in the original shootings, and clothes that matched those reportedly worn by the killer. Christopher was found to be mentally competent, and was sentenced to sixty years. The psychiatrist who examined him was amazed how closely Christopher fit Douglas's profile, even to the collection of weapons—which Christopher had inherited from his father.

Christopher had joined the army on November 13, but was on leave from December 19 until January 4, when he had launched his second murder spree. In an interview with Buffalo journalists after his conviction, Christopher estimated that his murder spree had cost at least thirteen lives.

Asked about the heart-removal murders of the two black taxi drivers, Christopher neither confirmed nor denied them. Douglas remains convinced that these two murders are not part of the sequence, because their MO is so completely unlike that of the earlier shootings. Yet it could be argued that the use of a knife connects them to the Midtown Slasher crimes, and that the mutilations of the taxi drivers reveals the same "signature"—hatred of blacks—as all the other crimes.

11

The Cases That Awakened America

11

The Cases That Awakened America

The Atlanta child murders lasted from July 1979 until June 1981, reached a figure of twenty-one (or twenty-nine, depending on which estimate you prefer to believe), and ceased with the arrest of the chief suspect, Wayne Williams. Roy Hazelwood and John Douglas were both called to Atlanta to work on the murders, and it was a suggestion by Douglas that led to Williams being detained for the first time.

The case began, almost unobtrusively, on July 28, 1979, when a woman searching for empty bottles to recycle for cash noticed a disgusting smell near some roadside undergrowth in a slum neighborhood of southwestern Atlanta, Georgia. When she spotted a leg sticking out of the tangle, she reported her find to the police, who uncovered the body of fourteen-year-old Edward Smith. He had been shot in the head with a .22-caliber gun. The last time he had been seen was a week earlier, when he left a skating rink after meeting his girlfriend there.

The buzzing of flies led the police to another body, fifty feet away in the woods—another black youth, Alfred Evans, thirteen, who had disappeared four days earlier. Partial decomposition made it hard to determine the cause of his death, but it could have been strangulation.

The boys were friends, although they lived in different parts of town. There was no sign of sexual assault upon either boy, but Smith's football shirt was missing; so were his socks. Evans was wearing a belt that was not his own. In each case, this could imply that the boy had been undressed.

Because both victims were black, even the double murder failed to attract widespread attention. The police hinted that the deaths were "drug-related."

Milton Harvey, fourteen, lived in a pleasant middle-class neighborhood in northwest Atlanta, a far cry from the slums in which Evans and Smith lived. On September 4, Harvey cycled to the bank on an errand for his mother, and disappeared. His bicycle was found a week later on a deserted dirt lane.

On October 21, 1979, a neighbor asked nine-year-old Yusuf Bell to fetch her a box of snuff. Yusuf, the son of an ex–civil rights worker, Camille Bell, was an unusually gifted child whose hobby was mathematics, and who read encyclopedias for recreation. He also disappeared, and was reported to have been seen getting into a blue car. This time, the event stirred up some media excitement, since Camille Bell was a well-known figure in the Mechanicsville neighborhood where she lived, and made on-air pleas to the abductor to release her son. A week later, a decomposed corpse was found near College Park; it proved to be the missing Milton Harvey. Then Yusuf's body was found stuffed into the crawl space of an abandoned elementary school. He had been strangled. Although he had been missing for ten days, it was clear that he had not been dead for more than half that time. His clothes had been cleaned, and the body washed. His funeral became a media event, with black leaders and politicians in attendance. They all promised a full investigation into Yusuf's death. His had not yet been linked to the three other boys'—although Camille Bell and her friends saw a definite connection.

In early March 1980, a twelve-year-old black girl, Angel Lenair, was found tied to a tree with panties that were not her own stuffed down her throat; her hymen had been broken and minor abrasions to the genitals suggested sexual attack, but police concluded that she had not been raped. It was difficult to assess whether this murder was related to the other killings, since the assumption was that the killer—now known to black children as "the Man"—was homosexual. Cause of death was strangulation by an electrical cord.

The day after Angel's body had been found, ten-year-old Jefferey Mathis left home to buy cigarettes for his mother from a nearby store; he also vanished. After his family had searched all night his mother rang the missing person's department, but they paid little attention, the assumption being that a missing child was probably a runaway. But a witness later reported seeing the child get into a blue car, possibly a Buick.

The vanishings continued. On May 18, Eric Middlebrooks, fourteen, received a phone call at 10:30 at night and, grabbing his tools, told his foster mother that he was going out to repair his bike. His bludgeoned body was found early the next morning. On June 9, twelve-year-old Christopher Richardson disappeared on his way to a swimming pool in nearby middle-class Decatur.

A seven-year-old girl, LaTonya Wilson, was carried from her bedroom during the early morning hours of June 22, presumably by someone who knew the house well. Like the murder of Angel Lenair, authorities assumed that this abduction had no connection to the previous disappearances and deaths of young boys.

The day after Wilson's kidnapping, the body of ten-year-old Aaron Wyche was found under a railway bridge in DeKalb County; police said he had died of an accidental fall, but his parents insisted that he was terrified of heights; a second autopsy concluded he had died violently.

Although the Atlanta police department was receiving its share of criticism for its inability to solve any of these murders, in mid-June, Deputy Chief Morris Redding had decided to consult the Behavioral Science Unit at Quantico. When Roy Hazelwood arrived in Atlanta, the police were still insisting that the murders were unconnected, citing the high crime rates in their city. Hazelwood had immediate experience of the high Atlanta crime rate when his wallet was stolen before he could even leave the airport, and he had to borrow $200 from a friend at the Atlanta FBI.

His review of the murders so far left him convinced that a serial killer was at work, although he doubted that the two girls were his victims. A few of the murders struck him as possible copycat killings. But his most important conclusion was that the killer was black. As he took a drive with black officers in an unmarked car through one of the neighborhoods from which children had disappeared, people stopped whatever they were doing to stare at him; obviously, a strange white man would have been noticed instantly.

By the beginning of July 1980, in what was later aptly labeled the "Summer of Death," the murders had continued for a year, and seven black children had been murdered and three had vanished. Understandably, there was outrage on the part of the African American community, which still assumed that the killer was a white man who hated blacks. One outrageous rumor asserted that scientists needed the penises of recently dead blacks to make the protein interferon for combating cancer. But a far more widespread rumor was that the Ku Klux Klan was behind the murders. Blacks all over the country were convinced that a white racist was responsible. Camille Bell and the mothers of two other murdered children, Mary Mapp and Venus Taylor, mobilized a group of parents who had lost children, and in early July the newly formed STOP called a press conference to protest police inaction, arguing that even if the killer was an African American, the police were dragging their feet because the victims were not white children.

Two more children vanished that month: On July 6, nine-year-old Anthony Carter, who was found behind a warehouse near his home the next day. He had been stabbed to death. On July 13, eleven-year-old Earl Terrell vanished after leaving the South Bend Park swimming pool. His aunt received a call from a man claiming that he had the boy with him in Alabama and demanding $200 for his return.

The crime of kidnapping and transporting a person across state lines falls under FBI jurisdiction. It was soon decided, however, that the ransom call had been a hoax; nevertheless, Agent John Douglas went down to join Hazelwood. Meanwhile, the task force had been increased from five members to twenty-five. Civic groups raised a $100,000 reward for the killer, and a plan was set up to promote athletic and cultural programs to keep young blacks off the streets. Later, a curfew on children would be imposed.

Some blacks held a theory that the killer was a policeman, but the police argued that he was more likely to be a black teenager, who would be trusted by other teens. The belief that the killings were racially motivated was strengthened by the fact that, with the exception of Angel Lenair, none of the victims had been sexually assaulted.

The last killing of the summer was that of thirteen-year-old Clifford Jones, who was visiting his grandmother in Atlanta. His strangled body was found in a Dumpster on August 20. He was dressed in clothes that were not his own.

On September 14, fourteen-year-old Darron Glass disappeared. By then, although many of the killings were still considered unconnected, authorities knew they had a crisis on their hands. Mayor Maynard Jackson asked the White House for help, but it was still a question of whether there had even been any interstate violations to justify the FBI's involvement in the situation. Nevertheless, Douglas and Hazlewood began their joint investigation using the methods of the BSU—studying crime-scene photographs, interviewing family members, studying the dumpsites.

Their problem was to put themselves into the mind of the killer, and they even took a test under a psychologist to try to view the world through the eyes of a paranoid schizophrenic—the psychologist was deeply impressed by their results.

As had Hazelwood, Douglas concluded that this killer was a young black man, probably about twenty-nine years of age. This would explain why the children would trust him enough to accept a lift. He would be a "police buff," who enjoyed posing as a police officer and probably carried a badge. He might even have a police-type dog.

As to motivation, the killer would be homosexual, attracted to young boys, but sexually inadequate, which would explain why there had been no rapes. He would probably have some kind of practiced ruse to attract the kids, and Douglas thought that he might pose as a music promoter. He hypothesized that the children probably knew their killer, and trusted him—these were not casual pickups.

The Atlanta Police Department checked through their records of known pedophiles, and ended with a list of fifteen hundred possible suspects. But not all Atlanta cops were impressed by the profile—one black officer told Douglas, "I've seen your profile and I think it's shit."

In Conyers, a small town twenty-five miles away, police thought they had a lead when they received a tape from someone who claimed to be the killer, declaring that he had left a body on Sigmon Road. He sounded like a white man with strong racist views. Douglas said immediately: "This is not the killer, but you have to catch him because he'll keep on calling and distracting us until you do." He then suggested how this could be done. The taunting tone implied that the man saw the police as idiots. Douglas advised them to go and search Sigmon Road, and make sure that they looked incompetent and failed to follow the caller's instructions. Just as he expected, the man rang to tell them what fools they were; they were waiting for his call, traced it, and arrested him in his own house—from which he had been stupid enough to make the call.

The killing went on. After Darron Glass, twelve-year-old Charles Stevens disappeared on October 9; his body was found the next day, suffocated. Nine days later, a search of woodland area revealed the body of the missing LaTonya Wilson, but the body was too badly decomposed for the cause of death to be determined.

Wayne Williams poses along the fence line at Valdosta State Prison in Georgia. His 1982 conviction for the slayings of two adults, and the decision by authorities to blame him for the murders of twenty-two others without taking him to trial for those crimes, officially ended what became known throughout the world as the "Atlanta child murders." (Associated Press)

By then, the Atlanta police chief, George Napper, was admitting that all leads had been exhausted. Fearing a Halloween attack on trick-or-treaters, the mayor initiated a citywide curfew, and police patrols were beefed up. Nonetheless, the suffocated body of nine-year-old Aaron Jackson was found on November 2. Although he had been a friend of an earlier victim, Aaron Wyche, there was still no clue to the identity of the killer. On November 10, sixteen-year-old Patrick Rogers disappeared. Rogers had once had a crush on Aaron Jackson's older sister. His body was found on December 21, facedown in the Chattahoochee River. A blow to the head had killed him. On January 4, 1981, Lubie Geter disappeared from a shopping mall. Five days later, police found the badly decomposed bodies of two missing children in a wood south of Atlanta—Christopher Richardson and Earl Terrell. Lubie Geter was found in early February.

DESPITE MASSIVE MEDIA ATTENTION AND REWARDS OFFERED FOR ANY HELP IN CAPTURING THE KILLER OR KILLERS, THE BODY COUNT CONTINUED TO RISE.

Also in early February 1981, the Task Force received a call from eleven-year-old Patrick Baltazar, saying that he thought the killer was coming after him. Unfortunately, the detectives failed to ask him why he thought so, and when Baltazar vanished on February 6, it was too late. His body was found a week later in an office car park, strangled with a rope. It was announced that a hair fiber found on his body matched that found on five previous victims.

On February 22, fifteen-year-old Terry Pue was last seen at a hamburger restaurant; he was a friend of Lubie Geter. An anonymous white caller told the police where his body could be found on Sigmon Road, in Rockdale County. The body was found there, strangled with a rope, and police announced that they had been able to raise a fingerprint from the flesh, but no match proved to be on record.

Douglas recalled that there had been another Sigmon Road in the case, and that the police search there had been widely publicized. Was it possible, he wondered, that the killer was carefully following the press reports, pleased at the level of interest he was generating, and that he dumped the last body in another Sigmon Road as if making the point that he could abandon bodies wherever he liked? The two Sigmon Roads were more than twenty miles apart, so the killer had a long drive in order to make his point. Might it be possible to manipulate the killer through publicity? Would he now start dumping bodies in the river, to wash away evidence? Douglas's insight proved correct; the next body to be found, thirteen-year-old Curtis Walker, was in the South River. That same day, the remains of Jefferey Mathis, who had been missing for more than a year, were finally uncovered. His funeral made national news.

FBI agents now strongly advised that a surveillance team should be set up to watch the rivers, particularly the Chattahoochee, Atlanta's main waterway. This was not easy, since it involved several police jurisdictions. It took the best part of two months to organize it, but by April it was in operation.

After Curtis Walker, the next two bodies, fifteen-year-old Joseph "Jo-Jo" Bell and his friend Timothy Hill, thirteen, were found in the Chattahoochee River, Timothy on March 30, Jo-Jo on April 19. Like Patrick Baltazar, both boys had been stripped of their outer garments. Two days after he had gone missing on March 2, a coworker of Bell had told his manager at the seafood restaurant where they worked that Jo-Jo had called him and told him that he was "almost dead" and pleaded for his help.

These were the last child victims. For reasons unknown, the killer now moved on to adults. Yet it is possible that the reason for the choice of the first adult victim, Eddie Duncan, twenty-one, was once again dictated by publicity. Residents of the Techwood Homes housing project took to the streets to protest that the police force was not doing its job. Residents decided to form a patrol carrying baseball bats. It was on the day this "bat patrol" started, March 20, 1981, that Duncan, who was both physically and mentally disabled, disappeared. His body was found in the Chattahoochee River on April 8.

Despite massive media attention and rewards offered for any help in capturing the killer or killers, the body count continued to rise. Twenty-year-old Larry Rogers was the second adult added to the list of victims. As was Duncan, Rogers was retarded. His strangled body was found in an abandoned apartment. Next came twenty-three-year-old Michael McIntosh, who had known Jo-Jo Bell and was pulled from the Chattahootchee River in April. John Porter was twenty-eight when he was found stabbed to death that same month. The body of twenty-one-year-old Jimmy Ray Payne was also found floating in the Chattahoochee that April. In May, seventeen-year-old William Barrett was found strangled and stabbed after leaving home to pay a bill for his mother.

On May 22 came the break. Police posted close to the Parkway Bridge over the Chattahoochee River spotted headlights, heard a splash, and saw a man climb into a station wagon. They stopped it, and found that it was driven by a plump young black man who identified himself as Wayne Williams, age twenty-three. He claimed to be a freelance photographer and music promoter, traveling across the bridge to audition a woman named Cheryl Johnson. In fact, her phone number was incorrect and her address did not exist. Williams was questioned for an hour, but the police could see no reason to detain him, so he was allowed to go, and placed under constant surveillance.

Two days later, the body of twenty-seven-year-old Nathaniel Cater, the oldest victim, was found floating in the river. Dog hairs found on the body matched those found in Williams's station wagon and in his home. One witness testified to seeing Williams leaving a theater hand in hand with Cater just before his disappearance. Another witness testified to seeing Williams in the company of another of the victims, Jimmy Ray Payne, also found in the river. A young black who knew Williams well testified that Williams had offered him money to perform oral sex, and another described how, after he had accepted a lift, Williams had fondled him through his trousers, then stopped the car in secluded woods; the teenager had jumped out and run away. He also said that he had seen Williams with Lubie Geter. When laboratory examination established that fibers and dog hairs found on ten more victims were similar to those found in Williams's bedroom, the police decided to arrest him. He was charged only with the murders of Nathaniel Cater and Jimmy Ray Payne.

Wayne Bertram Williams was the only child of two schoolteachers, Homer and Fay Williams, in their mid-forties when he was born on May 27, 1958. He was a brilliant and spoiled child. He studied the sky through a telescope and set up a home-built radio station. When his transmitter was powerful enough to reach a mile, he began selling advertising time. He was featured in local magazines and on TV. When he left school at eighteen he became obsessed by police work and bought a car that resembled an unmarked police car.

The prosecution later described him as the typical "Manichean" personality (the Manichees were world-haters): intelligent, literate, and "talented, but a pathological liar" ("a bullshitter" as one friend described him). He was a frustrated dreamer, and a man who felt himself to be a failure. He was obsessed by a desire for quick success, and first became a photographer, studying television camera work. He claimed to be a talent scout, trying to set up a pop group to sing soul music. He seemed to hate other blacks, according to several witnesses, referring to them as "niggers." Yet he distributed leaflets offering blacks between the age of eleven and twenty-one "free" interviews about a musical career. One of the victims, Patrick Rogers, was a would-be singer.

The evidence was, as the prosecutor conceded in the trial that opened on December 28, 1981, entirely circumstantial, and it was with some reluctance that the judge, Clarence Cooper, allowed it to be strengthened by details relating to other murders besides those with which Williams was charged.

Carpet fiber was a key component of the prosecution's case. Fibers found on the bodies of the victims were similar to fibers found in Williams's home and automobile—twenty-eight fiber types linked to nineteen items from the house, bedroom, and vehicles driven by Williams.

Five bloodstains were also found in Williams's station wagon, matched to the blood of victims William Barrett and John Porter.

Another telling argument by the prosecution was that Williams had lied extensively about the evening he stopped on the bridge, offering various alibis that proved to be false.

The trial began in January 1982, and ended in March when, after twelve hours' deliberation, the jury found him guilty of the two murders. He was sentenced to two consecutive life terms.

John Douglas comments: "Wayne Williams fit our profile in every key respect, including his ownership of a German shepherd. He was a police buff who had been arrested some years earlier for impersonating a law officer. After that, he had driven a surplus police vehicle and used police scanners to get to crime scenes to take pictures. In retrospect, several witnesses recalled seeing him along Sigmon Road when the police were reacting to the phone tip and searching for the nonexistent body. He had been taking photographs there, which he offered to the police."

Too little is known about Wayne Williams and his motivations, which is why many writers on the case—including novelist James Baldwin—have doubted his guilt. In the last analysis, the story of the Atlanta child murders is as frustrating as a jigsaw puzzle with a crucial piece missing. But the missing piece may well have been destroyed by Williams himself. According to Chet Dettlinger in his book *The List,* in the days following the incident on the bridge, Williams and his father "did a major cleanup job around their house. They carried out boxes and carted them off in the station wagon. They burned negatives and photographic prints in the outdoor grill." Photographs of what? They may have been anything from innocent shots of young blacks he had auditioned to photographs of actual murder victims, or even of the bodies.

The picture of Williams that emerges is of a "wannabe" with a strong desire to impress, bringing to mind in many respects "Hillside Strangler" Kenneth Bianchi. But if the motive behind the murders was not sex, then what was it?

The descriptions of the bodies seem to provide a clue. This killer committed strangulation again and again and again. Many of the victims still had the rope around their throats. Is it possible that this is the answer? In a case of the 1870s—recorded by the psychologist Krafft-Ebing—an Italian youth named Vincent Verzeni committed two strangulation murders and attempted more. Krafft-Ebing notes: "As soon as he has grasped his victim by the neck, sexual sensations are experienced . . . accompanied by erection and ejaculation. Usually simply choking them satisfied him, and then he allowed his victims to live . . ."

The same was true of the German mass murderer of the 1920s, Peter Kürten. Throttling was a crucial part of his sexual pleasure, and if it brought a climax before the victim died, he let her go. Even when being examined in prison by a psychiatrist, he admitted that the white throat of the stenographer produced a powerful desire to squeeze it.

Is this the reason that two of the victims had premonitions they were going to die? Had Williams already practiced throttling on them?

Whether or not the prosecution established the guilt of Wayne Williams beyond doubt, one thing is clear: after his arrest, the Atlanta child murders ceased.

Although the Atlanta child murders made a worldwide sensation, it was another case that finally made the American public aware of what was meant by the term "serial killer."

Over a period of months, a drifter named Henry Lee Lucas confessed to committing 360 murders. If true, this would make him the worst serial killer in American history—in fact, in world history.

The story that was to make world headlines began on June 15, 1983, when Joe Don Weaver, the jailer on duty in the Montague County Jail, Texas, was told by a five-foot eight-inch drifter, who was in jail for a minor weapons offence: "Joe Don, I done some pretty bad things."

Weaver said sternly, "If it's what I think it is, Henry, you better get on your knees and pray."

Lucas said, "Joe Don, can I have some paper and a pencil?"

Half an hour later, Lucas handed the letter out through the hole in his cell door. It was addressed to Sheriff Bill F. Conway, and began:

> *I have tryed to get help for so long, and no one will believe me. I have killed for the past ten years and no one will believe me. I cannot go own [sic] doing this. I allso killed The only Girl I ever loved . . .*

Weaver hurried to the telephone. He knew this was the break Sheriff Conway had been waiting for.

The unshaven, smelly little vagrant who now waited in his dark cell had been a hard nut to crack. Since the previous September, he had been suspected of killing eighty-year-old widow Kate Rich, who had vanished from her home; Sheriff Conway had learned that she had been employing an odd-job man called Henry Lee Lucas, together with his common-law wife, fifteen-year-old Becky Powell. Lucas had left Mrs. Rich's employment under a cloud, and gone to live in a local religious commune. Not long after that, Becky had also disappeared.

Lucas insisted that he knew nothing about the disappearance of Kate Rich. As to Becky Powell, he claimed that she had run off with a truck driver when they were trying to hitchhike back to her home in Florida. He had passed several lie-detector tests, and the sheriff had finally been forced to release him. Then a week later he was arrested for owning a gun—which, since he was an ex-convict, was against the law.

A few hours later, Henry Lee Lucas sat in Sheriff Conway's office, a large pot of black coffee and a packet of Lucky Strikes in front of him. He was a strange-looking man, with a glass eye, a thin, haggard face, and a loose, down-turned mouth like a shark's. When he smiled, he showed a row of rotten, tobacco-stained teeth. In the small office, his body odor was overpowering.

"Henry," said the sheriff kindly, "you say in this note you want to tell me about some murders."

"That's right. The light told me I had to confess my sins."

"The light?"

"There was a light in my cell, and it said: 'I will forgive you, but you must confess your sins.' So that's what I aim to do."

"Tell me what you did to Kate Rich."

There followed a chillingly detailed confession—Lucas seemed to have total recall—of the murder of the eighty-year-old woman and the violation of her dead body. Lucas described how he had gone to Kate Rich's house and offered to take her to church. She had asked him questions about the disappearance of his "wife" Becky Powell, and at some point, Lucas had decided to kill her. He had taken the butcher's knife that lay between them on the bench seat of the old car, and suddenly jammed it into her left side. The knife entered her heart and she had collapsed immediately. Then, speaking as calmly as if he was narrating some everyday occurrence, Lucas described how he had dragged her down an embankment, undressed her, and raped her. After that, he hauled her to a wide section of drainpipe that ran under the road, and stuffed her into it. Later, he had returned with two plastic garbage bags, and used them as a kind of makeshift shroud. He buried her clothes nearby. He drove back to his room in the religious hostel called House of Prayer, made a huge fire in the stove, and burned the body. The few bones that were left he buried in the compost heap outside.

Conway then asked him what had happened to Becky Powell. This time the story was longer, and Lucas's single eye often overflowed with tears. By the time it was over, Conway was trying to hide his nausea. Lucas had met Becky Powell in 1978, when she was eleven years old; she was the niece of his friend Ottis Toole, and Lucas was staying at the home of her great-aunt in Jacksonville, Florida. Becky's full name was Frieda Lorraine Powell, and she was mildly retarded. Even at eleven she was not a virgin. The family situation was something of a sexual hothouse. As a child, Ottis Toole had been seduced by his elder sister, Drusilla (who was Becky's mother). He grew up bisexual, and liked picking up lovers of both sexes—including Henry Lee Lucas. And he liked watching his pickups make love to Becky or her elder sister, Sarah.

Ottis had another peculiarity; he liked burning down houses because it stimulated him sexually.

In December 1981, Drusilla committed suicide, and Becky and her younger brother, Frank, were placed in juvenile care. Lucas decided to "rescue" her, and in January 1982, he and Ottis fled with Becky and Frank; they lived on the proceeds of robbery—mostly small grocery stores. Lucas felt heavily protective about Becky, he explained, and she called him "Daddy." But one night, as he was saying good night to her, and he was making her shriek with laughter by tickling her, they began to kiss. Becky had raised no objection as he undressed her, and then himself. After that, the father-daughter relation changed into something more like husband and wife. At twelve, Becky looked as if she was nineteen.

But Becky had suddenly become homesick, and begged him to take her back to Florida. Reluctantly, Henry agreed, and they set out hitchhiking. Later, in the warm June night, they settled down with blankets in a field. But when they began arguing about her decision to go home, Becky had lost her temper and struck him in the face. Instantly, like a striking snake, Lucas grabbed a carving knife that lay nearby, and stabbed her through the heart. After that he violated her body. And then, since the ground was too hard to dig a grave, he cut her into nine pieces with the carving knife, then scattered the pieces in the thick undergrowth. He told people who knew her that she had run away with a truck driver. His sorrow was obviously so genuine that everyone sympathized with him. In fact, Lucas told the lawmen, he felt as if he had killed a part of himself.

After this second confession, the sheriff asked: "Is that all?"

Lucas shook his head. "Not by a long way. I reckon I killed more 'n a hundred people."

If he was telling the truth—and Conway was inclined to doubt it—he was far and away the worst mass murderer in American criminal history.

The first step was to check his story about Kate Rich. Lucas had pointed out the spot he'd stashed her body on a map. Conway and Texas Ranger Phil Ryan drove there in the darkness. They quickly located the wide drainage pipe that ran under the road, and lying close to its entrance, a pair of knickers, of the type that

IN THE FIELD WHERE LUCAS SAID HE HAD KILLED BECKY POWELL, THEY FOUND A HUMAN SKULL, A PELVIS, AND VARIOUS BODY PARTS IN AN ADVANCED STAGE OF DECOMPOSITION.

would be worn by an old woman. On the other side of the road, they also found broken lenses from a woman's pair of eyeglasses.

In the House of Prayer, near Stoneburg, they searched through the unutterably filthy room that Lucas had occupied in a converted chicken barn, and in the stove, found fragments of burnt flesh, and some pieces of charred bone. On the trash heap they found more bone fragments.

In the field where Lucas said he had killed Becky Powell, they found a human skull, a pelvis, and various body parts in an advanced stage of decomposition. Becky's orange suitcase still lay nearby, and articles of female clothing and makeup were strewn around.

Even after killing Becky, Lucas told them, he had murdered another woman. He had drifted to Missouri, and there he saw a young woman waiting by the gas pumps. He went up to her, pushed a knife against her ribs, and told her he needed a lift, and would not harm her. Without speaking, she allowed him to climb into the driver's seat. All that night he drove south towards Texas, until the woman finally fell into a doze. Lucas had no intention of keeping his promise. He wanted money—and sex. Just before dawn he pulled off the road, and as the woman woke up, plunged the knife into her throat. Then he pushed her out on to the ground, cut off her clothes, and violated the body. After that, he dragged it into a grove of trees, took the money from her handbag, and drove the car to Fredericksburg, Texas, where he abandoned it.

Lucas was unable to tell them the woman's name, but his description of the place where he abandoned the car offered a lead. In fact, the Texas Rangers near Fredericksburg were able to confirm the finding of an abandoned station wagon the previous October. And a little further checking revealed that the police at Magnolia, Texas, had found the naked body of a woman with her throat cut, at about the same time. Again, it was clear that Lucas was telling the truth.

On June 17, 1983, Henry Lee Lucas appeared in the Montague County Courthouse, accused of murder and of possessing an illegal firearm. A grand jury indicted him on both counts.

On Tuesday, June 21, 1983, the unimpressive little man who looked like an out-of-work road sweeper was led into the courtroom between two deputies. Judge Frank Douthitt listened to the indictment concerning Kate Rich, and then asked the prisoner if he understood the seriousness of the indictment against him. Lucas replied quietly: "Yes, sir, I have about a hundred of them."

On request he clarified the point: yes, he meant that he had killed a hundred people.

The judge asked him if he had ever had a psychiatric examination. The little man nodded. "I tell them my problems and they didn't want to do anything about it . . . I know it ain't normal for a person to go out and kill girls just to have sex with them."

The following morning, the Austin newspapers carried head-lines that were a variant of a single theme: DRIFTER CONFESSES TO A HUNDRED MURDERS. The wire services immediately picked up the story, and by evening it was on front pages all over the country.

For the preceding ten years, the American public had been kept in a state of shock at the revelations about mass murderers: Ted Bundy, Ed Kemper, Dean Corll, John Wayne Gacy, the Hillside Stranglers, the Atlanta child murderer. And now a wandering vagrant was admitting to a total that surpassed them all. And in Quantico, where the NCAVC, the National Center for the Analysis of Violent Crime, had just been launched, it was clear that it was not a moment too soon. The "wandering killer" was obviously a new variety of menace. Suddenly, every newspaper in America was talking about serial killers.

Meanwhile, the cause of all this excitement was sitting in his jail cell in Montague County, describing murder after murder to a "task force" headed by Sheriff Jim Boutwell and Texas Ranger Bob Prince. It soon became clear that a large number of these murders had not been committed on his own, but in company with his lover, Ottis Elswood Toole.

Toole, who had a gap in his front teeth and permanent stubble on his chin, looked even more like a tramp than Lucas. And even before Lucas was arrested in Texas, Toole was in prison in his hometown of Jacksonville, Florida. He was charged with setting fires in Springfield, the area where he lived. On August 5, 1983, he was sentenced to fifteen years for arson.

One week later, in a courtroom in Denton County—where he had killed Becky Powell—Lucas staggered everybody by pleading not guilty to Becky's murder. He was, in fact, beginning to play a game that would become wearisomely familiar to the police: withdrawing confessions. It looked as if, now that he was in prison, the old Henry Lee Lucas, the Enemy of Society, was reappearing. He could no longer kill at random when he felt the urge, but he could still satisfy his craving for control over victims by playing with his captors like a cat with mice.

It did him no good. On October 1, 1983, in the courtroom where he had been arraigned, Lucas was sentenced to seventy-five years for the murder of Kate Rich. And on November 8, 1983, he was sentenced to life imprisonment for the murder of Becky Powell. Before the courts had finished with him, he would be sentenced to another seventy-five years, four more life sentences, and an additional sixty-five years, all for murder. For good measure, he was also sentenced to death.

When Henry Lee Lucas began confessing to murders, it seemed to be a genuine case of religious conversion. Later, when he was moved to the Georgetown Jail in Williamson County, he was allowed regular visits from a Catholic laywoman who called herself Sister Clementine, and they spent hours kneeling in prayer. He was visited by many lawmen from all over the country, hoping that he could clear up unsolved killings. Sometimes—if he felt the policeman failed to treat him with due respect—he refused to utter a word. At other times, he confessed freely. The problem was that he sometimes confessed to two murders on the same day, in areas so wide apart that he could not possibly have committed both. This tendency to lie at random led many journalists to conclude that Lucas's tales of mass murder were mostly invention.

None of the officers who knew him believed that for a moment. Too many of his confessions had turned out to be accurate.

For example, on August 2, 1983, when he was being arraigned for the murder of a hitchhiker known simply as "Orange Socks," Lucas was taken to Austin for questioning about another murder. On the way there, seated between two deputies, Lucas pointed to a building they passed and asked if it had been a liquor store at one time. The detectives looked at one another. It had, and it had been run by Harry and Molly Schlesinger, who had been robbed and murdered on October 23, 1979. Lucas admitted that he had been responsible, and described the killings with a wealth of detail that only the killer could have known. He then led the deputies to a field where, on October 8, 1979, the mutilated body of a young woman named Sandra Dubbs had been found. He was also able to point out where her car had been left. There could be no possible doubt that Lucas had killed three people in Travis County in two weeks.

When asked if Ottis Toole had committed any murders on his own, Lucas mentioned a man who had died in a fire set by Toole in Jacksonville. Toole had poured gasoline on the man's mattress and set it alight. Then they hid and watched the fire fighters; a sixty-five-year-old man was finally carried out, badly burned. He died a week later. Police assumed he had accidentally set the mattress on fire with a cigarette.

Lucas's description led the police to identify the victim as George Sonenberg, who had been fatally burned in a fire on January 4, 1982. Police drove out to Raiford Penitentiary to interview Toole. He admitted it cheerfully. When asked why he did it, he grinned broadly. "I love fires. Reckon I started a hundred of them over the past several years."

There could be no possible doubt about it: Toole and Lucas had committed an astronomical number of murders between them. At one point, Lucas insisted that the total was about 360—he went on to detail 175 he committed alone, and 65 with Ottis Toole.

In prison after his original convictions, Lucas seemed a well-satisfied man. Now much plumper, with his rotten teeth replaced or filled, he had ceased to look so sinister. He had a special cell all to himself in Sheriff Boutwell's jail—other prisoners had treated him very roughly during the brief period he had been among them, and he had to be moved for his own safety. And he was now a national celebrity. Magazines and newspapers begged for interviews, television cameras recorded every public appearance. Police officers turned up by the dozen to ask about unsolved murder cases, and were all warned beforehand to treat Lucas with respect, in case he ceased to cooperate. Now, at least, he was receiving the attention he had always craved, and he reveled in it. And some visitors, like the psychiatrist Joel Norris, the journalist Mike Cox, and the crime writer Max Call, came to interview him in order to learn about his life, and to write books about it. Lucas cooperated fully with Call, who was the first to reach print—as early as 1985—with a strange work called *Hand of Death*.

Here, for the first time, the American public had an opportunity to satisfy its morbid curiosity about Lucas's rampage of crime. The story that emerged lacked the detail of later studies, but it was horrific enough.

Lucas, Call revealed, had spent most of his life from 1960 (when he was twenty-six years old) to 1975 in jail. After his release he had an unsuccessful marriage—which broke up when his wife realized he was having sex with her two small daughters—and lived for a while with his sister Wanda, leaving when she accused him of sexually abusing her young daughter. He seems to have met Ottis Toole in a soup kitchen in Jacksonville, Florida, in 1978. Ottis had a long prison record for stealing cars and petty theft, and he invited Lucas back home, where he was soon regarded as a member of the family.

According to Lucas, he had already committed a number of casual murders as he wandered around. These were mostly crimes of opportunity—as when he offered a lift to a young woman called Tina Williams, near Oklahoma City, after her car had broken down. He shot her twice and had intercourse with the body. Police later confirmed Lucas's confession.

Even so, the meeting with Toole seems to have been a turning point. Now, according to both of them, they began killing "for fun." According to Toole's confession, they saw a teenaged couple walking along the road in November 1978, their car having run out of fuel. Lucas forced the girl into the car, while Toole shot the boy in the head and chest. Then, as Toole drove, Lucas repeatedly raped the girl in the back of the car. Finally, Toole began to feel jealous about his lover, and when they pulled up, shot her six times, and left her body by the road. The police were also able to confirm this case: the youth was called Kevin Key, the young woman Rita Salazar.

The case was the first of more than a score of similar murders along Interstate 35 that kept Sheriff Boutwell, now chief investigator, busy for the next five years. The victims included teenaged hitchhikers, elderly women abducted from their homes, tramps, and men who were killed for robbery. Lucas was later to confess to most of these crimes.

Lucas and Toole began robbing convenience stores, forcing the proprietor or store clerk into the back. Lucas described how, on one occasion, they tied up a young female clerk, but she continued to try to get free. So he shot her through the head, and Toole had intercourse with her body.

On October 31, 1979, the naked body of a young woman was found in a culvert on Interstate 35, her clothes missing, except for a pair of orange socks laying by the body. After his arrest, Lucas described how he and Toole had picked up "Orange Socks," who was hitchhiking, and when she had refused to let Lucas have sex with her, he strangled her. Lucas would eventually receive the death sentence for the murder of the still unidentified young woman.

When Lucas and Toole abducted Becky and her brother, Frank, in January 1982, they took the kids with them when they robbed convenience stores; Becky looked so innocent that the proprietor took little notice of the two smelly vagrants who accompanied her—until one of them produced a gun and demanded the money from the till. And, according to Lucas, Becky and Frank often became witnesses to murder—in fact, in one confession he even claimed that they had taken part in the killings.

Eventually, Frank and Toole returned home to Florida, while Becky and Lucas continued "on the road." In January 1982, a couple named Smart, who ran an antiques store in Hemet, California, picked them up, and for five months Lucas worked for them. When the Smarts asked Lucas if he would like to go back to Texas to look after Mrs. Smart's mother, Kate Rich, he accepted their offer. Yet after only a few weeks, the Smarts received a telephone call from another sister in Texas, telling them that the new handyman was spending Mrs. Rich's money on large quantities of beer and cigarettes in the local grocery store. Another sister who went to investigate found Mrs. Rich's house filthy, and Lucas and Becky drunk in bed.

Lucas was politely fired. But his luck held. Only a few miles away, he was offered a lift by the Reverend Reuben Moore, who had started his own religious community in nearby Stoneburg. Moore also took pity on the couple, and they moved into the House of Prayer. There everyone liked Becky, and she seemed happy. She badly needed a home and security. Both she and Henry became "converts."

Becky nonetheless began to feel homesick, and begged Henry to take her back to Florida. A few days later, pieces of her dismembered body were scattered around a field near Denton. And Lucas's nightmare odyssey of murder was drawing to a close.

The American public, which at first followed Lucas's confessions with horrified attention, soon began to lose interest. After all, he was already sentenced. So was Ottis Toole (who would also be later condemned to death for the arson murder of George Sonenberg). And as newspapers ran stories declaring that Lucas had withdrawn his confessions yet again, or that some police officer had proved he was lying, there was a growing feeling that Lucas was not, after all, the worst mass murderer in American history.

It was a couple named Bob and Joyce Lemons who first placed this conviction on a solid foundation. An intruder had murdered their daughter, Barbara Sue Williamson, in Lubbock, Texas, in August 1975. Lucas confessed to this murder when asked about it by Lubbock lawmen. When the Lemons heard the confession they felt sure it was a hoax. Lucas said he recalled the house as being white, that he had entered by the screen door, and killed the newly married woman in her bedroom. It was a green house, the screen door had been sealed shut at the time, and Barbara had been killed outside.

The Lemons went and talked to Lucas's relatives, and soon came up with a list of the periods when he had stayed in Florida, which contradicted dozens of his "confessions." But when they confronted Texas Ranger Bob Prince with these discoveries, he became hostile and ordered them out of his office.

Unsurprisingly, Ressler's own attitude toward Lucas is skeptical. In *Whoever Fights Monsters,* he writes:

> *By the time I interviewed Lucas, years after the controversy had died down, the dust had settled and Lucas said that he had actually committed none of the murders to which he had previously confessed. Under closer questioning, he did admit that since 1975 he had "killed a few," fewer than ten, perhaps five. He just wasn't sure. He had told all those lies in order to have fun, and to show up what he termed the stupidity of the police.*
>
> *This figure, however, is obviously as much an underestimate as Lucas's original claim of 350 (or even, at one stage, 650) was an exaggeration. As noted above, many of Lucas's claims were confirmed on investigation. It seems, on the whole, that he was probably telling something like the truth in his first statement that he had killed "about a hundred."*

Ressler adds:

> *It took several years for the Lucas fiasco to be resolved. The task-force member had been right, though: If we had had VICAP up and running at the time Lucas made his first startling admission, it would have been easy to see what was truth and what was falsehood in his confession. First, we would have asked the police departments to fill out VICAP forms on their unsolved murders and enter them into the computer system. Then we would have analyzed them by date, location, and MO, and would quickly have been able to show that several of them had been committed on the same date in widely separated locations, thus eliminating the possibility that they were committed by the same man. By such processes of elimination, we would have narrowed the field very quickly and allowed investigators to concentrate on the real possibilities.*

Lucas, sentenced to several life terms as well as to death in the 1980s, began the usual process of appeal, then spent thirteen years on death row. By June 1998, when it seemed that he could no longer delay the death sentence, then Governor George Bush commuted it to life imprisonment.

Ottis Toole died in September 1996 of cirrhosis of the liver.

12

The Most Evil?

12

The Most Evil?

Sadism, the enjoyment of another person's suffering, is a relatively rare perversion. As Roy Hazelwood told Stephen Michaud, however, ". . . those who harbor it are the most dangerous of all aberrant offenders. They are the great white sharks of deviant crime."

He was referring to Mike DeBardeleben, whose criminal career spanned eighteen years. When he was arrested on May 25, 1983, it was not for murder or rape—although in both these fields he was a repeat offender—but passing counterfeit bills.

By 1980, one of the Secret Service's serious headaches was a counterfeiter agents called the "Mall Passer," who they had been trying to find for three years. The Mall Passer unloaded fake $20 bills in shopping malls all over the country by handing them over in exchange for small items, such as cigarettes and men's socks, and taking the change. He obviously drove far and wide; in one year, he traveled to thirty-eight states and unloaded as much as $30,000 in fake bills. It was the task of the hunters, led by Secret Service agents Greg Mertz, Dennis Foos, and Mike Stephens, to try to discern some kind of pattern in his crimes and lay a trap. The number of fake bills passed in the Washington D.C. and northern Virginia area suggested that this might be where he lived.

Police artist drew up sketches of the Mall Passer based on the descriptions of store clerks who had seen him, and these were passed to every mall he had ever visited. In the late afternoon of Thursday, April 25, 1983, staff of the Eastridge Mall in Gastonia, North Carolina, was on the lookout for the Mall Passer, since a local FBI agent had worked out that this might well be his target that month.

When a customer offered a $20 bill in payment for a paperback book, the clerk thought he recognized the wanted man, and noted that the $20 bill did not seem genuine. At the first opportunity he called the security guard, only to discover that his cell phone was out of order. But the Mall Passer had now moved on to other stores, where he continued to pass counterfeit bills. Finally, the Mall Passer—a thin, dark-haired man with a tight, straight mouth—was followed to his car. Some sixth sense must have told the fugitive that he was being observed, for one clerk noticed that he was so nervous that he was shaking. The police arrived shortly after he had driven away.

A month later, on May 25, the Passer was recognized by a bookstore clerk in West Knoxville, Tennessee, who dialed the police. The man had realized he was being tailed, and broke into a run, with two agents after him, when he found himself confronted by two policemen who had been summoned by radio.

But the thin, tight-lipped man was uncooperative with the police, even though he knew that they had found more phony bills and stolen license plates in his car, as well as a large quantity of pornography.

His wallet identified him as Roger Collin Blanchard, but his car was registered to a James R. Jones of Alexandria, Virginia. Fingerprint identification, however, revealed him to be James Mitchell DeBardeleben II, known as "Mike," and that in 1976 he had spent two yeas in jail for passing dud $100 bills.

In his apartment, investigators discovered a Yellow Pages directory with a tiny slip of paper slipped between the pages listing storage facilities. And a visit to the one nearest his home uncovered a storeroom full of the kind of items that indicated a car thief, and someone who posed as a policeman—a police badge, bubble lights, handcuffs, and a siren. And together with more pornography, they found dozens of photographs of women in various stages of undress, many looking terrified and battered. There could be little doubt that these latter were not posed by models—a bag containing bloodied panties, a chain, handcuffs, a dildo, and a lubricant suggested why the women looked so terrified. There were also tapes that made it clear that DeBardeleben enjoyed having women at his mercy—and forcing them to say that they were enjoying the rapes and tortures he was inflicting on them.

In his study of DeBardeleben, *Lethal Shadow,* Stephen Michaud remarks that investigators concluded that he was "the most dangerous felon ever at large in America." Michaud also comments: "For

Mike DeBardeleben, possession meant a live victim, suffering under his control." "There is no greater power over another person than that of inflicting pain on her," DeBardeleben wrote in his private journal. "To force her to undergo suffering without her being able to defend herself. The pleasure in the constant domination over another person is the very essence of the sadistic drive."

The problems with chronicling DeBardeleben's criminal career were, as Michaud soon discovered, enormous. Even with the help of Roy Hazelwood, who had collected all of the evidence that figured in DeBardeleben's trials (no less than six), and which finally sent him to prison for 365 years, there was no possibility of constructing a timeline of DeBardeleben's criminal activities. He had covered his trail far too well. Ted Bundy—about whom Michaud also wrote a book—continued to deny his guilt until his death sentence produced a state of desperation in which he was willing to bargain for time with confessions dribbled out piecemeal. DeBardeleben was never under this pressure, and so had no motivation to tell the whole truth. Michaud, like the police investigators, had to work backwards, telling the story in reverse order. For practical purposes, this began with DeBardeleben's release from prison in May 1978, where he had spent two years for passing counterfeit bills.

In the early hours of Sunday, September 4, 1978, DeBardeleben passed a nineteen-year-old nurse (whom Michaud calls "Lucy Alexander") who had quarreled with her boyfriend and was walking towards her home. He politely asked if he could help. She climbed into his luxury car. Minutes later he produced a police badge and told her she was under arrest for hitchhiking. He snapped handcuffs on her wrists, and gagged and blindfolded her with adhesive tape. Two hours later they stopped at a house and he took her indoors. On a mattress on the floor he undressed her, leaving the blindfold in place, and then raped her for an hour without reaching a climax. He then sodomized her, ordering her to call him "Daddy." After a sleep, he drank root beer, smoked a cigarette, and forced her to fellate him. As she did this he abused her verbally—obviously an integral part of the pleasure of the rape.

In lulls between further rapes, he told her about his former wife; "all she did was spend money." During the next eighteen hours she was raped four times vaginally and anally. Finally, he allowed her to dress, drove her to an isolated area, and released her.

On the afternoon of February 4, 1979, DeBardeleben went into the trailer sales office of a real estate company, and told the realtor, thirty-one-year-old Elizabeth Mason (again a pseudonym), that he was a federal employee about to be transferred to Arlington, Virginia, and was looking for a home for himself and his wife. He asked her to take him to see some houses in the $100,000 range. Finally, in an empty house, he pointed a .389 automatic at her. Recalling an article she had read by the TV hostess Carol Burnett, she decided to scream and yell and flail at him.

DEBARDELEBEN WAS NEVER UNDER THIS PRESSURE, AND SO HAD NO MOTIVATION TO TELL THE WHOLE TRUTH. MICHAUD, LIKE THE POLICE INVESTIGATORS, HAD TO WORK BACKWARDS, TELLING THE STORY IN REVERSE ORDER.

He tried to shoot her, but the gun jammed. He then began hitting her with the gun. Eventually, declaring that he only wanted her purse and that he would then leave, he got her to agree to being tied up. This proved to be a mistake; when she was tied, he throttled her, banging her head on the floor and shouting, "Pass out, bitch." Finally she did.

When she woke up, her slacks had been removed, and the man had taken her car. She was in such a state of trauma that it was two days before a detective could question her. Her head required thirty-one stitches. It was not until she was in the hospital that she realized that her sanitary pad was still in place and that she had not been raped.

On June 1, 1979, a twenty-year-old woman (Michaud calls her "Laurie Jensen") was on her way home toward midnight from the convenience store she managed when a sedan pulled up and the driver said, "Police," and ordered her into the car. Then he told her she was suspected of being an accomplice in a burglary.

Soon he abandoned the pretense, and handcuffed, blindfolded, and gagged her. A two-hour drive followed, which ended when he made her walk into a house. There he undressed her and ordered her to perform oral sex. She noticed the small size of his penis. After achieving an erection with difficulty he sodomized her, ordering her to call him "Daddy" as he did so.

DEBARDELEBEN'S NEXT ATTEMPT AT ABDUCTION SHOWED HOW HIS HATRED OF WOMEN COULD EXPLODE IF HE WAS RESISTED.

That afternoon he made her pose for photographs, tape-recorded her as she was forced to tell him how much she enjoyed what he was doing to her, and then locked her in a closet. He told her that he was resentful about a previous wife and wanted "to get back at all women." After keeping her for twenty-four hours, with more sodomy and oral sex, he drove her to within a few blocks of her home.

Frustrated investigators consulted the Behavioral Science Unit at Quantico, and it was John Douglas who profiled the rapist. What he said was to prove remarkably accurate when DeBardeleben was finally arrested. Douglas said that a man who did this kind of thing was raised by an overbearing, domineering mother, and had a passive father. He had probably been arrested in his teens, had been in the military, but would have such problems adjusting to discipline that he would probably have been discharged. He would also be sexually inadequate.

DeBardeleben's next attempt at abduction showed how his hatred of women could explode if he was resisted. On November 1, 1980, a twenty-five-year-old named Diane Overton was pulled over at 4 a.m. by a man who claimed to be a policeman. He ordered her out of the car, and when she opened the door, snapped handcuffs on her wrists. When he put his hand over her mouth she bit him hard. She then began screaming and honking her horn. But in spite of being in the middle of a residential district, no one responded. He dragged her into his car, but she stalled it by kicking it out of gear. Then she managed to open the door and fell out. The open door hit a cement wall and jammed. He managed to get it free and drove at her; she twisted out of the way, but he turned at a closed gas station and drove at her again. She succeeded in escaping by hiding under a concrete stairway, until her attacker finally drove off. She was lucky to escape; in his fury, DeBardeleben would undoubtedly have tortured as well as killed her.

Ten days after this attempted kidnapping, he went into a clothing store in southern New Jersey and abducted the clerk, an Italian-American Michaud calls "Maria Santini." In the car, she was ordered to crouch with her head on the seat. In his home he undressed her and tied her up with rope, explaining that he was "into bondage." He then told her he was a transvestite, and proved it by disappearing into the next room and returning wearing a miniskirt and high heels. After taking photographs of her in various poses that he arranged, he moved her into the bedroom and took more bondage photographs, explaining that his method was known as a "Chinese hog-tie." Then, after lying beside her, kissing her breasts, and fondling her vagina, he allowed her to dress, even giving her the sweaty turtleneck he had been wearing to replace a blouse he had cut off her. After that he drove her to some woods and left her.

These were just a few of the crimes DeBardeleben committed between May 1978 and his arrest as the Mall Passer.

After DeBardeleben's capture, investigators—still unaware that he was more than a skillful counterfeiter—began checking his background. Born in 1940, he was first arrested at age sixteen was for carrying a concealed weapon. He had subsequently been arrested on charges of sodomy, murder, and attempted kidnapping. But he had been in prison only twice, once for a parole violation and once for counterfeiting. A large part of the material seized in his storage facility consisted of handwritten pages in which he spoke about himself and his plans at length—one document described his long-term ambition to buy himself a house in a remote spot, where he was not overlooked by neighbors, and turn it into a place where he could bring captive women and make them obey his every whim.

Incredibly, it looked as if the authorities might be willing to forget all of his criminal activities except passing dud bills. The reason, simply, was that following up his criminal career looked as if it was likely to be a long and costly exercise. The Secret Service's responsibilities began and ended with the counterfeiting case. Agent Jane Vezeris, in overall charge of the investigation, was outraged by the idea, and went to see her boss, Acting Assistant Director Joe Carlon. She took with her a tape in which DeBardeleben could be heard making various sadistic demands, while his victim screams in anguish.

By chance, the director of the Secret Service, John R. Simpson, dropped in during the meeting, and heard the tape. When it was over, Simpson told Carlon, "Give them whatever they want," and left.

The first step agents Foos and Mertz took was to dispatch a Teletype about DeBardeleben's arrest to all field offices. Soon they had a break. Agent Harold Bibb, of Shreveport, Louisiana, thought he recognized the photograph of DeBardeleben, and after staring at it for a quarter of an hour, recalled that it resembled an artist's impression of a man who was wanted for the murder of a real estate agent, Jean McPhaul, in 1982. The man had asked her to show him properties in Bossier City; he called himself "Dr. Zack." On April 27, the attractive forty-year-old had left her office in the morning, and when she failed to return, colleagues went looking for her. They found her in an attic, suspended by the throat from a rafter, drenched in blood from two knife wounds.

The killing seemed motiveless—she had been neither raped nor robbed.

Moreover, the investigators heard of another murder of a realtor dating back to 1971 in Barrington, Rhode Island; she was fifty-two-year-old Edna ("Terry") Macdonald, and had set out for an evening appointment with a customer who called himself Peter Morgan, and failed to return. She was found in a basement, a cord around her neck and tied to an overhead pipe. She had been strangled, and again, rape and robbery were ruled out as motives. The description of Peter Morgan sounded like DeBardeleben.

Enquiries about DeBardeleben went on pouring in from all over the country—Mertz and Foos were astonished at the sheer volume of unsolved murders—and one of these indicated another level of DeBardeleben's criminal activities: a kidnapping for ransom. On April 13, 1983, David Starr, manager of the Columbia Savings Bank in Greece, near Rochester, New York, had taken his sick housemate, Joe Rapini, to the hospital. On arriving home, they were held at gunpoint by a ski-masked intruder, who proposed to take Rapini hostage in his own car while Starr went to his bank and collected $70,000. When the money was paid, Rapini would be left in the trunk of the car. Starr was able to collected only $37,900, which he left near a burnt-out house. Twice Starr saw a woman driving a small white car, and it appeared later that she was the accomplice who collected the ransom. But when Rapini was found in the trunk of his car later that day, he had been shot through the heart, as well as beaten about the head and face.

INCREDIBLY, IT LOOKED AS IF THE AUTHORITIES MIGHT BE WILLING TO FORGET ALL OF HIS CRIMINAL ACTIVITIES EXCEPT PASSING DUD BILLS.

DeBardeleben's writings had indicated an interest in banks. And a teller at the Columbia Savings Bank recognized a photograph of him as a man who had been hanging around there.

The next task was to try to identify photographs of forty women among DeBardeleben's seized possessions, whose positions and expressions suggested that they had been victims of the same kind of sexual violence as rape victims Lucy Alexander, Elizabeth Mason, and Laurie Jensen. The identity of most of them would remain unknown, as did the question of how many of them survived their ordeals. One or two were identified by one of DeBardeleben's former wives as women who had worked for a nude modeling photographic studio he had run in 1972. Others were obviously in a state of terror, a few looked drugged, and others dead. The only thing that was absolutely clear was that DeBardeleben had spent much of his life raping, torturing, and terrifying women.

The reason for this hatred of women emerged when investigators spoke to his previous wives. The root of the trouble was his mother Mary Lou (whom he called Moe). Theirs was the classic Freudian love-hate relationship. When she had met DeBardeleben's father (also called Mike) in the early 1930s, he was a serious-minded young engineer; she was a pretty, bubbly legal secretary who loved to party. Her own mother had died giving birth to her, and she had been adopted (twice) but never felt loved. So she had little love to give her children. When stressed she tended to drink, and so soon lost her hourglass figure. She was undoubtedly responsible for turning her son into a sociopath, and the investigators came to believe that he had murdered realtor Terry Macdonald because she resembled his mother. He grew up narcissistic, cruel, and demanding—an archetypal Right Man.

HIS FIRST POLICE MUG SHOT—ON A CARELESS DRIVING CHARGE—SHOWS HIM WEARING A LEATHER JACKET, DARK GLASSES, AND A BORED SNEER.

His father also seems to have had some Right Man tendencies, in that he was strict and bad-tempered, and "made everyone miserable" according to his daughter Beal. "His wife and children were made to feel inadequate," and Mike was frequently punished, on one occasion by having his head held under water. Parents like these can be almost guaranteed to turn a strong-willed son into a sociopath.

By the time he was sixteen his mother had become a drunk, and his "physical assaults on her were routine." His first police mug shot—on a careless driving charge—shows him wearing a leather jacket, dark glasses, and a bored sneer. Soon after that he was expelled from high school.

He was in the air force for a brief period, but was court-martialed for disorderly behavior, and a psychiatrist described him as "a verbose young man of superior intelligence who gave an extensive history of repetitive acts of an egocentric and antisocial nature." He was soon discharged. He went back to high school and was soon expelled again. An attempt to rob a service station led to him firing at the attendant and then fleeing empty-handed. He was sentenced to five years' probation. By this time his first marriage—to a girl called Linda—was also over. He soon married again—a pretty schoolgirl—but this also broke up. By now, his parents were terrified of him. And his younger brother, Ralph, whose upbringing had been equally loveless and equally traumatic, committed suicide. After he threatened his mother with a hatchet, his parents had him committed to a mental hospital, where he spent six weeks.

He forced his third wife, a pretty beautician named Faye, to pose for pornographic photographs, including bondage. He also pressured her to become his partner in crime. Her job was to locate lonely elderly women. DeBardeleben would then call a target, claiming to be a "Federal Bank Examiner," explain that her account was being tampered with, and that in order to help him catch the culprit, she had to withdraw money from her account; when she did this, the "Examiner" would arrive at her house with a briefcase and dark suit, and convince her that he had to take the money away, but that it would be returned shortly. Faye estimated that the husband-and-wife team did this about thirty times and took around $1,200 on each occasion—although on one occasion it was as high as $3,500.

His next moneymaking scheme involved the crimes of kidnapping and extortion, using the same basic scheme as in the extortion that had ended in the murder of the bank manager's male partner. This brought $60,000. Soon after this incident, Faye learned she was pregnant, refused his demand that she have an abortion, and left him.

His fourth wife was another pretty schoolgirl named Caryn, and the marriage began auspiciously when he returned to college (he was now thirty) and took courses in philosophy, history, and government. But soon he was treating her as he treated Faye, and forcing her to become his accomplice in another extortion—a bank manager's wife was held at pistol point and made to telephone her husband and tell him she would be killed unless he delivered $60,000 to a pickup point. In fact, he was able to raise only half this sum, which Caryn retrieved.

Under the stress of being married to DeBardeleben, acting as his accomplice in crimes, and taking part in strange sexual games that involved bondage and beatings, Caryn developed acute nervous problems, including multiple personality disorder (which usually develops as an attempt to escape an intolerable reality). And, eventually, Caryn did something that Right Men hate and fear more than anything else: she left him, and so became the object of an almost insane hatred. She, it seems, was the wife he was punishing vicariously when he kidnapped and raped women such as Laurie Jensen, Elizabeth Mason, and Maria Santini.

Eventually, investigators would discover at least one occasion when this hatred led to murder. On April 27, 1983, in Beaumont, Texas, Rhoda Piazza, a twenty-two-year-old topless dancer, was seen with a tall white male in a club called The Foxy Lady. Two days later, her naked body, raped, sodomized, and brutally beaten, was found beside a country road. Investigators connected DeBardeleben to this murder because among the many stolen license plates found in his storage unit was one from Beaumont, Texas, stolen just before the dancer disappeared; he had been passing counterfeit bills in a nearby town soon after. Marks on the body showed that she had been suspended in a harness and then lashed, beaten, and tortured with cigarette burns. The position of one burn suggested it had been made while she was being anally raped.

The two detectives who had traveled from Texas to Virginia to interview him only met with frustration. As soon as they identified themselves as being from Beaumont, Texas, DeBardeleben stood up and walked out of the interview room. The inference seems to be that he had no desire to discuss Beaumont, Texas.

Roy Hazelwood, who was asked to survey the sexual materials seized from the storage facility—photographs, audiotapes, sheaves of notes and diary entries—concluded that DeBardeleben was the most self-documented sadist since the Marquis de Sade.

He also noted that DeBardeleben was a totally narcissistic egomaniac, and that his decision to act as his own defender—a typical decision for a narcissist—led to his downfall as much as any other factor. (As we have seen, Ted Bundy would have escaped execution if he had left the conduct of his trial to his lawyers.)

DeBardeleben's major mistake came when he was cross-examining nineteen-year-old Lori Cobert, who had been pulled over by a "police officer" on February 5, 1981. The "officer" had made her fellate him before he let her go. In the courthouse at Manassas, Virginia, DeBardeleben took her through the crime in detail, so that spectators felt he was relishing it.

UNDER THE STRESS OF BEING MARRIED TO DEBARDELEBEN, ACTING AS HIS ACCOMPLICE IN CRIMES, AND TAKING PART IN STRANGE SEXUAL GAMES THAT INVOLVED BONDAGE AND BEATINGS, CARYN DEVELOPED ACUTE NERVOUS PROBLEMS, INCLUDING MULTIPLE PERSONALITY DISORDER

"During the incident in this man's car, it was dark all the time, wasn't it?"

"I could see."

"The interior lights were not on, were they?"

"No."

"And there were no overhead interior lights, were there?"

"No.

"The only lights they had there were these little small ones next to the door at the bottom of the door, right?"

"Correct."

Prosecutor Miliette would point out to the jury that DeBardeleben's question revealed a knowledge of the car that indicated that it was his own. The panel required just thirty-eight minutes to convict.

But it was not simply mistakes like this that led to the guilty verdict. Everything about his presentation underlined an overblown ego and conviction of his own cleverness. At his sixth and final trial, for the abduction and rape of Laurie Jensen, he was sentenced to 60 years, bringing the total to 375.

In 1987, too late to help in the prosecution of DeBardeleben, law enforcement agencies gained a new tool with the introduction of genetic fingerprinting, discovered by the British scientist Dr. Alec Jeffreys in 1984. This was founded on the recognition that every cell in our bodies is as individual as a fingerprint, so that a rapist can be identified from his semen, a fragment of skin under the victim's nails, or even by a hair root. There are stretches in the DNA molecule (three feet long) where the genetic code differs dramatically for each individual (except identical twins), and which is therefore a "fingerprint." It was used in the United Kingdom in November 1987, to identify the rapist of a forty-five-year-old disabled woman in Bristol. After that, it was used to establish the culprit in a case where two schoolgirls had been raped and murdered. All males in a whole country area near Leicester were asked for blood samples. In fact, the rapist, a bakery worker named Colin Pitchfork, was not caught by his blood sample, but by his attempt to avoid giving it; he persuaded a friend to take the test for him, and the friend was overheard boasting about it. Pitchfork was questioned and confessed.

In Virginia at that time there was a far more brutal and dangerous rapist and killer. He took as much pleasure in raping and slowly strangling his victims, using a lubricant, as the Hillside Stranglers. Pettechial hemorrhages—small blood spots—under the eyelids revealed that he had tortured his victims with a tourniquet for up to an hour, repeatedly throttling them and then allowing them to breathe again.

The first victim had been thirty-five-year-old Debbie Davis, who was asleep when the rapist broke into her apartment in Richmond, Virginia, on September 19, 1987. Two weeks later, on October 3, thirty-two-year-old neurologist Dr. Susan Hellams was attacked in her bedroom, subjected to lengthy rape and torture with a tourniquet, and then strangled with a belt; her husband, a law student, found her bound body in a wardrobe in the bedroom.

On November 22, the killer moved twenty miles away, to the home of a fifteen-year-old Korean student, Diane Cho, where she lived in Chesterfield County with her family. Her death had not even been noticed for most of a day because the killer had climbed through her bedroom window when she was asleep—she had removed the screen—and gagged her with duct tape before subjecting her to the lengthy rape and strangulation. The rapes, both vaginal and anal, had been exceptionally brutal, tearing her flesh. Since Diane had been working late at night on some assignment, her parents and brother assumed that she was sleeping late, and did not investigate until mid-afternoon.

Police went to the home of forty-four-year-old Susan Tucker after a call from her husband, who was away in his native Wales and was unable to get an answer to his phone calls; she was a government employee, and they had no children. She was found facedown in the bedroom, naked except for a sleeping bag that covered her lower body; the rope around her wrist was also looped around her neck, so that any struggles would cause her to strangle herself. Semen was found on her nightdress, and two black pubic hairs. The contents of her handbag had been scattered on the floor, yet there was no sign that anything had been taken.

Detective Joe Horgas was reminded of a similar murder in Arlington three years earlier—that of thirty-two-year-old attorney Carolyn Hamm, who had also been raped and strangled. Strangulation was obviously a part of the killer's obsession; he had looped a rope around Carolyn Hamm's neck, taken it over a ceiling pipe, and tied it to the bumper of a car in the garage.

A suspect named David Vasquez, thirty-seven, had been arrested. Neighbors had noticed him hanging around her house on the two days preceding the murder. A search of his apartment revealed girly magazines of the *Playboy* sort, one containing a picture of a woman bound and gagged. He was not a highly intelligent individual, and the evidence suggested that he was a Peeping Tom who liked to take photographs while he was doing it. The semen evidence did not link him to the crime, but police theorized that he was one of two intruders. Under interrogation he confessed, and was confined to prison.

A blood test on the semen on Susan Tucker's nightdress revealed that the blood was type O, as in the Hamm case; but since that was the most common type, this was of little help.

It was at this point that Horgas heard about the three rape-murders in nearby Richmond, and wondered if there was a connection. The MOs were very similar. He had also just learned about Alec Jeffreys's discovery in England, and instantly saw that genetic fingerprinting might be his solution. The only laboratory in the United States that was performing DNA testing was Lifecodes of New York. And it was to them that the five semen samples were sent.

In 1987, the tests took about ten weeks. Meanwhile, Horgas learned of a series of rapes that had preceded the murders in Richmond. These had started early in 1983, but had then stopped. The probable reason, Horgas suspected, was that the rapist had been sent to prison. The first of three 1983 rapes had taken place in the Richmond suburb of Green Valley. Horgas reasoned that this was probably close to the rapist's home, since a first rape is often committed where the rapist feels comfortable and knows his escape route.

Thousands of names of criminals were run through the computer. Then Horgas came upon a case with which he had been involved in the early 1980s—a young black burglar named Timothy Spencer, who had started his career with arson. Horgas had been to the home of Spencer's mother to investigate a burglary in which Spencer—born 1962—was a possible suspect. And although Spencer had not been charged, Horgas had entered his name into the system.

Now Horgas realized that he had a hit. Spencer had gone to jail in January 1984 for burglary, and had been released to a halfway house in Richmond two weeks before the murder of Debbie Davis. When Horgas checked the dates Spencer had signed out of the halfway house, each was the date of a murder. And when Susan Tucker was murdered in Arlington in December 1987, Spencer had been allowed back to his home in Washington on furlough for Thanksgiving.

When the DNA test results came back from Lifecodes, they showed that the same person had committed all of the five rapes.

Spencer was picked up for questioning in January 1988. When authorities requested a blood sample, he asked: "What has blood got to do with rape?" But no one had mentioned rape.

His blood sample had the same genetic code as that of the Susan Tucker rapist, and he was charged with her murder.

The defense took the line that DNA fingerprinting was new and untested, and therefore unreliable. The prosecution replied that in that case, they would have to submit the evidence from the other rape-murder cases to prove their point. Understandably, the defense team dropped their objection.

Timothy Spencer was found guilty in July 1988 and sentenced to death; he was executed in the electric chair on April 27, 1994.

In due course, the efficiency of DNA testing improved until results came back in a matter of days rather than weeks. It also became possible to make copies of the DNA molecule, so that in cases where only a small quantity was available, an indefinite amount could be created. In the case of Gary Ridgway, the Green River Killer (see chapter 14) this was to prove crucial.

It also became possible to open up "cold cases" that had long ago been abandoned, so that most police departments created Cold Case teams to look into murders that might be several decades old.

The Virginia police files provide a striking example.

On July 25, 1980, forty-seven-year-old Dorothy White was found stabbed and raped in her trailer; her throat had also been slashed. But a careful search by the physical evidence recovery team failed to find any clues to her murder. Although unmarried, she had been for years in a stable relationship with a used-car salesman, who was eliminated from the enquiry. Dozens of possible suspects were interviewed, but none detained. Over the years the case went cold.

In 1999, nineteen years after the murder, the victim's sister-in-law, Doris White, telephoned the local police department to ask whether they might try DNA fingerprinting. She spoke to Detective Sergeant Edgar Browning, who had worked on the case. Browning went back to the file for the original "perk" kit (physical evidence recovery) and sent off the swabs taken from Dorothy White to the laboratory for testing.

Immense strides had been taken in DNA testing since Timothy Spencer had been convicted ten years earlier. In those days, a fairly large quantity of semen was required—enough to cover a nickel. Now a spot almost invisible to the eye was sufficient, for it was possible to churn out copies by a method know as STR, or short tandem repeats (also known as PCR, polymerase chain reaction).

Since 1989, Virginia had also started to build a DNA fingerprint database, which now contained samples from 100,000 offenders.

Almost immediately, Browning had a match—a man named William Morrisette. He had, in fact, been among the suspects originally interviewed, for he did odd jobs for Dorothy White's boyfriend, and occasionally mowed her lawn.

Morrisette was in the database because in 1985, he had approached a woman called Virginia Brown, who had been sitting in her car waiting for her daughter to come out of school. Morrisette had tried to gag her, and forced his way into the car, with the obvious intention of abducting and raping her; she had thrown her keys out of the car window. The approach of another car motivated him to run away. Arrested a few days later, he had been sentenced to eight years for attempted abduction. But it was not until after his release, when he was re-arrested for parole violation, that Browning had asked for a blood sample to enter into the database.

AFTER LISTENING TO GASKINS'S HORRIFIC STORIES FOR MONTHS, HE SANK INTO A STATE OF STRESS AND ANXIETY THAT WRECKED HIS MARRIAGE AND LED TO A NERVOUS BREAKDOWN.

Morrisette was found guilty of Dorothy White's murder on the DNA evidence and sentenced to death.

In 1993, I became involved—retrospectively—in the case of a man who may be the worst serial killer of all time. If sadistic killers are the great white sharks of deviant murder, then Donald ("Pee Wee") Gaskins probably qualifies as its Jaws. Yet until 1992, a year after his execution, his name remained completely unknown to the public at large. This changed with the publication of *Final Truth: The Autobiography of a Serial Killer,* whose descriptions of his crimes were so horrific that when I first tried to read it, I gave it up after a few dozen pages.

In the summer of 1993, I was working as a contributing editor on a part-work called *Murder in Mind*. (A part-work is a magazine published in single issues, which the reader can collect and bind together in a series of folders.) I suggested Gaskins as the subject of an issue, but this soon ran into problems. Most of the photographs of Gaskins were the copyright of the author of *Final Truth,* Wilton Earle Hall, a South Carolina writer who wrote under the pen name Wilton Earle. He not only owned the photographs, but he also felt that, since he had "discovered" and researched the case, copyright on its details belonged to him. He had successfully sued one writer who had used his work.

When the publisher of *Murder in Mind* spoke to Earle on the telephone, he learned that he was an admirer of my books, and so asked me to ring him and see if I could persuade him to allow us to go ahead. Later that day I spoke to him from the publisher's office, and immediately established a warm relationship that has lasted to the present time.

What he had to tell me was this:

Pee Wee Gaskins had come to Earle's attention when he was under sentence of death in the Broad River Correctional Institution in Columbia, South Carolina, for murdering a fellow prisoner. He had been sentenced originally for killing a number of "business associates," people involved with him in a racket involving respraying and selling stolen cars. Earle wrote to ask him if he would like to collaborate on his autobiography. Gaskins invited Earle to visit him in prison, and in unsupervised conversations revealed that he was a sadistic killer who had often cooked and eaten parts of his victims—sometimes while they were still alive. And since he was scheduled for execution, Gaskins had decided to tell the whole story, which involved around 110 murders.

But listening to this recital of torture and murder proved more than Wilton Earle had bargained for.

In *Whoever Fights Monsters,* Ressler writes:

> *Nearly everyone in our unit fell victim to its situational stress. One woman profiler bailed out after a few years because the work was giving her nightmares. She found herself unable to deal rationally with cases in which someone broke into a house and raped a woman; she, too, went on to other work for the FBI. Several of our people developed bleeding ulcers and three had anxiety attacks that were so severe that they were initially misperceived as heart attacks. Four of us, myself included, had periods of rapid and unexplained weight loss, some twenty to forty pounds in six-month periods. We went for batteries of tests, including the standard gastrointestinal series, and no purely physical reasons for the weight loss were discovered; it was all stress-related.*

Something of the sort had happened to Earle. After listening to Gaskins's horrific stories for months, he sank into a state of stress and anxiety that wrecked his marriage and led to a nervous breakdown. Even after Gaskins had been executed, the problems continued—at which point medical tests revealed that Earle was suffering from cancer. He regards this as one outcome of those days spent closeted with the man who told him: "My name is going to live as long as men talk about good and evil."

A harmless-looking little man with a high voice, Gaskins enjoyed torturing his victims, mostly hitchhikers, to death.

Born in the backwoods of South Carolina in 1933, Gaskins had been sent to reform school for burglary as a teenager, and had been gang-raped by twenty youths; this was the first of many terms in prison, although he later compelled the respect of fellow inmates when he murdered a particularly dangerous fellow prisoner, one of the jail's "power men." After a prison sentence for raping an underage girl, he resolved in future to kill women he raped and to hide the bodies. The first time he did this he was so carried away by the sensation of power that he began doing it regularly.

It seems likely that his predisposition to sadism was inborn. When he was a five-year-old, he went to a carnival where he saw a cobra in a glass cage kill a rat with a single strike of its fangs, and he found that the sight gave him an erection.

I suspect (as does Earle) that if Gaskins had been subjected to a postmortem, he would have been found to be brain damaged. As noted in an earlier chapter, a significant number of violent killers have suffered brain lesions due to blows to the head or birth defects.

The human brain has the consistency of jelly, and a violent blow—particularly on the forehead—can cause it to surge forward against the skull, creating scars. Such people often experience a total personality change, becoming prone to explosions of violence. It seems plausible that this may explain what Gaskins called his "bothersomeness"—a feeling as if he had a ball of molten lead in his stomach, which created tension and severe pain.

In *Final Truth,* Gaskins says:

> *When I was younger, there was always one or another of a bunch of different step-daddies around. I called them all sir and never bothered to learn most of their names because I knew my Mama wasn't married to them, and they wouldn't likely be around for long. The one she finally did marry was one mean son-of-a-bitch. He used to backhand me and knock me clean across the room just for practice. But then everybody knocked me around: my uncles, my other step-daddies, and nearabout all the boys and girls I played with and went to school with. They beat up on me just because I was so damned little.*

When Donald "Pee Wee" Gaskins was arrested on November 14, 1975—charged with contributing to the delinquency of a minor—it was for suspected involvement in the disappearance of Kim Ghelkins, a thirteen-year old girl last seen leaving her home in Charleston with an overnight bag.

Kim's parents told the police of a married man named Donald Gaskins, whose stepdaughter was a friend of Kim's.

Twelve years before this, Gaskins had been imprisoned for the statutory rape of a twelve-year-old girl named Patsy. A week later, he had escaped by jumping from an open window of a second-storey waiting room in the Florence County courtroom. He was at liberty for six months before being recaptured and sentenced to four years in the South Carolina Central Correctional Institution. In November 1970, he was again questioned by the police, this time about the disappearance of his own fifteen-year-old niece, Janice Kirby, but denied all knowledge of her whereabouts.

A month later, he had again been under suspicion—this time, of a horrifying sex murder. Peggy Cuttino, the thirteen-year-old daughter of a prominent local politician, had disappeared in the small town of Sumter; her mutilated and tortured body was found in a ditch. Again, Gaskins was questioned and released.

It was when some of Kim Ghelkins's clothes were found in a mobile home rented by Gaskins that a warrant was issued for his arrest. Yet even when taken into custody, police were unable to find enough evidence to charge him. Just as they were preparing to release him, his trusted friend and fellow convict Walter Neely experienced a sudden conversion as a born-again Christian, and decided to tell everything he knew about Gaskins. That same afternoon—December 4, 1975—he led the police to the graves of two young men who had been shot in the head and buried in the swamp. The following day he led them to four more corpses, two men and two women. On December 10, he was able to help them locate two more graves.

GASKINS DISLIKED HIS LOSS OF CELEBRITY STATUS AS SOUTH CAROLINA'S WORST MASS MURDERER; HE FELT HE DESERVED TO BE FAMOUS.

On May 24, 1976, Gaskins went on trial in the Florence County Courthouse, and was sentenced to die in the electric chair.

On death row, Gaskins began to think hard about how he could escape execution. One possibility was to confess to more murders, and engage in plea-bargaining. So he confessed to the murder of his niece, Janice, and her friend, Patty Ann Alsbrook. He claimed he had killed them as a result of an argument when he had caught them taking drugs. (In fact, as he later admitted to Wilton Earle, both had been sex crimes.) In exchange for his confession, Gaskins's death sentence was commuted to life imprisonment. With a known score of eleven murders, he prepared to face a lifetime behind bars.

In late 1980, there came a welcome diversion. He was asked if he would undertake to murder a fellow prisoner, Rudolph Tyner, a twenty-four-year-old black drug addict, who had killed an old couple in the course of holding up their grocery store. Now Tyner was on death row, hoping that the sentence would be commuted to life.

The son of his victims, Tony Cimo, was embittered at the thought of Tyner escaping the electric chair, and decided to take justice into his own hands. Through a friend of a friend, he approached Gaskins. Bored and frustrated in prison, Gaskins rose to the challenge of committing a murder under the nose of the wardens.

The first step was to get to know Tyner and gain his trust, which Gaskins did by slipping him reefers. The murder itself was brilliant in its ingenuity. Gaskins suggested he install a homemade telephone between their cells, running through a heating duct. Tyner's phone contained plastic explosive, supplied by Tony Cimo. When, at a prearranged time, Tyner said, "Over to you," Gaskins plugged his end of the wire into an electric socket, and the explosion rocked the whole cellblock. Tyner was blown to pieces.

At first the authorities believed that it had been an accident. Then rumors of murder began to spread. Soon, Tony Cimo was arrested, and confessed everything. He and Gaskins stood trial for the murder of Rudolph Tyner. Cimo received eight years. Gaskins was sentenced to the electric chair.

During his early days in prison, after his arrest for the murder of Kim Ghelkins, Gaskins had often been interviewed by reporters; now he was almost forgotten—a mere car thief and contract killer who had murdered a number of crooked business acquaintances. One or two criminologists had talked about writing about him, but it had all come to nothing. Gaskins disliked his loss of celebrity status as South Carolina's worst mass murderer; he felt he deserved to be famous.

So in 1990, when Wilton Earle, who felt that his story might be worth telling, approached him, Gaskins cautiously agreed. He was running out of appeals, and his appointment with the electric chair could not be long delayed—a year at the most. As he came to trust him, Gaskins agreed to tell Earle what he called "the final truth." But there was one stipulation: that nothing should be published until after Gaskins had been executed. Among other things, his rape of a small child would disgust his fellow prisoners.

Earle agreed. What he did not know when they made the agreement was that he was about to hear the most appalling and terrifying story of serial murder in the history of twentieth-century crime. What was revealed over many sessions with the tape recorder was that Gaskins was not simply a killer of crooked business associates; he was a compulsive and sadistic sex killer, whose list of victims amounted to three figures. The story of "the final truth" was so nauseating that Earle must have doubted many times whether it could be published.

Gaskins's problem, as it emerged in the tapes, had always been an overdeveloped sex-impulse. His need for sex was so powerful and compulsive that, whenever it came on him, he experienced a heavy feeling that rolled from his stomach up to his brain, and down again. He compared it to the pain women suffer before menstruation. When this happened, he would drive up and down the coastal highway cruising for female hitchhikers.

But having served two terms for rape, he had vowed it should never happen again. His solution was simple: to kill his victims. And having raped and killed his first with a knife, he discovered, like so many serial killers before him, that torture and murder were an addiction. "I felt truly the best I ever remembered feeling in my whole life."

With his next female hitchhiker, "I took my time and did some of the extra things I had thought up, so I enjoyed myself more, and after I finished, I felt the same good relief I felt the first time."

These "extra things" soon came to include melting lead and pouring it on his victims' flesh.

After a while, it made no difference whether the hitchhiker was male or female; it was the torture—and the sense of power—that gave the pleasure. In effect, he became a character out of one of the novels of the Marquis de Sade, working out new ways to satisfy his desire to torture and degrade.

Gaskins estimated that in the six years between September 1969 and his arrest in November 1975, he committed between eighty and ninety "coastal kills," an average of fourteen a year. He distinguished these murders of hitchhikers picked up on the coast road from his "serious murders," those committed for business or personal motives such as revenge.

Hours before his execution, Gaskins tried to commit suicide with a razor blade that he had swallowed the previous week, and then regurgitated. He was found in time, and given twenty stitches.

He had assumed that Earle would attend his execution, as his "official witness," so that he could die looking at a friendly face. But Earle, who had been forced to conceal his feelings of revulsion during the tape-recorded confessions, had no intention of giving Gaskins this comfort. At their final meeting, he told Gaskins: "You are mistaken, Pee Wee, if you think I was ever your advocate. Not for a moment did I ever approve of you." Gaskins tried to get at him from around the conference room table, but Earle was cautious enough to keep it between them (and proved to be correct—Gaskins had a concealed razor blade).

"I TOOK MY TIME AND DID SOME OF THE EXTRA THINGS I HAD THOUGHT UP, SO I ENJOYED MYSELF MORE, AND AFTER I FINISHED, I FELT THE SAME GOOD RELIEF I FELT THE FIRST TIME."

Soon after midnight on September 6, 1991, Donald Gaskins walked into the execution chamber without help, and sat in the electric chair. After his wrists and ankles had been strapped, a metal headpiece was placed on his skull, with a wet sponge inside it. Before the black hood was placed over his head he gave a thumbs-up salute to his lawyer. Three buttons were then pressed by three men—so that none of them would be sure who had been responsible for the execution.

His body was handed over to his daughter, and was later cremated.

13

Slaves

13

Slaves

In a chapter on the history of sex crime in *I Have Lived in the Monster,* Robert Ressler writes about the rise of serial murder: "Perhaps it is because modern society has thrown up many young men who were loners as children. They turned to fantasy as a result of physical and mental abuse during childhood, and were mentally unable to participate in normal consensual sexual relationships as young adults." And he adds: "The lethal fusing of sexual and aggressive impulse that characterize serial killers seems to occur in most modern societies . . ." And he cites Ed Kemper, who told a psychiatrist: "I have fantasies about mass murder—whole groups of select women. . . . Taking life away from them . . . and having possession of everything that used to be theirs—all that would be mine. Everything."

Unlike DeBardeleben, Kemper is not the kind of aggressive sadist who enjoys inflicting pain and humiliation on living victims. His dream is about sex slaves, with whom he can do whatever he likes because they are dead. With a slightly different temperament, such as that of William Heirens, he might have released his tensions in underwear fetishism.

Ressler then discusses a serial killer who followed this route. Jerry Brudos, an electrician of Salem, Oregon, had been stealing shoes and panties for most of his life when, on January 26, 1968, he received a visit from Linda Slawson, a twenty-two-year-old encyclopedia saleswoman. He invited her into his garage, knocked her unconscious with a piece of wood, and then strangled her. He was not interested in rape, but in dressing and undressing her as if she were a doll, using a box of stolen panties and bras. That night he threw her in the Long Tom River, south of Corvallis, Oregon. He kept only one thing—her foot for trying shoes on—in his garage freezer.

The following November, Brudos succeeded in luring another victim into his garage, twenty-three-year-old student Jan Whitney. He strangled her from behind, and then once again "played dolls." This time he also raped her, then suspended her by the wrists from a hook in the ceiling—the archetypal "sex slave" position. He kept her there for several days, using her as a plaything, and even removed her breast and tried to turn it into a paperweight with a resin hardener. He left her there while he took his family for a Thanksgiving trip, and was dismayed on his return to find that a corner of his garage had been demolished by a car that had run out of control. Fortunately for him, the police who were called to the accident had failed to look inside.

Once more he disposed of the body in the river.

But he was growing bored with passive slaves. On March 19, 1969, he abducted a nineteen-year-old student, Karen Sprinker, from a parking lot by pointing a gun at her and promising not to hurt her. After raping her on his garage floor, he made her pose for photographs in her white cotton bra and panties, and then in more glamorous underwear from his box. Finally he tied a rope around her neck, pulled her clear of the ground, and watched her suffocate. He then violated the corpse, cut off her breasts, and disposed of the body in the river.

With his next—and final victim—Brudos used the same abduction technique. Linda Salee, a twenty-two-year-old office worker, was climbing into her car, loaded with parcels, when Brudos showed her a police badge and told her he was arresting her for shoplifting. He took her back to his garage and tied her up, then left her while he went and ate dinner. He then went back to the garage and strangled her with a leather strap; he was in the act of raping her as she died. Later, he once more disposed of the body in the river.

The finding of bodies in the river triggered the search for the killer. Detective Jim Stovall decided to start at the Oregon State University campus in Corvallis, eighty miles south of Portland, where Karen Sprinker had been a student, and spent two days questioning every female student. The only promising leads were several mentions of a stranger who made a habit of telephoning the residence hall, asking girls their first names, then talking at length about himself, claiming to be psychic and to be a Vietnam veteran. He usually asked for a date, but seemed unoffended when he was refused. It was when one of the girls mentioned that she had agreed to meet the "Vietnam veteran" that Stovall's attention suddenly increased.

The man had seemed intrigued when she mentioned that she was taking a psychology course, and told her that he had been a patient at the Walter Reed Hospital, where he had learned about some interesting new techniques. When he suggested meeting her at the dorm for a coffee, the girl agreed.

The man's appearance had been a disappointment. Overweight and freckled, he looked to be in his thirties. He had a round, unprepossessing face and narrow eyes that gave him an oddly cunning look, like a schoolboy who is planning to steal the cookies. But he seemed pleasant enough, and they sat in the lounge and chatted at some length. Nevertheless, she had the feeling that he was a bit "odd." This suddenly came into focus when he placed a hand on her shoulder and remarked: "Be sad."

"Why?"

"Think of those two girls whose bodies were found in the river . . ."

When he left, he asked her to go for a drive, and when she declined, made the curious comment: "How do you know I wouldn't take you to the river and strangle you?" Stovall began to feel excited when the girl told them that the "Vietnam veteran" had mentioned that he might call again.

"If he does, would you agree to let him come here? Then call us immediately?"

The girl was reluctant, but agreed when the police told her that they would be there before the man arrived. She merely had to make some excuse to delay him for an hour.

A week later, on Sunday, May 25, 1969, the Corvallis Police Department received the call they had been hoping for. The girl told them that the "Vietnam veteran" had telephoned a few minutes ago, asking if he could come over. She told him she wanted to wash her hair, and asked him to make it in about an hour.

When the overweight, freckle-faced man in a T-shirt walked into the lounge of Callaghan Hall, two plainclothes policemen walked up to him and produced their badges. The man seemed unalarmed; he gave his name as Jerry Brudos, and said that he lived in Salem; the only sign of embarrassment was when he admitted that he had a wife and two children. He was now in Corvallis, he explained, because he was working nearby—as an electrician. Because Brudos had committed no offence for which he might be arrested, or even taken in for questioning, the police let him go.

A preliminary check showed that he was what he claimed to be—an electrician working in Corvallis. But when Stovall looked into his record, he realized that he had a leading suspect. Jerome Henry Brudos, thirty, had a record of violence towards women, and had spent nine months on the psychiatric ward of the Oregon State Hospital. Moreover, at the time of the disappearance of Linda Slawson, Brudos had lived in Portland, in the area where she was trying to peddle encyclopedias.

The first thing to do was to check him out. Stovall called on Brudos at his home in Center Street, Salem, and talked to him in his garage. Stovall's colleague, Detective Jerry Frazier, also went along, and noted the lengths of rope lying around the room, and the hook in the ceiling. He also noticed that one of the ropes was knotted, and the knot was identical to one that had been used to bind the corpses in the river.

This, Stovall decided, had to be their man. Everything fit. He worked as an electrician and car repairman. He had been working at Lebanon, Oregon, close to the place where Jan Whitney's car had been found. And he had been living close to the place from which Karen Sprinker had disappeared in Salem.

There was another piece of evidence that pointed to Brudos. On April 22, an overweight, freckled man holding a gun grabbed a fifteen-year-old schoolgirl as she hurried to school along the railroad tracks; she had screamed and succeeded in running away. She immediately picked out the photograph of Jerry Brudos from a batch shown to her by the detectives.

Except for this identification, there was no definite evidence against Brudos for the murders. Stovall was therefore reluctant to move against him. But five days after Brudos had been questioned in Corvallis, Stovall realized that he could no longer take the risk of leaving him at large. As he was on his way to arrest Brudos for the attempted abduction of the schoolgirl on the railway tracks, he received a radio message saying that Brudos and his family had left Corvallis, and were driving towards Portland. Shortly after this, a police patrol car stopped Brudos's station wagon. At first it looked as if Brudos was not inside; but he proved to be lying in the back, hidden under a blanket.

Back at the Salem police station, Brudos was asked to change into overalls. When he removed his clothes, he was found to be wearing women's panties.

When Stovall first questioned Brudos, he failed to secure any admissions. It was the same for the next three days, Stovall did not ask outright if Brudos had murdered the girls; he confined himself to general questions, hoping to pick up more clues. But at the fifth interview, Brudos suddenly began to talk about his interest in female shoes and underwear. Then he described how he had followed a girl in attractive shoes, broken into her home through a window, and made off with the shoes. Soon after this, he described how he had stolen the black bra—found on Karen Sprinker's body—from a clothesline. Now, at last, he had virtually admitted the killing. Then, little by little, the rest came out—the curious history of a psychopath who suffered from the curious sexual abnormality for which the psychologist Alfred Binet coined the word *fetishism*.

In Jerry Brudos's case, it first showed itself at the age of five, when he found a pair of women's patent leather shoes on a rubbish dump, and put them on at home. His mother was furious and ordered him to return them immediately; instead he hid them and wore them in secret. When his mother found them, he was beaten and the shoes were burned.

THE DESIRE FOR A LIVING TOY WAS CARRIED TO AN ABSURD EXTREME WHEN CAMERON HOOKER, A BESPECTACLED, MILD-LOOKING TIMBER WORKER, KIDNAPPED A HITCHHIKER AND KEPT HER IN A BOX FOR SEVEN YEARS.

When he was sixteen—in 1955—he stole the underwear of a girl who lived next door. Then he approached the girl and told her he was working for the police as an undercover agent, and could help her to recover the stolen articles. She allowed herself to be lured into his bedroom on an evening when his family was away. Suddenly, a masked man jumped on her, threatened her with a knife, and made her remove all her clothes. Then, to her relief, he merely took photographs of her with a flashbulb camera. At the end of the session, the masked man walked out of the bedroom, and a few minutes later, Jerry Brudos rushed in, claiming that the masked intruder had locked him in the barn. The girl knew he was lying, but there was nothing she could do about it.

In April 1956, Brudos invited a seventeen-year-old girl for a ride in his car. On a deserted highway, he dragged her from the car, beat her up, and ordered her to strip. A passing couple heard her screams, and rescued her.

A psychiatrist determined that he was sane and had no violent tendencies. Back in his home, police found a large box of women's underwear and shoes. They sent him to the Oregon State Hospital for observation, and he was released after nine months.

A period in the army followed, but he was discharged because of his bizarre delusions—he was convinced that a beautiful Korean girl sneaked into his bed every night to seduce him.

Back in Salem, he attacked a young girl one night and stole her shoes. He did it again in Portland. Then, just as it looked as if nothing could stop him from turning into a rapist, he met a gentle seventeen-year-old named Darcie (a pseudonym) who was anxious to get away from home, and who got herself pregnant by him. Once married, she was sometimes a little puzzled by his odd demands—making her dress up in silk underwear and high-heeled shoes and pose for photographs—but assumed that most men were like this.

While his wife was in the hospital having a baby, Brudos followed a girl who was wearing pretty shoes. When he broke into her room that night, she woke up, and he choked her unconscious. Then, unable to resist, he raped her. He left her apartment carrying her shoes.

He was now a time bomb, waiting for another opportunity to explode. It happened when an encyclopedia saleswoman knocked on his door one winter evening . . .

Because he pleaded guilty to four counts of murder, Jerry Brudos was sentenced without a trial to life imprisonment.

* * * * *

The desire for a living toy was carried to an absurd extreme when Cameron Hooker, a bespectacled, mild-looking timber worker, kidnapped a hitchhiker and kept her in a box for seven years. No case better illustrates Hazelwood's comment that sex crime is not about sex, but about power.

On May 19, 1977, twenty-year-old Colleen Stan was hitchhiking from Eugene, Oregon, to Westwood in Northern California when she was offered a lift by a young couple with a baby. When they suggested turning off the main road to look at some ice caves, she raised no objection. In a lonely place the man placed a knife to her throat, handcuffed her, and then confined her head into a peculiar boxlike contraption that left her in total darkness. Hours later, he took her into the cellar of a house, stripped her, suspended her from the ceiling with leather straps, and whipped her. Then the couple had sex under her feet. After that, the head-box was clamped on again and she was placed in a larger wooden box, about three feet high, for the night.

The next day she was chained by her ankles to a rack, and given food. When she showed no appetite, he hung her from the beam again and whipped her until she was unconscious. Later the man made her use a bedpan, which he himself emptied. Again she was locked up in the box.

This went on for weeks. When she became dirty and unkempt, he made her climb into the bath. He raised her knees and held her head under water until she began to choke. He did this over and over again, taking snapshots of the naked, choking girl in between. After that, her female jailer tried to comb her hair, then gave up and snipped off the knots and tangles with scissors.

Cameron Hooker had been born in 1953. He was a shy, skinny boy who had no close friends. When he left school he went to work as a laborer in a local lumber mill. His only reading was pornography, particularly the kind that dealt with flagellation and bondage. His daydream was to flog nude women who were tied with leather straps. When he was nineteen, he met a plain, shy fifteen-year-old named Janice. She was delighted and grateful to be asked out by this quiet, polite youth who drove his own car and treated her with respect. So far she had fallen in love with boys who had ignored her or treated her badly. Cameron was marvelously different. When he explained that he wanted to take her into the woods and hang her up from a tree, she was frightened but compliant. It hurt her wrists, but he was so affectionate when he took her down that she felt it was worth it. In 1975 they married, and she continued to submit to strange demands, which included tying her up, making her wear a rubber gas mask, and choking her until she became unconscious. Finally, he told her of his dream of kidnapping a young woman and using her as his "slave." Eventually, she agreed. She wanted a baby, and longed to live a normal life; perhaps if Cameron had a "slave," he would stop wanting to whip and choke her. That is how it came about that Colleen Stan was kidnapped, and taken to their basement in Oak Street, Red Bluff, where she was to spend the next seven years.

After a month or so, Janice felt she could no longer stand it. The idea of holding someone captive sickened her. What was worse was that the captive was an attractive young woman. Even though her husband had agreed that there would be no sex between him and his "slave," it was obvious that he was deriving from Colleen the same sexual satisfaction that he derived from tying her up. Janice decided to weaken the ties with her husband. She went to stay with a sister, and found herself a job in Silicon Valley. She returned every weekend, but this brought about the situation she had been trying to avoid. Left alone with his "slave" for the whole week, Cameron gave way to temptation. He forced Colleen to perform oral sex on him, reasoning that he was not going back on his bargain so long as there was no vaginal intercourse. He also burned her with a heat lamp, administered electric shocks, and choked her until she blacked out. Six months after the kidnapping, he started giving her small tasks, such as shelling walnuts or crocheting. The Hookers sold the results of her labors in the local flea market.

Early in 1980, after nearly three years of captivity, Colleen was allowed an amazing excursion. She was permitted to dress up in some of Janice's clothes, make up her face, and accompany Janice to a dance. There they met two men and went home with them. Janice vanished into the bedroom with one of them, while Colleen stayed talking to the other. Cameron apparently suspected nothing, and his wife's liaison continued for the next two months, until it fizzled out. After that, Janice, still unsuspected, had another short affair.

In January 1981, Hooker discovered an article in an underground newspaper about a company of white slavers who forced girls to sign a slavery contract, and decided that Colleen should do the same. On January 25, Colleen was made to sign a long document declaring that she handed herself over, body and soul, to her Master, Michael Powers (alias Cameron Hooker), but her true owner was a company affiliated with the Mafia. She was to agree never to wear panties, and always to sit with her legs open. She was told that her new name was Kay Powers.

Now she was allowed upstairs to help with household chores, but if Cameron came in and shouted "Attention!" she had to strip off her clothes and stand on tiptoe with her hands above her head. Soon after this, Janice herself suggested to her husband that he should have sex with his slave. Perhaps she was hoping that he would cite his original agreement and refuse; in fact, he promptly brought Colleen up from the basement, spread-eagled her naked on the bed, with a gag in her mouth and her wrists and ankles tied to the corners, and then raped her. Janice, meanwhile, rushed off to vomit.

The Hookers decided to move to a more secluded place. He bought a trailer on some land beyond the city limits, and underneath a large waterbed, constructed a kind of rabbit hutch, which was to be Colleen's home. Colleen was moved in—blindfolded and handcuffed—one afternoon, and immediately confined in her new quarters.

Life became a little freer. She was let out for an hour or so every day to perform her ablutions and help with the chores. She made no attempt to escape—Hooker had told her all kinds of horror stories about what happened to "Company" slaves who tried to run away: having their fingers chopped off one by one was the least of them. To remind her that she was his slave he periodically hung her from the ceiling and flogged her with a whip. He also burned her breasts with lighted matches.

There were compensations. In the autumn, Hooker went up into the mountains to cut wood on the land of the company that employed him; he took his slave with him. He made her work; he also made her swim in a pond and run along a dirt road. When she was "disobedient," he tied her down on a kind of mediaeval rack and "stretched" her. This excited him so much that he stripped naked and made her perform oral sex. On another occasion he raped her on the "rack." Janice was not told of these sexual episodes. Soon after this, the slave was made to drink most of a bottle of wine, then perform oral sex on Janice; it made her sick.

Colleen was also allowed more freedom—she was allowed to go out and jog on her own. Incredibly, she still made no attempt to escape—Hooker had brainwashed her into seeing herself as a well-behaved and loyal slave. As a reward for obedience, she was allowed to write to her sister—without, of course, including a return address—and even, on one occasion, to telephone her family, with Hooker standing beside her monitoring everything she said. She told them she was living with a couple who were "looking after her." When they wanted to know more, her Master made her hang up. Soon after that he took her on a visit to his own family, on their ranch outside town. This passed off so well that he decided to take the ultimate risk, and allow her to go and see her own parents, who lived in Riverside, California. In March 1981, he drove her to Sacramento, and ordered her to wait in the car while he went into an office block that belonged to the sinister Company who owned her. When he came back, he told her that they had granted permission to visit her family. The visit to Riverside was brief, but went off perfectly. Hooker was introduced as her fiancé Mike, who was on his way to a computer seminar. Colleen Stan spent the night in her father's home, and then visited her mother—who lived elsewhere—without divulging where she had been for four years, or why she had failed to keep in touch. The following day, her Master rang her and announced that he would be arriving in ten minutes to take her home. Colleen was upset that Hooker had broken his promise to allow her to spend a full weekend with her family, and sulked all the way back to Red Bluff. When they got back, the Master decided that enough was enough. The slave's period of liberty came to an end, and she was put back into the box.

This period lasted another three years, from 1981 until 1984. The relationship between Hooker and his wife was becoming increasingly tense—she disliked being tied up and whipped. At one point she left him for a few days and went to stay with her brother. When she came back, she and Cameron had a long, honest talk; she confessed her two affairs—her husband seemed indifferent—while he admitted that he had been having sex with Colleen. (This deeply upset Janice.) Then, in an attempt to repair their marriage, they began reading the Bible together. Colleen had already found refuge in the religion of her childhood, and now she joined in the prayer sessions. Cameron, meanwhile, worked on a kind of underground bunker that would be a dungeon for the slave. It was completed in November 1983, and Colleen was installed inside. When the winter rains came, however, the dungeon began to fill with water, and they had to take her out again and let her back indoors.

Janice and Colleen, whose relationship in the past had often been stormy—Janice was inclined to boss

Colleen around—had now become close friends as well as fellow Bible students. Cameron still flogged his slave—on "Company orders"—but was also treating her better, giving her more food, and allowing her to babysit his two daughters. And in May 1984, seven years after her abduction, he sent her out to find a job. She was hired at a local motel as a maid, and proved to be such a hard worker that she soon received a promotion.

Colleen believed implicitly that she was the slave of "the Company"; she often mentioned it to Janice, and Janice felt increasingly guilty and uncomfortable at having to support her husband's lies. Her new religious faith made it difficult. It became harder still when she and Colleen—with Cameron's permission—began to go to the local church together. Cameron tried to turn the Bible to his own advantage, quoting the passage from Genesis in which Abraham went to bed with his wife's maid, Hagar, and suggesting that Janice should take the same liberal attitude towards Colleen. As usual, he finally got his way; he even persuaded Janice to share the bed, and entertain him with lesbian acts with Colleen. Janice was so upset by the new situation that she asked Cameron to strangle her—something he did frequently, but only to the point of unconsciousness. He agreed, but either lost courage, or was suddenly struck by the thought of the inconvenience of disposing of the body; at all events, Janice woke up to find herself still alive.

On August 9, 1984, Janice made her decision. She went to speak to Colleen at work, and told her the truth: that there was no "Company," that she was not a slave, that Cameron was merely a pervert. Colleen was stunned. Her first reaction was to quit her job. Then she and Janice called on the pastor of their church, and gave him a confused outline of the story. He advised them to leave Cameron. But it was too late in the day for Colleen to take a bus to her family in Riverside. Instead, they picked Cameron up from work as usual, and went back to the mobile home. That night Janice pleaded that she felt ill, and she and Colleen slept on the floor together. As soon as Cameron had gone to work at 5 a.m., they began packing, and fled to the home of Janice's parents. Then Colleen went home, told her parents the whole story but—after a phone conversation with a tearful Cameron, agreed not to go to the police.

In a sense, the story was now over. Cameron Hooker was not arrested immediately; it took some time for Janice to make up her mind to turn him in. And when she eventually did so, what she had to tell the police was not simply the story of Colleen Stan's seven-year ordeal. She had been keeping a more sinister secret. In January 1976, more than a year before Colleen had been abducted, they had offered a lift to a young woman in the nearby town of Chico. She told them her name was Marliz Spannhake, and that she was eighteen years old. When the time came to drop her off at her apartment, Hooker had grabbed her and driven off to a lonely spot, where the young woman had been tied up, and her head clamped in the "head-box." Back at home, Hooker stripped off her clothes and hung her from the ceiling. Then, perhaps to stop her screams, he cut her vocal cords with a knife. He tortured her by shooting her in the abdomen with a pellet gun, and finally strangled her. In the early hours of the morning, they drove into the mountains, and Hooker buried Marliz Spannhake in a shallow grave.

The police were able to verify that a young woman named Marie Elizabeth Spannhake had indeed vanished one evening in January 1976; but although Janice accompanied them up into the mountains, they were unable to locate the grave. That meant that there was not enough evidence to charge Cameron Hooker with murder. Two detectives flew down to Riverside to interview Colleen Stan, and as they listened to the story of her seven years in a box, they soon realized that they had enough evidence to guarantee Cameron Hooker at least several years in jail. Hooker was arrested on November 18, 1984.

The trial, which began on September 24, 1985, caused a nationwide sensation; the "Sex Slave" case seemed specially designed to sell newspapers. The jurors learned that Hooker was to be tried on sixteen counts, including kidnapping, rape, sodomy, forced oral copulation, and penetration with a foreign object. The prosecutor, Christine McGuire, had hoped to be able to introduce the Spannhake murder as corroborative evidence of Hooker's propensity to torture, but had finally agreed to drop it if Hooker would plead guilty to kidnapping. On October 28, 1985, the jury retired; on October 31—Halloween—they filed in to deliver their verdict. Cameron Hooker had been found guilty on ten counts, including kidnapping, rape, and torture. On November 22, Judge Clarence B. Knight delivered the sentence. After describing Cameron Hooker as "the most dangerous psychopath that I have ever dealt with," he sentenced him to several terms of imprisonment amounting to 104 years.

One question remains unanswered—the question that Christine McGuire raises on the last page of her book about the case, *Perfect Victim*: how did Cameron

Hooker develop his peculiar taste for torturing women? She has an interesting comment from someone on the case who wished to remain anonymous:

> *People like to believe in an Einstein or a Beethoven—geniuses—but they hate to believe in their opposites. A genius is a mutant, something unnatural. But just as some people are born with extra intelligence, others are born without much intelligence or without fingers or limbs or consciences. The human body is phenomenally complex, with trillions of cells, and trillions of things can go wrong. Cameron Hooker is a fluke, an accident of internal wiring. His instincts are simply the opposite of yours and mine.*

But is it as simple as that? Surely this element of conquest is present in all male sexuality? If it were absent, the male would find the female totally undesirable. In "normal" relationships, protectiveness and affection outweigh the desire for conquest, but it does not replace it.

In a fantasist such as Cameron Hooker—and, like Brudos, he had been a shy and introspective child—the dominance fantasy had been cultivated until it had grown out of all proportion, producing a grotesque, lopsided monster.

The world learned of the existence of another such monster—perhaps the worst serial killer since Pee Wee Gaskins—in early June 1985, after a group of detectives from the San Francisco Missing Persons Department drove out to a remote cabin near Wilseyville, Calaveras Country, together with Claralyn ("Cricket") Balasz, the ex-wife of its deceased owner, Leonard Lake. In the master bedroom the bed had electric cords attached to its posts. Hooks in the ceiling and walls suggested that it was some kind of torture chamber, while a box full of chains and shackles could have only one use: to immobilize someone on the bed. A wardrobe proved to contain numerous women's undergarments and some filmy nightgowns. In a dresser drawer was an assortment of women's lingerie, some of it soiled with dark red stains. The mattress was stained dark brown.

Next to the cabin there was a concrete building that ran back into the hillside. When Balasz refused to give them access, the police obtained a search warrant.

At first sight the interior looked harmless enough—a workshop with power tools. But closer inspection revealed that some of these were encrusted with a dark substance that looked like dried blood. The shelves of the tool rack at the rear proved to cover a secret door that led into a small room with a bed and reading lamp. A wooden plaque was inscribed with "The Warrior's Code," and above it, in red ink, the words "Operation Miranda." The wall contained twenty-one "candid" photographs of girls in various stages of undress. (Further investigation would reveal that these had been taken by Lake, whose lifelong hobby was photography, and that all the girls were still alive.)

Again, a bookcase proved to be a false front that led into the next room, which was little more than a deep closet, and which contained a narrow bed. A one-way mirror on the wall meant that someone in the next room could survey it. Under the bed they found a book that proved to be the diary of Leonard Lake. It was this that provided the evidence that Leonard Lake and his close associate, Charles Ng, were serial killers.

This story had begun two days earlier, on Sunday, June 2, when a shop assistant at the South City lumberyard in San Francisco noticed that a young man was leaving without paying for a $75 vise. The assistant hurried outside to speak to Police Officer Daniel Wright, and by the time the young man—who looked Asian—was putting the vise in the trunk of a car, the officer was right behind him. When he realized he was being followed, the man fled. Wright gave chase, but the skinny youth was too fast for him, and vanished across a main road.

When Wright returned to the car—a Honda Prelude—a bearded, bald-headed man was standing by it. "It was a mistake," he explained, "He thought I'd paid already. But I have paid now." He held out a sales receipt.

That should have ended the incident—except for the fact that the young Asian had fled, ruling out the possibility that it was merely an honest mistake. Wright wondered if anything else in the car might be stolen. "What's in there?" he asked, pointing at a green holdall.

"I don't know. It belongs to him."

Wright found that it contained a .22 revolver, with a silencer on the barrel. Americans have a right to own handguns, but not with silencers—such attachments being unlikely to have an innocent purpose.

The bearded man explained that he hardly knew the youth who had run away—he had just been about to hire him to do some work.

"I'm afraid I'll have to ask you to come down to headquarters to explain this."

Lonnie Bond and Brenda O'Connor hold their son, Lonnie Bond Jr. All three are believed to have been murdered by Charles Ng and his accomplice Leonard Lake. One of California's longest and costliest homicide cases started in 1998, more than thirteen years after Charles Ng's arrest for shoplifting led to his prosecution for serial murder. (Associated Press/*Detroit Free Press*)

At the police station, the man handed over a driver's license to establish his identity; it indicated that he was Robin Scott Stapley. But when asked various simple questions, such as his birthdate, he was unable to answer. Clearly, the license was someone else's, and he had failed to memorize the details.

"We'll have to do a computer check on the car. But you'll probably have to post bond before you can be released."

"Stapley" asked if he could have some paper and a pencil, and a glass of water. When the policeman returned with these items, he scribbled a few words on the sheet of paper, tossed two capsules into his mouth, and swallowed it down with water. Moments later, he slumped forward on the tabletop.

Assuming it was a heart attack, the police called an ambulance. The hospital rang them later to say that the man had been brain-dead on arrival, but had been placed on a life-support system.

The medic added that he was fairly certain the man had not suffered a heart attack; it was more likely that he had swallowed some form of poison. In fact, the poison was soon identified as cyanide. The note "Stapley" had scribbled had been an apology to his wife for what he was about to do. Four days later, removed from the life-support system, the man died without recovering consciousness.

By this time, the police had determined that he was not Robin Stapley. The real Robin Stapley had been reported missing in February. But soon after, there had been a curious incident involving his camper, which had been in collision with a pickup truck. The young Chinese man who had been driving the camper had accepted responsibility and asked the other driver not to report it. But since it was a company vehicle, the driver was obliged to report the accident.

The Honda the two had been driving proved to be registered in the name of Paul Cosner. And Cosner had also been reported missing. He had told his girlfriend that he had sold the car to a "weird-looking man" who would pay cash, and driven off to deliver it; no one had seen him since. The Honda was handed over to the forensic experts for examination; they discovered two bullet holes in the front seat, two spent slugs, and some human bloodstains.

If the bearded man was not Robin Stapley, who was he? Some papers found in the Honda bore the name Charles Gunnar, with an address near Wilseyville, in Calaveras County, 150 miles northeast of San Francisco. Inspector Tom Eisenmann was assigned the task of heading to Wilseyville to check on Gunnar. There he spoke to Sheriff Claude Ballard, and learned that Ballard already had his suspicions about Gunnar, and about the slightly built Chinese youth, Charles Ng (pronounced "Ing"), with whom he lived. They had been advertising various items for sale, such as television sets, videos, and articles of furniture, and Ballard suspected that they were stolen. Nonetheless, checks on serial numbers had come to nothing. What was more ominous was that Gunnar had offered for sale furniture belonging to a young couple, Lonnie Bond and Brenda O'Connor, who had lived next door, explaining that they had moved to Los Angeles with their baby and had given him the furniture to pay a debt. No one had heard from them since. And at a nearby campsite at Schaad Lake, another couple had simply vanished, leaving behind their tent and a coffee pot on the stove.

By now, a check on the dead man's fingerprints had revealed that he had a criminal record—for burglary and grand larceny in Mendocino County—and had jumped bail there. His real name was Leonard Lake.

Eisenmann's investigation into Lake's background convinced the detective that this man seemed to be associated with numerous disappearances. His younger brother, Donald, had been reported missing in July 1983 after setting out to visit Lake in a "survivalist commune" in Humboldt County. Charles Gunnar, whose identity Lake had borrowed, had been best man at Lake's wedding, but had also vanished in 1985. Together with Stapley and Cosner and the Bond couple and their baby, that made seven unexplained disappearances.

Police also found some expensive video equipment. This led Eisenmann's assistant, Sergeant Irene Brunn, to speculate whether it might be connected with a case she had investigated in San Francisco. Harvey and Deborah Dubs had vanished from their apartment, together with their sixteen-month-old baby son, Sean, and neighbors had seen a young Chinese man removing the contents of their apartment—including an expensive video recorder. She had recorded the serial numbers in her notebook. Her check confirmed her suspicion: this was the missing equipment.

Deputies came in to report that they had been scouring the hillside at the back of the house, and had found burnt bones that looked ominously human. Ballard noted a trench that seemed to have been intended for a telephone cable; he ordered the deputies to dig it up.

A filing cabinet in the cabin proved to be full of videotapes. Eisenmann read the inscription on one of these—"M. Ladies, Kathy/Brenda"—and slipped it into the recorder. A moment later, they were looking at a recording of a frightened young woman handcuffed to a chair, with a young Asian man—obviously Charles Ng—holding a knife beside her. A large, balding man with a beard enters the frame and proceeds to remove the young woman's handcuffs, then unshackles her ankles, and orders her to undress. Her reluctance is obvious, particularly when she comes to her panties. The bearded man tells her: "You'll wash for us, clean for us, fuck for us." After this, she is made to go into the shower with the Asian man. A later scene showed her strapped naked to a bed, while the bearded man tells her that her boyfriend, Mike, is dead.

After "Kathy" the video showed "Brenda"—identified by Sheriff Ballard as the missing Brenda O'Connor from next door—handcuffed to a chair, while Ng cuts off her clothes. She asks after her baby, and Lake tells her that it has been placed with a family in Fresno. She asks: "Why do you guys do this?" and he tells her: "We don't like you. Do you want me to put it in writing?" "Don't cut my bra off." "Nothing is yours now." "Give my baby back to me. I'll do anything you want." "You're going to do anything we want anyway."

Another tape showed a woman Sergeant Brunn recognized as Deborah Dubs.

Lake's accomplice, Charles Ng, was now one of the most wanted men in America, but had not been seen since his disappearance from the South City parking lot. Police had discovered that he had fled back to his apartment, been driven out to San Francisco International Airport by Cricket Balasz, and there bought himself a ticket to Chicago under the name "Mike Kimoto." Four days later, a San Francisco gun dealer notified the police that Ng had telephoned him from Chicago. The man had been repairing Ng's automatic pistol, and Ng wanted to know if he could send him the gun by mail, addressing it to him at the Chateau Hotel under the name Mike Kimoto. When the gun dealer explained that it was illegal to send handguns across state lines, Ng cursed and threatened him with violence if he went to the police. By the time Chicago police arrived at the Chateau Hotel, the fugitive had fled. From there on, the trail went dead.

Meanwhile, the team excavating the trench had discovered enormous quantities of bones, chopped up and partly burnt. Tracker dogs were brought in to sniff for other bodies. They soon located a grave that proved to contain the remains of a man, a woman, and a baby. These could be either the Dubs family or the Lonnie Bond family—they were too decomposed for immediate recognition. A bulldozer removed the top layer of earth to make digging easier.

The discovery of the cabinet of videos was followed by one that was in some ways even more disturbing: Lake's detailed diaries covering the same two-year period. The first one, for 1984, began: "Leonard Lake, a name not seen or used much these days in my second year as a fugitive. Mostly dull day-to-day routine—still with death in my pocket and fantasy my goal."

The diaries made it clear that his career of murder had started before he moved into the ranch on Blue Mountain Road. He had been a member of many communes, and in one at a place called Mother Lode, in Humboldt County, he had murdered his younger brother, Donald. A crude map of Northern California, with crosses labeled "buried treasure," suggested the possibility that these were the sites of more murders; but the map was too inaccurate to guide searchers to the actual locations.

Who was Leonard Lake? Investigation of his background revealed that he had been born in 1946 in San Francisco, and that he had a highly disturbed childhood. His father was unstable and workshy, and he and Lake's mother fought all the time. Lennie was only six when his parents, loaded with debt, decided they could not keep him, and he was sent to live with his grandmother, a strict disciplinarian. Both his father and mother came from a family of alcoholics. The alcoholic grandfather was a violent individual who subjected the child to a kind of military discipline. Lake's brother, Donald, his mother's favorite, was an epileptic who had suffered a serious head injury; he practiced sadistic cruelty to animals and tried to rape both his sisters. Lake protected the sisters "in return for sexual favors."

From an early age Lake had displayed the sexual obsession that seems to characterize serial killers. He took nude photographs of his sisters and cousins, and later became a maker of pornographic movies starring his wife, Cricket. She was "into" S&M and kinky sex with chains and handcuffs.

Lake had compensated for the emotional aridity of his childhood by living in a world of fantasy, both sexual and heroic. But the greatest single influence on his fantasy life was a novel, *The Collector* by John Fowles, in which a mentally disturbed lepidopterist chloroforms and kidnaps Miranda, a pretty art student, and keeps her captive in a farmhouse—Fowles admitted that it was based on his own "Bluebeard" fantasies of imprisoning one of his students. This novel became the basis of Lake's adolescent fantasies, and explains the "M" on the videotapes, and "Operation Miranda" on the plaque—it stood for his Miranda project—kidnapping and enslaving young women.

Lake had been in the marines for seven years, and had even served in Vietnam; but he had finally showed signs of being deeply mentally disturbed and was discharged on his second tour of duty. According to his sister, this, as much as any other problem, was the foundation of his insecurity and sense of betrayal. But his hatred of women, she said, was due to his mother's early rejection, and the fact that this first wife had divorced him.

Yet he was skillful in hiding his abnormality, teaching grade school, working as a volunteer firefighter, and donating time to a company that provided free insulation in old people's homes. He seemed as exemplary a citizen as John Wayne Gacy of Chicago. But his outlook was deeply pessimistic, convinced that World War III would break out at any moment. Like other "survivalists," he often dressed in combat fatigues, and talked of living off the land. Once out of the marines, his behavior became increasingly disturbed and psychotic.

It was while living in an isolated village called Miranda in the hills of Northern California—obviously chosen for its name—that Lake thought out Operation Miranda. It was to stockpile food, clothing, and weapons against the coming nuclear holocaust, and also to kidnap women who would be kept imprisoned and used as sex slaves. "The perfect woman," he explained in his diary, "is totally controlled. . . . A woman who does exactly what she is told to and nothing else. There is no sexual problem with a submissive woman. There are no frustrations—only pleasure and contentment."

Lake's accomplice, Charles Ng, was born in Hong Kong on December 24, 1961, the son of a wealthy businessman, who believed that children had to be brought up strictly, and often beat Charles. After being expelled from several schools for stealing and arson, he was sent to a school in Yorkshire, England, where an uncle taught. He was soon expelled for thieving. At eighteen, he traveled to the United States on a student visa, and spent a semester in Notre Dame College in Belmont, California, before boredom set in. After being convicted of a hit-and-run accident in which he was ordered to pay damages, he joined the marines, claiming to be a U.S. citizen. But when he and three accomplices stole military equipment in Hawaii, he escaped to California, where he met Lake through an ad in a survivalist magazine.

He and Lake formed a close friendship, in which Lake, sixteen years Ng's senior, became a kind of father figure, and for a while Ng moved in with Lake and Cricket. Then the military authorities caught up with him, and he was sentenced to two years in Leavenworth.

Lake by then was involved as an accomplice, and decided to go into hiding, sewing cyanide capsules into the lapel of his jacket, which he swore to use rather than go to prison. And it was when Ng emerged from prison that the two once more went into partnership, moved out to the property in Wilseyville—purchased by Balasz's parents—and set about turning "Operation Miranda" into a reality.

Lake's journal left no doubt about his method of collecting his sex slaves. He made a habit of luring people

THE WORLD SUDDENLY BECOMES A MUCH MORE DANGEROUS PLACE.

to the house, often inviting them—as he did the Bond family—to dinner. The husband and the baby were then murdered, probably almost immediately. The woman was stripped of her clothes, shackled, and sexually abused until her tormentors grew bored with her. Then she was killed and buried or burned.

One other thing emerged clearly from these journals, and was noted by psychiatrist Joel Norris, who published a study of Lake in his book *The Menace of the Serial Killer*: when Lake killed himself, he was in a state of depression and moral bankruptcy. "His dreams of success had eluded him, he admitted to himself that his boasts about heroic deeds in Vietnam were all delusions, and the increasing number of victims he was burying in the trench behind his bunker only added to his unhappiness. By the time he was arrested in San Francisco, Lake had reached the final stage of the serial murderer syndrome: he realized that he had come to a dead end with nothing but his own misery to show for it."

In mid-June 1985, two weeks after the digging began, the police had unearthed nine bodies and forty pounds of human bones, some burnt, some even boiled. The driving licenses of Robin Stapley and of Ng's friend Mike Carroll (the boyfriend of another victim,

Kathy Allen), and papers relating to Paul Cosner's car, confirmed that they had been among the victims.

When the "survival bunker" itself was finally dismantled and taken away on trucks, it seemed clear that the site had yielded up most of its evidence. This suggested that Lake had murdered and buried twenty-five people there. The identity of many of the victims remained unknown. The only person who might be able to shed some light on it was the missing Charles Ng.

On Saturday, July 6, 1985, nearly five weeks after Ng's flight, a security guard in a department store in Calgary, Alberta, saw a young Chinese man pushing food under his jacket. When he challenged him, the youth drew a pistol; as they grappled, he fired, wounding the guard in the hand. He ran away at top speed, but was intercepted by other guards. The youth obviously had some training in Japanese martial arts, but was eventually overpowered and handcuffed. Identification documents revealed that he was Charles Ng.

FBI agents hurried to Calgary, and were allowed a long interview. Ng admitted that he knew about the murders, but put the blame entirely on Lake. And before the agents could see him again, Ng's lawyers—appointed by the court—advised him against another interview. After a psychiatric examination, Ng was tried on a charge of armed robbery and sentenced to four and a half years. But efforts by California Attorney General John Van de Kamp to make sure that he was extradited after his sentence, met with frustration. California, unlike Canada, still had the death penalty, and the extradition treaty stipulates that a man cannot be extradited if he might face the death penalty. In November 1989, after serving three and a half years of his sentence, Ng was ordered back to California to face the murder charges against him, yet the possibility of the death sentence would impede his extradition for another six years. Ng was eventually returned to California on September 26, 1991.

What followed was the most drawn-out and costly American legal proceeding in U.S. history, the bill soon passing $14 million. His lawyers were able to further delay his trial for another eight years, until October 1998. It was finally moved to Santa Ana, in Orange County, on the grounds that most people in San Andreas, Calaveras County, believed Ng guilty.

The accused had now ceased to be slimly built and become rotund. But he still continued to insist that he should not be on trial at all, since it was Lake who was entirely responsible for the murders. The problem about that defense was that he could be seen on videotape cutting off the clothes of one of the victims, and joining with Lake in making fun of her distress. Worse still, part of the evidence against him was a cartoon he had drawn showing himself dropping a baby by its leg into a kind of wok over a fire. An accompanying cartoon shows him holding the baby upside down and breaking its neck with a karate chop.

Four months later, on February 24, 1999, the jury returned a verdict of guilty on eleven of the twelve counts of murder in the first degree. Judge John J. Ryan sentenced Charles Ng to death.

Ng's complaints of unfair treatment are perhaps not entirely without foundation. In practically all known cases in which two people participate in murder, there is a leader and a follower. In this case there can be no doubt that Ng was the completely besotted follower. Yet it is also certain that the murders could never have taken place without his presence from the beginning. As noted earlier, psychiatrists use the phrase *folie à deux*, a mental disorder shared by two in association, such as Leopold and Loeb, Fernandez and Beck, Bianchi and Buono. In most such cases, the presence of the follower is the catalyst that sparks the leader to kill. The two then murder as a matter of joint purpose. But the follower adds some essential psychological element to the partnership.

In the case of Lake and Ng, the joint purpose was sealed by their sense of having been treated badly in childhood; both saw themselves as victims of the adult world represented by their parents. That is how Lake came to hate happy families. And this is why, in his case, the normal inhibition against harming children was suspended. We only have to look at the photograph of the families he destroyed—of Brenda O'Connor, Deborah Dubs, Kathy Allen—to understand how a man who felt he had been denied a normal family life must have envied and hated them.

Then why was it Ng who provided emotional fuel that energized the *folie á deux*, rather than Cricket Balasz? To that the answer is undoubtedly that she was more dominant than Lake, a leader, not a follower. Photographs of Lake reveal a man who is undermined by lack of self-esteem. It was Ng who provided Lake with the unqualified admiration that he needed. The envy and hatred that triggered twenty-five murders might have remained isolated in the vacuum of Lake's enormous self-pity if he had not met someone else who shared his feelings. When two paranoid and self-pitying individuals share the same vision of the world, the world suddenly becomes a much more dangerous place.

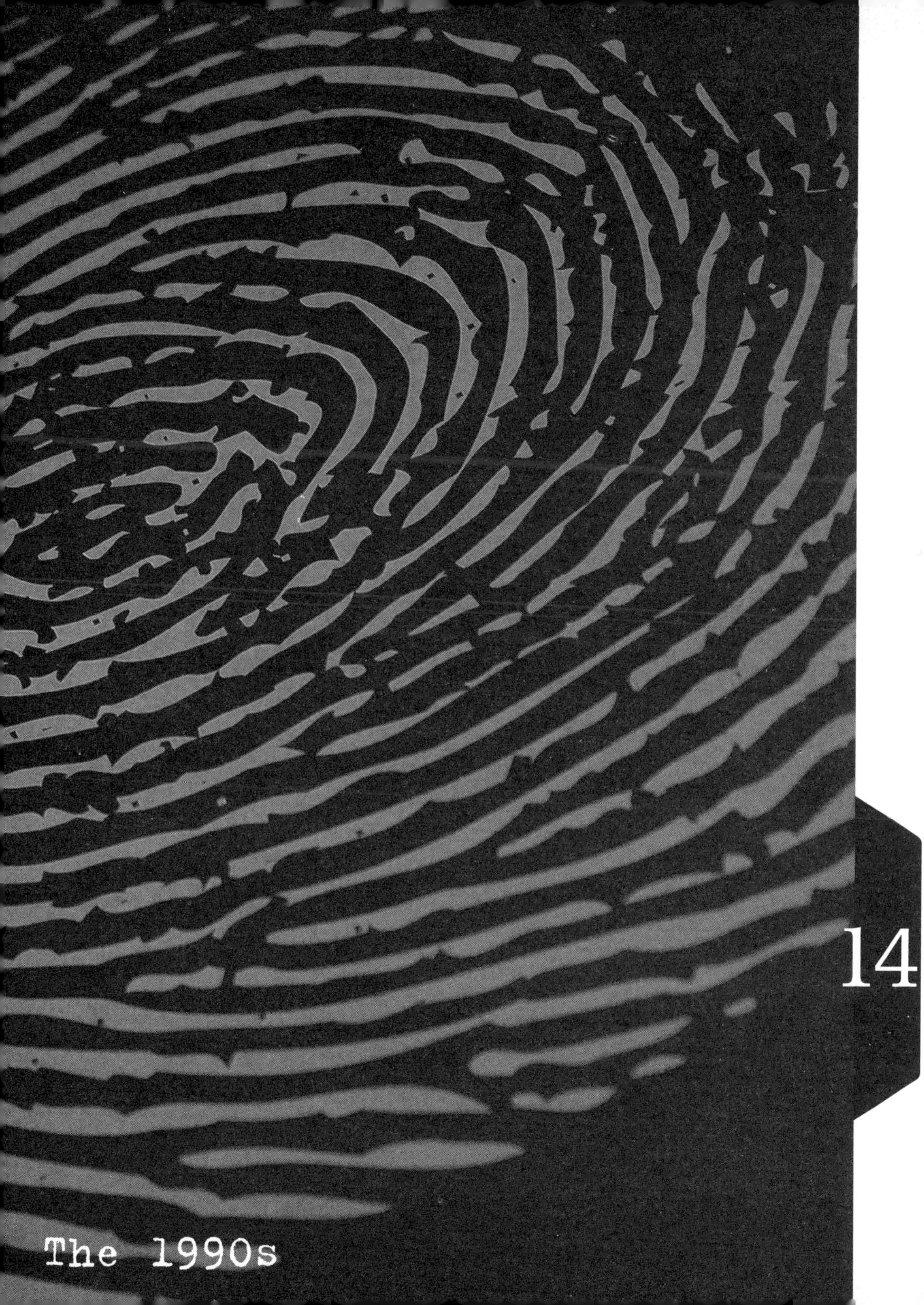

14

The 1990s

14

The 1990s

In 1946, the British novelist George Orwell wrote an essay in which he lamented the decline of the British murder since prewar days. The "classic" cases, he said, such as Jack the Ripper, Dr. Crippen, the Brides in the Bath, have a gruesome or dramatic quality that touches the imagination of novelists and film producers. With these Orwell contrasts the "Cleft Chin Murder" of 1944, in which an American GI named Karl Hulten teamed up with a striptease dancer, Betty Jones, and set out on what was intended to be a rampage of crime that would bring 1920s Chicago to London. They shot and robbed a hired car driver and dumped his body in a ditch, then drove around all weekend in his car until they were caught. Both were sentenced to death, although she was reprieved. Orwell complains that, as the most talked-about murder of recent years, it is oddly commonplace and unmemorable.

He would probably have had something similar to say about the rise of the serial killer—Manson, Corona, Mullin, Kemper, Frazier, Corll, Gacy—for all these certainly lack the quality of the classic American murder case from Professor Webster to Lizzie Borden. And this is simply because killers who are demented by drugs or suffering from clinical psychosis are bound to be less interesting than killers who are basically normal but are driven to kill by some negative or twisted emotion we can understand.

This complaint will certainly be echoed by any future criminologist who attempts to tell the story of serial murder in retrospect. The interest of the tale lies mainly in the advances that have been made in forensic and psychological detection—in short, in the manhunt. Corll, Gacy, Henry Lee Lucas, clearly belong to the story, but only because their cases have been landmarks in the history of mass murder. As to the dozens of killers known by acronyms such as the Night Stalker, the Green River Killer, the Skid Row Slasher, the Trashbag Killer, the Sunset Slayer, the Trailside Killer, the Freeway Killer—they will probably be relegated to a few paragraphs describing the number of their crimes and how they were caught. There is something oddly anonymous about such murderers.

In the case of the Night Stalker, this sense of anonymity persisted even after he had been caught. Yet the crimes themselves were hideous enough. He would break into a house, creep into the bedroom and shoot the husband in the head, before raping and beating the wife. On one occasion when a woman refused to tell him where to find the valuables, he put out her eyes with a knife and took them away with him. He also occasionally raped or sodomized children.

The intruder had already been described by the roommate of a woman he killed in her condominium in Los Angeles on March 17, 1985; Maria Hernandez said he was a long-faced young man with black curly hair, bulging eyes, and rotten teeth.

In that spring and summer there were more than twenty attacks, most of them involving both rape and murder. By the end of March the press had picked up the pattern and splashed stories connecting the series of crimes. After several abortive nicknames, such as the "Walk-In Killer" or the "Valley Invader," the *Herald Examiner* came up with the "Night Stalker," a name sensational enough to stick.

By August things were obviously getting difficult for the Night Stalker. The next murder that fit the pattern occurred in San Francisco, the shooting of sixty-six-year-old Peter Pan and his wife on August 17, showing perhaps that public awareness in Los Angeles had made it too taxing a location. This shift also gave police a chance to search San Francisco hotels for records of a man of the Night Stalker's description. Sure enough, while checking the downmarket Tenderloin district police learned that a thin Hispanic man with bad teeth had been staying at a cheap local hotel periodically over the past year. On the last occasion he had checked out the night of the San Francisco attack. The manager commented that his room "smelled like a skunk" each time he vacated it and it took three days for the smell to clear.

The Night Stalker's next shift of location was to bring about his identification. A young couple in Mission Viejo were attacked in their home. The Night

Stalker shot twenty-nine-year-old Bill Carns through the head while he slept, and then raped his partner on the bed next to the body. He then tied her up while he ransacked the house for money and jewelry. Before leaving he raped her a second time and force her to fellate him with a gun pressed against her head. After making her repeat that she loved Satan, he left.

A thirteen-year-old boy, James Romero, was repairing his motorcycle when he noticed an orange Toyota driving slowly past, and the driver peering around as if looking for a place to rob. And when he saw the car a second time half an hour later, he made a note of its license plate number. When he heard about the rape, he alerted the police. LAPD files showed that the car had been stolen in the Los Angeles Chinatown district while the owner was eating in a restaurant. The Night Stalker abandoned it soon after the attack, and it was located two days later in a car park in the Los Angeles Rampart district. It was taken away for forensic testing, and a single fingerprint was successfully raised from behind the rearview mirror.

The identification was described by the forensic division as "a near miracle." The computer system had only just been installed, and this was one of its first trials. Furthermore, the system only contained the fingerprints of criminals born after January 1, 1960. Richard Ramirez was born in February 1960.

The police circulated the photograph to newspapers, and it was shown on the late evening news. At the time, Ramirez was in Phoenix, buying cocaine with the money he had stolen in Mission Viejo. On the morning that the papers splashed his name and photograph on the front pages, he was on a bus on the way back to Los Angeles, unaware that he had been identified.

In the bus station he went into the men's room to finish off the cocaine, and then into a liquor store to buy Pepsi and sugared donuts. Waiting for his change, he saw his own face looking up at him from a newspaper, and as someone said, "It's him," he ran from the shop. Stimulated by the cocaine, he raced two miles, and into the Hispanic district. In a parking lot he tried to drag a woman from her car, but was chased by passers-by. Seeing a red Mustang in a yard he jumped into it, but the owner, who was underneath it, emerged and grabbed him by the collar. Ramirez reversed into the garage wall and the car stalled. Once again he began running. He tried to pull another woman from her car, but failed and fled, now pursued by a crowd. Racing ahead, he stopped to stick out his tongue at his pursuers. Minutes later, he was caught, and dragged down by a crowd. At that moment, a young policeman arrived, and Ramirez shouted, "Save me before they kill me."

In his hometown of El Paso, on the Texas-Mexico border, acquaintances said Ramirez had become a Satanist in negative reaction to Bible-study classes, and that he had spent his teens as a loner, smoking marihuana and listening to heavy metal music

In spite of his own desire to plead guilty, his lawyers entered a plea of not guilty. The defense strategy was to play for delays, and the case came to trial only after three and a half years, in October 1988. Ramirez was finally sentenced to death in November 1999, telling the court, "You maggots make me sick."

At a second trial in San Francisco, he was besieged by enthusiastic female groupies who lined up to visit him in jail. He married one of his admirers in October 1996.

The kind of good fortune that identified Richard Ramirez from a single fingerprint failed to favor the police in the case of Gary Ridgway, the Green River Killer, which illustrates the difficulty of capturing an elusive criminal in a crowded urban area. In a deal to save himself from the death penalty, he offered to give the details of fifty-nine murders. In fact, he admitted that the actual number was closer to ninety.

The first corpse was discovered in the slow-flowing Green River, near Seattle, Washington, on July 15, 1982, and was identified as a sixteen-year old prostitute, Wendy Coffield.

The second, twenty-three-year-old Debra Lynn Bonner, known as "Dub," was a stripper with a list of convictions as a prostitute. Her body was found on August 12, 1982, also in the Green River. Between then and March 21, 1984, forty victims were found in the Seattle-Tacoma area, many from the strip around Sea-Tac airport, known as a haunt of prostitutes.

Within three days of the finding of Dub Bonner, Dave Reichert, the detective in charge of the case, heard that two more bodies had been found in the Green River. Both women were black, both were naked, and they had been weighted down to the river bottom with large rocks. They were only a few hundred yards upstream from the spot where Dub had been found, and had almost certainly been there at the time.

As Reichert walked along the bank toward that site, he discovered another body. Like the other two, she was black, and was later identified as sixteen-year-

Gary Ridgway prepares to leave the courtroom where he was sentenced in King County, Washington. Ridgway received a life sentence for each of forty-eight counts of murder in what became known as the "Green River Killer" serial murder case that began in 1982 and was the largest unsolved serial murder case in American history. (Associated Press/Joshua Trujillo, *Seattle Post-Intelligencer*)

old Opal Mills. The fact that rigor mortis had not yet disappeared meant that she had been left there in the past two days—which in turn meant that if the police had kept watch on the river, the killer would have been caught before this young woman had died.

It was the first of a series of mischances that would make this one of the most frustrating criminal cases in Seattle's history. The next—and perhaps the worst mischance—occurred two days later, when a local TV station announced that the riverbank was now under round-the-clock surveillance, thus destroying all chance of catching the killer on a return visit.

No less than twenty-six women vanished in 1983, and the remains of eight of them were found near Sea-Tac Airport or close by. In March, special investigator Bob Keppel, known for his brilliant work on the Ted Bundy case, was asked to write up a report on the investigation. It was devastating, with hundreds of examples of incompetence and failure to follow up on leads. For example, when the driving license of one victim, Marie Malvar, was found at the airport, and the police notified, they did not even bother to collect it—although it might well have contained the killer's fingerprint.

In 1984, four victims were found together on Auburn West Hill, six more in wooded areas along State Route 410, and two near Tigard, Oregon, the latter giving rise to the speculation that the killer had moved. In January, a Green River Task Force of thirty-six investigators was formed, with a $2 million budget. (By 1988 the bill would have reached $13 million.)

Among the hundreds of suspects interviewed by the police was Gary Leon Ridgway, thirty-five, a short, mild-looking man with fishlike lips, who worked for the Kenworth Truck Plant and was known to pick up hookers—he even admitted to being obsessed by them. He also confessed to choking a prostitute in 1982, but claimed this was because she bit him.

By 1986, with the investigation stalled. Ridgway's file was reopened, and his ex-wife interviewed about his preference for sex in the open, often near the Green River. Ridgway was placed under surveillance. And still women disappeared—although no longer with quite the same frequency. And so throughout the 1990s, the case marked time, while Reichert, the chief investigator, admitted that his obsession with the killer had caused serious problems in his marriage.

Since genetic fingerprinting had first been used in 1988 to convict the South Side Rapist, Timothy Spencer, it had led to the solution of many murders. The main problem was likely to occur if there was not enough DNA material for testing, or if it was old. In 2001, a major breakthrough came when the Washington State crime lab acquired the equipment to extract usable DNA from old samples and multiply the quantity by the method known as STR, or short tandem repeats. Now a major review of samples of semen evidence began. And by September 2001, it had paid off. Semen

NO LESS THAN TWENTY-SIX WOMEN VANISHED IN 1983, AND THE REMAINS OF EIGHT OF THEM WERE FOUND NEAR SEA-TAC AIRPORT OR CLOSE BY.

samples, taken from Opal Mills, Marcia Chapman, and Carol Christensen, three of the earliest victims, proved to be from Gary Ridgway. Paint fragments and fiber evidence taken from the grave of Debra Estes in 1988 were also linked to Ridgway. When Ridgway was finally arrested on November 30, 2001, he was charged with four counts of murder.

At first pleading innocent, he later agreed to change his plea to guilty to avoid the death penalty.

Ridgway's account of how he became a serial killer occupies the most fascinating chapter of Reichert's book *Chasing the Devil*. As with so many killers, the problems started with a domineering mother. Born in 1949, he was a chronic bed wetter, and she would drag him out of bed and parade him in front of his brothers, and then make him stand naked in a tub of cold water. His father seems to have been a timid nonentity. But as an employee of a mortuary he strongly influenced his son's fantasies by describing at length interrupting someone having sex with a corpse. Ridgway began to fantasize about this. When he saw his mother sunbathing he had imagined having sex with her, but now he dreamed of killing her and violating the body. All this seems to imply some inbuilt or genetic tendency to sexual violence.

Like so many serial killers he was sadistic to animals, and once killed a cat by locking it in a refrigerator. He also claimed that, as a teenager, he drowned a little boy by wrapping his legs around him and pulling him under the water. And later he would stab and injure another boy, because, he said, he "wanted to know what it was like to kill someone," although he was never caught.

Sent to the Philippines as a sailor, he began to use prostitutes, and they quickly became a lifelong obsession.

He had discovered he enjoyed choking when he was quarrelling with his second wife, Marcia, and wrapped his arm round her neck from behind (a method also used by the Boston Strangler). In addition he enjoyed tying her up for sex. In 1975 they had a son, Matthew, whom he adored. A religious phase lasted until 1980, when they divorced. But during their marriage, he still hired prostitutes.

He embarked on killing them after his divorce. Because he seemed a "milquetoast," they felt no alarm about him, and allowed him to get behind them. He often took them back to his house, had sex, and then killed them. Later, he found he preferred to kill them first and have sex with the bodies. He also confessed to revisiting bodies several times for more sex.

On one occasion, he even took his son with him in his pickup truck when he went into the woods with a prostitute; when the boy asked what had happened to her, Ridgway told him that she lived nearby and had decided to walk home.

He even admitted to a scheme—never carried out—to overpower a prostitute and then impale her with an upright pole in her vagina—a favorite practice of the original Dracula, Vlad the Impaler.

And so this apparently harmless little man was able to carry on killing for many years. Reichert emphasizes that Ridgway was full of self-pity, regarding himself as the helpless victim of these sinister urges. On November 5, 2003, Ridgway pleaded guilty to forty-eight murders, and received forty-eight life sentences.

Joel Rifkin bore a certain physical resemblance to Gary Ridgway and, like him, had a curious urge to kill the prostitutes who exercised such a fascination over him.

In late June 1993, soon after dawn, two New York State troopers patrolling Long Island's Southern State Parkway noticed that a station wagon ahead of them lacked a license plate. When they signaled it to stop, it swerved off the freeway into the streets of Wantaugh. The troopers pursued—reaching speeds of ninety miles an hour—with sirens wailing. Five additional police cars joined the chase before the station wagon veered out of control and hit a telephone pole. The driver proved to be bespectacled thirty-four-year-old Joel Rifkin. He claimed to have no explanation for his wild flight, but when the troopers noticed a foul order emanating from the car, they checked the back of the wagon. There, wrapped in tarpaulin, was the naked, decomposing corpse of a woman. She was a twenty-two-year-old prostitute named Tiffany Bresciani, who had vanished three days earlier. Rifkin confessed to strangling her as they had intercourse, and taking her back to the house in East Meadow, Long Island, where he lived with his mother and sister.

It was hot weather and the corpse began to decompose quickly, so he decided to dump it among some bushes on rough ground near the local airport. And he went on to admit that he had made a habit of picking up prostitutes and strangling them—seventeen in all. (The police decided the number was actually eighteen, and that Rifkin had simply lost count.)

Rifkin was an unemployed landscape gardener, and he had been picking up prostitutes on average three times a week since he was eighteen. In his bedroom, police found victims' ID cards, driving licenses, credit cards, and piles of women's underwear: panties, bras, and stockings. In the garage, which smelt of decaying flesh, they found the panties of his last victim, Tiffany Bresciani.

As information about Rifkin began to emerge, it became clear that—once more—he was basically an inadequate. An illegitimate child, he had been adopted a few weeks after his birth in January 1959 by a Jewish couple, Ben and Jeanne Rifkin, who also adopted a girl.

The children seemed to have been well treated, but Joel was backward at school; he mumbled, walked with hunched shoulders, and was dyslexic. (As with Bundy, there was probably a lack of "bonding" with his mother immediately after birth.) His schoolfellows called him "turtle" and made fun of him. When he left home he tried various jobs, on one occasion working in a record store, but he was usually late, and would turn up with rumpled clothes and dirty fingernails.

Rifkin's dream was to become a famous writer, and it could be argued that he had the right kind of preparation—a certain amount of childhood and adolescent frustration often seems to be good for writers. Rifkin spent hours writing poetry in his bedroom. But a few half-hearted attempts at further education fell through because he had no ability to concentrate. He began to work as a landscape gardener, but with such inefficiency that he usually lost his customers within days.

He was already in his late twenties when his stepfather was diagnosed as suffering from prostate cancer, and committed suicide because he could not bear the pain. Jeanne Rifkin was shattered and went into a depression.

Not long after, Rifkin met an attractive blonde in a coffee shop; he was scribbling, and they began a casual conversation; he was impressed when she told him she was writing a film script.

He told her—untruthfully—that he was also writing a film script, and that he was a university student. When she took a small apartment, she even invited him to move in, to help her with her script. Rifkin had hoped that this was the beginning of a love affair; but she refused even to let him kiss her. A few weeks later, she tired of his laziness and untidiness and threw him out. After Rifkin's arrest it was reported that she had worked as a streetwalker, and was suffering from AIDS, although it is not clear whether he was aware of either of those facts.

What is certain is that he began to kill prostitutes in 1989, picking them up on Manhattan's Lower East Side. Many prostitutes turned him down because he looked and smelled peculiar. But one with whom he had sex on two occasions said he seemed perfectly ordinary and normal, and made no odd sexual demands. Another prostitute, however, refused when he asked for oral sex.

Rifkin continued to commit murder after murder for almost five years, killing seventeen or eighteen prostitutes, many of them drug addicts. He may well have had sex with the corpses since he often took them home and kept them for days before he disposed of them. One body that he tossed on waste ground near JFK Airport was still there, more than a year later, under a mattress. Other bodies were placed in metal drums and thrown in the East River.

Rifkin's motivation has never been adequately explained. What is clear is that he was, like so many serial killers, an inept underachiever, a person who found life too much for him. As one of his schoolmates told a reporter, he was a lifelong loser. We can only assume that he killed because violence satisfied some long-held fantasy, and because it gave him a bizarre sense of achievement, a feeling that, in spite of a habit of failure, he was a "somebody," a multiple killer, a man to be reckoned with.

Yet soon after his arrest, one of the policemen involved in the chase commented that he had probably wanted to be caught, since driving with a corpse in a car without license plates seems to be asking for trouble.

AS INFORMATION ABOUT RIFKIN BEGAN TO EMERGE, IT BECAME CLEAR THAT—ONCE MORE—HE WAS BASICALLY AN INADEQUATE.

On May 9, 1994, Joel Rifkin was sentenced to 203 years in prison.

Probably the most widely publicized American case of the 1990s was that of Jeffrey Dahmer, a homosexual killer who murdered and cannibalized seventeen young men.

Dahmer, born in 1960, was arrested on July 22, 1991. Late that evening, a slim black man ran out of the Oxford Apartments in a rundown area of Milwaukee, shouting for help, and waved a police car to a stop. He was wearing a handcuff on one wrist, and explained that a white youth was trying to kill him.

The police went up to Apartment 213, and the door was answered by a tall, good-looking young man who apologized for causing a disturbance. His manner was so believable that the police were about to go away when one of them noticed a strong smell of decay emanating from the flat. As they tried to force their way in, the young man—Dahmer—became hysterical. When a policeman opened the door of the refrigerator, he found himself looking at a decapitated human head. They found another severed head in the freezer, three skulls in a filing cabinet, and four more elsewhere around the flat. A kettle contained severed hands and male genitals, and packets of meat that proved to be of human flesh. The man who had raised the alarm, Tracy Edwards, thirty-two, described meeting Dahmer in a shopping mall. Dahmer invited him to a party, but there was no one else in the apartment when they arrived. Edwards accepted several drinks, after which he became sleepy. Then Dahmer snapped a handcuff on his wrist and held a butcher's knife against his throat, forcing him to sit still as he watched a videotape of *The Exorcist*. When Dahmer said he intended to kill Edwards and eat his heart, Edwards managed to kick him and run for the door.

At the police station, Dahmer seemed glad that it was all over, and admitted that he was a cannibal and had been obsessed by dissection ever since he was a teenager, and had enjoyed stripping birds and small animals of their flesh to preserve their skeletons. And later, the same morbid obsession with dead things had led him to kill human beings.

He was eighteen, he explained, when he committed his first murder—when his parents were away, he had picked up a nineteen-year-old hitchhiker, Stephen Hicks, who sexually attracted him, and they sat in Dahmer's home drinking beer and smoking pot. When Hicks said he had to go, Dahmer became oddly hysterical—he obviously found it worrying to be left alone—and struck Hicks on the head with a dumbbell. Then he undressed him and masturbated on the corpse. After dark he buried the body in the crawl space under the house, but later transferred it to a remote spot. He was almost caught when police stopped him for driving over the central line, but fortunately—for him—they failed to notice the parcels in the rear.

Unlike the majority of serial killers, who for the most part are from working-class backgrounds, Dahmer came from a comfortable middle-class home. But his parents quarreled constantly. He obviously suffered from a deep sense of insecurity and inferiority, partly because they seemed to prefer his younger brother, Dave.

After his first murder, Dahmer joined the army, but was discharged for drunkenness. He had always been a heavy drinker, obviously finding it an escape from reality. He moved in with his grandmother in West Allis, near Milwaukee, and took a job in a chocolate factory. He had recognized his homosexuality in his early teens, and his strange inner compulsions meant that he preferred to be alone, rather than trying to join the gay community. But in Milwaukee, where he was known as a monosyllabic loner, he was banned from a gay bar for slipping knockout drugs into drinks.

In 1986, when he was in his mid-twenties, he was arrested for exposing himself to two boys, and placed on probation. In September of the following year, he committed his second murder, going to a hotel room with a man named Stephen Tuomi, and apparently having normal sex with him before they fell asleep. In the middle of the night, Dahmer strangled Tuomi—he claimed that he had no memory of the murder, but simply woke up and found himself in bed with the body.

The murder certainly seems to have been unpremeditated. Dahmer had to go out and purchase a large suitcase, in which he succeeded in taking the body back to the basement of his grandmother's house. There he dismembered it, and then left it out in garbage bags for collection. This was typical of the fifteen murders that followed between January 1988 and July 1991. He would pick up a young male, usually black, and invite him home—either to his grandmother's or, after she had asked him to leave, to his own apartment on North Twenty-fourth Street. There the victim was rendered unconscious with a strong dose of a knockout drug in his alcohol, and undressed and strangled. Dahmer then dismembered the body, and disposed of it in garbage bags—although he also stored some of it in his refrigerator for cooking and eating.

Dahmer had already come close to being caught in September 1988, when he had picked up a thirteen-year-old Laotian boy named Keison Sinthasomphone and raped him in his apartment, after giving him drugged coffee. But the boy had succeeded in staggering out into the street and back to his home. The police were notified, and Dahmer was charged with second-degree sexual assault and sentenced to a year in a correction program, which allowed him to continue working in the chocolate factory.

Yet three years later, on May 26, 1991, Dahmer was able to pick up the younger brother of his earlier victim, Conerak Sinthasomphone, in the same shopping mall where he later picked up Tracy Edwards. Conerak was also given drugged coffee, and then stripped and raped. But when Dahmer went out to buy beer, the naked boy succeeded in escaping from the apartment, and stood talking to two black teenage girls, begging for help. Dahmer tried to grab the boy, but the girls clung on to him, and one of them succeeded in ringing the police. Two squad cars arrived shortly, but when Dahmer explained plausibly that the young man was his lover and that this was merely a lover's quarrel, the police escorted Conerak back to Dahmer's apartment and left him there to be murdered and dismembered.

When this was finally revealed after Dahmer's arrest, it caused a scandal that shook the Milwaukee Police Department.

In March 1990, Dahmer was released from the correctional center in which he was serving his sentence for the earlier rape. By that time he had already killed five times. On March 13, 1990, he moved into the Oxford Apartments, and during the next eighteen months killed twelve more victims, the last two in just over two weeks, between July 5 and July 22, 1991, the day of his arrest.

Dahmer had almost been caught after his second murder, that of Eddie Smith, on June 14, 1990. He had invited a fifteen-year-old Hispanic youth back to his apartment, but, for some reason, decided to try to knock him unconscious with a rubber mallet instead of the usual drugged drink. The youth fought back, and managed to reach the door. Dahmer let him go after making him promise not to tell the police. The young man broke his promise, but when he begged the police not to let his foster parents know that he was gay, they decided to do nothing about it. So once more, Dahmer managed to escape to kill again.

In the summer of 1991, the revelations about the apartment full of corpses filled the front pages week after week, and made worldwide headlines. In January 1992, Dahmer appeared in court charged with fifteen murders. He made no attempt at defense, and was sentenced to fifteen terms of life imprisonment. Asked how he felt about being in prison, he remarked: "I couldn't find any meaning for my life when I was out there. I'm sure as hell not going to find it in here."

Robert Ressler happened to be in Milwaukee lecturing at a university at the time of Dahmer's arrest, and was asked if he would testify for the defense, who had decided on an insanity plea. His own feeling was that although Dahmer was not entirely innocent, the odd mixture of "organization" and "disorganization" in his crimes made it arguable that he was not entirely sane. This is why he went twice to interview Dahmer in prison. The result shed some interesting light on Dahmer and his motivation. One of the most interesting comments entered the conversation almost by accident. He asks Dahmer if he ever committed violence in his early years, to which the reply was no, but there was violence against him, and he went on to tell how, on his way home from school he was approached by three seniors, and had a feeling that they were hostile. "Sure enough, one of them just took out a billy club and whacked me on the back of the head." Ressler does not pursue this. But when, a few moments later, he asks when Dahmer became interested in dissecting animals, Dahmer says that it was at the age of sixteen, after he had been hit on the head. It started in a biology class, when they were dissecting a baby pig.

Since so many serial killers have received skull injuries, it is inevitable to wonder if the beginning of his obsession with death and corpses was the blow on the head. By coincidence it was also the end. Dahmer

DAHMER WAS MURDERED IN A WISCONSIN JAIL ON NOVEMBER 28, 1994; HE WAS STRUCK ON THE HEAD WITH AN IRON BAR BY A FELLOW CONVICT CALLED CHRISTOPHER SCARVER, WHO EXPLAINED THAT HE BELIEVED HE WAS THE SON OF GOD.

was murdered in a Wisconsin jail on November 28, 1994; he was struck on the head with an iron bar by a fellow convict called Christopher Scarver, who explained that he believed he was the Son of God.

In the 1990s, I became involved in correspondence with the "Gainesville Ripper," Danny Rolling, who, when he was in jail, had become engaged to Gerard Schaefer's one-time fiancée Sondra London, now a well-known crime writer. He had written to her from Florida State Prison, where he was serving time for an attempted robbery of a supermarket store in Ocala, Florida.

It was not until January of the following year that the police had administered a blood test. Rolling's DNA revealed that he was the man who had been involved in the sex murder of four young women on the campus of the University of Florida at Gainesville in the previous August. The crimes had caused such fear that half the students had gone home.

Sondra and Rolling entered into correspondence, and by Christmas 1992 had decided that they were in love. Finally, she was allowed to visit him, and the meeting confirmed their feelings. There was, she told me, an instant and powerful physical attraction. Soon after this they announced their engagement.

This announcement, in February 1993, was featured in some newspapers next to a story claiming that he had confessed to the Gainesville murders to a fellow inmate, Robert Fieldmore Lewis.

Rolling looked an unlikely serial killer, thirty-eight years old, tall, good-looking, and articulate, a talented artist and guitar player, who looked more like a schoolteacher in his horn-rimmed glasses. But in due course he confessed to the Gainesville murders, and eventually, to three more.

Through Sondra, I came to write an introduction to Rolling's autobiography, *The Making of a Serial Killer*, which is how I came to exchange a few letters with him. He told me that had no doubt that he had been possessed by some demonic force when he committed the murders. It sounds like the typical excuse made by a killer; yet after studying the case, I came close to believing him.

Rolling was born in 1954 in Shreveport, Louisiana, the son of a police sergeant who had been a war hero. Unfortunately, James Rolling was also another of Van Vogt's Right Men. Such men, as already noted, are usually family tyrants. Rolling senior seems to have had no love for his son, and lost no opportunity of telling him he was stupid and worthless.

Rolling also went into the military, but just before he was scheduled to go to Vietnam, was caught with drugs and discharged. He was dismayed, for he had been enjoying military life. His father was furious and disgusted with him. But Danny then had a religious conversion, and married a fellow member of the Pentecostal Church. Unfortunately, he was unable to get rid of a habit he had acquired in childhood of peering through windows at women undressing. When he was caught, the marriage began to disintegrate.

On the day he was served his divorce papers, he committed his first sex attack, breaking into a house and raping a young woman who was alone. He felt so remorseful that the next morning he made his way back to her house to apologize—then saw two grim, powerfully built men come out, and changed his mind. But soon after that he committed his first armed robbery. And it was not long before he was serving his first jail term.

The brutality and violence of prison life in the South shocked him. Blacks and whites hated one another and often killed one another. He was nearly gang-raped in the shower by a group of blacks.

Free once more, he now experienced a compulsion to commit rape. He admits in his book that what he enjoyed was the surrender of the terrified girl, the sense of power; it was balm to his bruised ego. Another period in jail only confirmed his self-image as a desperate criminal.

Back in his hometown in 1989, he began peeping through the window of a pretty model named Julie Grissom. One day, after missing work for three days in a row, he was fired from his job in a restaurant. He reacted just as he had reacted years earlier to his divorce papers. On November 1989, he crept into the backyard of the Grissom household, where he had formerly played Peeping Tom. Undeterred by the fact that there were three people in the house—Julie Grissom's father and her eight-year-old nephew—he burst in and tied up all three at gunpoint with duct tape. Then he stabbed to death the boy and the elder man, dragged Julie into the bathroom and raped her against the sink, forcing her to say, "Fuck my pussy, daddy." After making her climb in the bath so he could wash out her vagina with a hosepipe, he stabbed her to death. He left after taking $200.

By now he was convinced that he had two "demons," one a robber and rapist called "Ennad," and the other a killer called "Gemini."

A violent quarrel with his father ended with James Rolling trying to shoot him, and with Danny shooting his father and leaving him for dead. In fact, James Rolling survived, minus one eye. Rolling committed more armed robberies and rapes, and then traveled to Gainesville, where he bought a tent and pitched it in the woods.

There were more voyeuristic activities—on some occasions he stripped naked while he peeped. On August 24, 1990, he broke into an apartment shared by two seventeen-year-olds, Christina Powell and Sonja Larson, who were both asleep. He stabbed Sonja to death in her bed. Then he went downstairs and woke up Christina on the sofa, and at gunpoint taped her hands. After raping her he stabbed her to death, making her lie on her face while he did it. He left both bodies positioned for maximum shock value.

Two evenings later he broke into the apartment of eighteen-year-old Christa Hoyt (on whom he had been spying), and waited for her to return home. When she did, he overpowered her, and raped and stabbed her to death, also disemboweling her and cutting off her head. When police arrived on the scene, they were horrified to find her headless body seated on the edge of her bed, her severed nipples beside her.

Two days later, Rollings broke into an apartment shared by two students, Tracy Paules and Manuel Taboada, both twenty-three. The latter was stabbed as he lay asleep. Tracy Paules heard sounds of struggle and came to see what was happening. Rolling chased her to her bedroom, tied her up and raped her, afterwards stabbing her to death as she lay facedown.

The murders caused widespread panic; thousands of students left campus for Labor Day weekend; only seven hundred returned. By then Rolling had already moved south, living by burglary and armed robbery.

On August 27, 1990, a bare-chested, ski-masked bandit robbed the First Union Bank a half mile down the road from Hoyt's apartment. Two witnesses later recognized Rolling from the muscle-definition of his chest.

On September 7, driving a Ford Mustang taken after his last burglary, Rolling stopped in Ocala, Florida, and walked into the crowded Winn-Dixie supermarket at midday. He strolled up to the location manager, Randy Wilson, pointed a .38 at his head and demanded the money from the cash drawer. Then he called to the girls to empty their registers.

Rolling asked: "Where's the safe?"

"In my office."

"Let's go." They went up two steps into the office.

Meanwhile, the store's bookkeeper, who was returning from an errand, was notified at the entrance that the store was being robbed. She ran into the dry cleaner next door. "Can I use your phone? We're being robbed."

As Rolling left the store with a bag of money, the manager followed him, and watched him turn into the back lot behind the store. A crowd of shoppers pointed. "He went that way." By now a police car had arrived and Wilson directed them.

When Rolling reached his stolen car, the police were right behind him. The high-speed chase that followed ended when Rolling wrecked the car. He fled into a nearby building, through to the back, and into the parking lot. The police were there waiting for him. He ignored their order to freeze, and ran on. Finally, a tackle brought him down, and moments later he was in a squad car. Behind, in his stolen car, was the $4,700 he had taken. Within an hour he was behind bars.

It was in Florida State Prison that he met Robert Lewis, who had written a screenplay. When Danny asked him who was the Sondra London mentioned on the title page, Lewis explained that she was his editor. Danny, who felt that he too could become a writer, to while away the long years behind bars, asked for her address, and wrote to her.

In his hometown of Shreveport, authorities had noted the similarity between the murder of the Julie Grissom family and the Gainesville murders. Now the FBI's VICAP came into operation, detailing the similarities.

In January 1991, Rolling was asked for a blood sample. The result revealed that the Gainesville Ripper and the killer of the Grissom family were the same person. Tried for the Gainesville murders in 1994, he was given five death sentences.

And why am I prepared to take seriously his claim of being "possessed" by a demonic entity?

In *The Making of a Serial Killer*, Rolling tells how he tried to enter the apartment of Christina Powell and Sonja Larson and found the door locked. He claims that he then prayed to "Gemini," his demon, and that when he tried the door again, it was unlocked. And in a letter to me he described how, in his cell, a kind of gray gargoyle had leapt onto his chest, held him down with its claws, and thrust its tongue down his throat. All this may, of course, be invention. Or it may be that Rolling really believes what he says. I am inclined to think that he does.

After thirty years studying the paranormal, I have slowly come to accept that "possession" can actually occur, and that it is not a fantasy dreamed up by the feeble-minded and the sex-starved.

But whether Rolling was possessed by some unpleasant paranormal entity is perhaps beside the point. As in the case of Ted Bundy, Rolling's life typifies the development of a sex killer: the childhood voyeurism culminating in his first rape (which was committed in a state of rage at the prospect of divorce); the murder of the Grissoms, again committed in a state of anger and defiance; and then the orgy of rape and murder at Gainesville. It seems clear that, as in the case of Ted Bundy, rape and murder proved addictive. In a sense, Rolling was possessed—by his craving to violate and kill.

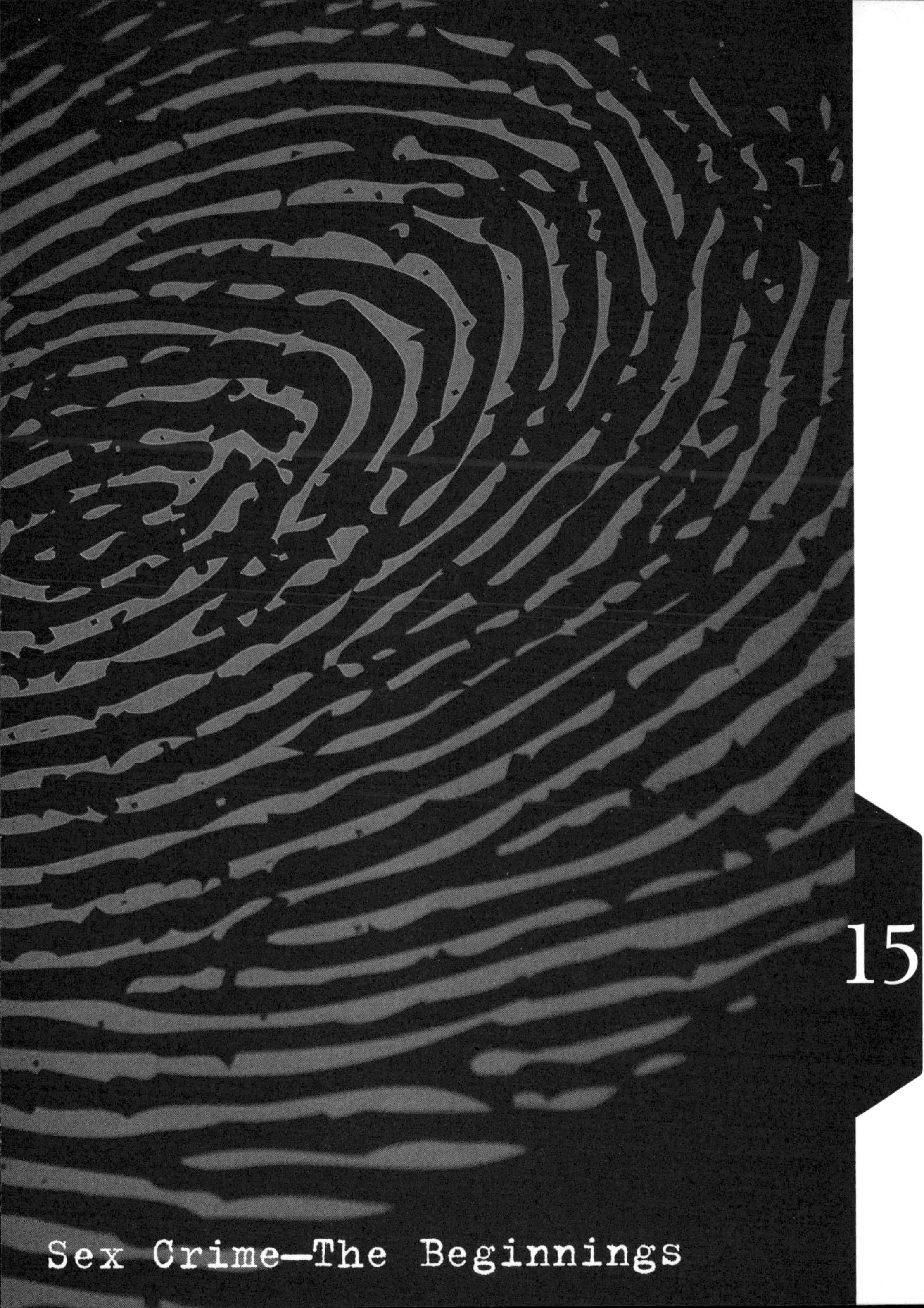

15

Sex Crime—The Beginnings

15

Sex Crime—The Beginnings

The Jack the Ripper murders, which took place in the East End of London in the autumn of 1888, are generally acknowledged to be the first sex murders in our modern sense of the term. But a century before that date, London was also the scene of the first crimes that we would regard as sexually abnormal—the series of knife attacks on women by a man who became known as the "London Monster."

In the words of the chronicler J. W. von Archenholtz, he committed "nameless crimes, the possibility of whose existence no legislator has ever dreamt of." These nameless crimes amounted to creeping up behind fashionably dressed women and slashing at their clothing with a sharp knife, which occasionally caused painful wounds; it was also alleged that he would hold out a nosegay to young ladies, and as they bent to sniff it, would jab them in the face with a "sharp pointed instrument" hidden among the flowers. He was also known to jab bosoms.

During the months he was attacking women, the London Monster created a reign of terror: rewards were offered for his capture and walls covered in posters describing his activities.

It seems that he became obsessed with the pretty daughter of a tavernkeeper, Anne Porter, and followed her in Saint James's Park, making obscene suggestions. On the night of January 18, 1790, when she was returning from a ball with her two sisters, he came up behind her, and she felt a slashing blow on her right buttock. Indoors, she discovered that she had a nine-inch-wide knife wound that was four inches deep in the center. Six months later, out walking with a gentleman named Coleman, Anne recognized the Monster in the park. Coleman followed the man to a nearby house, accused him of being the attacker, and made a kind of "citizen's arrest." The man adamantly denied being the Monster, but Anne fainted when she saw him.

The Monster proved to be a slightly built man young man named Renwick Williams, twenty-three, a maker of artificial flowers. It seemed that Williams was from Wales, had received some education, and come to London under the auspices of a gentleman who was a patron of the theater. Williams was hoping to become an actor or dancer, but proved to lack the talent and application. Instead he dressed "above his station" and aspired to become a ladies' man, drinking rather too much. So the picture we form of him is of an introspective "wannabe," dreaming of fame, and sexually stimulated by fashionable young ladies, whose bare arms and half-covered bosoms must have struck a country-bred youth as wickedly exciting. Slashing these provocative garments—and penetrating the body underneath—probably induced a sexual climax.

At his trial, Williams insisted that it was a case of mistaken identity; and even offered an alibi. The jury chose to disbelieve him, however, and he was sentenced to six years in prison for "damaging clothes." The prosecuting counsel talked of "a scene that is so new in the annals of humanity, a scene so inexplicable, so unnatural, that one might have regarded it, out of respect for human nature, as impossible." All of which demonstrates that the eighteenth century was very far from any comprehension of sex crime.

That is understandable because, for all practical purposes, the nineteenth century saw the real beginning of the "age of sex crime." Before that, a majority of crime was motivated by profit. But already, by 1790, Renwick Williams was becoming so excited by the provocatively clad ladies of London that he became the first "sadistic piqueur."

In 1807 and 1808, Andrew Bichel a peasant in Regensdorf, Bavaria, murdered two young women, apparently for their clothes, then dismembered their bodies and buried them in his woodshed. He later tried unsuccessfully to lure other women to his cottage. It is not clear whether, as did the London Monster, he had a fetish for female dress, but when dogs sniffed out the women's remains, Bichel was tried for murder and beheaded.

In 1867, as noted earlier, the clerk Frederick Baker, murdered eight-year-old Fanny Adams in Alton, Hampshire, and wrote in his diary: "Killed a young girl yesterday—it was fine and hot."

In 1871, a French youth, Eusebius Pieydagnelle, begged the jury to sentence him to death for four murders of girls, and explained to them that he had become fascinated by the smell of blood from the butcher's shop opposite his home in Vinuville, and persuaded his middle-class father to allow him to become an apprentice there. In the slaughterhouse, he drank blood and secretly wounded the animals. When his father removed him and apprenticed him to a lawyer, he went into deep depression, and began killing people, including a fifteen-year-old girl and his former employer.

In April 1880, twenty-year-old Louis Menesclou admitted to murdering four-year-old Louise Dreux and sleeping with the body before he attempted to burn it; he was executed.

But it was the five Jack the Ripper murders, which happened between August and November 1888, that achieved worldwide notoriety, and made the police aware that they were confronted by a new kind of problem: a killer who struck at random.

The first victim, a prostitute named Mary Ann Nicholls, was found in the early hours of the morning of August 31, with her throat cut; in the mortuary, it was discovered that she had also been disemboweled. The next victim, another prostitute, Annie Chapman, was found spread-eagled in the backyard of a slum dwelling, also disemboweled; the contents of her pockets had been laid around her in a curiously ritualistic manner—a characteristic that has been found to be typical of many serial killers.

The two murders engendered nationwide shock and outrage—nothing of the sort had been known before—and this was increased when, on the morning of September 30, 1888, the killer murdered two pickups in one night. A letter signed "Jack the Ripper," boasting of the "double event," was sent to the Central News Agency within hours of the murders. When the biggest police operation in London's history failed to catch the killer, there was unprecedented public hysteria. As if in response to the sensation he was causing, the Ripper's next murder was the most gruesome so far. A twenty-four-year-old prostitute named Mary Jeanette Kelly was killed and disemboweled in her room; the mutilations that followed must have taken several hours. Then the murders ceased—the most widely held theories being that the killer had committed suicide or was confined in a mental home.

From the point of view of the general public, the most alarming thing about the murders was that the killer seemed to be able to strike with impunity, and that the police seemed to be completely helpless.

Robert Ressler wrote in *I Have Lived in the Monster*: "Sexual satisfaction for Jack the Ripper, and others of his ilk, derives from seeing the victim's blood spilt" and pointed out that cutting out uteruses and opening the vagina with his knife leaves no doubt that the crimes were sexual (by which, presumably, he means that they were accompanied by orgasm).

FROM THE POINT OF VIEW OF THE GENERAL PUBLIC, THE MOST ALARMING THING ABOUT THE MURDERS WAS THAT THE KILLER SEEMED TO BE ABLE TO STRIKE WITH IMPUNITY, AND THAT THE POLICE SEEMED TO BE COMPLETELY HELPLESS.

In 1988, a century after the Ripper murders, a television company in the United States decided to do a two-hour live special on the case, and asked John Douglas and Roy Hazelwood to participate. Their provocative conclusions are described in *Dark Dreams* by Hazelwood and Michaud.

To begin with, Douglas and Hazelwood were interested to learn of the vast amount of evidence that would be available to them, from coroner's reports, witnesses' statements, and police files; there were even photographs. In addition, they were presented with a list of five favorite suspects, which included Queen Victoria's physician Sir William Gull; the heir to the throne Prince Albert Victor; Roslyn Donston, a Satanist and occultist who lived in Whitechapel; Montague Druitt, a melancholic schoolmaster who drowned himself soon after the last murder; and a psychotic Polish immigrant named Aaron Kosminski. The latter two were listed as leading suspects in a private memorandum by Sir Melville Macnaghten, who had been assistant chief constable at Scotland Yard soon after the murders. Most of these suspects were dismissed on various grounds—for example, Sir William Gull had suffered a stroke that paralyzed his right side a year before the murders and would have been in no condition to prowl the streets, while Prince Albert Victor had solid alibis.

But the most interesting part of the program was the analysis presented by the profilers:

> *[John] explained that Jack was like a predatory animal who would be out nightly looking for weak and susceptible victims for his grotesque sexual fantasies. Douglas told the TV audience that with such a killer, you do not expect to see a definite time pattern because he kills as opportunity presents itself. He added that such killers return to the scenes of their successful crimes.*
>
> *He surmised that Jack was a white male in his mid-to-late-twenties and of average intelligence. John and I agreed that Jack the Ripper wasn't nearly as clever as he was lucky. I then said that we thought Jack was single, never married, and probably did not socialize with women at all. He would have had a great deal of difficulty interacting appropriately with anyone, but particularly women.*
>
> *I said Jack lived very close to the crime scenes because we know that such offenders generally start killing within very close proximity to their homes. If Jack was employed, it would have been at menial work requiring little or no contact with others.*
>
> *I went on to say that, as a child, Jack probably set fires and abused animals and that as an adult his erratic behavior would have brought him to the attention of the police at some point.*
>
> *John added that Jack seemed to have come from a broken home and was raised by a dominant female who physically abused him, possibly even sexually abused him. Jack would have internalized this abuse rather than act it out toward those closest to him.*
>
> *John described Jack as socially withdrawn, a loner, having poor personal hygiene, and a disheveled appearance. Such characteristics are hallmarks of this type of offender. He said that people who know this type of person often report he is nocturnal, preferring the hours of darkness to daytime. When he is out at night, he typically covers great distances on foot.*
>
> *I said that Jack simultaneously hated and feared women. They intimidated him, and his feeling of inadequacy was evident in the way he killed. I noted that the Ripper had subdued and murdered his victims quickly. There was no evidence that he savored this part of his crime; he didn't torture the women or prolong their deaths. He attacked suddenly and without warning, quickly cutting their throats.*
>
> *The psychosexually pleasurable part came for him in the acts following death. By displacing or removing his victims' sexual parts and organs, Jack was neutering or de-sexing them so that they were no longer women to be feared.*

I find this profile convincing and impressive. It sounds, of course, oddly like Ramirez, the Night Stalker. The skill of Douglas and Hazelwood in profiling killers has been so fully demonstrated in this book, it seems to me probable that this is as accurate a profile of the Ripper as we shall ever get.

It should be noted that the profilers do not feel that it is likely that Jack the Ripper was a "gentleman," as so many theorists have suggested since the time of the murders. They see him as working class.

That also rules out the suspect suggested by the crime novelist Patricia Cornwell—that the Ripper was the artist Walter Sickert. I would also rule out Sickert on other grounds. This kind of murder is an explosion of frustration—this is why we so often say that a killer is a "walking time bomb." No artist or creative person is likely to experience this degree of mental stress and frustration. In fact, I have pointed out in *A Criminal History of Mankind* that no creative artist has ever committed a murder. A few have killed in the course of quarrels or duels, such as Ben Jonson and Caravaggio, or to revenge honor, like the composer Gesualdo, but never a premeditated crime of violence.

The only remaining Ripper suspect of the five named above is Aaron Kosminski, a Jewish hairdresser who came to England in 1882 in his late teens, and who spent a number of periods in an insane asylum. He died in 1919.

This is not to suggest that Kosminski has to be Jack the Ripper. There are a number of other candidates, including a homicidal Russian doctor named Michael Ostrog, also on Sir Melvile Macnaghten's list. And there may be some so-far unknown who fits the FBI profile even better. But it probably does mean that we should not be looking for suspects who do not qualify as "gentlemen."

Despite royal conspiracy theorists claims, and a number of books that name him as a plausible suspect, Prince Albert Victor, Duke of Clarence, was not Jack the Ripper. Reputable historians and most "Ripperologists" discount these theories as highly unlikely, if not downright preposterous.

From the end of the Victorian age until the beginning of World War II there were no British serial killers. In London in early 1942, a member of the Royal Air Force named Gordon Cummins became known as the Blackout Ripper when he took advantage of the London blackout to murder four women. Although the motive seems to have been primarily robbery, there was also a sadistic sexual element in that he mutilated one woman with a can opener and two with razor blades. He was arrested on February 15 after a passer-by interrupted an attack, and he fled, leaving his gas mask with his service number on it. He was later hanged.

Another airman, Neville Heath, would undoubtedly have gone on to become a serial killer if he hadn't been caught after his second murder in July 1946. On June 21, 1946, he had escorted a model named Margery Gardner to a London hotel; Gardner had masochistic tendencies and Heath had a taste for flogging women. But he seems to have become over-excited and left her dead and mutilated. Two weeks later, staying in a hotel in Bournemouth, he insisted on accompanying twenty-one-year-old Doreen Marshall back to her hotel. He then murdered and mutilated her in a wooded gorge. He was arrested, and a jeweler identified him as the man who had sold him Doreen Marshall's watch; Heath was hanged at Pentonville Prison on October 16, 1946.

Britain's first true serial killer since Jack the Ripper was the middle-aged John Reginald Halliday Christie, who committed eight sex murders in London's Notting Hill between 1943 and 1953. To his neighbors, the most irritating thing about Christie was his authoritarian personality. As a special reserve constable during World War II, he became notorious for his officiousness—he enjoyed reporting people for minor blackout offences.

A sexually frustrated loner who suffered from bouts of impotence, his solution was to persuade women to inhale a nasal decongestant called Friar's Balsam, which is added to boiling water, and then breathed in with a towel covering the head. Christie would then introduce a rubber pipe attached to the gas supply, which quickly induced unconsciousness, after which the women were strangled as he raped them. This is the method he employed with his first two victims, an Austrian part-time prostitute named Ruth Fuerst, twenty-one, strangled in September 1943, and a fellow-employee at a radio factory, Muriel Eady, thirty-one, killed three months later. In his confession, Christie would declare that after killing her, "I felt that quiet, peaceful thrill. I had no regrets."

On both occasions his wife, Ethel, was away in Sheffield visiting her family.

Christie's next murder, in 1949, was that of Beryl Evans, twenty-two, the wife of a Welsh laborer, Timothy Evans, twenty-seven, who lived in the upper floor of the slum terrace house at 10 Rillington Place, Notting Hill. The Evanses had a year-old baby, Geraldine. Lack of money caused frequent quarrels, and when Beryl found she was pregnant again, she decided to have an abortion. Christie claimed to be a skilled abortionist. On the morning of November 8, 1949, Christie went up to her flat, and told her to lie on a quilt in front on the fire, and take a few sniffs of gas to anaesthetize her. Then he strangled her and almost certainly raped her.

When her husband came home from work, Christie told him that this wife had died during the attempted abortion, and said they would both face criminal charges when her death was discovered. Evans was of subnormal intelligence, and the likeliest scenario is that Christie somehow persuaded him to kill baby Geraldine. Then both bodies were concealed in the outside washhouse. Somehow, Evans was convinced that he had to sell his furniture and flee to Wales. There he went to the police station and confessed to "disposing of" his wife, and to strangling her and his daughter. By the time he was tried for their murder, he had changed his mind and accused Christie of strangling his wife and child, but the jury did not believe him, and he was hanged. Christie was a witness against him and was commended by the judge.

Ethel Christie had a strong suspicion, amounting to a certainty, that her husband was somehow involved in the murders—she had noticed his extreme nervousness at the time. She confided her belief to a neighbor, and when Christie came in and caught them discussing the case, he flew into a rage. This could explain why, on December 14, 1952, he strangled Ethel in bed. It could also have been that he experienced a compulsion to commit more sex crimes, and that Ethel stood in his way. Christie told her family in Sheffield that she was unable to write because she had rheumatism in her fingers.

In mid-January 1953 Christie picked up a prostitute called Kathleen Maloney in a pub in Paddington, and invited her back to his flat. As she sat in a deckchair in the kitchen, he placed the gas pipe under the chair; she was too drunk to notice. When she was unconscious, he raped and strangled her and put her in the closet

The next victim, Rita Nelson, was six months pregnant; Christie may have lured her back with the offer of an abortion. She also ended in the cupboard—the second body.

About a month later, Christie met a girl called Hectorina Maclennan, who told him she was looking for a flat. She and her boyfriend actually spent three nights in Christie's flat, now devoid of furniture (Christie had sold it). On March 5, Hectorina made the mistake of going back to the flat alone. She grew nervous when she saw Christie toying with a gas-pipe and tried to leave; Christie killed her and raped her. When her boyfriend came to inquire about her, she was in the cupboard, and Christie claimed not to have seen her. As Christie gave him tea, the boyfriend noticed "a very nasty smell," but had no suspicion he was sitting within feet of her corpse.

During the next few months, the squalid little flat was allowed to become filthy and untidy. Christie had no job and made no attempt to find one. A week later, he sublet the flat to another couple, collected £7 13s. for rent in advance, and wandered off, leaving the decomposing bodies in the closet that was now disguised by a layer of wallpaper. The owner of the house, finding the flat sublet, ordered the new tenants to leave, and looked into the closet. In spite of the hue and cry that followed, Christie made no attempt to escape from London, even registering at a cheap doss house under his own name. He walked around, becoming increasingly dirty and unshaven, until a policeman recognized him on Putney Bridge. What happened to him in those last weeks of freedom? It is tempting to suppose that he ceased to be responsible for his actions. Yet he continued to plan and calculate: even when on the run, he met a pregnant young woman in a café, and told her he was a medical man who could perform an operation . . .

He was tried for only one murder, that of his wife, and pleaded insanity. Found guilty, John Reginal Christie was hanged on July 15, 1953.

Christie seems to have been a highly neurotic since his early days in Halifax, in the north of England, when a sexual failure in adolescence caused him to be labeled "Reggie-no-dick," and "Can't-do-it Christie" But the determining factor that finally turned him into a sex killer may well have been an accident he suffered when he first came to London in 1922; he was struck by a car and was unconscious when taken to hospital—one more to add to the list of serial killers with suspected head injuries.

The series of unsolved murders known as the "Thames Nude Murders" deserves a place in any history of manhunting because the detective who led the investigation believes that it was his game of psychological cat and mouse that drove the killer to suicide.

Between February 1964 and January 1965, the bodies of six women, mostly prostitutes, were found in areas not far from the Thames. The first of the bodies, that of a thirty-year-old prostitute by the name of Hanna Tailford, was found in the water near Hammersmith Bridge. She was naked except for her stockings, and her panties had been stuffed into her mouth. On April 18, the naked body of Irene Lockwood, a twenty-six-year-old prostitute, was found at Duke's Meadows, near Barnes Bridge. She had been strangled and, like Hanna Tailford, had been pregnant. A fifty-four-year-old Kensington caretaker, Kenneth Archibald, confessed to her murder, and he seemed to know a great deal about the victim, but at his trial it was established that his confession was false. Archibald was acquitted.

There was another reason for believing in his innocence: while he was still in custody, another naked woman was found in an alleyway at Osterley Park, Brentford. This was only three weeks after the discovery of Irene Lockwood's body. The dead woman—the only one among the victims who could be described as pretty—was identified as twenty-two-year-old prostitute and striptease artist Helen Barthelemy. There were a number of curious features in the case. A line around her waist showed that her panties had been removed some time after death, and there was no evidence of normal sexual assault. But four of her front teeth were missing. Oddly enough, the teeth had not been knocked out by a blow, but deliberately forced out—a piece of one of them was found lodged in her throat. Medical investigation also revealed the presence of male semen in her throat. Here, then, was the cause of death: she had been choked by a penis, probably in the course of performing an act of fellatio. The missing teeth suggested that the killer had repeated the assault after death. It was established that she had disappeared some days before her body was found. Where, then, had her body been kept?

Flakes of paint found on her skin suggested the answer, for it was the type of paint used in spraying cars. Clearly, the body had been kept somewhere near a car-spraying plant, but in some place where it was not likely to be discovered by the workers.

Enormous numbers of police were deployed in the search for the spray shop and in an attempt to keep a closer watch on the areas in which the three victims had been picked up, around Notting Hill and Shepherd's Bush. Perhaps for this reason, the killer decided to take no risks for several months.

The body of the fourth victim—Mary Fleming, thirty, was found on July 14, 1964. Her false teeth were missing, there was semen in her throat, and her skin showed traces of the same spray paint found on Helen Barthelemy. She had vanished three days earlier.

Her body was found in a half-crouching position near a garage in Acton, and the van that took her there was actually seen leaving the scene of the crime. A motorist driving past Berrymede Road, a cul-de-sac, at 5:30 in the morning, had to brake violently to avoid a van that shot out in front of him. He was so angry that he contacted the police to report the incident, but had failed to take note of the license plate number. A squad car that arrived a few minutes later found Mary's body in the forecourt of a garage in the cul-de-sac.

The near miss probably alarmed the killer, for no further murders occurred that summer. Then, on November 25, 1964, another naked corpse was found under some debris in a car park in Hornton Street, Kensington. It was identified as Margaret McGowan, twenty-one, who had disappeared more than a month before her body was found, and there were signs of decomposition. Again, there were traces of paint on the body, and a missing front tooth indicated that she had died in the same way as the previous two victims.

The last of the "Jack the Stripper" victims was a prostitute named Bridie O'Hara, twenty-eight, who was found on February 16, 1965, in some undergrowth on the Heron Trading Estate, in Acton. She had last been seen on January 11. The body was partly mummified, which indicated that it had been kept in a cool place. As usual, teeth were missing and sperm was found in the throat. Fingermarks on the back of her neck revealed that, like the other victims, she had died in a kneeling position.

Detective Chief Superintendent John du Rose was recalled from his holiday to take charge of the investigation in the Shepherd's Bush area. The Heron Trading Estate provided the lead they had been waiting for. Investigation of a paint spray shop revealed that this was the source of the paint found on the bodies—chemical analysis proved it. The proximity of a disused warehouse solved the question of where the bodies had been kept before they were dumped. The powerful spray guns caused the paint to carry, with diminishing intensity, for several hundred yards. Analysis of paint on the bodies enabled experts to establish the spot where the women must have been concealed: it was underneath a transformer in the warehouse.

Yet even with this discovery, the case was far from solved. Thousands of men worked on the Heron Trading Estate. (Oddly enough, John Christie had been employed there). Mass questioning seemed to bring the police no closer to their suspect. Du Rose decided to throw a twenty-mile cordon around the area, to keep a careful check on all cars passing through at night. Drivers who were observed more than once were noted; if they were seen more than twice, they were interviewed. Du Rose conducted what he called "a war of nerves" against the killer, dropping hints in the press or on television that indicated the police were getting closer. They knew he drove a van and they knew he must have right of access to the trading estate by night. The size of the victims, who were all small women, suggested that the killer was under middle height. As the months passed, and no further murders took place, du Rose assumed that he was winning the war of nerves. The killer had ceased to operate. He checked on all men who had been jailed since mid-February, all men with prison records who had been hospitalized, all men who had died or committed suicide. In his book *Murder Was My Business*, du Rose claims that a list of twenty suspects had been reduced to three when one of the three committed suicide. He left a note saying that he could not bear the strain any longer. The man was a security guard who drove a van, and had access to the estate. At the time when the women were murdered, his rounds included the spray shop. He worked by night, from 10 p.m. to 6 a.m. He was unmarried.

The Moors Murder case was one of the most notorious British murder cases of the twentieth century.

Ian Brady, the illegitimate son of a waitress, was born in a tough Glasgow slum in 1938, and was farmed out to foster parents. He was intelligent and a good student, and at the age of eleven he won a scholarship to an expensive school. Many of his new fellow students came from well-to-do families, and—like so many serial killers—he developed a fierce resentment of his own underprivileged position. He began committing burglaries, and at thirteen was sentenced to two years' probation for housebreaking; as soon as this ended he was sentenced to another two years for ten burglaries. He also practiced sadistic cruelty to animals. When his mother moved to Manchester with a new husband, he took a job in the market there, but was picked up by the police for helping to load stolen goods on to a truck. Since this was in violation of his probation, he was sentenced to a Borstal institution, a punishment he regarded as so unfair that he decided that from then on he would "teach society a lesson."

At twenty-one, he became a clerk in Millwards, a chemical firm in Gorton, and began collecting books on the Nazis, and reading the Marquis de Sade—virtually the patron saint of serial killers. His books give expression to their basic belief that the individual owes nothing to society, and has the right to live in it in a kind of subjective dream world, treating morality as an illusion. Brady experienced a kind of religious conversion to these ideas. So far he had seen himself merely as a criminal; now—like Leonard Lake—he began to see himself as the heroic outcast, the scourge of a hypocritical society.

It was at about this point in his life that Myra Hindley entered the story. She was a completely normal working-class girl, not bad-looking, inclined to go in for blonde hairdos and bright lipstick, interested mainly in boys and dancing. She was a typical medium-dominance female, who would have been perfectly content with a reasonably hard-working boy-next-door. When she came to work at Millwards, she was fascinated by Brady's sullen good looks and moody expression. But Brady was undoubtedly one of the dominant 5 percent (see chapter 4); he recognized her as a medium-dominance type and ignored her; at the end of six months he had not even spoken to her. Without encouragement Myra filled her diary with declarations of love: "I hope he loves me and will marry me some day." Finally, Brady decided it would be a pity not to take advantage of the maidenhead that was being offered, and invited her out. Soon after this Myra surrendered her virginity on the divan bed in her gran's front room.

For criminal couples, the combination of high- and medium-dominance egos usually produces an explosive mixture—as in the case of the Hillside Stranglers or Lake and Ng. The high-dominance partner finds himself regarded with admiration that acts as a kind of superfertilizer on his ego; in no time at all he develops a full-blown case of the Right Man syndrome. Brady found it intoxicating to have an audience; he talked to Myra enthusiastically about Hitler, and nicknamed her "Hessie"—from pianist Dame Myra Hess and the führer's deputy Rudolf Hess.

But her sexual submission was not enough; it only intensified his craving to be a "somebody." He announced that he was planning a series of payroll robberies, and induced her to join a local pistol club to gain access to guns. He also took photographs of her posing with crotchless panties and, using a timing device, of the two of them having sex. In some of the photographs—which Brady tried to sell—she has whip marks across her buttocks.

BRADY'S MOTIVATION LAY IN HIS OBSESSIVE NEED TO TASTE THE DELIGHTS OF DOMINATING ANOTHER PERSON, AND THE SADISM THAT HAD DEVELOPED IN HIM SINCE CHILDHOOD.

Some time in 1963—when he was twenty-five and she twenty-one—he induced her to join with him in the murder of children. It is hard to understand how a typical medium-dominance woman allowed herself to be persuaded. But the answer undoubtedly lies in the curious chemistry of religious conversion. The love-struck Myra became the archetypal convert. Her sister Maureen would later describe in court how Myra had changed from being a normal young woman who loved children and animals to someone who was hostile and suspicious and said she hated human beings.

Brady's motivation lay in his obsessive need to taste the delights of dominating another person, and the sadism that had developed in him since childhood. Myra became his "slave." And when, in July 1963, he told her he wanted to rape Pauline Reade, a sixteen-year-old neighbor, Myra agreed to lure Pauline up on to the moor. Brady then arrived on his motorbike, and raped and strangled Pauline. Myra then helped Brady bury her on Saddleworth Moor.

In the next two years, he and Myra would commit four more murders. On October 23, 1963, they drove to the market at Ashton-under-Lyne, where twelve-year-old John Kilbride had been earning pocket money by doing odd jobs for stallholders. On that dark and foggy night a "kind lady" asked him if he wanted a lift. It was the last time John was seen alive. When his body was found two years later, his trousers had been pulled down to his knees. The police found the grave because Brady had taken a photograph of Myra Hindley kneeling on it.

On June 16, 1964, another twelve-year-old boy, Keith Bennett, vanished on his way to visit his grandmother in Manchester. His body has never been found.

On December 26, 1964, Myra arranged for her grandmother to stay with relatives for the night. At six o'clock that evening, she approached ten-year-old Lesley Ann Downey at a fair and offered her a lift home. Lesley was taken back to the grandmother's house, and forced to undress, after which Brady tape-recorded her pleas to be allowed to go home, and took photographs of her with a gag in her mouth. Brady raped her, but would later claim that it was Myra who strangled Lesley with a piece of cord. They kept the body in the house overnight before burying it on the moor.

Brady would later admit that committing so many murders had given him an odd sense of meaninglessness, of futility, which may be why he allowed almost a year to elapse before he killed again. This crime was not for "pleasure," but to entrap Myra's brother-in-law, David Smith, a young man who regarded Brady with hero worship, into becoming an accomplice. On October 6, 1965, the couple picked up a seventeen-year-old homosexual, Edward Evans, and took him back to the house. Then Myra called at her sister's flat, and asked Smith to walk her home. As Smith stood in the kitchen, he heard a scream, and Myra pushed him into the sitting room, yelling. "Help him, Dave." Brady was hacking at Evans with a hatchet. When Evans was dead, Brady handed the bloodstained hatchet to Smith, saying: "Feel the weight"—he wanted Smith's fingerprints on it. But Smith was sickened and horrified by what he had seen (the FBI profiling team could have told Brady that a teenager would panic), and after drinking tea and agreeing to return the next day with a pram and help dispose of the body, he went home to his wife and vomited. Smith and his wife then went to the police. The next morning, a policeman dressed as a baker's roundsman called at the house, and the body was found in a locked bedroom. Brady was arrested, and Myra was arrested the next day. Photographs of the graves led the police to uncover the bodies of two of the victims on Saddleworth Moor. In May 1966, both were sentenced to life imprisonment. Myra Hindley died in prison in November 2002.

By that time I had been in correspondence with Ian Brady for ten years. This came about because soon after Easter 1990, an attractive girl named Christine arrived at my house, explaining that she was a friend of Brady; she wanted to ask my advice about an autobiography she was writing, and whether she could quote his letters to her. I explained that Brady's letters were his copyright, and that she could not quote them without his permission. A few weeks later, I received a letter from Brady, who was now in the Ashworth High Security Hospital near Liverpool, asking if it was true that I was helping Christine to write a book about him. I replied explaining the true situation, and Brady and I continued to correspond. In fact, I had always been curious about him, because it was obvious from the trial evidence that he was highly intelligent, and I was baffled by the way that he had converted ordinary Myra to becoming his accomplice in killing children.

My correspondence with Brady was my first contact with the mind of a serial killer. He was, in fact, as intelligent as I had supposed. But I quickly became aware that there were certain important factors that I had left out of account. William James wrote an essay called "On a Certain Blindness in Human Beings." And I soon came to recognize that a highly intelligent person can suffer from it just as much as a stupid person.

Brady was obsessed by the notion that the criminal has the right to be a criminal because society—particularly people in authority—commits far worse crimes. (He would cite the atom bomb and napalm.) It was no good pointing out to him that, even if that were true, two wrongs do not make a right. Brady's hatred of authority was so absolute that he would not even consider the argument. Myra Hindley would describe how, after burying one of the victims, Brady shook his fist at the sky and shouted: "Take that, you bastard."

Most of us can recognize how anger and humiliation makes us irrational, but even when cursing with fury, a part of us recognizes that we are being illogical, and surrendering to negative emotion. Brady seemed to possess a psychological mechanism that completely blocked any such notion. I once asked him if he ever thought about his victims; he replied: "That would be the quickest way to mental suicide."

He obviously meant the same thing when he admitted to a journalist: "I felt old at twenty-six. Everything was ashes. I felt there was nothing of interest—nothing to hook myself on to. I had experienced everything."

I suspect that this odd sense of moral bankruptcy affects most serial killers, and sometimes explains why they make mistakes that lead to their arrest.

Brady often told me that there had been a "hidden agenda" behind the murders, and that if I read certain of his letters carefully enough, I would grasp what it was. He would never explain himself further, and I came to suspect that it was merely some form of self-justification. I was inclined to believe that he was hinting at a factor that is the essence of sex crime: that sense of power that Hazelwood talks about. Christie experienced it after he had strangled and raped Muriel Eady: " . . . once again I experienced that quiet, peaceful thrill. I had no regrets."

Psychologist Mihály Csíkszentmihályi has labeled this feeling "the flow experience." He recognizes that human beings need the flow experience to change and evolve. Our energies could be compared to a river flowing over a plain. If the flow is too slow, the river begins to meander as it accumulates silt and mud. But a violent storm in the mountains can send down a roaring torrent that sweeps away the silt and straightens out the bends, so that once again, the river flows straight and deep. This is why all human beings crave the flow experience.

The flow experience also brings the recognition that human beings possess powers and capabilities of which they are not normally aware. Again, it is James who catches this insight when he says that the problem with most of us is "a habit of inferiority to our full selves."

But by the "hidden agenda" Brady may have meant something more straightforward. In January 2006,

Brady's mental health advocate, Jackie Powell, who had to visit him regularly in Ashworth, gave a newspaper interview in which she said that he had explained his motives to her, and that what he wanted was "to commit the perfect murder." "That's what it was all about. He saw it as the ultimate act of being above the law."

My quarrel with Brady was in the nature of a misunderstanding. During the course of our correspondence, I persuaded Brady to write a book about serial killers based on his own insights. The typescript was called *The Gates of Janus*, and at first glance I felt fairly convinced that no publisher would touch it, since its first part consists of seven chapters in which he explains why no criminal behind bars is as wicked as our corrupt society. The second part, on the other hand, seemed to me full of interesting comments on killers such as Bundy, Gacy, Sutcliffe, and the Hillside Stranglers. I sent it to Adam Parfrey, the California publisher who had brought out Gerard Schaefer's stories and Danny Rollins's autobiography, and he accepted it on condition that I wrote an introduction. The book was published in the United States in 2001.

Before it could be distributed in the United Kingdom, however, Ashworth Hospital, where Brady is imprisoned, got wind of it, and demanded to see it. I had no objection, for I was aware that Brady does not even mention Ashworth. On the other hand, I had talked about the result of the government enquiry into Ashworth, the Fallon Report that spoke of "years of abuse, corruption, and failure," and recommended that it should be closed down.

The authorities at Ashworth demanded various changes to my introduction, all of them trivial, and mostly disputable. This was out of the question, since the book was already in print. I was all for ignoring their demands, but the British distributor was afraid of legal action. Finally I satisfied both Ashworth and the distributor by agreeing to insert an erratum slip listing their objections. The result was that *The Gates of Janus* was published in the United Kingdom in November 2001.

As far as Brady was concerned, this erratum slip was the last straw. When his solicitor, Benedict Birnberg, went to Ashworth to see him, shortly after *Janus* was published, he told me that Brady had shrieked obscenities for an hour without stopping. At first I found this baffling, for the erratum slip is only a few lines long, and makes it clear that my own "apology" was tongue-in-cheek and that I retracted nothing.

Then I understood. Brady has spent years in a battle with the Ashworth authorities, and with authority in general. He had done his best to convince himself that the Moors murders were no more criminal than acts carried out by society every day. Not long before the publication of *Janus* he had written to me saying that he was looking forward to seeing the book in print, and finally being allowed the satisfaction of denouncing our corrupt society as it deserves. Instead, he obviously felt that his triumph had been tainted, and that Ashworth had won.

THE CHARACTER FLAWS THAT TURNED BRADY INTO A RAPIST AND KILLER WOULD PREVENT HIM FROM EVER ACHIEVING THE KIND OF SELF-DISCIPLINE TO SEE HIMSELF OBJECTIVELY.

After that traumatic afternoon with Brady, Benedict Birnberg advised me not to write to him—that if Brady felt in a forgiving mood, he would no doubt write to me when he felt like it. But the truth was that I had no particular motivation in wanting to renew a correspondence with Brady. Ten years of exchanging letters had taught me something I should have realized sooner—that even an intelligent criminal remains trapped in the vicious circle of his own criminality, and cannot escape. The character flaws that turned Brady into a rapist and killer would prevent him from ever achieving the kind of self-discipline to see himself objectively. So my notion that his negative feelings could be diverted into creativity was wishful thinking.

At least he had taught me something fundamental about the serial killer.

16

Profiling Comes to Britain

16

Profiling Comes to Britain

In England, psychological profiling suddenly came into its own with the arrest of the "railway rapist" John Duffy, one of the most sadistic rapists since the Hillside Stranglers. (It would later emerge that Duffy, like Bianchi, was only half of a rape-and-murder team, the other half being a childhood friend, David Mulcahy.) The profiler involved was David Canter, then a professor of psychology at the University of Surrey.

The London police did not even become aware they had a problem until July 1985, after the rapists had attacked three women in three hours. The first, a twenty-two-year-old dancer, was grabbed in the Euston Road and dragged into Warren Mews at 1:15 in the morning. She was sexually assaulted but not raped. An hour later, two men brandishing knives dragged a twenty-year-old woman into a doorway in Kentish Town, but she escaped. An hour later still they dragged a twenty-four-year-old secretary into an underground car park at Chalk Farm, and both of them raped her. The triple attack led police to look for similar offenses on their computer, and they soon recognized a pattern involving no less than twenty-seven rapes that had been going on since 1982.

The rapes had begun at half past midnight on June 10, 1982, when two men in balaclavas grabbed a twenty-three-year-old woman in North End Road, Hampstead, dragged her under the railway bridge, and raped her. One rapist was tall, the other short. There was another similar rape in July, and another in August, and then three rapes in September. On one occasion the rapists attacked two foreign au pair girls on Hampstead Heath. In the following year, 1983, there was only one attack, in March—the 10th—but by the end of the next year, the number had reached twenty-five. In one of these, on June 6, the shorter rapist operated on his own. He threatened his victim with a knife, tied her hands, and raped her with a great deal of violence.

On December 1985, a nineteen-year-old secretary, Alison Day, left her home in Hackney Wick, East London, to meet her fiancé, an out-of-work printer; she never arrived for their date. Seventeen days later her body was found in a nearby canal, weighted down with stones. Alison had been raped and beaten on the head with a brick. Her hands were tied behind her back, and her attacker had ripped a strip from her tartan shirt, tied it round her neck, and then twisted a stick in it to make a tourniquet.

More rapes followed, then, on April 17, 1986 a fifteen-year-old schoolgirl, Maartje Tamboezer, set out on her bicycle to the sweetshop in the village of East Horsley, near Guildford. Her father, a Dutch executive, had only just come to England to work. She took a shortcut down a narrow lane through some woodland beside East Horsley station, and ran into a nylon cord stretched across the road, which swept her off her bicycle. She was bludgeoned, and then her hands tied behind her before she was raped and strangled. This time the killer stuffed paper tissues into her vagina, then set them alight, obviously in an attempt to eliminate semen. Witnesses spoke of sightings of a small wiry man in a blue parka running for the 6:07 to London. Two million railway tickets were collected and examined for the suspect's fingerprints without result.

The rapists would commit one more murder. On May 18, 1986, Ann Lock, twenty-nine, a secretary at London Weekend Television, took her usual late-evening train to Brookman's Park, North London, where she usually collected her bicycle, and cycled home to join the husband she had only recently married. She vanished, and it was not until July 21 that her decomposed body was found. An attempt to burn it suggested that she was a victim of the killer of Alison Day and Maartje Tamboezer.

A year earlier, in 1985, Detective Chief Superintendent Thelma Wagstaff had given some thought to the notion of trying to set up a London equivalent of the Behavioral Science Unit at Quantico, and asked the advice of Professor David Canter, of the University of Surrey, who was invited to lunch at Scotland Yard in November 1985. At that time he had never heard of psychological profiling. But in January 1986, he saw an article about the rapists in the *London Evening Standard*, and made up a table of the attacks, set out in two columns labelled "Two Attackers" and

"One Attacker." The result was that he was asked to visit Hendon Police College in North London, where an incident center had been set up. By this time, the police forces involved had decided to link their computers, and the result was a list of 4,900 sex offenders, soon reduced to 1,999. The police had noted the similarities in method between the murders of Alison Day and Maartje Tamboezer—the ligature and the gag cut from the clothing, and had tentatively linked these crimes to the North London rapes.

Canter was assigned two police officers as assistants, and began to computerize the data. One of his assistants, Detective Constable Rupert Heritage, had marked the location of all the rapes and murders on a map. As Canter looked at it, he pointed to an area in the center of the first three rapes and said: "He lives there, doesn't he?" He was, in effect, noting what Detective Horgas would deduce about the case of Virginia's South Side Rapist—that a rapist usually starts close to home.

Canter then went on to make a number of other observations, such as that the rapist had lived in the same area since 1983, and that his knowledge of the railway system—which had led journalists to label him the "Railway Rapist"—possibly indicated that he had worked for the rail network.

In the list of 1,999 suspects, a man named John Duffy occupied number 1,594; he was included because he had been charged with raping his ex-wife and attacking her lover with a knife. The computers showed that he had also been arrested on suspicion of loitering near a railway station. (Since the blood group of the Ann Lock strangler had been the same as that of the Railway Rapist, police had been keeping a watch on railway stations.) Duffy had been called in for questioning, and his similarity to descriptions of the Railway Rapist noted. (Duffy was small, ginger-haired, and pockmarked.) But when the police tried to conduct a second interview, Duffy was in the hospital suffering from amnesia, alleging that muggers had beaten him up. The hospital authorities declined to allow him to be interviewed. And since he was only one of two thousand suspects, the police did not persist.

Studying the map of the attacks, Canter concluded that the rapist probably lived within three miles of the Finchley Road area of North London. He also concluded that he'd been a semiskilled worker, and that his relationship with his wife had been stormy. (The violence of the rapes suggested a man burning with anger.) When Canter's analysis was matched up against the remaining suspects, the computer immediately threw up the name of John Duffy, who lived in Kilburn. He was small, wiry, and had what some of the victims called "laser eyes." He was also a martial arts expert, and had worked on the railways.

Police kept him under surveillance until they decided that they could no longer take the risk of leaving him at liberty—another schoolgirl had been raped with typical violence since Duffy was committed to the hospital (but had been allowed to go in and out)—and they arrested him. When a fellow martial arts enthusiast, Ross Mockeridge, admitted that Duffy had persuaded him to beat him up so he could claim loss of memory, the police were certain that he was the man they were seeking.

Five of the rape victims picked him out at a lineup, and string found in the home of his parents proved to be identical with that which had been used to tie Maartje Tamboezer's wrists. When forensic scientists matched fibers from Alison Day's sheepskin coat to fibers found on one of Duffy's sweaters, the final link in the chain of evidence was established.

Duffy's wife, Margaret (who divorced him in 1986), added further useful information. She had married Duffy, who had been a former altar boy, in June 1980, when he was twenty. But she seemed unable to conceive, and it embittered their relationship; he seemed to feel that his failure to procreate was a kind of personal insult, and their sex life took on a sadomasochistic element. He liked to tie her hands as if he was raping her; the more she struggled the more he liked it. His obsession with bondage, and his violence led to angry quarrels. This was the period when he and Mulcahy began their series of rapes. In the autumn of 1983 Duffy and his wife had attempted a reconciliation, which accounted for the lull in the attacks. But in June 1985, there was a total breakdown in the marriage. "The nice man I had married had become a madman with scary, scary eyes," said his wife. Although Duffy continued to refuse to admit or deny his guilt, he was sentenced at the Old Bailey to life imprisonment on February 27, 1988—life meaning a minimum of thirty years.

David Canter has described the techniques he used to pinpoint where the railway rapist lived:

> *Many environmental psychology studies have demonstrated that people form particular mental maps of the places they use. Each person creates a unique representation of the place in which he lives, with its*

own particular distortions. In the case of John Duffy, journalists recognized his preference for committing crimes near railway lines to the extent that they dubbed him the "railway rapist." What neither they nor the police appreciated was that this characteristic was likely to be part of his way of thinking about the layout of London, and so was a clue to his own particular mental map. It could therefore be used to see where the psychological focus of this map was and so specify the area in which he lived.

After his conviction, Duffy remained sullen, stubborn and unrepentant. But at some point he had confessed to a prison counselor that he had had an accomplice in the attacks. It was probably resentment that his accomplice was living a happy family life outside that made him decide to betray him. In 1999, he decided to "clear his conscience" by naming his fellow rapist as his schoolfriend David Mulcahy, a married father of four.

During the earlier rapes, the "taller rapist" had been described by some of the victims as the less violent of the two. He had more than once gone back to the bound victim to see if she was all right, and even apologized. When the gag was too tight he sometimes loosened or removed it. But it seemed that since those early days he had become more brutal; after Ann Lock had crawled out of the canal into which they had thrown her, Mulcahy raped her again, and it was he who murdered her. So now, on February 2, 2001, he was given three life sentences for the rape and murder of Alison Day, Maartje Tamboezer, Anne Lock, and for seven other rapes.

Duffy's decision to turn in his friend had also cost him dear; several more rapes were disclosed, and Duffy was given an additional sixteen years.

The next major British murder case, that of Fred West, would achieve worldwide notoriety in 1994, when the local police discovered a number of female corpses buried in the back garden and concreted under the floor of his house at 25 Cromwell Street, Gloucester. Of all the serial killers in this book, West was probably the one who can most literally be described as a "sex maniac," since those who knew him well noted that he seemed to eat, think, and dream sex from morning until night.

West was a swarthy, slightly simian-looking man with long sideburns, piercing blue eyes, and a gap between his front teeth. There were several children in his family, ranging in age from babies to teenagers—three of them very obviously not his; they were clearly of mixed race.

His wife, Rose, many years his junior, had once been pretty; now she was plump and bespectacled. There were rumors in the area that she worked as a prostitute—large numbers of men were seen coming and going from their house, many of them black.

One day in May 1992, Rose had gone out shopping, leaving her husband alone in the house with the five younger children. West asked his fourteen-year-old daughter to make him a cup of tea, and then to bring it up to his room on the second floor, which was also a bar. Once there, the girl was undressed and raped in front of a video camera, sodomized, and then raped again—West was obviously in a fevered state of sexual excitement. He left her crying, and went downstairs.

When Rose returned, her daughter told her that her father had raped her. Rose's only comment was: "Oh well, you were asking for it."

The distraught daughter told a school friend, who in turn mentioned it to a policeman. On the morning of August 6, 1992, police made a thorough search of 25 Cromwell Street, and found an extraordinary assortment of pornographic videos and sex aids, including whips, dildos, chains, and handcuffs.

The following day, the police arrived with a social worker to take the children into care. They arrested Fred West. Detective Constable Hazel Savage, the policewoman who was dealing with the case, went to call on the West's eldest daughter, Anne Marie, who had left home when she was fifteen because her father had made her pregnant. At the police station, Anne Marie described how Fred had raped her for the first time when she was nine years old. Her stepmother, Rose, had looked on, laughing. After that, her father had regular sexual intercourse with her, and also allowed his younger brother, John, a dustman, to join in. Anne Marie also mentioned that she was worried about her younger half-sister, Heather, who had vanished from her home in May 1987. Fred sometimes joked that she was buried under the patio. But by the time the rape case came up in court, Anne Marie had changed her mind about giving evidence in court, and Fred West was acquitted.

Hazel Savage now tried to persuade her superiors to dig up the garden and look under the patio. Finally, with a great deal of difficulty—they were afraid of being sued—she succeeded. On February 24, 1994, four policemen with a warrant arrived at 25 Cromwell Street. They told West's daughter Mae that they intended to dig up the garden in search of Heather's body. Fred was arrested the following day. That evening, he admitted

A marriage truly made in hell. Pictured here during happy times are serial killers Rosemary and Fred West. The couple took pleasure in molesting their own daughters, raping young women, and together killing at least twelve victims, including Fred's daughter Heather. West hanged himself in his jail cell and Rosemary was sentenced to life imprisonment with no chance of parole. (Associated Press)

to murdering his sixteen-year-old daughter. The next morning, the police uncovered Heather's remains. But the pathologist was puzzled to discover an extra femur—a thighbone—among the remains. Another body had to be buried somewhere.

Confronted with this evidence, Fred now admitted that, in fact, there were two more bodies buried in the garden. The police soon uncovered these, and identified them as Shirley Ann Robinson, a former lodger of the Wests, and Alison Chambers, a sixteen-year-old schoolgirl called who had vanished in 1979. Shirley Ann had been the lover of both Fred and Rose, and a fetus found nearby was later admitted by Fred to be his own child.

The police now moved their search to the basement, and found five more dismembered corpses under the floor. Another was discovered under the bathroom floor, and identified as Lynda Carol Gough, who had been a regular visitor to the Wests' home before she vanished in April 1973. That brought the total up to nine bodies.

The search was moved to a field near West's former home in the village of Much Marcle, and located the body of West's first wife, Rena. They also found the body of Rena's daughter, Charmaine, underneath the kitchen of their former home at 25 Midland Road, Gloucester. Finally, another body, that of one of West's former girlfriends, Anne McFall, was found buried in a field, bringing the body count up to twelve.

As Fred West's story began to emerge, it became clear that he had been operating longer than any serial killer in criminal history. His first murder—that of Anne McFall—seems to have taken place eighteen years earlier, in 1967.

Fred had been born in a farm cottage in Much Marcle, a small Herefordshire village, in 1941, the son of a farm laborer. It later emerged that, in the West household, incest was common, and that his father frequently told his three daughters, "I made you—I'm entitled to touch you." West was later to take exactly the same attitude towards his own daughters. West's mother retaliated by seducing Fred when he was only twelve years old.

Fred was a mild, unaggressive teenager. When he was seventeen, he swerved his motorbike to avoid a girl on a bicycle, and hit his head against a wall. He was unconscious for almost a week, and one leg healed permanently shorter than the other. It was after this accident that his brothers observed a change in his disposition. He became moody, and had sudden fits of rage.

Two years later, when he was nineteen, he was standing on the platform of a fire escape outside a youth club and tried to put his hand up the skirt of a girl he had invited outside; she gave him a push and he fell over the rails, striking his head. He was unconscious for twenty-four hours.

Shortly before this accident, he had met a sixteen-year-old Glasgow delinquent named Katherine Costello, known as Rena, who, even at that age, had worked as a prostitute. Soon they were having sex in fields, and Rena was convinced that she was in love. Nevertheless, she went back to Glasgow, returned to prostitution, and was soon pregnant by her black pimp.

Unhappy at the unwanted pregnancy, she returned to Gloucestershire, and Fred tried to abort her, without success. Apparently unconcerned that she was pregnant by another man he married her in November 1962. He had always been excited at the idea of women being possessed by other men—preferably while he was watching.

They went back to Glasgow, where he ran an ice cream van, but their marriage quickly deteriorated, and he began to beat her. Rena also confided to a friend that Fred's sexual demands were "weird." She may have meant that he liked to tie her up.

After accidentally killing a child when backing up in his ice cream van, West returned to Much Marcle, and found work as a butcher in an abattoir. This job may also have influenced his sexuality—a friend at the time recounts that West plied a trade as an abortionist, and had a collection of "gruesome polaroid photographs of blood-stained women." West obviously found blood exciting.

Soon, Rena rejoined her husband, bringing with her two Scots girlfriends, one of whom was the teenaged Anne McFall. All four of them—and Rena's baby, Charmaine—went to live in a small trailer. And although Fred frequently beat Rena, Anne nevertheless fell in love with him. When Rena decided to return to Glasgow, Anne stayed behind, and soon became Fred's mistress.

Why he murdered Anne is uncertain, since he later described her as "an angel." It may possibly have been because she told him she was pregnant. He strangled her in July 1967, and buried her in a nearby field.

Rena now came back to live with him. And in January 1968, West committed another murder. The victim was a fifteen-year-old waitress called Mary Bastholm, who knew West through the café where she worked—he had done some decorating there. On the night of January 6, 1968, she waited at a bus stop on her way to see her boyfriend, and then simply disappeared. Mary's body was never found, but when West was in prison, he told his son Stephen that he had killed her.

In November, West and Rena were again living apart, and Fred was occupying a trailer near the village of Bishop's Cleeve. It was there that he met Rose Letts, a fifteen-year-old schoolgirl who, it became clear, was already something of a nymphomaniac, and West had little trouble seducing her. In spite of the violent opposition of her parents—it later emerged that she had had an incestuous relationship with her father—she moved into the caravan with Fred as soon as she was sixteen. Rose's younger brother, Graham, later described how she had seduced him when he was twelve.

When she and Fred moved in together, he was soon persuading her to have sex with other men while he looked on. When they moved together into Gloucester, Fred put advertisements into sex magazines, with photographs of Rose displaying her naked breasts. Rena's daughter, Charmaine, and Fred's first daughter, Anne Marie, moved in with them. But Charmaine intensely disliked her stepmother, who reciprocated by beating her.

In the New Year of 1971, West was sent to prison for theft and fraud at a garage where he had worked, and it was while he was there that Charmaine disappeared. There seems to be little doubt that Rose killed her. From now on, Fred and Rose were bound together by their knowledge that the other was a killer.

At their first home, at 25 Midland Road, Gloucester, they made the acquaintance of a young married woman, Liz Agius, whose Maltese husband worked abroad. She began to make a habit of taking tea with them, and one day felt strangely drowsy; she woke up to find herself naked in bed between Fred and Rose—and Fred admitted that he had raped her. Oddly enough, it does not seem to have disturbed the friendship. It was also at about this time that Fred's wife, Rena, came to call on them at Midland Road, and simply disappeared. Her body was eventually found buried not far from that of Anne McFall.

The Wests' life seems to have become a nonstop sexual orgy. In September 1972, Fred and Rose, now married, moved to 25 Cromwell Street. They rented out cheap rooms to teenagers, and Rose was soon having sex with the male lodgers. Fred had no objection—when his wife returned from another man's bed, he flung himself on her with intense excitement. Rose also enjoyed sex with other women.

A teenage au pair, Caroline Raine, was hired, but when both Fred and Rose made sexual advances, she decided to move back to her parents. Four weeks later, on December 6, 1972, the Wests saw Caroline in nearby Tewkesbury, and offered her a lift home. She accepted, but soon regretted it because Rose, sitting in the back seat with her, tried to kiss her on the mouth. When it was clear she was going to be uncooperative, Fred stopped the car, and punched her until she lost consciousness.

Back at 25 Cromwell Street, West dragged Caroline upstairs, and Rose sat beside her on the settee and began fondling her breasts. She was given a cup of tea, which made her sleepy. Then the Wests tied her hands behind her, and gagged her with cotton wool. She was stripped naked and laid on the floor, where West beat her between the legs with the buckle end of a belt. After that, Rose, who had obviously become sexually excited, lay between her legs and performed oral sex, Fred meanwhile lying on top of Rose, having sex with her.

Later, while Rose was in the bathroom, Fred raped Caroline. He raped her a second time the next morning, when someone came to the door and Rose went downstairs to answer it.

The Wests now told her that they wanted her to return as their au pair, and Caroline, realizing this was her only chance of escape, agreed. In fact, she confessed what had happened to her mother as soon as she got home, and the Wests were arrested. But in court on January 12, 1973, they were charged only with indecent assault, the magistrate obviously believing their story that nothing more serious had taken place. Caroline had felt too traumatized to attend the hearing. The Wests were fined £25 and returned home with the knowledge that if they intended to silence future victims, it would be simpler to murder them.

This is exactly what they did. Lynda Gough, nineteen, was a girlfriend of one of their male lodgers, and had also slept with his roommate. (Rose had climbed into bed with both of the men on the first night they moved in.) In April 1973, Lynda left home, leaving her parents a note saying that she had found herself a flat. They never saw her again, although when Mrs. Gough called on the Wests to ask if they knew where her daughter was, she noticed that Rose was wearing Lynda's slippers. The Wests insisted that Lynda had simply gone to Western-Super-Mare looking for a job.

It was at about this time—mid-1973—that West began having sex with his nine-year-old daughter, Anne Marie. She was taken to the basement and hung up from the ceiling by her hands, while a dildo was inserted inside of her. After that, her father raped her regularly, sometimes even when she came home from school for lunch. Anne Marie was also made to submit to many of Rose's lovers while her father spied through a hole in the wall. At fifteen, Anne Marie became pregnant by her father, but had a miscarriage. It was at this point that she decided to leave home, and lived by prostitution.

During the next two years, the Wests murdered five more girls, and Fred concreted their bodies under the basement floor. These were:

Carol Ann Cooper, fifteen, who vanished on November 10, 1973, after going to the cinema with friends. It seems certain that the Wests offered her a lift, then took her home and killed her after forcing her to join their usual "sex games."

Lucy Partington, twenty-one, was a student at Exeter University and a niece of the novelist Kingsley Amis. She vanished on December 27, 1973, after spending the afternoon with a disabled friend. It seems likely that the Wests kept her prisoner for several days, raping and torturing her before killing her.

Therese Siegenthaler, twenty-one, was a Swiss student, who set out hitchhiking on April 15, 1974, to see a friend in Ireland. She disappeared, and her body was found in the Wests' cellar twenty years later.

Shirley Ann Hubbard, fifteen, had, like so many of the Wests' victims, been in foster care. She was working as a trainee shop assistant in Worcester, and disappeared on November 5, 1974, on her way to see her foster parents in Droitwich. When her body was found, her skull was completely covered with black adhesive tape, and plastic tubes had been inserted into her nostrils to enable her to breathe.

Juanita Mott, eighteen, was also the child of a broken home. She had been a regular visitor to the Wests' house in Cromwell Street, and it seems likely that she returned there one day to see a friend, and was raped and murdered.

There was a three-year gap between the death of Juanita Mott in April 1975 and that of the next victim, Shirley Ann Robinson, another child of a broken home who came to the Wests' house as a lodger. She entered into a lesbian affair with Rose and also became pregnant by Fred. She was obviously hoping to persuade Fred to abandon Rose and marry her. Shirley Ann disappeared on May 9, 1977, and was buried in the garden, since there was now no more room in the basement.

Alison Chambers, sixteen, had spent years in a children's home after her parents split up. In September 1979, she wrote a letter to her mother saying that she was living with "a really nice homely family." Her body was one of those found in the Wests' garden.

The last known victim was the Wests' own daughter Heather, sixteen, whose virginity West had taken when she was fourteen. She became deeply depressed, and it is conceivable that West thought she might start telling friends about the incest he continued to force on her. On June 19, 1987, West took the day off from his building work, and some time during that day, he and Rose murdered Heather. Her body was the last to be buried in the back garden.

ROSE MADE A BAD IMPRESSION ON THE JURY BY A BLANKET DENIAL OF KNOWING ANYTHING WHATEVER ABOUT THE CRIMES

Did West then stop killing? This seems doubtful. On the day the police went to 25 Cromwell Street with a search warrant, his son, Stephen, managed to contact him on his mobile phone, to tell him what had happened. West said that he would be home immediately—but in fact, took several hours. It seems likely that he went to check on bodies buried elsewhere, to make sure that they were not likely to be discovered. He also hinted to his son, when Stephen visited him in prison, that there were still many more bodies to be discovered. The evidence of the children made it quite clear that West's life revolved around sex. They noted that he thought and talked about sex all the time. Rose was almost as bad—West encouraged her to sleep with his brother John (who also had sex with Anne Marie), to continue her affair with her father, to work as a prostitute, and to take a series of black lovers, by whom she occasionally became pregnant.

Fred's second daughter, Mae, was raped at the age of eight, almost certainly by John, who would later commit suicide on the day before the jury was to return its verdict on the charge that he had been raping Anne Marie and "another girl."

After Fred's arrest in 1994, and the discovery of the twelve bodies, Rose was also charged with ten murders.

On New Year's Day 1995, Fred West committed suicide by hanging himself in his cell at Winson Green Prison, Birmingham, with strips of blanket from his bed, which he had plaited together. Anne Marie made a suicide attempt after hearing of her father's death. Rose, on the other hand, declared vociferously that he had got what he deserved. Her own story was that she was innocent, and knew nothing about the various murders committed by her husband when, she claimed, she was out of the house sleeping with clients.

The trial of Rose West began at Winchester Crown Court on October 3, 1995, and it was obvious that the defense pinned its hopes on the fact that there was no definite evidence to link her to any of the murders. Yet there was still ample evidence that Rose was capable of taking part in the rape of women such as Caroline Raine and a married neighbor named Liz Agius. Another young woman, known at the trial as Miss A, told how, as a teenager, she had called at 25 Cromwell Street, had been undressed by Rose, and then made to take part in an orgy in which she was tied down to a bed, while Fred raped and sodomized her.

Rose made a bad impression on the jury by a blanket denial of knowing anything whatever about the crimes—she even insisted that she had never met Caroline Raine, in spite of the evidence that she had helped to kidnap and sexually abuse her.

On November 21, 1995, Rose was found guilty of ten murders, and sentenced to life imprisonment, the judge, Sir Charles Mantell adding: "If attention is paid to what I think, you will never be released."

It seems very clear that what was basically responsible for turning West into a "sex maniac" was being born into a household that became a sexual free-for-all, with the father committing incest with his daughters, the mother with her eldest son, and the brothers and sisters joining in the sex games. (In his late teens Fred impregnated his thirteen-year-old sister.) All this, combined with West's serious head accidents in his teens, had the effect of turning normal sex into "kinky" sex, then into sadism. It became clear that West used his basement as a torture chamber, suspending the girls by their wrists, and cutting off fingers and toes. Even the body of his eldest daughter had missing fingers. It seems that what we are dealing with here is an extreme version of what Hazelwood meant when he said that sex crime is not about sex but about power. What West was seeking in hanging his victims from the ceiling was a sense of total control, of being the "master."

A search for utter control also seems to be the explanation in one of the most puzzling cases of multiple murder in the late 1990s: that of Harold Shipman, who is also Europe's most prolific serial killer.

Shipman, of Hyde in Cheshire, came under suspicion after the sudden death of an elderly patient, Kathleen Grundy, on June 24, 1998. Mrs. Grundy had apparently left a will in which her considerable fortune—over £300,000—was left to her doctor, Harold Shipman. But the will was carelessly typed, and two witnesses who had also signed it explained that they had done so as a favor to Dr. Shipman, who had folded the paper so that they could not see what they were signing.

Mrs. Grundy's daughter, Angela Woodruff, reported her suspicions to the police. Detective Inspector Stan Egerton noted that this looked like a case of attempted fraud. But could it be more than that? The death rate among Shipman's patients, especially elderly women, was remarkably high, but there seemed to be no other cases in which Shipman had actually benefited from the death of one of them.

In fact, the above-average death rate had been noted by one of Shipman's colleagues, Dr. Linda Reynolds. In 1997, she had realized that Shipman seemed to have been present at the deaths of an unusual number of patients—three times as many as might have been expected—and reported her suspicions to the local coroner. Yet these came to nothing; there seemed to be no logical reason why a popular GP should kill his patients. If the coroner had checked Shipman's criminal record, however, he would have learned that he had been arrested twenty years earlier, in 1976, for forging prescriptions for the drug pethidine, a morphine derivative, to which he had become addicted.

Mrs. Grundy's body was exhumed, and the postmortem showed that she had died of a morphine overdose. Another fourteen exhumations of Shipman's patients revealed the same cause of death. Moreover, it was clear that these were only a small proportion of Shipman's victims. After his conviction for fifteen murders on January 31, 2000, further investigation made it clear that the total could be as high as 260.

Shipman ran his practice alone, and was known to medical colleagues as a rude, overbearing man. His patients, however, found him kindly and patient, always willing to talk to them about their problems. But with people over whom he had authority, he was a bully. He was brutal to a young female pharmaceutical representative, out on her first assignment, and browbeat her until she was in tears. When a receptionist forgot his coffee, he went white with rage. When his wife rang him to say that she and the kids were hungry and waiting to eat dinner, he snapped: "You'll wait until I get there."

SHIPMAN SEEMS TO HAVE BEEN THE KIND OF MAN WHO URGENTLY NEEDED REASONS FOR A HIGH LEVEL OF SELF-ESTEEM, BUT SIMPLY LACKED SUCH REASONS.

When a man is as arrogant and impatient as Shipman, it seems obvious that he has an inflated opinion of himself. Shipman seems to have been the kind of man who urgently needed reasons for a high level of self-esteem, but simply lacked such reasons. The accounts of people he upset—always people who were weaker than himself—make is clear that he was a classic case of a Right Man. He had tried working in a practice with other doctors, but they found his self-opinionatedness intolerable.

But how do we make the leap from arrogance and frustrated craving for self-esteem to murdering patients with overdoses of morphine?

The first step is to recognise that Shipman was a member of the dominant 5 percent, while his wife, Primrose, was undoubtedly of medium to low dominance. Psychologist Abraham Maslow, who studied the role of dominance in sexual partnerships, observed that such an extreme mixture of high and low dominance seldom works.

So how did this curious relationship come about? Shipman's background offers a few clues. He was born in Nottingham in January 1946 of working-class parents. Harold, his mother's favorite, was not obviously talented, and less than brilliant at school; but his mother's expectations turned him into a hard worker, a "plodder." He was distinguished in only one respect—on the rugger field, where, a friend commented, he "would do anything to win."

When his mother died of cancer he was seventeen, and expressed his grief by running all night in the rain; but he did not even mention her loss at school. During his mother's painful last days, Shipman watched the family doctor administering increasingly large doses of morphine.

After an initial failure, hard work got Shipman into Leeds University Medical School. There he acquired himself a girlfriend who was living in the same students' lodging. Primrose Oxtoby was three years his junior, and has been described by writers on the case as "frumpish" and "a plain Jane"; even then she had a tendency to put on weight. Her background was even narrower than his; her parents had been so strict that she was not even allowed to go to the local youth club. But in less than a year, Shipman had—as he himself said later—"made a mistake." Primrose was pregnant. Her parents immediately broke ties with her. But she married Shipman, and as more children followed, any hopes he had entertained for an interesting future evaporated. Primrose was not even a good housekeeper, and policemen who came later to search their house were shocked by the dirt and general untidiness.

The Shipmans moved to Pontefract, where he became a junior houseman at the General Infirmary. Three years later, in 1974, they moved to Todmorden, in the Pennines, and he began injecting himself with pethidine, obtained on forged prescriptions, to stave off depression. When he was caught two years later, he was suspended, and Primrose and the children were forced to live with her parents. Shipman fought hard to save his job, but was fired from the practice. He obviously felt that he had been treated unfairly.

After his trial in 1976 for forging prescriptions, he was fined £658, which would be about twelve times as much in today's (2006) money. He must have felt that fate was grinding him into the ground. In the following year he became part of a practice in Hyde, Cheshire, and—the evidence seems to show—began his career as a murderer.

When he was questioned on suspicion of fifteen murders, Shipman angrily denied any wrongdoing, sure that he had covered his trail so carefully that he was safe. But the investigators soon discovered that he had made extensive changes in his patients' notes, to make them seem more seriously ill than they were. On October 7, 1998, Shipman was full of self-confidence during the police interview. But when a detective constable began to question him about changes he had made in the patients' records, he began to falter and flounder. That evening he broke down and sobbed. But he still refused to confess.

Why did Shipman kill? Could it have been because the Right Man needs a fantasy to justify his immense self-esteem, and dealing out death with a syringe provided that fantasy—the self-effacing GP who is actually one of the world's most prolific serial killers?

Or could it have been something as simple as a psychological addiction, like the escalating sadism the BSU noted in so many serial killers? At least one man in Todmorden, the husband of Eva Lyons—who was dying of cancer—believed that Shipman injected his elderly wife with an overdose of morphine in a mercy killing. Soon thereafter, eight more elderly patients were found dead after Shipman had been to see them. Had he discovered that watching someone die peacefully produced in him a sense of relief that was not unlike the effect of morphine? And was this ability to deal out death a godlike sensation that compensated for the failure of his life?

With most serial killers there is an overt sexual element in the murders. But the only hint of sexual frustration can be found in the case of seventeen-year-old Lorraine Leighton, who went to see him about a lump in her breast. Shipman's comments about the size of her breasts were so rude that she fled the surgery in tears.

One thing that seems clear is that Shipman felt no guilt about killing his patients. After his imprisonment, someone said something that implied a comparison with Myra Hindley, and Shipman snapped: "She is a criminal. I am not a criminal."

Shipman was given fifteen life sentences in January 2000 for murdering fifteen patients. On Tuesday, January 13, 2004, he was discovered hanging in his cell. An official report later concluded that he had killed between 215 and 260 people over a twenty-three-year period.

It was the chance intervention of a British witness that led to the conviction of Australia's worst serial killer, Ivan Milat.

In the early 1990s, it became obvious that a particularly sadistic killer was operating in southern Australia. Because his victims were usually hitchhikers, he became known as the "Backpacker Killer." Most of the disappearances occurred in New South Wales, not far from Sydney.

On September 19, 1992, two members of a Sydney running club, Ken Seilly and Keith Caldwell, were jogging in the forty-thousand-acre Belanglo State Forest. As Ken approached a boulder he was overwhelmed by a nauseating odor—what smelled to him like decaying flesh. A closer look at a pile of branches and rotten leaves revealed a human foot poking out. The two men carefully marked the position of the remains and set off to contact the authorities. When local policeman arrived at the scene they called in regional detectives, who then sent out a call to the Missing Persons Bureau. The corpse was identified as that of Joanne Walters, a British backpacker who, along with her traveling companion, had gone missing in April 1992. The next day, police investigators uncovered the body of Joanne's companion, Caroline Clarke. Caroline had been shot at least ten times in the head, as well as stabbed several times. Joanne had been viciously stabbed fourteen times in the chest and neck; the fact that she had not been shot, as had Caroline, suggested that there had been two murderers. There were no defensive wounds on their hands, which suggested that the young women had been tied up. And it was clear that the killers had taken their time; there were six cigarette butts, all of the same brand, lying nearby. The bodies were too decayed for forensic examination to determine if they had been raped.

A wide search of the Belanglo State Forest was immediately launched but failed to reveal additional bodies—hardly surprising given the vastness of the forest. More than a year later, however, on October 5, 1993, two lots of skeletal remains were found there; they proved to be those of two nineteen-year-olds, James Gibson and Deborah Everist, who had vanished on December 30, 1989, after setting out from Melbourne. Soon after this discovery, sniffer dogs unearthed the decomposed body of Simone Schmidl, twenty, a German tourist who had vanished on January 20, 1991. Three days later, the dogs located the bodies of two more German backpackers, Gabor Neugebauer, twenty-one, and his traveling companion, Anja Habscheid, twenty, who had vanished on December 26, 1991. Anja's body had been decapitated, and the angle of the blow made it clear that she had been forced to kneel while the killer cut off her head.

A special team, known as "Task Force Air," was set up to hunt the Backpacker Killers. When interviewing members of a local gun club, the task force received a strange report. A friend of one of the members claimed to have witnessed something suspicious in the forest the previous year. When contacted by the police, the man supplied them with a detailed description of two vehicles, one a Ford sedan and the other a four-wheel drive, that he saw driving down one of the trails into the forest. According to him, a man was driving the sedan while in the back seat two other men held between them a female with what appeared to be a gag in her mouth. In the second vehicle, he reported that he saw the same thing—a male driver and a bound female in the back with two males. The observer added descriptions of all the occupants—clothing, hair color, and approximate ages. He claimed to have noted the license plate number of the four-wheel drive, but had lost it. His official statement to the police was signed, "Alex Milat."

Although the task force methodically pursued the clues they had, they made no progress during the next six months. But following their "Milat" line of inquiry, they finally got their break: a workmate of Croatian-born Richard Milat reported that Milat had been heard saying: "Killing a woman was like cutting a loaf of bread." Police checked his work schedule against the presumed dates of the murders. Richard Milat was at work on all of those days, but his brother Ivan was not. And Ivan had a long police record, which included sex offenses.

Investigators now turned their attention to the Milat brothers, who were found to own property about twenty-five miles from Belanglo.

Once again, the case marked time. Then, in April 1994, the police uncovered a report that a young Englishman named Paul Onions had placed a call to the task force's hot line five months earlier. Here was the tip they had been hoping for. Onions, a student from Birmingham, had been attacked by a man who corresponded to Milat's description, near the Belanglo State Forest.

Onions had been hitchhiking from Sydney on January 25, 1990, when he had encountered a short, stocky man with a drooping moustache. The man asked him where he was heading, and offered him a lift in the direction of Melbourne. Onions was impressed by the stranger's car, an expensive-looking four-wheel drive Nissan. As they climbed into the car, the stranger introduced himself as "Bill," and said that he was Yugoslav.

As they passed the town of Bowral, Onions noticed that "Bill" kept glancing in the rearview mirror and slowing down. When he asked him why, "Bill" explained that he was trying to find a place where he could park for a while, and retrieve an audiocassette player out of the trunk. The layby was close to the turn off to the Belanglo State Forest. Some instinct told Onions to get out of the car at the same time as "Bill," which seemed to annoy his companion. "What are you doing out of the car?" he asked. And then, suddenly, he produced a black revolver, and the friendly manner vanished. "You know what this is—a robbery."

Onions tried to calm "Bill" down, then became more alarmed as the man reached into the back seat, and took out a bag containing rope. "That was enough," said Onions later. "I decided to leg it." Behind him he heard the man shout, "Stop or I'll shoot," and a bullet whizzed past his head. It had the effect of flooding him with adrenalin, and he ran even faster.

The man nonetheless caught up with him, and the two began to wrestle at the side of the highway, while cars drove on past them. Onions managed to break free, and scrambled over the top of the hill. He spotted a van driving towards him, and flung himself on the ground to force it to halt.

Behind the wheel was Joanne Berry, who had her sister and four children with her. Onions pleaded: "Give me a lift—he's got a gun." Berry, at first frightened by the seemingly crazy man in the road, noticed the true fear in his eyes, and allowed him to clamber into the back of the van through the sliding door.

When he told her what had happened, she drove him straight to the Bowral Police Station. There Onions reported the attack, and Berry told the police that she had also glimpsed the man running away, with his hand held low—obviously to hide the revolver. Incredibly, the Bowral police succeeded in losing the report on the attempted robbery, with the result that "Bill" was free to continue raping and murdering.

Four years later, however, the police lost no time in flying Onions to Sydney. There he identified Milat as the man who had fired his revolver at him. Onions had also left his backpack in Milat's car when he fled, and he later recognized a blue shirt found in Milat's garage as his own.

On May 22, 1994, police arrested fifty-year-old Ivan Milat in Eaglevale, a Sydney suburb. In Ivan Milat's garage, police found a bloodstained rope of a type that had been used to bind some of the victims, a sleeping bag that proved to belong to Deborah Everist, and a camera of the make owned by Caroline Clarke. The police also found spent cartridges similar to those found near Caroline in Milat's garage,

Milat had a long police record. Born in December 1944 to an Australian mother and Croatian father, he had been a member of a large family that had been repeatedly in trouble with the law. In his twenties he had been incarcerated several times for car theft and burglary.

In 1971, he had picked up two female hitchhikers, and had suddenly turned off the highway, produced a knife, and announced that he intended to have sex with them, or would kill them both. One of the girls, who was eighteen, allowed him to have sex with her on the front seat. Milat had then driven on to a petrol station, and she had taken the opportunity to run inside and tell the attendant that she had been raped, and that the driver was holding her friend. When several employees ran towards the car, Milat pushed the other girl out and drove off at high speed. Later on, he was pulled over by police, but there were no knives or rope in the car. Milat agreed that he had had sex with the girl, but insisted that it was with her consent. In any case, he said, both the girls were "screwy."

After this brush with the law, Milat had fled to New Zealand, to escape the rape charge, and also two charges of armed robbery. He was brought back and tried three years later, in 1974, but was cleared of all charges and freed. (One of his brothers went to prison for a bank robbery.)

In 1979, he again gave a lift to two women near the Belanglo State Forest, and suddenly pulled off the road. When he told them he intended to have sex with both of them, the women managed to jump out of the car, and hide in a ditch. Although Milat searched for them, cursing and swearing, for nearly two hours, he did not succeed in finding them. Unfortunately, neither of the women reported this attempted rape until years later, when the Backpacker Task Force was set up.

Milat's trial began in the New South Wales Supreme Court in Sydney on March 25, 1996. By that time, the press had dubbed him "Ivan the Terrible."

What emerged clearly during the trial was that Milat was a "control freak," whose chief pleasure was seeing his victims terrified and helpless. It also became apparent that with every killing, he became more sadistic, and relished taking his time over it. At one murder site, half a dozen cigarette butts were found. He paralyzed some of these female victims by stabbing them in the spine, so he could sexually attack them at his leisure. The injuries found on the victims were so appalling that the presiding judge refused to give details during the trial, in order to spare the relatives.

A friend of Milat's ex-wife, Karen, gave evidence that suggested that Milat was another Right Man, who demanded total obedience and submission. Milat was obsessive about keeping the house neat and tidy, and when Karen went shopping with a list, she had to stick to every item on it, or risk him flying into a violent rage. She had to ask him for every penny she spent, account for every minute of her time, and bring back receipts for every purchase. Milat's younger brother George reports that Milat would become enraged with his wife on the smallest provocation. When Karen finally walked out on him, and he could not find her, he burned down her parent's garage. And it was shortly after Karen left him in 1989 that Milat began his series of murders.

Milat's barrister suggested in court that the murders must have been committed by Milat's brothers Walter and Richard, and in a television interview on the day after the trial, the two brothers were accused on camera of being accomplices in the murders. Understandably, both men denied the allegations.

Milat was found guilty on July 27, 1996, and sentenced to life imprisonment on seven counts of murder. In the maximum-security wing of Goulburn Correctional Centre, only a short distance from Belanglo, where he eventually was transferred, he was placed in solitary confinement after a hacksaw blade was detected in a packet of cigarettes. He declared that he would continue to make every effort to escape.

His brother Boris, tracked down to a secret location by reporters, told them, "All my brothers are capable of extreme violence. The things I could tell you are much worse than Ivan is supposed to have done. Everywhere he's worked, people have disappeared."

Asked if he thought Ivan was guilty, he replied: "I reckon he's done a hell of a lot more." Pressed to put a figure on it, Boris Milat replied: "Twenty-eight."

17

Murder in Lonely Places

17

Murder in Lonely Places

In July 1960, I was in Leningrad—formerly Saint Petersburg—at an official reception at the Astoria Hotel, together with Patricia Pitman, my collaborator on *An Encyclopedia of Murder*. The guests were Russian writers and literary bureaucrats, and at one point I overheard Pat asking a stern-faced lady who spoke excellent English whether there were any important Soviet murder cases we ought to include. The lady snorted contemptuously that such crimes were symptomatic of Western decadence and were virtually unknown under communism.

It was precisely this attitude that would cost dozens of lives in southern Russia in the 1980s, when Andrei Chikatilo, Russia's worst serial killer, was operating.

In the autumn of 1990, a year before the dissolution of the Soviet Union, Ukrainian police were hunting a serial murderer who had been killing for at least ten years, and who was one of the worst sadists and sexual perverts in human history.

One of the main reasons the police found him so difficult to track down was the Soviet policy of giving little or no publicity to murder. While a wave of serial killings was taking place around Rostov-on-Don, the Soviet press continued to insist that Russia's crime rate was virtually nil. So Russian women or children who might otherwise have thought twice about accompanying a strange man to some lonely spot had no idea that they might be in danger.

To the police, the Rostov Ripper was known as the *lesopolosa* killer, or Forest Path Killer, because so many of the victims had been found in woodland. He killed children just as readily as adults, and boys as readily as girls. He preferred to pick up his victims on trains, or in public places such as bus stations, and then take them to some quiet place, where he strangled or stabbed them to death, performed horrific mutilations, and sometimes cooked and ate parts of the body. As far as Major Mikhail Fetisov, the head of the Rostov CID, was concerned, the murders had begun on June 12, 1982, when thirteen-year-old Lyubov Biryuk disappeared on her way home from an errand in the village of Donskoi. Thirteen days later, her body—reduced to little more than a skeleton by the heat—had been found behind some bushes. She had been stabbed twenty-two times, and chips of bone missing from around the sockets suggested that the killer had even stabbed at her eyes. Her state of undress indicated a sex crime. Because Lyubov was the niece of a police lieutenant, the case aroused more attention than it might otherwise have done, and Fetisov investigated it personally. From the fact that the killer had taken such a risk—the main road was a few yards away—Fetisov deduced that he was driven by an overpowering sex urge, while the number of stab wounds indicated a sadist for whom stabbing was a form of sexual penetration.

Thirty-four-year-old Vladimir Pecheritsa, a convicted rapist, was hauled in for questioning—he had been at a nearby venereal clinic on the day of the murder. Russian interrogation techniques, developed by the secret police, were designed to extract a confession in the shortest possible time. But instead of confessing, Pecheritsa went away and hanged himself, the first of five men who would end their lives after becoming suspects.

With Pecheritsa's death, Fetisov hoped that the case was closed. But before 1982 was over, two adult female bodies—reduced to unidentifiable skeletons—were discovered lying in woodland near Rostov. Both victims had been stabbed repeatedly, and stab marks around the eyes made it clear that these killings were the work of the same person as the others—the Forest Path Killer. Fetisov organized a special squad of ten detectives to hunt the maniac. It would later develop that the Forest Path Killer had killed another four victims that year: Lyuba Volubuyeva, fourteen; Oleg Pozhidayev, nine; Olga Kuprina, sixteen; and Olga Stalmachenok, ten. Many of the murders took place near the town of Shakhty, not far from Rostov. The newly formed "Red Ripper" unit therefore began by dispersing police over a wide area, hoping to come upon the murderer by chance.

During 1983, the Forest Path Killer kept up a steady pace of slaughter: June 18, Laura Sarkisyan, fifteen; August 8, Igor Gudkov, seven; August 8, Irina

Dunenkova, thirteen; and December 27, Sergei Markov, fourteen. By the next year, however, the killer seemed to be butchering in a frenzy. On January 9, he killed seventeen-year-old Natalya Shalapinia. On February 22, he killed a forty-four-year-old vagrant named Marta Ryabyenko, in Rostov's Aviator Park. Ten-year-old Dmitri Ptashnikov was found near Novoshakhtinsk on March 27. In early July, police found evidence of a double murder in woods near Shakhty—a woman whose skull had been smashed in, and a ten-year-old girl who had been beheaded. In late July, another woman's body as found in woods near Shakhty. On August 3, it was a sixteen-year-old girl named Natalia Golosovskaya, found in Aviator Park; on the 10th, seventeen-year-old Lyudmila Alekseyeva, in woods near the Rostov beach; on the 12th, a thirteen-year-old boy named Dmitri Illaryonov, who had been castrated; on August 26, an unidentified woman in woods thirty miles east of Rostov; on September 2, eleven-year-old Aleksandr Chepel; on September 7, twenty-five-year-old Irina Luchinskaya, again in Aviator Park. Twelve murders in eight months.

The police had one important clue. Semen found on the clothes of many of the victims revealed that the killer had blood type AB, the rarest blood group. Unfortunately, this seemingly ironclad clue would mislead investigators more disastrously than any other during the long investigation.

On a hot evening at the end of August 1984, Major Alexander Zanasovsky, one of the "murder squad" watching the Rostov bus station, spotted a tall, well-dressed man with a briefcase and thick glasses talking to a teenage girl. When she caught a bus, he then moved on to another. Zanasovsky decided to ask the man to step into the police office on the station. There the gray-haired suspect produced his identification papers, which showed him to be Andrei Romanovich Chikatilo—not a typical Russian name. His credentials seemed to be impeccable: he was graduate of the philological faculty of Rostov's university, a married man with two children, the head of the supply department of one of the city's main factories, and—most impressive of all—a member of the Communist Party. Chikatilo explained to Zanasovsky that he lived in Shakhty, and was about to return home. He had once been a teacher, he said, and simply enjoyed talking to kids. His story sounded reasonable enough, and Zanasovsky let him go. The soft-spoken man certainly did not look like a serial killer.

Zanasovsky asked the girl if Chikatilo had tried to persuade her to go with him; she said no, he just asked her about her studies.

But when, two weeks later—on August 13—Zanasovsky again spied Chikatilo approaching two teenaged girls in succession at the bus station, he decided that it might be worth following him. When Chikatilo boarded an airport bus, Zanasovsky was right behind him, together with a plainclothes colleague, and they watched him trying to catch the eye of female passengers. Two stops farther on, Chikatilo got off the bus and boarded another on the other side of the road. Here again he tried to engage female passengers in conversation—not with the irritating manner of a man looking for a pickup, but casually and kindly, as if he simply liked people. When he had no luck, he climbed on another bus. In two and a half hours he switched buses repeatedly, after which he tried to approach girls outside the Central Restaurant, and then sat on a park bench paying particular attention to female passers-by. At three in the morning, he was in the waiting room at the mainline railway station, attempting more pick-ups. Finally, when the station was almost deserted, he succeeded with a teenaged girl in a track suit, who was lying on a bench trying to sleep. She seemed to agree to whatever he was proposing, and he removed his jacket, and placed it over her head as she lay in his lap. Movements under the jacket, and the expression on Chikatilo's face, revealed that she was performing oral sex on him. After that, at 5 a.m., Chikatilo took the first tram of the day, and got off in the central market. Zanasovsky decided it was time to make an arrest, and placed his hand on the man's shoulder. Chikatilo recognized him, and his face broke into sweat; but he made no protest when Zanasovsky told him that he would have to accompany him to the nearest police station.

There the contents of the briefcase seemed to justify Zanasovsky's belief that he had arrested the Forest Path Killer. It contained a kitchen knife with an eight-inch blade, a dirty towel, some rope, and a jar of Vaseline.

Chikatilo's story was that he had missed his bus to Shakhty and was merely killing time. The knife, he said, was to slice sausage and other comestibles. He also agreed to take a blood test.

Zanasovsky was amazed when the test showed Chikatilo to be innocent. His blood group was A, not AB as was the semen found in the bodies. He was held, nevertheless, on an unrelated charge relating to the theft of a roll of linoleum that had vanished when Chikatiko was in charge of supplies to a factory. Three months later, he was released.

The murders near Rostov had stopped, but when a woman's corpse was found with similar mutilations near Moscow, there was fear that the killer had moved.

In fact, it soon became clear that the killer was still in the Rostov area when, on August 28, 1985, another mutilated corpse was found in the woods near Shakhty—an eighteen-year-old mentally retarded vagrant named Irina Gulyaeva

In retrospect, her death was a turning point in the investigation. In Moscow, the authorities decided that the case must be solved at all costs. The murder team was increased substantially with additional detectives and legal experts. And a new man had to be placed in charge of the new "Killer Department." He was Inspector Issa Kostoyev, known as one of the best detectives in Russia. It was Kostoyev who finally had the satisfaction of hearing the confession of the Forest Path Killer.

At the start of Kostoyev's investigation, all was frustration. The murders ceased for almost two years. But between May 1987 and November 1990 the body count rose by at least eighteen. During that time, Fetisov and Buratov used their greatly increased manpower to keep a watch on railway stations, bus stations, and trains. There was evidence that the killer had lured victims off trains at fairly remote stations—for example, two victims had been found in Donleskhoz, in the middle of a forestry commission area. Was there some method of persuading the Forest Path Killer to choose such a station, rather than Rostov or Shakhty? Suppose, for example, they placed uniformed policemen at all the large stations? Would that not encourage the killer to use the smaller ones?

The huge operation required 360 men, mostly placed prominently at large stations. But at three smaller stations—Donleskhoz, Kundryucha, and Lesostep—there would only be a few discreet plainclothes men.

On November 12, 1990, Fetisov reached a new low point in morale. Yet another body—this time of a young woman—had been found near Donleskhoz station, in spite of the plainclothes surveillance. Her name was Svetlana Korostik, twenty-two, and she had been disembowelled; her tongue had also been removed. She had been dead about a week.

But, explained the quite nervous and stammering plainclothesman, they had been taking names of all middle-aged men on the station during that time. They had a pile of forms, which they intended to send to Rostov very soon . . .

When the promised paperwork at last arrived, Fetisov ran his eye over the forms, noting the names. Suddenly, he stopped. He had seen this name before—Andrei Romanovich Chikatilo. He turned to Burakov. "Have you ever heard of this man?" Burakov had. He recalled that Fetisov had been on holiday when Chikatilo was arrested in 1984. Now he was able to tell his superior that Chikatilo had been cleared because he was of the wrong blood type. But Fetisov then recalled an interesting piece of information issued to all law enforcement agencies from the Ministry of Health in 1988: police should no longer assume that a sex criminal's blood type was the same type as his semen. Rare cases had been found of men whose blood and semen types differed. Both Fetisov and Burakov felt that Chikatilo had to be the man they were looking for. The first step was to find his address. It seemed that he no longer lived in Shakhty, but in Novocherkassk, and that he worked in a locomotive repair works in Rostov.

The entire investigation now focused on Chikatilo.

Fetisov learned that his job had once allowed him to travel widely, and that this was the period when victims were found over a wide area. When his job confined him to the Rostov area, the victims were found there. As a schoolteacher, he had been dismissed for child molesting. He had been dismissed from the Communist Party. And while he had been in prison for three months in 1984, the murders had stopped abruptly.

Now that they were almost certain that they had their man, it was tempting to shadow him and try to catch him in the act. But that entailed the obvious risk that he might kill before the tail could stop him. It would be safer to place him under arrest. Kostoyev, told of this development, agreed. He also agreed to allow Fetisov to conduct the preliminary interview.

At 3:40 on the afternoon of November 20, 1990, three plainclothesmen in an unmarked car drove to Novocherkassk, and waited at a point where—they knew from the surveillance team—Chikatilo would soon be passing. In fact, Chikatilo halted outside a café. The policemen approached him, and one asked his name. "Andrei Chikatilo," he replied.

"You're under arrest."

Without speaking, Chikatilo held out his wrists for the handcuffs.

The man who was brought into Mikhail Fetisov's office did not look like a mass murderer. He was tall—

about six feet—and thin, although obviously muscular, and his face had a worn and exhausted look. He wore glasses and certainly looked "respectable." His shoulders were stooped, and he walked with a shuffle, like an old man. The only sign of degeneracy was the mouth, with its loose, sagging corners, suggesting a weak character.

Chikatilo was subdued and politely uncooperative. He never looked Kostoyev in the eye. At first all he would say was that he had been arrested for the same crimes before, and had been released as innocent.

But Kostoyev had received a piece of information that left him in no doubt that Chikatilo was the Forest Path Killer. Comparison of his blood type and his semen—he had been masturbating behind a newspaper in his cell and left traces on his underpants—revealed that he was indeed one of those rare males whose blood type differs from his semen. His blood type was A, his semen AB—as was the killer's.

HE KILLED CHILDREN JUST AS READILY AS ADULTS, AND BOYS AS READILY AS GIRLS.

At the third interrogation, Kostoyev spoke to him kindly, and asked about childhood problems. Suddenly, Chikatilo asked if he could write a statement. In this, he spoke of having deranged sexual feelings, and "committing certain acts." The remainder consisted of self-pitying complaints about how he had felt degraded since schooldays, how everyone jeered at him, and how later employers had treated him with contempt. His "perverted sex acts," he said, were an expression of his fury at all this mistreatment. "I could not control my actions."

The next day, all the ground seemed to be lost as Chikatilo went back to fencing and evasions.

Time was running out. They had ten days to question a suspect before charging him, and this allotment was nearly up. Chikatilo did not take well to Kostoyev's approach—the approach of a top Soviet official who is accustomed to authority. And as it became clear that the ten days would not bring the confession they expected, Buratov made a suggestion—that Kostoyev should give way to someone with a "softer" approach. A local psychiatrist, Alexander Bukhanovsky, had already written his own detailed psychological portrait of the Forest Path Killer. He was now called in, and his more sympathetic approach soon produced results. As Bukhanovsky read his own words aloud, Chikatilo listened with a silence that had ceased to be hostile or noncommittal, and was obviously moved by the psychiatrist's insights into the lifetime of humiliation and disaster that had turned him into a killer. Soon he was holding back tears. Next he was telling the story of his life as if he was lying on a couch. Towards evening, he suddenly confessed to his first murder.

It was not, as Bukhanovsky had expected, that of Lyuba Biryuk in 1982, but of a nine-year-old child named Lena Zakhotnova, and it had taken place four years earlier, in 1978. In that year, Chikatilo explained, he had bought a dacha—hardly more than a wooden hut—at the far end of Shakhty.

Three days before Christmas 1978, when night had already fallen, he saw a pretty little girl dressed in a red coat with a furry collar and a rabbit-fur hat standing at a tram stop. He asked her where she had been until such a late hour, and she explained that she had gone to see a friend after school. As they talked, she found his friendly manner irresistible, and was soon admitting that she badly needed to find a toilet. Chikatilo told her that he lived just around the corner, and invited her to use his.

Inside the hut, he hurled her onto the floor, and with his hand over her mouth, tore at her clothes. His intention was rape, but he was unable to summon an erection. He ruptured her hymen with his finger—and immediately achieved a violent orgasm at the sight of the blood.

It was, he admitted to Bukhanovsky, a revelation. Now he suddenly understood: he needed to see blood to achieve maximum excitement. Still gripped by sexual fever, he took out a folding knife, and began to stab the screaming child in the stomach. It was then that he discovered something else about himself—that stabbing with a knife brought an even greater delight than normal sexual penetration.

He carried the girl's body and her clothes to the river, and hurled them in. They drifted under a bridge and were not found for two days.

Chikatilo was an immediate suspect. He was taken in for questioning nine times. Then he had an incredible piece of luck. Not far from his shack lived twenty-five-year-old Alexander Kravchenko, who had served six years in prison for a rape-murder in the Crimea. The police transferred their attention to Kravchenko, "interrogated" him, and soon obtained a "confession." Kravchenko was executed—by a pistol shot in the back of the head—in 1984.

From then on, Chikatilo admitted, he knew that his deepest sexual satisfaction could only come from stabbing and the sight of blood. But the unpleasant memories of the police interrogations made him cautious, and for almost three years he kept out of trouble. Meanwhile, he had been made redundant as a schoolteacher, and begun working as a supply clerk in Shakhty. This involved traveling all over the country, and offered him new opportunities. On September 3, 1981, he fell into conversation with a seventeen-year-old girl, Larisa Tkachenko, at a bus stop in Rostov. She was his favorite kind of pickup—a rebellious school dropout with a taste for vodka, who would offer sex in exchange for a meal. She agreed to accompany him to a local recreation area. There his control snapped. He hurled her to the ground, bludgeoned her with his fists, rammed earth into her mouth to stop her screams, and then strangled her. After that, he bit off her nipples and ejaculated on the naked body. Then he ran around the corpse, howling with joy, and waving her clothes. It was half an hour before he hid the body under branches.

And now he had crossed a kind of mental Rubicon.

He knew he was destined to kill for sexual enjoyment. Before he had finished, Chikatilo had confessed to fifty-three murders—a dozen more than anyone had suspected. He never admitted to cannibalism, although the fact that he took cooking equipment with him on his "hunting expeditions" leaves little doubt of it.

In mid-December 1990, the Russian public finally learned that the Forest Path Killer had been caught when Kostoyev called a press conference. Before the coming of Gorbachev and *glasnost*, the news would have been kept secret. Now this horrific story of a Russian Jack the Ripper quickly made headlines all around the world. This was the world's first intimation that the Soviet Union was not as crime-free as communist propaganda had insisted.

The trial of Andrei Chikatilo began in the Rostov courthouse on April 14, 1992. In any other country but Russia, it would have been regarded as a circus rather than an administration of justice. In any Western country, its conduct would certainly have formed grounds for an appeal that would have led to a second trial, and even possibly overturned the verdict.

Chikatilo, his head shaved and wearing a 1982 Olympics shirt, was placed in a large cage, to protect him from attacks by the public. This was a real possibility, since the court was packed with angry relatives, who frequently interrupted the proceedings with screams of "Bastard!" "Murderer!" "Sadist!"

Chikatilo confessed to all the crimes except the very first, that of the murder of Lena Zakhotnova. Kostoyev had no doubt that this was because pressure had been brought to bear; he had actually succeeded in obtaining

IT WAS THEN THAT HE DISCOVERED SOMETHING ELSE ABOUT HIMSELF—THAT STABBING WITH A KNIFE BROUGHT AN EVEN GREATER DELIGHT THAN NORMAL SEXUAL PENETRATION.

a posthumous pardon for the executed murderer, Kravchenko, but the legal authorities obviously felt that it would be better to let sleeping dogs lie.

On October 14, 1982, as Chikatilo received individual sentences for fifty-two murders, the court was filled with shrieks that often drowned out the judge's voice.

Sixteen months later, on February 14, 1994, Andrei Chikatilo was executed by a single shot in the back of the neck, fired from a small-caliber Makarov pistol.

Within two years of the execution of Andrei Chikatilo, a killer who seemed even more violent and ruthless than the Forest Path Killer threw the Ukraine into a panic. Chikatilo killed individuals; the murderer who was labeled "the Terminator" (after the Arnold Schwarzenegger film) killed whole families, including children. By the time of his arrest in April 1996, the

Terminator had killed forty victims. Later, he would confess to another dozen murders in an earlier orgy of killing that started in 1989.

On the morning of Sunday April 7, 1996, police investigator Igor Khuney, in the Ukrainian town of Yavoriv, received a phone call from a man called Pyotr Onoprienko, complaining about his cousin Anatoly, who had until recently lived in his home. Pyotr had evicted him after finding a stock of firearms in his room, and Anatoly had threatened to "take care" of Pyotr's family at Easter—which happened to be that day. Would the police go and see Anatoly? He was, said Pyotr, living with a woman in nearby Zhitomirskaya.

This caught Khuney's attention, for he had recently been informed of the theft of a twelve-gauge, Russian-made Tos-34 shotgun in that area. And in recent months there had been an outbreak of appalling murders of entire families, most of them involving a rifle or shotgun. On intuition, Khuney's superior Sergei Kryukov decided to interview Onoprienko. He took twenty policemen with him in squad cars.

They were taking no chances. When a small, balding man with piercing blue eyes opened the door, he was swiftly overpowered. Asked for identification, he led them to a closet. As a policeman opened the door, the man dived for a pistol, but failed to reach it.

When Onoprienko's woman friend returned home from church with her two small children, Kryukov told her that they thought her lover might be the suspected mass murderer. She broke down and wept.

In the apartment, police located 122 items that belonged to numerous unsolved murder victims, but the police still need a confession from their suspect. In police custody, Onoprienko refused to speak until he was questioned by a general. But when one was brought in—General Romanuk—Onoprienko confessed that he had used the stolen shotgun in a recent murder. Admissions to more than fifty murders then came pouring out.

The recent murders began on Christmas Eve 1995, in Garmarnia, a small village in central Ukraine, near the Polish border. A man entered the home of a forester, and killed him, his wife, and his two sons with a sawn-off double-barreled hunting rifle. He stole a few items of jewelry and a bundle of clothes before setting the house on fire. Five nights later he slaughtered another family of four—a young man, his wife, and her twin sisters. It was in Bratkovychi, another remote village near the Polish border. Again the killer stole items of gold jewelry and an old jacket and set fire to the house.

During the next three months there were eight similar attacks in two villages; twenty-eight people died, and one woman was raped. In Enerhodar, seven were killed. He returned to Bratkovychi on January 17, 1996, to kill a family of five. In Fastov, near Kiev, he murdered a family of four. In Olevsk, four women died. His usual method was to shoot the men, knife the women, and bludgeon the children to death.

There was panic, and an army division was called in to patrol the villages. An intensive manhunt was mounted—even greater than for Chikatilo. Finally, in April 1996, police arrested Onoprienko near Lvov. The thirty-six-year-old ex–mental patient was soon confessing to a total of fifty-two murders.

Born in 1959, Onoprienko began his career as a forestry student. He would confess: "The first time I killed I shot down a deer in the woods. I was in my early twenties, and I recall feeling very upset when I saw it dead. I couldn't explain why I had done it, and I felt sorry about it. I never had that feeling again."

Later he became a sailor on cruise liners. After giving up this well-paid job, he became a fireman. In 1989, he and an accomplice named Sergei Rogozin decided to commit a burglary, but were surprised by the householder, whom they then killed. Rogozin was his accomplice in eight additional murders motivated by theft.

It was during his later killing spree of 1995, he confessed, after a period in a mental hospital in Kiev when he was diagnosed schizophrenic, that he had raped a woman after shooting her in the face. During another spree, he had approached a young girl who had fallen on her knees to pray after seeing him kill her parents. He asked her to tell him where they kept the money, and she stared in his eyes and defiantly said: "No, I won't." Onoprienko killed her by smashing her skull; but he admitted later that although he was impressed by her courage he nonetheless still felt nothing during the murders. "To me, killing people is like ripping up a duvet," he told journalist Mark Franchetti, in his tiny prison cell in Zhitomir, Ukraine, where his trial had been held.

In 1989, "driven by a rage at God and Satan," he had killed a couple standing by their Lada on a motorway. He also killed five people in a car, and then sat in the car for two hours, wondering what to do with the corpses, which quickly began to smell.

The act of killing, he insisted, gave him no pleasure. On the contrary, he felt oddly detached from it. "I watched all this as an animal would stare at a sheep," he told police in a confession videotaped in 1997. "I perceived it all as a kind of experiment. There can be no answer in this experiment to what you're trying to learn." He said he felt like both perpetrator and spectator.

Onoprienko claimed that he was driven by some unknown force, and that voices ordered him to kill. "I'm not a maniac," he insisted to Franchetti, "I have been taken over by a higher force, something telepathic or cosmic, which drove me." But he had to wait for this force to give him orders. "For example, I wanted to kill my brother's first wife, because I hated her. I really wanted to kill her, but I couldn't, because I had to receive the order first. I waited for it, but it did not come.

"I am like a rabbit in a laboratory, a part of an experiment to prove that man is capable of murdering and learning to live with his crimes. It is to show that I can cope, that I can stand anything, forget anything."

His trial began in Zhitomir in late November 1998. The delay was due to a lack of funds. The authorities could not afford to try him because his crimes had covered such a wide area. Eventually, after two years, his judges appeared on television to appeal for money, and the Ukrainian government contributed the $56,000 for the trial.

As had Chikatilo, Onoprienko was confined in a metal cage in the courtroom. Sergei Rogozin, the accused accomplice in nine of the killings, stood trial with him. The trial ended four months later, on March 31, 1999, when Onoprienko was found guilty and sentenced to death. Rogozin received thirteen years. Because there is a moratorium on capital punishment in Russia, Onoprienko is still alive and may never be executed. Leonid Kuchma, the Ukrainian president, however, spoke of temporarily lifting the moratorium in order to execute him.

For his part, Onoprienko declared that he wished to die. "If I am not executed, I will escape and start killing again. I am being groomed to serve Satan." He believed that he was destined to kill a large number of people, perhaps 350, and that if his sentence is commuted to life—which in Russia means at most twenty years—he would go on to fulfill his destiny after his release (by which time he would be sixty).

The judge who sentenced him, Dmitri Lipski, said: "He is driven by extreme cruelty. He doesn't care about anything—only about himself. He is egocentric, and has a very high opinion of himself."

What motivated all of these murders?

Psychiatrists who examined Onoprienko stated that he was not insane. He was brought up without parents, and his elder brother allowed him to be taken into an orphanage. This, psychiatrists suggested, may

"If I am not executed, I will escape and start killing again. I am being groomed to serve Satan."

be why he has chosen to kill whole families. His worst killing spree occurred at the time he moved in with his girlfriend and her children and it seems possible that this sight of a happy family triggered the resentment that is the key to virtually all serial killers.

Although he proposed to his girlfriend by offering her a ring he had just cut off the finger of a corpse, she insists that he was very tender and loving with the children. Here again we encounter the split personality that seems so typical of a certain type of serial killer.

I have left one of the most interesting profilers of the Behavioral Science Unit to the end. This is partly because Gregg McCrary was relatively a latecomer to the BSU, joining in 1990, but also because two of his three best-known cases—the Toronto Rapist and the poet-killer Jack Unterweger—occurred outside the United States, and are thus appropriate for this final chapter.

A high school teacher and wrestling coach who joined the FBI in 1969—when he was twenty-four—Gregg McCrary spent years working in Michigan, the Midwest, New York, and Buffalo before John Douglas recruited him for the NCAVC. But he proved to be oddly suited to the BSU because he had studied the Japanese martial art of Shorinji Kempo, which emphasizes thinking past the present situation to future strategy—excellent training for out-thinking the criminal mind. He liked what he had seen and heard of the Behavioral Science Unit, and two years before John Douglas became chief in 1990, he applied to join—one of thirty or so who were after the same job. McCrary landed it.

I became acquainted with Gregg in 1989, when a London publisher asked me to write a book about serial killers. I asked a friend who lived nearby, Donald Seaman, if he would like to collaborate with me. As an ex-reporter, the first thing he wanted to do was visit the FBI Academy at Quantico for himself. I rang there, explained I was writing a book about serial murder, and asked if I could speak to someone in the Behavioral Science Unit. A few minutes later, Agent Gregg McCrary was on the line, and when I explained what I wanted, he said that he would see what he could do to arrange it. His intervention was so effective that a few weeks later Don was in Virginia, being guided around the Academy by Gregg—to whom, in due course, we dedicated *The Serial Killers*. This is how Don describes Gregg in the book:

> *He stands some six feet in height, a spare, upright figure with a pale face, a carefully trimmed moustache, and brown hair flecked with grey. As with all personnel in the NCAVC he is smartly dressed, reflecting the evident high morale. Equally, this is the FBI at work; McCrary's dark blue blazer reveals no sign of the Smith & Wesson 9mm semi-automatic below, fully loaded with twelve rounds in the magazine, plus one (for emergency) already in the chamber.*

Gregg was kind enough to send me a copy of the useful FBI handbook *Criminal Investigative Analysis* (1989) by Ressler, Douglas, Anne Burgess, and others. And Don passed on to me a letter from Gregg, in which he discusses my comment that there is a basic suicidal impulse in serial killers, which explains why so many of them make absurd mistakes that land them in the gas chamber. (I had pointed out that one-third of all murderers commit suicide.)

In the letter, dated October 1989, Gregg commented that, being egocentric psychopaths, most serial killers are unfortunately not the suicidal type. "They don't want to deprive the rest of us of the value of their company." He goes on:

> *The exception is the sexually sadistic serial killer. His crimes involve the infliction of physical and psychological terror on his victims. He may use weapons or instruments to torture the victims before death and be involved in experimental sexual activity. He abducts his victims and keeps them for hours, days, months, etc.*
>
> *While they represent a minority of serial killers, they are the most horrific due to the ante-mortem activity. Examples would be Christopher Wilder, Leonard Lake and Charles Ng, etc.*
>
> *Most serial killers (Bundy, Gacy, Kemper, etc.) kill their victims quickly in a brutal blitz style of attack. Sexual assaults and dismemberment are post-mortem. These types of killers who do not inflict torture prior to death are far less inclined to be suicidal than are the sub group of sexually sadistic serial killers.*

This is a point worth underlining. Killers such as Dean Corll and John Wayne Gacy are not remotely suicidal because they are so self-absorbed. They remain lifelong adolescents. On the other hand, Henry Lee Lucas confessed because he was overtaken by a kind of religious conversion, and the Boston Strangler because he somehow "outgrew" murder.

On the other hand, I am inclined to wonder if there is such a clear distinction between sadists and non-sadists. Lake committed suicide because he was trapped and faced life in jail. Chris Wilder, a spree killer who murdered and raped half a dozen women on a cross-country rampage in the spring of 1984, turned his gun on himself when cornered. But at least one thing is clear: sex murder is addictive, which is why most sex murderers carry on until they are caught, even if, like Rolling and Onoprienko, they come to feel that they are serving some evil force.

One of McCrary's first major cases at Quantico is a good example of obsessive addiction—in this case to a kind of necrophilia. The man who became known as the "Genesee River Killer" murdered eleven women in the Rochester area of New York in the late 1980s. In trying to profile the man responsible, McCrary was struck by the evidence of one prostitute who recognized his picture as a client who had wanted her to "play dead." Like Christie, this man had problems raising an erection with a conscious woman.

Noting that the murders continued even though there was panic in the red-light district, McCrary deduced that the killer seemed so ordinary and nonthreatening that prostitutes saw him as harmless. He probably drove a nondescript car. From behavioral evidence he was probably in his late twenties, or perhaps early thirties. He would work at some menial job, and might well be a fisherman, since so many victims had been found in the Genesee River Gorge, known for its good fishing.

In many of the eleven murders, there were signs that the killer had returned, probably to have sex with the body. But in the case of the last but one, he had also disemboweled his victim. It was this victim, June Stott, who proved to be the turning point in the case, because this lead the local authorities to call in the FBI—and Agent McCrary. For McCrary, the Stott murder showed that the killer was "growing into this. . . . Killing wasn't enough. He had to come back and cut her open."

The police decided to make use of helicopters, since the gorge has so many twists and turns where a body might be dumped (it is sometimes called the Grand Canyon of the East). After much frustrating searching, a pilot spotted the body of a woman, clad only in a white shirt, half-concealed by a bridge, and above it, a man who was either urinating or masturbating. The helicopter followed the man and he drove away to the town of Spencerport, where he parked close to a nursing home. The airborne observers watched the heavily built, middle-aged man go inside. After alerting troopers on the ground, the helicopter flew off to protect the crime scene, while the troopers confronted the driver. Lacking I.D, he nonetheless admitted that he was Arthur Shawcross, forty-four, who had once served fifteen years for murdering two children.

When arrested, Shawcross at first denied his guilt. But when asked whether his mistress—who worked in the nursing home—was involved in the murders, he hung his head, and said: "No, I was the only one involved."

McCrary's profile proved remarkably accurate—the killer's appearance, the kind of car he drove, the love of fishing in the gorge, the fact that Shawcross returned to the scenes of his crimes to masturbate. It was not murder that he found most satisfactory; that was merely a means of rendering his victims passive. Like Christie, Shawcross needed an unconscious woman.

The only inaccuracy was the killer's age—he was forty-four, not twenty-nine or thirty. Then it struck McCrary that Shawcross had been in jail for fifteen years, and that in a sense his development had been on hold during that time. Forty-four was therefore not a bad estimate after all.

Arthur Shawcross, who earlier in life had suffered a number of severe head injuries, one involving a blow from a sledgehammer, was sentenced to a total of 250 years in prison.

This notion of murder as an addictive drug also seems to apply to another case that McCrary profiled, the "Scarborough Rapist," Paul Bernardo, whose case would have fit perfectly into the chapter on sex slaves except that Bernardo's three murders do not qualify him as a serial killer.

The rapes began in May 1987. The perpetrator, who was described as young and white, would follow women who alighted from buses in the Scarborough area of east Toronto, attack them from behind, and make sure that they did not see his face. Scarborough is a middle-class area, and he sometimes dragged them behind bushes on the edge of lawns, or between the houses. He called them foul names, and used more violence than was necessary—in one case he broke the victim's shoulder bone, and smeared her hair with dirt. He raped and sodomized them, and then force them to give him oral sex.

McCrary profiled him as a young man who lived in the area—hence his care in making sure that his victims did not see his face. He felt hatred and resentment towards women. He was probably incapable of sex unless he was inspiring fear, and he was most likely unmarried and lived at home, since as a young man he would be unable to afford his own house in Scarborough.

The rapes had reached a total of fifteen when, in June 1991, fourteen-year-old Leslie Mahaffy disappeared. Two weeks later, parts of her body, encased in concrete, were found on the edge of Lake Gibson, Saint Catherine's. Then, in April of the following year, a fifteen-year-old schoolgirl, Kristen French, vanished on her way home from school. A witness who had seen a cream-colored car speeding away left the police in no doubt that she had been abducted, almost certainly by two people. Two weeks later her body was found dumped down a side road. She had been beaten and strangled.

The killer was arrested in late January 1993. It happened after DNA profiling had finally identified the Scarborough Rapist. There had been 224 suspects, among these Paul Bernardo, who resembled an identikit drawing of the rapist. Bernardo had given blood, hair, and saliva samples to be compared with the rapist, but had heard nothing further in two years, and assumed he was in the clear. In fact, the DNA testing had proceeded slowly, and Bernardo was among the last five suspects whose body samples were tested. It was only then that the police knew that Paul Bernardo was the Scarborough Rapist they had been seeking for more than five years. The person who revealed him as the killer of Leslie Mahaffy and Kristen French was his wife—and accomplice in the murders—Karla.

Once again, Gregg McCrary's profile of the rapist proved remarkably accurate. Bernardo lived in the Scarborough area, was then twenty-three, and was living at home with his parents.

Although she presents an image of blonde sweetness, driven by a desire to present her fiancé with a "surrogate virgin," Canada's most notorious female criminal, Karla Homolka, presented her husband, Paul Bernardo, with schoolgirls to rape—and then kill. (Associated Press/Frank Gunn)

The story, as it then emerged, began when Paul Bernardo, a handsome young businessman of twenty-three met the seventeen-year-old blonde Karla Homolka in a Howard Johnson's in 1987, and the two lost no time in climbing into bed. Later, it became clear that their affinity was based upon the fact that his sexual tastes veered towards sadism, and hers towards masochism. At sixteen, Karla had allowed a boyfriend to tie her up with his belt and slap her during sex, and discovered that she enjoyed it. The first time she and Paul were alone in her bedroom, he found handcuffs in her pocket, and asked: "Are these for me?" He then handcuffed her to the bed and pretended that he was raping her. As their relationship progressed, she had to dress up as a schoolgirl—with her hair in pigtails tied with ribbons—and he also liked her to wear a dog collar round her neck when they had sex. If she failed to comply with his demands, he beat her. She soon became expert at explaining away her bruises to friends.

THEIR AFFINITY WAS BASED UPON THE FACT THAT HIS SEXUAL TASTES VEERED TOWARDS SADISM, AND HERS TOWARDS MASOCHISM.

When she met Bernardo, Karla was unaware that he was the Scarborough Rapist, whose attacks continued for years after they had met and become engaged.

Sometime before Christmas 1990, Karla had asked Bernardo—by now her fiancé, and living in her home—what he wanted for Christmas, and he had replied: "Your sister, Tammy." Tammy was fifteen, and still at school. Desperate to please Bernardo, Karla obtained sedatives from the animal clinic where she worked, and on the evening of December 23, 1990, invited Tammy to join them in watching a film after midnight in the basement "den." They plied the unsuspecting girl with drugged drinks and, when she fell unconscious, Bernardo undressed her and raped her on the floor.

It was while Bernardo was raping Tammy—filmed by Karla—that he noticed that she had stopped breathing, and her face had turned blue. The couple's attempts to revive her failed so they re-dressed her and called an ambulance. No suspicion fell on Karla or Bernardo; the inquest ruled the death accidental. It was assumed that she drank too much and choked on her own vomit.

In June 1991, a fourteen-year-old schoolgirl named Leslie Mahaffy arrived at her home at 2 a.m. to find herself locked out. Bernardo came across her sitting disconsolately on a bench in her backyard, and offered her a cigarette. Then he held a knife to her throat, and took her back to the house that he and Karla shared—they were due to get married in two weeks. There he raped her and videotaped her urinating.

The next day Karla had to join in, having lesbian sex with the schoolgirl while Bernardo videotaped them. Leslie was raped repeatedly. When left alone with Karla, Leslie begged her to let her go; Karla replied that if she did, she would be beaten. She gave Leslie two sleeping tablets to "make her feel better," and while Leslie was asleep, Bernardo looped electrical cord around her throat and strangled her.

Two days later, he dismembered the body with an electric saw, encased the pieces in quick-drying cement, and then dropped them off a bridge into Lake Gibson, with Karla acting as lookout.

Bernardo now decided to seduce a fifteen-year-old schoolgirl, Jane, who had been a friend of Tammy's, and who bore a remarkable resemblance to the dead girl. As a "wedding present" for her husband, Karla invited Jane to their house. Jane was flattered by the attention of two adults, and developed a schoolgirl crush on Karla. Once there, the newlyweds served her drugged liquor, and after she fell asleep Karla anaesthetized her with halothane, again obtained from the animal clinic. Bernardo then raped and sodomized her while Karla videoed the acts; Bernardo was particularly delighted to find that Jane had been a virgin. Fortunately for her, she remained unconscious during the rape.

On April 6, 1992, ten months after the murder of Leslie Mahaffy, Karla accompanied Bernardo as they drove in search of another victim. They passed fifteen-year-old Kristen French, walking alone on her way home from school, and Karla called out to ask her directions. The girl came over to their car as Karla produced a map. Bernardo then moved behind her and forced her into the car at knifepoint. After three days of being repeatedly raped and forced to take part in videotapes in which she had to address Bernardo as "master," Kristen, like Leslie Mahaffy, was murdered. Her naked body was thrown on a dumpsite full of old washing machines.

During the New Year 1993, Bernardo beat Karla more violently than usual, clubbing her with a rubber flashlight and blacking both her eyes. Finally, her mother and sister called when Bernardo was out, and insisted on taking her to hospital. After that she agreed to go home with them. To prevent Bernardo from discovering her whereabouts, she moved in with an aunt and uncle.

Instead of arresting him immediately, the police went to interview Karla. She refused to admit that she knew her husband was the rapist, but when they had gone, blurted out to her uncle and aunt: "Christ, they know everything." Pressed by her aunt, Karla finally told her about the murder of the two schoolgirls.

Bernardo was arrested on February 17, 1993.

When he finally met the killer, McCrary was able to gauge the remarkable accuracy of his profile. Bernardo hated women because he hated his hostile, neurotic mother, who had told him when he was ten that he was a bastard fathered by her lover. His sex life was therefore dominated by a desire to humiliate and punish woman. His preferred method of sex was to beat a woman as he sodomized her.

In due course, Karla turned state's evidence, in exchange for a promise of a lighter sentence. She was tried first, for manslaughter, and was sentenced to twelve years. She was released from prison in July 2004. On September 1, 1995, Paul Bernardo was sentenced to life imprisonment, with the proviso that he should serve a minimum of twenty-five years before he could apply for parole.

Perhaps the most fascinating of all the cases that McCrary profiled was that of Jack Unterweger, poet, dramatist, and TV celebrity. He was also Austria's first serial killer.

In the summer of 1992, McCrary received a phone call from Vienna. A man was about to go on trial for the murders of eleven women. Would he be willing to profile the case? He replied that if they had the right man, a profile would be unnecessary, and that a signature crime analysis would be more to the point. A "signature" means certain typical elements in a criminal's modus operandi—for example, the way he ties a knot or takes a certain kind of "trophy."

Two leading investigators on the case, Ernst Geiger, the policeman who had put the suspect behind bars, and Thomas Muller, chief of the Psychiatric Service, agreed to travel to Quantico. McCrary mentioned in advance that he wanted to know nothing whatever about their suspect—just about the crime scenes.

When Geiger and Muller arrived, the three men devoted several days to studying the files. The murders had taken place in Austria, Czechoslovakia, and Los Angeles. The women had all been beaten, and then strangled with an item of their underwear, either bras or pantyhose. No semen was found, either in the bodies or on them. The victims were often killed in woodland, near water, and left covered in leaves.

When McCrary had studied the files, and established that the MOs seemed to indicate the same killer, they turned to the man who had been arrested: Jack Unterweger, ex-convict and now one of Austria's best-known writers.

Born in 1950, the son of a prostitute and, according to rumor, an American GI, Jack had been abandoned by his mother. He was brought up by an alcoholic grandfather, who often brought prostitutes to the small hut where they lived in a single room. In his teens, Jack was in trouble repeatedly for offenses such as burglary and car theft, and became a pimp who was known for beating up his hookers. Then, in 1974, he was arrested for two murders. The first was of eighteen-year-old Margaret Schaefer, who happened to be a friend of a prostitute named Barbara Scholz. As Unterweger and the latter drove past her in the street, Unterweger invited the girl into the car, and then decided on impulse to rob her and her family's home. After that he took her to the woods, forced her to undress, and demanded oral sex; when she refused, he beat her unconscious with a steel pipe and then strangled her with her bra. Barbara Scholz gave him away, and he was arrested.

The second victim, a prostitute named Marcia Horveth, had been strangled with her stockings and dumped in a lake. Unterweger was not charged with this murder, because he had already confessed to the first and had been sentenced to life. He pleaded guilty, claiming that as he was having sex, he had seen the face of his mother before him. A psychologist had diagnosed him a sexually sadistic psychopath with narcissistic tendencies.

When he went to jail for murder, Unterweger had been illiterate. He had already been in prison fifteen times. But condemned to life, he set about learning to read and write. He then edited the prison newspaper, started a literary review, and wrote his autobiography, a book called *Purgatory* (*Fegefeur*), in which he professed to be completely rehabilitated, and explained that he had killed the prostitute because he hated his mother.

Purgatory was a literary sensation, and intellectuals began to lobby for his release. He was paroled on May 23, 1990, after sixteen years behind bars. And he quickly became prosperous as his book climbed to the top of the best-seller charts, and then was filmed. He wrote plays, gave readings of his poetry, and appeared as a guest on talk shows. A small, handsome man who wore white suits and drove expensive cars, his face was soon familiar to everyone in Austria.

Then women began to disappear. The first, a shop assistant, Blanka Bockova, was found on the banks of the Vltava River, near Prague, on September 14, 1990. She had been beaten and strangled with a stocking.

On New Year's Eve 1991, in a forest near Graz, Austria, nearly three hundred miles south of Prague, another woman was found strangled with her pantyhose. She was Heidemarie Hammerer, a prostitute who had vanished from Graz on October 26, 1990. Five days later, the badly decomposed body of a woman was found in a forest north of Graz. She had been stabbed, and probably strangled with her pantyhose. She was identified as Brunhilde Masser, another prostitute. The decomposed body of a prostitute named Elfriende Schrempf was found eight months later, on October 5, in a forest near Graz. When four more prostitutes, Silvia Zagler, Sabine Moitzi, Regina Prem, and Karin Eroglu disappeared in Vienna during the next month, it looked as if the killer had changed his location.

And at the point, the police were given their vital lead. Ex-policeman August Schenner, retired for five years from the Vienna force, was reminded of the MO of the prostitute-killer Jack Unterweger sixteen years earlier. Police who checked upon his tip were at first skeptical—Unterweger was rich, famous, and had plenty of girlfriends. Would such a man murder prostitutes? Moreover, as a magazine writer, Unterweger had interviewed prostitutes about the killer the press had labeled the "Vienna Courier," and been critical of their failure to catch him. If they treated him as a suspect, would it not look as if they were pursuing a vendetta?

Yet as they reviewed the evidence, the Vienna police—and especially Detective Ernst Geiger—decided that the case against Unterweger looked highly convincing. A check on his credit card receipts revealed that his travels had invariably taken him to the same areas where the women were killed. He had been on a magazine assignment in Los Angeles, interviewing prostitutes, when three of them were strangled there in a manner that recalled the Vienna murders. He had even persuaded the Los Angeles Police Department to drive him around red-light districts in their patrol cars.

As his investigation continued, Ernst Geiger learned from prostitutes who had been picked up by Unterweger that he liked to handcuff them during sex—which was consistent with some of the marks on the wrists of victims. Police tracked down the BMW that Unterweger had bought on his release from prison, and found in it a dark hair with skin on the root. It was tiny, but using the PCR technique to make multiple copies of DNA, they were able to identify it as belonging to victim Blanka Bockova. When a search of his apartment revealed a red scarf whose fibers matched those found on her body, they decided to arrest their suspect.

They interviewed Unterweger on October 2, 1991. Naturally, he denied everything. Moreover, he renewed criticism of the police for their failure to catch the Vienna Courier. And support for him among Viennese intellectuals and his society friends remained strong. How could they admit that their enthusiasm for his writing had unleashed a killer on Vienna? Was it not more likely, as Unterweger told them, that the authorities were persecuting this ex-criminal who had now become their scourge?

It was time to bring the suspect into custody. In February 1992 a judge signed the warrant. But when the police arrived at his apartment, Unterweger had already left. They learned from his friends that he had gone on holiday with his latest girlfriend, eighteen-year-old Bianca Mrak, whom he had picked up in a restaurant, and with whom he had been living since the previous December.

It seemed they had gone to Switzerland, and then, when friends tipped him off by telephone that there was a warrant out for him, to New York.

Before leaving Europe, Unterweger had telephoned Vienna newspapers to insist that the police were trying to frame him. He also made an offer: if the officer in charge of the case would drop the warrant for his arrest, he would return voluntarily to "clear his name." He had alibis, he said, for all of the murders—on one occasion he had been giving a reading of his work.

Unterweger and Bianca moved to Miami, Florida, and rented a beach apartment. They were running short of cash, and Bianca took a job as a topless dancer. Her mother kept them supplied with money by telegraph.

When the police learned about this, they called on the mother, and prevailed on her to inform them the next time her daughter made contact. And when Bianca asked her mother to telegraph more cash to the Western Union office in Miami, two agents were waiting for them. The alert Unterweger spotted them and fled, urging Bianca to head in another direction. But he was caught after running through a restaurant, creating havoc. Out in the back, an armed agent arrested him. When told he was wanted for making a false customs declaration in New York—he had failed to admit his prison record—he looked relieved. But when they added that he was also wanted in Vienna for murder, he began to sob.

Learning that he was also wanted in California, he chose to resist extradition to Europe and opt for a Los Angeles trial; however, when informed that California had the death penalty, he changed his mind.

The trial began in Vienna in April 1994, and in spite of overwhelming circumstantial evidence, the result was by no means a foregone conclusion. Unterweger had hundreds of admirers, who were convinced that the police had picked on him because they were blinded with prejudice by his past criminal record. And there was virtually no forensic evidence to link him to the crimes—merely a few red fibers that matched his scarf.

The part McCrary played in the prosecution proved to be central and vital. It was his task to explain to the court that the "signature" evidence amounted to overwhelming proof of Unterweger's guilt. It was almost impossible, he told them, for eleven unconnected murders to be committed with an almost identical pattern—strangulation by underwear tied in a unique knot, and disposal in woodland in the same manner.

McCrary had even fed the "signature analysis" into the VICAP computer, which covered nearly twelve thousand murders from all over the United States. He had expected dozens of matches; instead, it came up with only four, one of which had been solved. The other three were the murders attributed to Unterweger.

When the defense asked him whether he had ever come across another case of a man who had frequent consensual sex getting involved with prostitutes, he was able to cite the case of Arthur Shawcross who, like Unterweger, had been in prison for fifteen years for murder, been released, and then murdered eleven prostitutes—in spite of having a wife and a girlfriend. The amazing parallel produced an obvious effect on the jury.

As the trial dragged on for two and a half months, McCrary watched Unterweger's support eroding away as the public realized the strength of the evidence against him. In a speech in his own defense, Unterweger did not even attempt to counter it. He merely repeated his assertion that he had no reason to kill women, since he had every reason to stay out of jail. He conceded that he had once been "a primitive criminal who grunted rather than talked, and an inveterate liar." But, he declared with passion, he was no longer that person.

But McCrary's evidence left little doubt that he was exactly that person. And on June 28, 1999, the jury found Unterweger guilty on nine of the eleven counts of murder—in the remaining two cases the jury reasoned that the bodies were too decomposed for the cause of death to be established. Unterweger was obviously stunned; he had confidently expected an acquittal.

HE CONCEDED THAT HE HAD ONCE BEEN "A PRIMITIVE CRIMINAL WHO GRUNTED RATHER THAN TALKED, AND AN INVETERATE LIAR."

McCrary had one more contribution to make to the case. By now he knew enough about Unterweger to know that an ego like his would find it virtually impossible to accept the verdict. He had sworn that he would never return to prison. This time it would be for life; there would be no second chance of parole. Suicide would be his last defiant act, his last great "Fuck you!"

Unfortunately, this warning was not passed on to the prison guards. That night Jack Unterweger hanged himself in his cell with the cord of his jumpsuit.

For McCrary, the moral of the story is also the moral of this book: It is almost impossible for serial killers to change their spots.

Epilogue: An End in Sight?

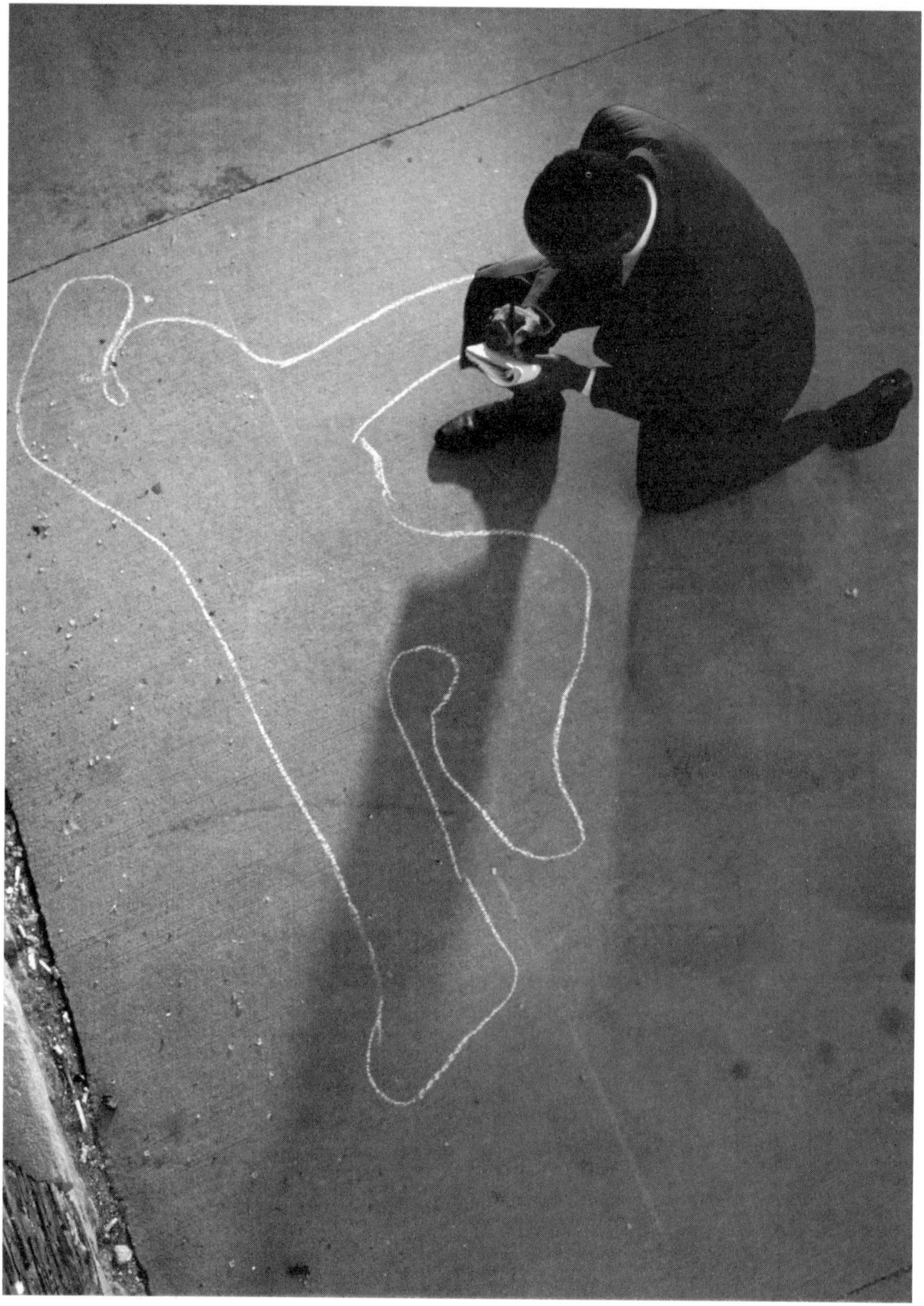

Epilogue: An End in Sight?

A book like this is hardly the place for philosophical reflection, but in these final pages perhaps I might permit myself some latitude.

On a hot Monday in June 1955, an ex-con named Willie Cochran saw fifteen-year-old Patty Ann Cook sunbathing in a black swimsuit in her front yard in Dallas, Georgia, and offered her a lift to the swimming pool. When she accepted, he drove her to a spot beside the Etowah River, raped her, and then shot her through the head. Since Cochran was a sex offender who had taken that day off from work, he was questioned by the police and confessed to the crime. He was duly executed in Reidsville's electric chair.

What stuck in my mind about the case was a comment made by the presiding judge, J. H. Paschall: "The male sexual urge has a strength out of all proportion to any useful purpose that it serves."

I suspect that comment contains the solution to the rise of the serial killer. In the West we live in a society that has seen a steady rise in the level of sexual stimulation. By the 1930s advertisements already made use of attractive young women in swimsuits, and in the postwar years these images extended to women clad only in their underwear. Nowadays anyone can access pornographic pictures on the Web. If Patty Ann had been wearing a Victorian bathing costume with a woollen skirt down to the knees, Cochran would have driven past.

Which might seem to imply that unless we revert to a Victorian code of advertising, there is no end in sight to the rise of sex crime and serial murder. This conclusion, however, is not as inevitable as it looks. There is, I would suggest, a way forward. And Christie's remark about the "quiet, peaceful thrill" he felt after killing Muriel Eady offers a starting point for trying to explain what it is. Christie's remark had always reminded me of a phrase used by D. H. Lawrence in *Lady Chatterley's Lover* when the gamekeeper first makes love to Lady Chatterley: "He had come in to her at once, to enter the peace on earth of her soft, quiescent body."

Roy Hazelwood's comment that sex crime is about power is obviously true, but it is not the whole truth. Equally important is that sense of "peace on earth."

Now Lawrence was a true descendant of those nineteenth-century writers and artists we call Romantics, a movement that began in Germany in the late eighteenth century, at the time of Goethe. And fifty years ago, they were the starting point of my first book *The Outsider*. As a teenager in the 1940s, I had been fascinated by the high rate of suicide among the Romantics, as well as deaths by tuberculosis that seemed to be part of the syndrome of misery and defeat.

The reason for the misery and defeat was their feeling of the painful contrast between "peace on earth," and the madness of our materialistic world. This I saw as the basic "Outsider problem," which was succinctly expressed in Villiers de L'Isle Adam's play *Axel* when the hero tells the heroine: "As for living, our servants can do that for us." He is embracing her as he speaks, and then goes on to propose that the solution would be suicide. This is the conclusion reached by so many of the Romantics. What I wanted to demonstrate was why this is illogical, and why, when we recognize this, we can also see a way forward for our chaotic civilization.

To me, it seemed obvious that the answer was for the "Outsider" to stop feeling sorry for himself, and

IF PATTY ANN HAD BEEN WEARING A VICTORIAN BATHING COSTUME WITH A WOOLLEN SKIRT DOWN TO THE KNEES, COCHRAN WOULD HAVE DRIVEN PAST.

get on with the job of trying to change the world. If he didn't do it, then nobody else would.

At about this time, 1960, I received a letter from Abraham Maslow, an American professor of psychology. He explained that he had got tired of studying sick people, because they talked about nothing but their sickness, and decided to study healthy people instead. And he quickly learned something that no one had discovered so far: healthy people had with great frequency what they called "peak experiences," experiences of sudden tremendous happiness. Typical was his story of a young mother who was watching her husband and children eating breakfast when she suddenly thought, "My God, aren't I lucky?" and went into the peak experience.

He also made another interesting discovery: when he talked to his students about peak experiences, they began remembering and talking about their own peak experiences, and they began having peak experiences all the time. The capacity for peak experiences is obviously quite basic and normal in human beings. Until we recognize this, we are selling ourselves short.

But Maslow said something else that struck me as relevant to the problem of crime. He talked about what he called the "hierarchy of needs." As they evolve, human beings pass through certain levels of need. If you are so poor that you have difficulty getting enough to eat, then you will find it hard to think about anything but food. But when people have enough to eat, then the next level emerges: for a roof over your head. Every tramp dreams of retiring to a cottage with roses round the door.

If that need is satisfied, then the next level emerges—the sexual level. This is not merely the need for sex, but the need to love and be cared for.

If this is satisfied, the next level is self-esteem, the need to be liked and respected by one's fellows, and if possible to be admired. This is the level of the "wannabe" that we have encountered so frequently in this book. As I thought about this, I saw the same levels emerging in the development of society in the past few centuries—and in the types of crime in those societies.

In the eighteenth century, the majority of people were at that basic level, the need to get enough to eat. So crime was also basic, most of it connected with robbery.

In the nineteenth century, things had advanced, and there was now a middle class whose chief needs were connected with their homes and domestic security. The crime historian thinks of the mid-nineteenth century as the age of domestic murder. But a new level is also emerging—the sexual level. In the United States, a doctor named H. H. Holmes lures women into his "murder castle"—complete with hidden doors and secret rooms—to violate them and dispose of their bodies, and Sunday school teacher Theodore Durrant murders and rapes two young women in San Francisco. In England there is Jack the Ripper, in France, Joseph Vacher, a mentally deranged journeyman who rapes and mutilates peasant women. The age of sex crime has begun, and it escalates in the twentieth century into serial murder.

Self-esteem criminals need to impose their will on other people.

In the 1920s, the next level, the self-esteem level, makes its tentative appearance with Leopold and Loeb, the wealthy students who wish to see themselves as intellectual supermen. But self-esteem crime gets into its stride in the 1950s, with Melvin Rees, and in the 1960s with the Moors Murders and Charles Manson. Self-esteem criminals need to impose their will on other people. DeBardeleben belongs to this type; so does Leonard Lake and Jack Unterweger.

But beyond that, Maslow posits the next level of the hierarchy of needs: self-actualization. Not all people rise to this level, but in our society, the number of self-actualizers increases steadily. It is, of course, the creative level, but not necessarily artistic or intellectual creation. It may be somebody who enjoys putting ships in bottles or making dolls. Maslow knew a woman who was so good at bringing up children that when her own were grown up she went on adopting more, just for the sheer pleasure it gave her.

And of course, there is no category of violent crime associated with the self-actualization level. The two are a contradiction in terms. This explains why no creative artist has ever committed a premeditated murder—which would seem to imply that at the next level of social evolution, crime will naturally decrease.

There is another interesting mechanism of change that points towards the same conclusion: what the biologist Rupert Sheldrake calls "formative causation," which, in effect, guarantees the increase in the number of self-actualizers. Formative causation takes place through the influence of a factor that Sheldrake has labeled "morphogenetic fields," which you might compare to the field around a magnet, which can be communicated to other magnets.

The wing of a bird or the tentacle of an octopus is shaped by a kind of electrical "mold"—just like the molds into which we pour jellies—which is why many creatures can regrow a limb that has been cut off. These "molds" seem to be magnetic fields, which shape the living molecules just as a magnet can "shape" iron filings into a pattern. Sheldrake suggests that these "fields" can be used to explain some rather odd observations made by biologists.

For example, in 1920 the psychologist William McDougal performed an experiment at Harvard to see if baby rats could inherit abilities developed by their parents (the "inheritance of acquired characteristics" that Darwinists regard as such a fearful heresy). He put white rats into a tank of water from which they could escape up one of two gangplanks. One gangplank had an electric current running through it, and the first generation of rats soon learned to choose the other one. Then McDougal tried the same experiment on their children, and then on their grandchildren, and so on. And he found that each generation learned more quickly than its parents—that is, he had proved that the inheritance of acquired characteristics does occur.

Now when a scientist performs an experiment on a group of animals, he always keeps an exactly similar group who are not subjected to experiments; these are called the "control group"—the purpose being to have a ready standard of comparison. When a colleague of McDougal's—W. E. Agar of Melbourne—repeated his experiment, he also decided to test the control group at the end of several generations. To his baffled astonishment, these also showed the same ability to learn more quickly. And that was impossible, for they had merely been sitting passively in cages. It looked as if the control rats had learned by some kind of telepathy.

Not telepathy, says Sheldrake, but by "morphic resonance." The control group of rats "picked up" the morphogenetic field of the trained rats in the same way that an iron bar can pick up the electrical field of a coil of wire and turn into a magnet: simple induction.

Incredibly, this seems to work not only with living creatures but with crystals. New chemicals, when synthesized for the first time, are often extremely difficult to crystallize. But as soon as one of them has been crystallized in any laboratory in the world, it becomes easier to crystallize in all the others. At first, it was suspected that scientists traveling from one laboratory to another might be carrying fragments of crystals in their clothes or beards—or even that tiny quantities are carried in the atmosphere. Both explanations seem highly unlikely. The likeliest, Sheldrake suggests, is a process of "induction" through morphogenetic fields.

A series of experiments has been performed to test the Sheldrake hypothesis and has produced positive results. At Yale, Professor Gary Schwartz found that people who do not know Hebrew were able to distinguish between real words in Hebrew and false words—because Jews all over the world already know the genuine words. Alan Pickering of Hatfield Polytechnic obtained the same result using Persian script. In another experiment, English-speaking people were asked to memorize two rhymes in a foreign language—one a well-known nursery rhyme, one a newly composed rhyme. The result—as the hypothesis of formative causation predicts—is that they learned the traditional rhyme more easily than the newly composed one.

We can see that this must also be true of self-actualization. When the number of self-actualizers in a society has increased beyond a certain critical mass, it will go on increasing by the action of morphogenetic fields.

Which explained why, on the whole, I do not share the current pessimism about the way the world is going. Human beings seem to have an odd ability to solve apparently intractable problems with a mixture of determination and serendipity; faced with such problems, they seem to have the ability to set unknown forces in motion. Or, as Buckminster Fuller put it: "I seem to be a verb."

Crime is a disintegrative force. Self-actualization is an integrative force. And the lesson of history is that it is the integrative force that finally prevails.

Index

E

F

G

H

I

J

K

L

M

N

O

P

R

S

T

U

V

W

ACKNOWLEDGMENTS

In writing this book I have had some distinguished helpers, including Steve Band, who was the chief of the FBI Behavioral Science Unit from 1998 until 2005, and its newly appointed chief Harry Kern. This book also owes a major debt to Robert K. Ressler, and to FBI Agent Gregg McCrary.

I also wish to thank Sondra London for reading and making suggestions for the sections on Gerard Schaefer and Danny Rolling.

My friend Wilton Earle, the chronicler of the crimes of "Pee Wee" Gaskins, has also contributed his own invaluable insights into the case.

Finally, I also owe a debt of gratitude to Britain's first and still its most distinguished criminal profiler, Professor David Canter.